MILITARY HISTOI

OF THE

UNITED STATES

(Early Exploration through American Civil War)

Rodger Woltjer

Military History of the United States, – 1513 - 1865

Published by Merriam Press
489 South Street, Hoosick Falls NY 12090

Photos are that of the author unless otherwise shown.
Text Photo: Battle of the Brandywine, PA, 9/11/1777 Library of Congress, Prints & Photographs Division

Published in the United States of America

 ISBN 9781576386491
 HISTORY / MILITARY / UNITED STATES
 Library of Congress Control Number 2018932689

Dedication

This work is dedicated to many military service members who have served the United States through time both in the development of our nation and preservation of its sovereignty!

Special Dedication

A special dedication to my young granddaughter, Madison Josephine Lewis, who has an avid interest in history that may come from her possible ancestral connection to the American explorer, soldier, and politician Meriwether Lewis!

Contents

Timeline of the

Military History of the United States

French and Indian Wars (1689 -1763)

The Revolutionary War (4/19/75 – 9/3/1783)

The War of 1812 (6/1/1812 – 1/8/1815)

Native American Indian Wars (1513-1865)

Texas War w/ Mexico (10/2/1835 – 4/21/1836)

Mexican War (6/1846 – 2/2/1848)

American Civil War (4/9/1861 – 5/10/1865)

Author's Note

Accuracy in reporting facts regarding historical events is the goal of this work as it should be in each and every written work. Sometimes resources are negligent is following this principle for whatever reason. Where there is doubt, every effort will be made to insure the information is as accurate as possible before citing such. This effort may mean using the best consensus available, but it will be done with utmost care to preserve the TRUE HISTORICAL FACTS!

Preface

THE military history of the United States is much maligned in the minds of far too many Americans these days and unfortunately so is much of history in general. In its place textbooks focus on mundane issues that have little relevance to our past and will do little or nothing for our future! When someone is asked what year the War of 1812 occurred and has no answer that pretty much tells you that we are marching down a slippery path that may well have catastrophic outcomes! The same is true when a person who should know can't state the countries we faced in World War II other than to mention France who was an ally!

This total lack of historical knowledge is frightening when one considers the words of George Santayana in his work *"The Life of Reason"* where he wrote: *"Those who cannot remember the past are condemned to repeat it."* Others more recently have made similar phrases that say much the same. Yet, the younger generation either does not care to hear our historical past or are denied the facts by our out-of-touch education system. More attention is given to the type of foods served in the school cafeterias than how our nation has progressed through time.

Patriotism has largely been replaced with notions of diversity and social matters that have little or no meaning to what our founding fathers put forth in both the Declaration of Independence and the United States Constitution. Individuals burn the U. S. Flag or defame our country on one accord and suck up the freedoms offered by our laws on the other as if they are entitled to those same rights!

The object of this work is to focus on the military history of our nation from its earliest beginnings to the end of the American Civil War. Military history of the United States does not mean only organized armies. From the time of Spanish exploration of North America there have been conflicts that required a response that was military in some sense. The progression of that response comes from crews aboard ships, individuals taking up arms, quasi-military groups, organized State militias, and to fully constituted nation armies. The first conflicts in North America involved the Native American Indians against small groups or individuals, not armies, but that would change as this nation grew in population. Countries like France and Great Britain would send their military troops to these shores for territorial gains changing the scope to full military involvement. The stage was set for the beginning of the United States Military!

Landing of Spanish Explorer Hernando de Soto in Florida, 1539
Library of Congress, Prints & Photographs Division, LC-USZ62-3031

The French and Indian Wars

THE French and Indian Wars fought between the French and English began in 1689 long before this nation was established and continued for seventy-four years with intervals of peace only to again flair into conflict finally ending in 1763. Obviously the wars did not involve the United States Military, but are included here for three reasons. They occurred on what would eventually become the land of this nation, they involved Native American Indians of which future conflicts would occur between the United States Military as early as 1816 in the First Seminole Indian War, and they involved colonists from both countries some of whom would become famous American citizens.

The French and Indian Wars involved Native American Indians allied with the French against the British and their Native American Indian allies. There were actually four named wars during the seventy-four years of conflict. Three were named after British royalty, not French, while the last and most important was named *The French and Indian War*.

King William's War

The first war was called *King William's War* that occurred from 1689 to 1697. It was named for King William III who ruled England from 1869 - 1702. King William III was also known as William of Orange. Struggles in Europe precipitated the events in the New World. The *War of the League of Augsburg* was one such struggle that involved England, Spain, The Netherlands, the Holy Roman Empire, and parts of Germany all against France. The French with their Indian allies attacked the colonies in New York and New England established by the English. The British garnered their forces and fought back against the French over the next eight years with neither side achieving much of anything. The war ended with Louis XIV of France signing the *Treaty of Ryswick* agreeing to the terms of the European powers returning most of whatever gains they had achieved during the conflict.

Queen Anne's War

The second war was called *Queen Anne's War* fought from 1702-1713. Queen Anne reigned over England from 1702 - 1714. In 1707, Queen Anne became the first monarch of the newly formed Great Britain that combined the Kingdom of England and Wales with the Kingdom of Scotland having agreed to the *Act of Union*. Little did this matter as struggles in Europe continued. This time it was the *War of the Spanish Succession* that impacted events in Colonial America. Unlike King William's War that took place in New York and New England, this war spread to sites such as St. Augustine, Florida, and Charleston, South Carolina. The war ended with the signing of the *Treaty of Utrecht* in 1713 in Utrecht, Holland. The treaty changed both the map of Europe and the control of nations as well as territories in the New World. Great Britain acquired Gibraltar and the island of Minorca from Spain and Nova Scotia, Newfoundland, and the Hudson Bay Territory in the New World from France. France retained Quebec (New France). Spain relinquished other European regions as a part of the Treaty. Britain's territorial gains from the French in North America were so ill defined that it led to the third war.

King George's War

King George's War was the next war to be part of the French and Indian Wars. It took place from 1744-1748. King George II ruled Great Britain from 1727-1760. Not unlike the previous two wars, Europe once again was the instigator of events in North America. The *War of the Austrian Succession* in Europe fueled the power struggle between France and Great Britain. French Fort Louisbourg on Cape Benton Island, Nova Scotia, was attacked and seized by loyal British colonists in 1745. Little else was gained by either side during this four year conflict, and the *Treaty of Aix-la-Chapelle* resulted in the end of hostilities. When all was said and done, the fort was returned to the French as if nothing had taken place.

The French and Indian War

The last and most important of the four *French and Indian Wars* was itself called *The French and Indian War*. It occurred from 1754 to 1763. Unlike the three previous, this war between the French and the English began in North America and produced the *Seven Years' War* in Europe! Land boundaries in the New World were again the cause of the war. As both English and French communities advanced into new regions, territorial conflicts became more prevalent. Previous agreed upon boundaries were either ignored or disputed and the expansion into new territories resulted in claims by both sides. Disputes raged as far west as the Great Lakes and south into today's Pennsylvania.

Much of North America's east coast region was under British occupation while the French held Canada, the Great Lakes, and the Allegheny region west to the Mississippi river. The northern portion of New York was under French control and the British held the lower.

Each country established forts to defend their acquisitions against attack. The French forts ranged from Nova Scotia to the Ohio River Valley. Some of the more important were Forts Louisbourg (Nova Scotia), Beausejour (Arcadia), Ticonderoga (New York), Fontenac (Ontario), Oswego (New York), Niagara (New York), Presque Isle (Ohio), Le Boeuf (Pennsylvania), Machault (Pennsylvania), and Duquesne (Pennsylvania). The British established forts of their own. Here too some of the important are Fort Prince George (Pennsylvania) captured and destroyed by the French before it was completed. Fort Hanger (Pennsylvania) was also captured and destroyed by the French. Fort Necessity (Pennsylvania) would exist for only two months before it was attacked and destroyed by the French. Fort William Henry (New York) would play a major role in the war. French Fort Duquesne would be attacked by British troops in 1758 and destroyed. The British would construct Fort Pitt near the site of the former Fort Duquesne. All total, both the French and British constructed nearly seventy forts comprised of various shapes and sizes.

The British were not alone in their territorial war against the French in North America. The English colonists took action against the French as early as 1753 due to land acquisitions and the building of forts from Lake Erie in the north to the Allegheny River region in the south. Fort Le Boeuf established by the French in the Ohio River Valley was on land claimed by Virginia. As early as 1752, representatives of the Ohio Company who were active in trading with the Indians in the Ohio Valley had made arrangements to build a trading settlement and fort at or near the confluence of the Allegheny and Monongahela Rivers. Actions by the French to build forts in the territory claimed by Virginia prompted Lieutenant Governor Robert Dinwiddie of Virginia to send twenty-one year old militia Major George Washington (who may have volunteered) along with no less than seven others to warn the French they were on territory that belonged to Virginia.

Major Washington set out from Williamsburg, Virginia, in late October 1753, in what would become an arduous trek across unfamiliar and dangerous territory. One of the men accompanying Major Washington was Jacob Van Braam, a friend and former military man who had mentored Washington in the art of military ways and who was knowledgeable in the French language. He would serve as interpreter. Another member of the group was Christopher Gist, a frontiersman and Ohio Company agent commissioned a lieutenant would act as guide.

Upon arriving at the future site of the trading settlement and fort, Washington noted that the site was well suited for its intended purpose. As this was the month of December, it could not be known that the ground was wet and flooding was surely possible situated along the rivers. Moving on, Washington stopped at the village of Iroquois Nation Chief Tanacharison also known as Half-King who was allied with the British. Tanacharison accompanied Washington on the rest of the journey to the French position. The group first arrived at Fort Machault near present day Franklin, Pennsylvania, on December 4th. There they were told by French Captain, Phillippe-Thomas de Joncaire that he did not have the authority to act on their request and directed Washington to proceed to Fort Le Boeuf near current Erie, Pennsylvania. Here they arrived on December 11th and delivered their message to the French commander of Fort Le Boeuf, Captain Jacques Legardeur de Saint-Pierre, who politely but adamantly refused to leave the territory claimed by Virginia.

Hand-drawn map by George Washington, accompanying a printing of the journal he kept of his 1753 expedition into the Ohio Country. The writings of Washington in the inset are shown below.

"The French are now coming from their Forts on Lake Erie & on the Creek, to Venango to erect another fort__And from thence they design to the Fork's of Monogahela and to the Logs Town, and so to continue down the river building at the most convenient places in order to prevent our settlements. A little below Shanapins Town in the Fork is the place where we are going immediately to Build a Fort as it commands the Ohio and Monongahela."

Library of Congress, Geography and Map Division, g3820.ct00036

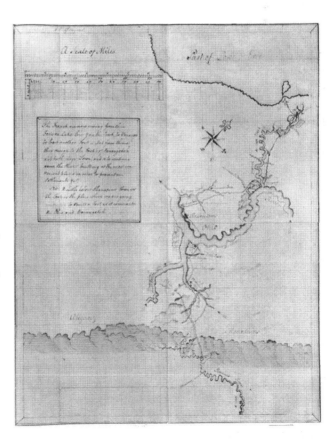

"Washington and Gist Visit Queen Alliquippa"

Queen Alliquippa was the leader of a band of Seneca Indians living in December 1753 near the Monogahela and Youghiogheny Rivers close to the route Washington took on his journey to meet the French.

Washington wrote in his journal of the visit --

"As we intended to take horse here [at Frazer's Cabin on the mouth of Turtle Creek], and it required some time to find them, I went up about three miles to the mouth of the Youghiogheny to visit Queen Alliquippa, who had expressed great concern that we passed her in going to [Fort Le Boeuf]. I made her a present of a match-coat and a bottle of rum, which latter was thought much the better present of the two."

Library of Congress, Prints & Photographs Division, LC-USZ62-42855

The request to leave the territory claimed by Virginia and rejected by the French prompted Major Washington to leave Fort Le Boeuf on December 16 and return to Williamsburg where he arrived January 16, 1754. Before Lieutenant Governor Dinwiddie knew of the French refusal to leave the territory claimed by Virginia, Governor Dinwiddie had organized and sent a small force of Virginia militia soldiers under the leadership of Captain William Trent to build a fort at the confluence of the Allegheny and Monongahela Rivers with the Ohio River in present-day Pittsburgh, Pennsylvania

William Trent was a fur trader and business entrepreneur familiar with the site who was given a commission as Captain in the Virginia Provincial Militia. Captain Trent with his force of forty-one men began construction on the fort in early February 1754. On April 18, 1754, before the fort was completed, it was attacked by the French and destroyed. At the time of the attack, Captain Trent was some 70 miles southeast at Wills Creek, currently Cumberland, Maryland. His second in command, Lieutenant John Fraser, was at his plantation on Turtle Creek located along the Mononghela River. The fort was left to the

US Military History – French and Indian Wars

command of Ensign Edward Ward who had little chance of defending the fort against upwards of 1,000 French soldiers commanded by Claude-Pierre Pecaudy de Contrecoeur. The Virginia Militia force was released to return to Virginia.

Prior to the events affecting the capture of Fort Prince George, Major George Washington upon his return to Williamsburg, Virginia, in January 1754 received a promotion to Lieutenant Colonel and was directed to raise a militia force and embark to the site of the new fort under construction by Captain Trent. His mission was to provide security at the fort and protect Virginia's land claim. Washington recruited 160 men for his new command and set out in April 1754 for the site of the new fort. Long before reaching the fort, word was received the unfinished fort had been captured by the French, but Washington was determined to continue to the region perhaps to stop the French from further land acquisitions.

On May 28, 1754, Lieutenant Colonel Washington's militia force reached an area called the Great Meadows. This was a large grass clearing with adequate supply of water approximately 50 miles south of the former British fort now in the hands of the French on which they were constructing Fort Duquesne. While at the Great Meadows, Washington began building a fort of his own and was alerted to an encampment of French soldiers nearby.

Considering the French a threat, Washington set out with his militia force to stop what turned out to be a scouting party of French soldiers and a fight ensued. Ten French soldiers were killed, one was wounded, and twenty-one captured losing only one militia soldier. One of the French soldiers killed was Ensign Joseph Coulon de Villers de Jumonville. Accounts of how Ensign Jumonville's died are disputed depending on the source. The French claim that he was "massacred" in the process of surrendering. Others claim that while in the custody of Lieutenant Colonel Washington, Jumonville was murdered by Tanaghrisson, the Iroquois Indian supporting the militia effort. This episode in history is called the *Battle of Jumonville Glen*. Regardless of the actual facts, the results of this military action set off the *French and Indian War*!

Knowing that the French would not take lightly to the outcome of events affecting their soldiers, Lieutenant Colonel Washington returned to the Great Meadows and hastily finished constructing the unfinished fort that was completed on June 2, 1754. The fort was nothing more than a log stockade that would provide only marginal protection. The fort was appropriately named Fort Necessity.

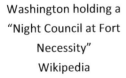
Washington holding a "Night Council at Fort Necessity" Wikipedia

Within a month's time (July 3), a French force of some 700 would surround Fort Necessity and force the surrender of Lieutenant Colonel Washington, his Virginia Militia, and a small force of British Regulars after a brief fight.

In the terms of the surrender, Washington was allowed to return to Virginia with his militia and British Regulars. Thirty or so of Washington's men were killed in the attack on Fort Necessity. They were buried in the Great Meadow on the morning of July 4th before surrendering the fort. Fort Necessity was burned soon after capture by the French. Today, Fort Necessity National Battlefield marks the site of the reconstructed fort and Visitor Center.

Meanwhile, the French were busy building their Fort Duquesne on the site of the burned British Fort Prince George. The fort design was similar to many of the French forts of star shape exterior with a square interior and triangular bastions on each of the corners. It was named in honor of Marquis Duquesne, the governor-general of New France. The fort was meant to deny the British use of the rivers for trading with the Indians.

The *Battle of Jumonville Glen* in 1754 may have started the *French and Indian War*, but more conflicts would occur for the next eight years. In an attempt to oust the French from their new fort and rid them of all their gains in the Ohio Valley, British Major General Edward Braddock led a force of nearly 2,200 British Regulars and Colonial Militia to retake the territory that had been lost a year earlier. George Washington would accompany Major General Braddock as a volunteer aide. The force left Cumberland, Maryland, on May 29, 1755, with much artillery and supply wagons that slowed the march due to rough and narrow roadways hindering the pace. To speed progress, Major General Braddock split his force leaving the slower assets and moved forward with approximately 1,300 of his men that spelled doom for the mission.

Before the British could reach Fort Duquesne, the French received word of the pending march and left the fort with their Indian allies to surprise the attackers. On July 9th, the *Battle of the Monogahela* occurred also known as the *Battle of Braddock's Field* or the *Battle of the Wilderness*. What ensued next was utter chaos and confusion on the part of the British soldiers unaccustomed to the war-like tactics of the Indians using cover of the woods to bring fire upon an enemy. In the end, nearly seventy-five percent of the British force was either killed or wounded. Major General Braddock himself was mortally wounded perhaps accidently at the hands of his own men and died four days later. This ended for the time being any attempt to retake the territory.

French Fort Duquesne

"Defeat of General Braddock, in the French and Indian War, in Virginia in 1755 / John Andrew, sc."
Library of Congress, Prints & Photographs Division, LC-USZ62-1473

Fort Duquesne would again be attacked on September 14, 1758, by British troops under the command of General John Forbes. That attack named the *Battle of Fort Duquesne* also led to defeat of the British. Eventually, the French decided to vacate Fort Duquesne due to overwhelming number of British soldiers in the region and the fort was torched on November 26, 1758. Arriving at the smoldering ruins of the fort, the British were aghast at the sight of beheaded British Highlanders with their heads on spikes at the hand of the Indians The British would construct their own fort on the site and name it Fort Pitt after William Pitt the Elder, 1st Earl of Chatham. Fort Pitt would see use during the American Revolutionary War.

A year before Fort Duquesne was abandoned, another historic event of the *French and Indian War* involved British Fort William Henry located on the south end of Lake George in New York. Fort William Henry was established in 1755 and named for the son of King George II, Prince William, the Duke of Cumberland, and for the grandson of the King,

Prince William Henry, Duke of Gloucester. The fort had an irregular shape of four sides most likely due to the terrain along the shoreline of Lake George. There were four pointed bastions at each corner of the fort. A dry moat covered the three land portions over which a bridge gave access to the fort and Lake George covered the fourth side. The walls were around 30 feet thick.

Fort William Henry would come under attack by French soldiers and their Indian allies in August 1757. The small force of British defenders were ill prepared for the artillery barrage they would receive from the French nor the large number of Indians in support of the French. After a two-day battle, the fort commander, Lieutenant Colonel George Monro (Munro), agreed to surrender with conditions. The garrison was to be paroled to Fort Edward (an other British fort to the South) under the protection of the French soldiers.

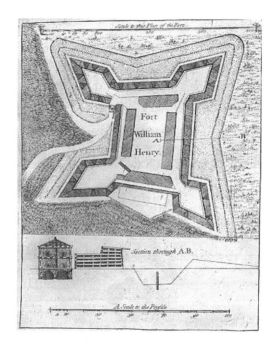

British Fort William Henry
Wikipedia

The Indians did not honor this agreement and harassed, murdered, scalped, and otherwise terrorized the British column from the time they surrendered the fort. The number of British soldiers, women, and children killed is speculation. In addition the Indians took a number of captives of which their fate is uncertain. James Fenimore Cooper's novel, *The Last of the Mohicans*, and the 1992 film of the same name, is based on the attack on Fort William Henry and the Indian massacre that followed. How much of both is based on fact is left to ones own liking, but is does parallel much of what history has reported. The treatment of the British soldiers and their families from this 1757 engagement would remain vividly in the minds of the British military and there would come a time for retribution. That time would come in 1758 and again in 1759.

Sketch of the Indian attack on the British column showing French General Louis-Joseph de Montcalm attempting to stop the attack.
Library of Congress, Prints & Photographs Division, LC-USZ62-120704

A number of Indians representing no less than twelve tribes in support of the French participated in the attack on Fort William Henry and the subsequent massacre of the British column as it evacuated the fort. Noteworthy tribes were the Huron, Algonquin, Iroquois, Menominee, Miami, and Ojibwe, although historians differ on which tribes actually supported the French. At various times during the occupation of North America by European countries the Indian tribes changed their support of one nation over the other depending on the circumstances.

Regardless, many of the tribes were indigenous to Canada or at least the far Northwest of North America. The British also had Indian support that is less well documented. That support may have come as scouts and guides rather than taking up arms in military engagements as did those who were aligned with the French. The five tribes of the Iroquois Nation supported the British at various times. There may have been other tribes from the southeast who also gave support.

About the same time the British constructed Fort William Henry, the French built a fort of their own named Fort Carillon today called Fort Ticonderoga. It was built on the west shore at the southern tip of Lake Champlain some distance north of Fort William Henry on Lake George. Fort Carillon was star shaped build between 1755 and 1757. There were two attacks on the fort in response to what had occurred at British Fort William Henry. The first attack occurred in 1758 at which time the 4,000 man French garrison faced 16,000 British troops and repelled the attack. The second attack occurred a year later at which time the British were successful in expelling the French. The fort renamed Fort Ticonderoga under British control would again see an attack in 1775 as a lead up to the American Revolution that is not part of the French & Indian War.

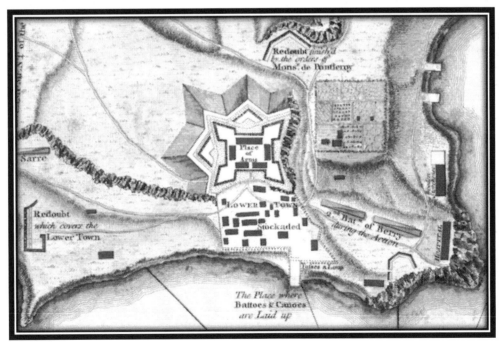

French Fort Carillon, British Fort Ticonderoga
Wikipedia

Military gains at French Fort Duquesne and later at Fort Carillon gave confidence to the somewhat beleaguered British Army who had suffered far too many defeats at the hand of the French and their Indian allies. The push would now reach into New York to the west where Fort Niagara was located along the shores of Lake Ontario. Fort Niagara was established in 1726, but a fort by another name was built by the French at the same site in 1678 named Fort Conti. Fort Conti itself would be replaced in 1687 by a fort called Fort Denonville that would last only one year due to the extremes of weather and disease. Fort Niagara of 1726 consisted of a single building called the "Maison a Machicoulis" that today is referred to as "The French Castle." In 1755 the fort was enlarged due to the events of the *French and Indian War*.

"The Maison a Machicoulis" or the Castle (2006)

Fort Niagara, East Wall (2006)

Fort Niagara
South Redoubt Gate

The Battle of Fort Niagara began on July 6, 1759. It was in fact a nineteen-day siege of the fort by British Regulars and New York Provincial Militia appropriately called the *Battle of Fort Niagara.* The French commander, Captain Pierre Pouchot, surrendered the fort on July 26 after French reinforcements failed to arrive. The French reinforcements were attacked and routed by British regulars along with their Iroquois allies on July 24, 1759, several miles before reaching Fort Niagara. British control of Fort Niagara would see expansion and serve the occupiers during the American Revolutionary War. Fort Niagara today is a National Historic Landmark and placed on the National Register of Historic Places in 1966. Fort Niagara will be revisited in the writing on the Revolutionary War.

Noteworthy is the establishment of another French establishment in 1745 along the Niagara River south of the future Fort Niagara. This consisted of a "small blockhouse and storehouse" known as Frenchman's Landing. This site would be moved slightly further south and Fort Little Niagara also called Fort du Portage would be constructed in 1750. Here too there were blockhouses surrounded by a palisade structure. With the approach of the British Army in 1759, the French destroyed Fort Little Niagara. The British would establish a fort of their own near the site in 1760 called Fort Schlosser. Similar to the larger Fort Niagara, Fort Schlosser would also play a role in the Revolutionary War.

Slowly but surely the French were being pushed north into the Colony of Canada or New France. Much of Great Britain's success was due to a concerted effort to send large numbers of military troops into the colonies along with financial support. The opposite was true for the French. French King Louis XV was reluctant to support the French colonies dealing with growing concerns at home part of which was the *Seven Years War*.

Along with the siege and eventual capture of Fort Niagara, the British command focused their attention on Quebec. Quebec in New France was a stronghold for the French protected with 15,000 troops under the command of Lieutenant General Louis-Joseph de Montcalm-Guzon Marquis de Saint-Veran. General Montcalm was in command of French troops in 1757 at the time British Fort William Henry was attacked and captured.

British Colonel James Wolfe was a distinguished military officer whose exploits came to the attention of the Prime Minister, William Pitt the Elder. William Pitt selected Colonel Wolfe for promotion to Brigadier General and dispatched him to North America where he took part in several campaigns against the French first at Fort Louisbourg (1758) followed by the expulsion of Acadians in the Gulf of St. Lawrence Campaign also in 1758. These actions further pleased William Pitt who then appointed Wolfe to Major General with the mission to take Quebec from the French.

Major General James Wolfe with a force of nearly 30,000 soldiers and sailors sailed up the St. Lawrence River from Louisbourg reaching Quebec in late June 1759. The British forces established themselves along the St. Lawrence River opposite Quebec and commenced bombing the city on July 12th. On July 31, the British attempted a landing at Beauport that was well defended by French forces who repelled the attackers. The British made a second assault on September 13 at l'Anse au Foulons a short distance east of Quebec that surprised the French. This landing was successful and British forces were soon on the plains above Quebec.

The *Battle of the Plains of Abraham* or *Battle of Quebec* occurred on September 13, 1759, on a plateau outside the walls of the city and lasted about fifteen minutes. The French troops were severely routed forcing them to abandon Quebec. The battle did not come without cost. French Major General Louis-Joseph, Marquis de Montcalm and British Major General James Wolfe were both mortally wounded in the short battle. Major General Wolfe would die from his wounds almost instantly while Major General Montcalm would succumb to his wounds the next day.

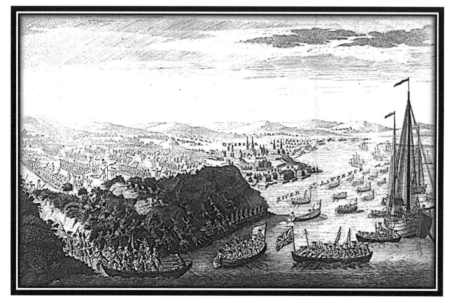

Scene showing the British attack on Quebec September 13, 1759
Library of Congress, Prints & Photographs Division, LC-USZ62-47

Painting showing Major General James Wolfe being attended to after falling
in the Battle of the Plains of Abraham
Library of Congress, Prints & Photographs Division, LC-DIG-ppmsca-03214

Print showing the death Major General Marquis de Montcalm during the siege of Québec.
Library of Congress, Prints and Photographs Division, LC-USZ62-106

Other engagements would occur in New France between the two countries during the next year that resulted in victories for each side, but the British assault on Montreal in September 1760 would largely put an end to hostilities in North America. French defenders of Montreal numbering around 2,000 were confronted by upwards of 17,000 British and Colonial Militia forces resulting in the surrender of the city on September 8, 1760. The Seven Years War in Europe would continue for three more years ending with the signing of the Treaty of Paris of 1763. The treaty essentially returned territories gained during the conflict to their previous owners with some exceptions. Great Britain would gain most of New France along with the eastern half of French Louisiana. Britain would also acquire Florida from Spain. There were other changes that occurred in Europe as a result of the treaty.

The military successes of Great Britain in the French and Indian War over their arch enemy France were achieved to some degree through support from the Colonial Militia. As the years of the war passed, so did the support from the militia forces and rightly so! The British Army gave little respect to their colonial fighters. Promotions in rank for Militia members were seldom if ever received and equal pay for equal rank to that of the British Regulars was never received. These circumstances along with an elitist attitude on both sides of the Atlantic by British citizens over the colonists would fester in the years from 1763 to the time of the Revolutionary War. Even George Washington who may have fashioned himself as a British officer only to be denied recognition as equal in rank and pay resigned his militia commission due to these inequities. Of course, the outcome of this situation would manifest itself in 1776 when George Washington would become the commanding general of the Continental Army fighting against the same British Army! Ironically, the colonist who

helped the British in their quest against the French, would take up arms against the British and receive support from the French!

———————————

Charleville Musket used by the French during the war. The British used the Bess Musket not unlike that of the French weapon.

The Revolutionary War

THE years following the French and Indian War saw a growing discontent among the inhabitants of the British Colonies due largely to ill-treatment and indifference at the hands of British authorities. The Colonial Militia forces had already experienced this impact toward their ranks by the British military during the war. Now, merchants, farmers, craftsmen, laborers, and all manner of men and women who were not British loyalists would come to experience the same. Individuals not born in the Colonies and who had come to this new land seeking a better life either for work or to express their religious freedom were also caught up in the same plight as the native born colonists. Neither group was in the mood for oppression from the British authorities or anyone else.

The colonists were hard working independent minded people who carved out their farms, villages, and towns from the forests and plains, built their homes, stores, stables, and churches with like-minded determination. They rallied with the British in their fight against France yet were unable to justify their existence with British authorities. In England the colonists would have been the "common people," subjects of the Crown! They would not have been land or property owners or even held positions of responsibility in their communities. In this new world an ocean away from long-standing traditions, people were able to think and act for the betterment of themselves. Perhaps it was this independence that threatened the Motherland. Whatever the reason and in spite of initial loyalty, Great Britain felt the need to suppress the independence common in the colonies by excessive laws and taxation that fueled to a large part the discontent that brewed in the years following the French and Indian War.

The many wars between Great Britain and France were costly to both countries and the French and Indian War was no exception. Large numbers of British military were sent to the colonies to fight in this war and stayed once it ended. This was an expense that would fall upon the shoulders of the colonial inhabitants through several tax laws. It wasn't enough to have just a costly standing army in the colonies, trade barriers were also imposed that hampered the independent thinking of the colonists.

On April 5, 1764, the British Parliament passed the *Sugar Act* known as the *American Revenue Act* or the *American Duties Act*. The primary purpose of this act was to raise money to support the ten thousand or so British troops permanently stationed in the colonies. Of course, this was a tax on the inhabitants of the British Colonies by the British Crown and would be one of many such infringements on the colonists. Previously there was the *Molasses Act of 1733* that did little to rile the inhabitants of the colonies largely because it was mostly ignored. The *Molasses Act* was to expire in 1763 thereby making way for the new *Sugar Act*.

The *Sugar Act* picked up where the *Molasses Act* left off. There would still be a tax on molasses, but half of what it was previously. However, certain other products were added to the list of taxed items to include lumber that was plentiful in the Americas and enforcement of the tax was also implemented. As much as the *Sugar Act* was unpopular, it would be out matched by its replacement, the *Stamp Act* or *Revenue Act of 1765*.

On March 22, 1765, Great Britain's Parliament passed the *Stamp Act*. This act was a direct tax on the British Colonies. It required that every document of every kind, contracts, newspapers, licenses, etc., show an official embossed stamp on government paper paid as a tax. The various stamps and stamped paper were to be made in England and shipped to the colonies. The stamps were to be sold by Stamp distributors selected by England. All monetary transactions were to be in British sterling and not Colonial currency. The tax collected was to pay for the British military stationed in the Colonies.

Two examples of the embossed stamps called for in the Stamp Act

The *Stamp Act* had about as much success as the previous Acts passed by the British Parliament, but it did cause much unrest among the colonists. So much so that it paved the way for the American Revolutionary War. Although the colonists were quasi-subjects of Great Britain, their true allegiance was to their colonial leaders and not the Crown! What followed were demonstrations, organizations that supported opposition to the *Stamp Act*, and efforts by colonial leaders such as Benjamin Franklin to petition Parliament to repeal the Act. The *Stamp Act* lasted only until March 18, 1766, but was followed by the *Declaratory Act* also known at *The American Colonies Act of 1766*.

The *Declaratory Act* was no more than a statement that *"The said colonies and plantations in America have been and are subordinate unto, and dependent upon the imperial crown and parliament of Great Britain; the King and parliament [has] full power and authority to make laws and statutes to bind the colonies and people of America, subjects of the crown of Great Britain, in all cases whatsoever."* Although this same Act no longer applied to the United States once recognized by Great Britain in 1783, it continued in other British colonies throughout the world until its repeal in 1964!

If the various Acts already mentioned were not enough control over the colonists, Britain earlier imposed the *Navigation Act of 1764* that regulated colonial shipping. Then there was *The Quartering Act of 1765* that required colonists to provide quarters (lodging) and other necessities for the British army stationed in the colonies. Next was the *Townsend Acts of 1767* named for Charles Townsend, the Chancellor of Exchequer. These Acts placed taxes on imports into the Colonies on paper, paint, lead, glass, and tea.

The *Townsend Acts* were actually a series of five separate Acts the first named the *Revenue Act of 1767*. The next four were the *Indemnity*

Act (1767), *Commissioners of Custom Act* (1767), the *New York Restraining Act* (1767), and finally the *Vice Admiralty Court Act* (1768). It was believed by Parliament that these five Acts would receive less opposition by the colonists because they were indirect taxes for the purpose of paying the salaries of governors and judges loyal to the Crown. The *New York Restraining Act* had the purpose of punishing New York for refusing to honor the *Quartering Act*. The result of the *Townsend Acts* was no different than those previous whether a direct or indirect tax. This led to the first major conflict of the pending American Revolutionary War – The Boston Massacre!

The Boston Massacre (Incident on King Street)

Boston was a major shipping port of both imports and exports. For this reason, taxes on goods in this town were felt more than other locations in the Colonies. The *Townsend Acts* had a direct impact on the residences of Boston especially the merchants. On March 5, 1770, what started as an unrelated incident to the Townsend Acts ballooned into an all out riot by a crowd of several hundred locals who were more upset by the presence of British troops than any other reason.

The incident on King Street (now State Street) started with a lone individual berating a British officer for not paying a bill due the man's employer. This escalated into taunting a nearby military sentry who then struck the man with the butt of his weapon. Soon others gathered to take up the taunt resulting in the arrival of more British troops to quell the crowd that did little to help the situation. It wasn't long before the crowd began throwing objects at the "redcoats" challenging them to fire their weapons at which time a soldier was hit by an object knocking him to the ground. Returning to his feet and retrieving his weapon, the soldier's anger is thought to have caused other soldiers to begin firing into the crowd. The result was three protesters who died instantly and two others a short time later. In addition, there were six injured in the volley of bullets fired. At least one of those wounded died ten years later caused it is said by his wounds inflicted on that fateful day!

Depiction of the Boston Massacre
March 5, 1770

Library of Congress, Prints & Photographs Division,
LC-USZ62-45554

An investigation began in the aftermath of the incident that included the arrest of eight British soldiers who took part in firing their weapons. To prevent further episodes of what had taken place, there was a call for the removal of all British troops from the immediate vicinity of Boston. At first this was rejected, but further reflection on the matter proved the best solution and the troops were removed to Castle William on Castle Island in Boston Harbor known today as Fort Independence.

On March 27, 1770, indictments for murder were brought against the eight soldiers and their Captain plus four civilians in the Custom House who were said to have fired shots. A trial occurred on November 27, 1770, for the eight soldiers at which time six of the soldiers were acquitted and two were convicted of manslaughter, but received reduced sentences ultimately resulting in the slapping of their hands. The four civilians were tried on December 13, 1770, and acquitted of all charges ending the Incident on King Street. Three years later Boston would again see a similar incident known as the Boston Tea Party.

The Boston Tea Party

The Parliament of Great Britain was not finished with imposing taxes on the British Colonies. *The Tea Act* was passed on May 10, 1773, that was essentially as extension of the *Townsend Acts* that had repealed all taxes but that on tea. The tax involved the East India Company that traded in many items to include tea, a commodity relished by the English.

A tax of any sort was against the belief by the American colonists that there be "no taxation without representation." Thus, on December 16, 1773, a group of individuals of the Sons of Liberty dressed as Native American Indians raided East India Company ships in Boston Harbor and dumped chests of tea into the harbor.

Scene of the Boston Tea Party, December 16, 1773
Wikipedia

The British Parliament responded with harsh steps in 1774 enacting the *Coercive or Intolerable Acts* that stripped among other things the Massachusetts Colony of all governing powers. There were four Acts from this legislation. The *Boston Port Act (1774)* that closed the Boston Port until the colonists paid for the destruction of the tea that had been dumped into the harbor. The *Massachusetts Government Act* took away the Massachusetts Charter. The *Administration of Justice Act* called for British loyalists accused of crimes in the colonies to be tried in Great Britain thereby protecting them from prosecution in the colonies where their crimes had occurred. Finally, the *Quartering Act* that was meant to put teeth into the earlier Act requiring the colonist to provide housing and amenities for British troops. These four Acts were direct punishment for what the colonists felt was exercising their rights under the various colonial charters. The time was ripe for direct confrontation with Great Britain.

The First Continental Congress

The crush of taxes and ill-treatment felt by the colonists in the British Colonies imposed by British authorities at all levels from the King down had come to a tipping point. As a result, the first step by the various Colonies toward resolution with Great Britain occurred in Philadelphia. Fifty-six delegates from twelve of the thirteen colonies (Georgia absent) gathered from September 5 to October 26, 1774, in what was the First Continental Congress. The Congress was called in response to the Coercive or Intolerable Acts enacted by the British Parliament. What response would the colonists take to change the current reprisals they faced? The delegates were of two mindsets. Some sought reconciliation with Great Britain while others wanted to form their own government free from oppression by England. The words of Patrick Henry, "*I know not what course others may take, but give me liberty or give me death*" became the battle cry for those who sought separation from Great Britain.

When all was said and done, the doves won the day and the First Continental Congress ended with a resolution to boycott British goods beginning that December. The boycott was effective for both imports and exports and England felt the impact that only caused a bigger rift between the two factions. The Congress also produced for the first time a universal agreement that showed unification among the Colonies. Finally, this Congress called for a Second Congress to meet in May 1775 that did occur, but only after was had begun.

Major Events of The American Revolutionary War

1775 –
Apr 19 - Battle of Lexington and Concord between Minutemen and British Redcoats.
May 10 – Capture of Fort Ticonderoga by Green Mountain Boys
Jun 17 – Battle of Bunker Hill, Minutemen driven from Breed's Hill by British.
Jul　3 – George Washington assumes command of the Continental Army.
Sep 25 – Battle of Longue-Pointe Canada

Nov 13 - Montreal, Canada, occupied by patriots
Dec 31 - Attempt to capture Quebec, Canada, by colonists failed.

1776 –
Feb 27 – Engagement at Moore's Creek Bridge routs colonists.
Mar　3 – The Continental Naval Fleet captured New providence Island in the Bahamas.

Mar 17 - British evacuate Boston Massachusetts

Jul 4 - Declaration of Independence adopted.

Aug 27 - Patriots defeated by the British on Long Island NY.

Sep 15 - British occupy New York City.

Oct 28 - Continental Army retreats from White Plains NY.

Nov 16 - British capture Fort Washington NY.

Dec 26 - Continental Army conducts a surprise attack on Trenton NJ.

1777 -

Jan 3 - Washington's Continental Army wins battle at Princeton NJ.

Aug 6 - British win temporary battle at Oriskany VA, then retreat.

Aug 16 - Patriots win a battle over the Hessians near Bennington VT

Sep 11 - British win the Battle of Brandywine PA

Sep 19 - First Battle of Freeman's Farm New York

Sep 26 - British occupy Philadelphia PA

Oct 4 - Patriot forces defeated in the Battle of Germantown PA

Oct 7 - Patriots repulse British in the Second Battle of Freeman's Farm, New York

Oct 17 - British Lieutenant General John Burgoyne surrenders 5,000 troops.

Dec 19 - Washington retires to Valley Forge PA for the winter

1778 -

Feb 6 - King Louis XVI of France recognizes United States and joins the war.

Jun 28 - Battle of Monmouth NJ ended in a draw.

Jul 4 - Lieutenant Colonel George Rogers Clark captures Kaskaskia IL, a French village.

Dec 29 - British enter Savannah GA

1779 -

Feb 23-25 - LTC George Rogers Clark captures Vincennes IN, a French village.

Jun 21 - Spain declares war on Great Britain on the European continent.

Jul 15 - Major General Anthony Wayne captures Stony Point on the Hudson River from the British.

Sep 23 - Captain John Paul Jones' *Bonhomme Richard* captured the British *Serapis.*

1780 -

May 12 - Charleston SC fell to the British.

Jul 11 - French troops arrive in Newport RI in support of American troops.

Aug 16 - British defeat Continental troops at Camden SC.

Oct 7 - American frontiersmen attack British loyalists at Kings Mountain SC.

1781 -

Jan 17 - American victory at Cowpens SC.

Mar 15 - British Lieutenant General Charles Cornwallis clashes with Major General Nathanael Greene at Guilford Courthouse NC.

Sep 15 - French Naval fleet drove a British naval force from Chesapeake Bay VA.

Oct 19 - British forces under Lieutenant General Charles Cornwallis surrendered at Yorktown VA

1782 -

Jul 11 - British evacuate Savannah GA

Nov 30 - Preliminary peace treaty between Americans and British signed in Paris, France.

Dec 14 - British leave Charleston SC

1783 -

Apr 15 - Congress ratifies the preliminary peace treaty.

Sep 3 - Final peace treaty signed between United States and Great Britain.

Nov 25 - British leave New York City.

Names of Key Participants in the Revolutionary War –

CONTINENTAL GOVERNMENT –

John Adams, Samuel Adams, Silas Deane, Benjamin Franklin, John Hancock, Patrick Henry, John Jay, Thomas Jefferson, Richard Henry Lee, Robert R. Livingston, George Mason, Robert Morris, James Otis, Thomas Paine, Paul Revere, Haym Salomon, and George Washington.

CONTINENTAL ARMY –

General George Washington
Major General Artemas Ward
Major General Philip Schuyler
Major General Benedict Arnold
Major General Horatio Gates
Major General Nathanael Greene
Major General Henry Knox
Major General Marquis de Lafayette
Major General Charles Lee
Major General Friedrich von Steuben

CONTINENTAL NAVY –

Commodore Esek Hopkins
Captain Joshua Barney
Captain John Paul Jones
Captain Thomas Truxtun

FRENCH TROOPS –

Comte de Rochambeau

GREAT BRITAIN GOVERNMENT–

King George III
Lord North, Prime minister to 1782
Marquis of Rockingham, Prime Minister thereafter
Edmund Burke

BRITISH ARMY –

Lieutenant General John Burgoyne
Lieutenant General Sir Guy Carleton
Lieutenant General Sir Henry Clinton
Lieutenant General Charles Cornwallis
Major General William Howe

BRITISH NAVY–

Vice Admiral Richard Howe, 1776-1778

Battles of Lexington and Concord

Before the Second Continental Congress could meet as planned, the Revolutionary War would begin. The first shots of the war between British "redcoats" and Massachusetts militia occurred at daybreak on April 19, 1775. The years of harsh British rule over the colonies from the end of the French and Indian War had come to war, but it might have been avoided except for a single shot or two on the Lexington Commons. Then again, perhaps it was inevitable in view of all that gone before.

British General Thomas Gage, military governor of Massachusetts and commander of British military forces garrisoned in Boston, devised a two-fold plan to capture activists Samuel Adams and John Hancock and to destroy supplies reported to be stockpiled by Massachusetts militia forces in Concord. Both Adams and Hancock among others were outspoken opponents to British rule and called for independence from Britain. A force of about 700 British soldiers lightly equipped under the command of Lieutenant Colonel Francis Smith were to march from Boston 40 miles west to Concord where it was believed the two men and supplies would be found. British Major John Pitcarin was assigned as executive officer under Lieutenant Colonel Smith. Unbeknown to General Gage, word of the British plan made its way to the people of Massachusetts long before the British troops embarked on their mission and efforts were initiated to deny the British any success. Efforts to contest British troop interventions in Colonial affairs were well under way long before April 1775. Militia groups were secretly organized and trained, supplies were stockpiled, a system of alerts established, all in anticipation of the exact thing that would occur on April 19, 1775.

With word the British would soon show their hand, Patriot Paul Revere instructed the sexton of Boston's Old North Church, Robert Newman, to display from the church belfry one signal lantern if the British troops were to move by land and two if by sea. In the early morning of April 19, 1774, two lanterns were seen indicating British troops were moving by way of water on the Charles River near Cambridge. Next, Paul Revere made his famous ride alerting the citizens along the route to Lexington that *"the Regulars are coming out"* and not as written in Henry Wadsworth Longfellow's poem *Paul Revere's Ride, "the British are coming.."* Paul Revere was not alone in his ride as others did the same to every farm, village, and home in the colony.

The pre-planned system of alerts was effective in turning out militia forces in every location in Massachusetts Colony. Colonial Militia formed on the Lexington Common awaiting the arrival of British troops. A force of some 80 Militia formed under the command of Captain John Parker. A number of spectators were also present as six companies of British Infantry numbering near 700 under Major Pitcarin approached Lexington on their way toward Concord. It was clear to Captain Parker that his small militia force were vastly outnumbered by the presence of the British "redcoats" and both he and Major Pitcarin issued orders not to fire unless fired upon. It is unclear to this day what exactly occurred on that early morning as the sun began to rise.

Written depositions from both sides after the incident gave differing accounts on what took place, but someone opened fire on the British that resulted in eight militia killed, ten injured with only one British soldier wounded. There is plausible reason to believe that a shot or two might have come from a spectator not affiliated with the militia that caused the mayhem. Regardless of who or how, war had begun. The British troops ordered the militia to lay down their arms and disperse, but confusion and seeing their comrades lying on the ground caused many to leave carrying their weapons to fight another day!

View of Boston's Old North Church center from which two signal lanterns were displayed indicating British troop were moving by water toward Lexington and Concord
Library of Congress, Prints & Photographs Division, LC-D419-80

News of the incident at Lexington reached the Militia forces at Concord where about 250 had mustered under Colonel James Barrett. A decision was made to march toward Lexington to meet the British head on. Seeing that there were too many British, the Militia returned to Concord where their numbers had swelled by the appearance of Militia from other nearby communities. Using fighting tactics common to American Indians, the Militia took up the fight from behind walls, trees, and any other disguised point not familiar to the British line tactic. This fight would continue throughout the day as the British forces retreated back to Cambridge and Boston. The British would be engaged nearly all the way as the fighting men of the Colony had risen to more than 2,000.

The British troops were tired, hungry, and short of ammunition due to the light amount they were issued for the mission plus they were harassed at every point on their retreat. When all was said and done, the Massachusetts Militia had surpassed their expectations in meeting and expelling the British forces from their towns and villages. The result, however, was not without cost in killed, wounded, and missing for both sides. Accounts may vary depending on the source, but the colonists lost forty-nine killed, thirty-nine wounded, and five were listed as missing. The British on the other hand lost 73 killed, 174 wounded, and fifty-three missing. Some in the Colonial ranks were called "Minutemen" for their rapid response and skill in defending a nation yet to be born! Those identified as "Minutemen" were generally young men part of organized groups, well trained in the tactics of warfare, and armed with the latest and best weapons. The symbol of a Minuteman of the Revolutionary War era exemplifies the National Guard of today!

The Battles of Lexington and Concord, if they can be called battles, occurred in one day and the first day of a war for independence that lasted at least until the British surrendered at Yorktown on October 19, 1881. This was over six years of conflict that would not be the end of differences between the new United States of America and the British Empire!

Statue of Minuteman in Concord, Massachusetts
Library of Congress, Prints & Photographs Division,
LC- DIG-det-4a25014

The Second Continental Congress

The Second Continental Congress convened on May 10, 1775, in Philadelphia. Its mission was clear as war had already begun. Delegates from Georgia were again absent at the opening of the session, but did have one representative who arrived a few days later. Even this delegate did not represent the whole of Georgia. That would come later in July when Georgia finally decided to be represented at the Congress.

The business of the Congress was first and foremost to manage the affairs of the war effort. One of the first actions was to establish the Continental Army that took place June 14, 1775. George Washington was appointed Commanding General of the Army and assumed command July 3, 1775. The military establishment was born even though it was still not called the United States Army!

The next action for the Second Continental Congress was to pave the way for the establishment of a government representing all thirteen colonies. Before that would occur, one final effort was made to resolve differences with Great Britain in the *Olive Brach Petition* passed on July 5, 1775. That effort failed to achieve positive results and Great Britain issued its own *Proclamation of Rebellion* against the colonists ending all chances of avoiding further conflict.

1775 – The Opening of the War

While the Second Continental Congress had barely begun its session in Philadelphia, the **Battle of Bunker Hill and Breed's Hill** occurred June 17, 1775. In the aftermath of the Lexington and Concord engagements, upwards of 15,000 Militia lay siege to the land region surrounding the Boston area denying the British access too much of the region. The British still controlled the waterways that provided necessary supplies and additional reinforcements, but that limited their control of the region.

The Boston of Colonial times differed in landmass from today. Boston was on a peninsula connected on the south by a narrow land strip to the mainland called Roxbury Neck. Charlestown to the north facing Boston across the Charles River was also on a peninsula that had several high points identified as Bunker Hill and Breed's Hill. Occupation of this high ground would give a strategic advantage to control the waters of Boston Harbor as well as Boston itself. Learning that the British were planning to occupy the high ground around Charlestown, Militia forces numbering over 1,000 under the command of Colonel William Prescott secured the area in an attempt to deny the British from doing the same. When the British learned that their plan had been discovered and Colonial Militia were already in place, they attacked at first with cannon fire from the British ships in the harbor. This was followed by ferrying troops across the harbor waters to the peninsula to take up the ground attack.

From fortified positions on the high ground of Breed's Hill, Militia firepower rained down on the attacking British with resounding results. A second attack resulted in the same result. This same scenario would have continued had it not been for the lack of ammunition available to the Militia forces. A third attack by the British was enough to drive those Militia still standing from Breed's Hill back across the Charlestown Neck to safety. The British had won the battle only to lose a substantial number of killed and wounded compared to the Colonial Militia.

The British lost over 1,000 men either killed or wounded, many of them officers to include Major John Pitcarin and Lieutenant Colonel James Ambercrombie. The Colonials on the other hand lost fewer than half those of the British, but Major General (Dr.) Joseph Warren, a well respected member and President of the

Massachusetts Provincial Congress, was among those killed. If there was one lesson from this battle it was that the Colonial Militia were up to the cause of defending their land!

Scene depicting the Battle of Bunker Hill, June 17, 1775
Library of Congress, Prints & Photographs Division, LC-DIG-ppa-00085

The Continental Army

The establishment of the Continental Army by the Second Continental Congress on June 14, 1775, was only the first step toward a unified military force. The next step was to establish an officer corps followed by enlistment of soldiers to fill up the ranks within the new military organization. George Washington was appointed Commander-in-Chief. He would be supported by the appointment of four Major Generals – Artemas Ward, Charles Lee, Philip Schulyer, and Israel Putnam. Eight Brigadier Generals received appointments – Seth Pomeroy, Richard Montgomery, David Wooster, William Heath, Joseph Spencer, John Thomas, John Sullivan, and Nathanael Greene. Seth Pomeroy declined his appointment and his position was left vacant.

The Continental Army would be the precursor to the United States Army, but not before reorganization in each of the next three years from its establishment, near disbanding in 1780-1781 due to the shortage of funds, and downsizing thereafter. A resolution passed by Congress June 3, 1784, established the United States Army. Even that name would see a name change to Legion of the United States before once again returning to the name United States Army

The first action of the Continental Army was to absorb into the ranks the militia troops from Massachusetts and New York. Next, it enlisted troops from Virginia, Maryland, Delaware, and Pennsylvania as infantry for one year formed into ten companies. This organization would become the First Continental Regiment in 1776. The organization of an army was not without debate among the delegates to the

Second Continental Congress and would continue far beyond July 4, 1776, the date of the Declaration of Independence!

The Army of 1775 under General George Washington would be organized into 38 regiments. Major General Artemas Ward was named second in command to General Washington. In the early stages of the army formation, Major General Ward was responsible for training the militia into a fighting force. When General Washington moved the Continental Army to New York in March 1776, Major General Ward was given command of the Eastern Department, the same department commanded by George Washington although is was not named as such at the time. It was essentially made up of the militia forces conducting the siege against Boston. Major General Ward remained in command of the Eastern Department for nearly a year at which time health issues forced his retirement. The Eastern Department remained in service to November 1779.

In addition to the Eastern Department, six other Departments were established during the tenure of the Continental Army. Each Department controlled a specific region with regard to administrative and operational matters if two or more regiments were assigned within its boundaries. A regiment was the only recognized type of unit, but terms such as brigade, division, and field army would be used on a temporary basis if the need occurred. Even the name battalion crept into the dialogue that had simultaneous meaning as regiment.

The New York Department under the command of Major General Philip Schuyler was the first to be organized on July 25, 1776. Its area of responsibility extended into Canada. The New York Department would evolve into the Northern Department April 14, 1776, under the same commander. The Northern Department would be formed from the Middle Department. The New York Department would also be the outshoot of the Canadian Department that was formally established January 17, 1776, although it is recognized as early as December 9, 1775, commanded by Brigadier General Richard Montgomery. The tenure of the Canadian Department would last only eight months. Devastating losses at Quebec and Montreal spelled its end.

The Middle Department was established February 27, 1776, the same time as another named the Southern Department. The Middle Department had responsibility for operations in New York, New Jersey, Pennsylvania, and Maryland. The Department was commanded by General George Washington and included the Main Army, or the original military organization. When the British army abandoned Boston on March 17, 1776, the Main Army belonging to the Middle Department moved to Long Island. It was at this time that the Northern Department was established and assigned to the territory north of the Hudson Highlands. The rest of New York would remain under the control of the Middle Department that continued until the end of the war.

War in the southern colonies prompted the establishment of the Southern Department on February 17, 1777, the same date as the Middle Department. Major General Charles Lee was assigned command. Major General Lee had a varied military career long before the Revolutionary War that included the British and Polish Armies before establishing his home in Virginia. Charles Lee felt he was the most qualified candidate to lead the Continental Army and failure to achieve this position did not set well with him. He is said to have despised his superior, George Washington! His early role in the Continental Army is not provided, but he assumed command of the Southern Department March 1, 1776. The Department remained in service to the end of the war and saw five command changes.

A region approximately 50 miles north of New York City was of critical importance to General George Washington. New York City was under the control of the British. Control of the Hudson River to the north was imperative to keep the British from advancing further. It was here that the Highlands Department was established November 12, 1776, commanded by Brigadier General William Heath while at the same time under the watchful eye of General George Washington and his Middle Department.

The seventh and final department was the Western Department covering the frontier regions beyond the Colonies to include the present States of Ohio, Indiana, Michigan, Illinois, and Wisconsin. Brigadier General Edward Hand took command of the Department on April 10, 1777. The Western Department has the distinction to be the only Department to remain after wars end. It would become the true United States Army!

As the years of war progressed, the Continental Army was plagued by logistical, monetary, and enlistment issues as well as one defeat after another. In the northern colonies, war was primarily determined by the months of the year. Spring through fall were the primary fighting times while year round engagements could take place in the south. There were, of course, exceptions to this at least in the north evidenced by the Battles of Montreal and Quebec followed by the Battles of Trenton and Princeton that will come to light shortly.

For the Continental Army to perform its mission in the Revolutionary War, it is vital to review the establishments of the various military service branches and departments authorized by the Second Continental Congress that would carry forward the war effort and beyond.

An army is not an army without weapons and ammunition defined as ordnance. The Second Continental Congress appointed a committee prior to June 14, 1775, to explore the methods of arms and ammunition in anticipation of the pending war. From this committee was established the Commissary General of the Artillery Stores although the exact date is not certain. Ezekiel Cheever was appointed the first Commissary General of the Artillery Stores on July 27, 1775. As the war effort progressed, improvements would occur to meet the needs.

Four departments or Corps were established on the same day, July 16, 1775. The first was the Quartermaster Department. This department was charged with supply matters to include camp and garrison equipment and transportation. Major Thomas Mifflin (later major general) was appointed the first Quartermaster General. Over the years, the Quartermaster Department would acquire further responsibilities than those of 1775.

The Department of Commissary Stores and Provisions, essentially the Subsistence Department, was next. This department was responsible for subsistence otherwise known as food or rations. Colonel Joseph Trumbull was appointed the first department commander. With little or no experience in the conduct of military endeavors, this department would undergo changes not unlike most of the departments when it was determined that new methods were necessary.

Congress established three companies of sappers and miners on June 16, 1775, that were the precursors to the Corps of Engineers whose official date of organization is March 16, 1802. Brigadier General Louis Lebegue du Portail was appointed commander of the three companies.

A military force cannot operate without revenue. The third department to be established on July 16 was the Pay Department. This department called for "one Paymaster General and a deputy. The first Paymaster was James Warren of Massachusetts appointed on July 27. He would not be the last to serve in this capacity during the Revolutionary War.

The organization of the Medical Department does not have the clean lines of establishment benefited by the previous five. Medical doctors were a reality of war regardless of government establishment. In the early years of this country, this situation was no less the case. It would take a military conflict in the early stages of the Revolutionary War in which casualties occurred to prompt Congress to take action. A Director-General was called for whose duties were to furnish bedding, medicines, and all other necessities. The first appointed to this position on July 27, 1775, was Doctor (Colonel) Benjamin Church. This department was plagued with problems that would have three directors before the end of the Revolutionary War.

In the coming months from the early days of the Second Continental Congress, the Continental Army would be joined by two other branches of military: the Continental Navy on October 13, 1775, and Continental Marine Corps November 10, 1775. Although the Navy consisted of private ships in the beginning, that would change in the years to come. The duties of the Continental Marines during the Revolutionary War were to provide security for Navy ships and conduct amphibious landings and raids. The Continental Marine Corps was disbanded at the end of the war in 1783 and reconstituted on July 11, 1798.

Capture of Fort Ticonderoga

Fort Ticonderoga along Lake Champlain was the scene of conflict in the French and Indian War. The British captured the fort from the French in 1759 after an attack a year earlier had failed. The fort was still in the hands of the British in 1775, but little had been done in the ensuing years from its capture to maintain its worthiness. The one thing of importance at the fort was armament.

Benedict Arnold was aware of the weapons at Fort Ticonderoga and convinced the Massachusetts Committee of Safety that capture of the fort and its assets could benefit the siege efforts on Boston by use of the weapons against the British. Arnold received approval to go forth with his plan, commissioned a colonel, provided with supplies and funds to raise a militia force of 400, and sent on his way.

Another group with an entirely different goal was already on its way to the site of Fort Ticonderoga. This was the Green Mountain Boys numbering about 100 and led by the flamboyant and charismatic Ethan Allen. The Green Mountain Boys were men from the New Hampshire Grant (future Vermont) organized into a militia group for the purpose of protecting their land from intrusion by New Yorkers. The lineage of the Green Mountain Boys today as the Vermont National Guard!

Word that Colonel Ethan Allen and the Green Mountain Boys were well on their way to attacking Fort Ticonderoga, Colonel Benedict Arnold raced ahead of his militia force to intercept Allen. The meeting resulted in a somewhat mutual agreement to consolidate forces although it is not certain that Colonel Arnold was given much support.

On May 10, 1775, after posturing for an attack, some of the militia reached the shoreline near the fort by boats used to cross Lake Champlain. Fearing that the element of surprise would be lost with militia still to cross the lake, an attack was made on the fort that completely overwhelmed the small British garrison of less than fifty men and half as many women and children. Not a shot was fired and British Captain William Delaplace surrendered the fort.

With Fort Ticonderoga in the hands of the militia, nearby Fort Crown Point garrisoned with only nine men was attacked and captured. Some indications point to the capture on the same day as Fort Ticonderoga, May 10, but others indicate May 11, 1775. The importance of Fort Crown Point was not for its weapons only to prevent its occupation by British reinforcements that might hinder control of Fort Ticonderoga.

Fort Ticonderoga would soon be occupied by as many as 1,000 patriots and held until the Saratoga campaign in July 1777 when it would fall once again to the British. The British stay at the fort was short ending with abandonment in November of that same year after British Lieutenant General John Burgoyne's surrendered at Saratoga (see Second Saratoga).

Battle of Montreal & Quebec

After Patriot successes involving the capture of Forts Ticonderoga and Crown Point in New York, a decision was made to make further advances against the British at points to the north in the region of Canada. Major General Philip Schuyler commanding the New York Department was granted permission by the Continental Congress to invade British strongholds at Montreal and Quebec both of which were home to many French people from the days of French occupation. The French inhabitants were not especially endeared to their British landlords. The colonists would take advantage of this situation and enlist the help of the French people against the British. Propaganda flyers were circulated to the French people calling on them to defy British occupation, establish militia to fight with the colonists, and provide intelligence that could aid the war effort. While these efforts achieved some success, the first attack on Montreal known as the *Battle of Longue-Pointe* resulted in the opposite outcome.

The Continental Army under Major General Schuyler reached Ile aux Noix, an island in the Richelieu River, on September 4, 1775. Ile aux Noix was south of British Fort Saint-Jean and even further south of the target of Montreal. Due to illness, Major General Schuyler turned command over to Brigadier General Richard

Montgomery with instructions to lay siege to Fort Saint-Jean that occurred on September 18 and would last for forty-five days. A week into the siege, Colonel Ethan Allen with a small contingent of Green Mountain Boys and Quebec Militia took it upon himself to attack Montreal or at least that was his plan. British Major General Carleton thought differently!

Major General Carleton, Provincial Governor of Quebec and Governor General of British North America, was in Montreal at the time of this siege. He had stationed the bulk of his force at Fort Saint-Jean in anticipation of a northward march by colonial forces. Catching wind of Allen's movement, he ordered British forces consisting mostly of militia to intercept the attackers.

The *Battle of Longue-Pointe* occurred on September 25, 1775. This battle was in essence an attack on Montreal that would be followed by a second attack later in 1775 as part of the overall plan to capture Quebec. Montreal in 1775 took up a small part of an island in the St. Lawrence River and Longue-Pointe was a site on the east end of the island. Colonel Allen's forces had crossed to the north side of the St. Lawrence River apparently believing that they could begin an attack from that point. Allen claims that he was to be reinforced by a force under the command of Major John Brown that did not happen. Allen and his militia forces were soon surrounded with only the water open to escape. Most of Allen's troops were able to return to safety by the south shore of the river, but he was captured and imprisoned in England at times before being exchanged in 1778 for a British officer.

The siege of Fort Saint-Jean lasted to November 1, 1775. Winter weather would influence military actions in this part of the country. If Montreal were to be captured, it would need to be now or wait for warmer weather. Brigadier General Montgomery set in motion the attack on Montreal that occurred on November 13, 1775, without incident.

British Major General Carleton had evacuated Montreal of all British forces prior to the arrival of the Continental Army and sailed for Quebec to establish defenses of that city. On December 31, 1775, the opposing armies would again meet in the *Battle of Quebec* resulting not only in the defeat of the Continental Army, but the loss of life of Brigadier General Richard Montgomery. Nearly half of the Continental Army (900) and its militia (300) would be killed, wounded, and captured. British losses were less than twenty total. The result of this battle would stop all Revolutionary War efforts in Canada and reduce British influence for at least the present.

The Death of Brigadier General Richard Montgomery, Battle of Quebec, December 31, 1775
Library of Congress, Prints & Photographs Division, LC-DIG-det-4a26292

Declaration of Independence

By the middle of 1776, The Continental Army had been in operation for a year, the Canadian Department had suffered a devastating defeat at the hands of the British in Quebec, the British had abandoned their presence in Boston, and the Second Continental Congress was still in session in Philadelphia. On July 4, 1776, nearly one month to the date of a proposal by Richard Henry Lee of Virginia that *"These United Colonies are, and of right ought to be, free and independent States"*; The Declaration of Independence that was actually named *The unanimous Declaration of the thirteen united States of America*, drafted largely by Thomas Jefferson, was adopted by the Congress. On August 2, 1776, fifty delegates signed the declaration with six others signing in the days and months to follow into 1781.

Battle of Long Island

The first major battle after the signing of *The unification Declaration of the thirteen united States of America* was fought on August 27, 1776. It was called the *Battle of Long Island*, but also went by the *Battle of Brooklyn* and *Battle of Brooklyn Heights*. It was fought for control of the city of New York. It was also a battle that saw the largest number of combatants in any battle of the Revolutionary War numbering close to 10,000 in the Continental Army and twice that number for the British.

Shortly after the British abandoned Boston on March 17, 1776, boarded ships anchored in the harbor and set sail for Halifax, Nova Scotia, to await reinforcements, General Washington moved his army to Long Island concerned that it would be the next move by the British. Here he ordered construction of a number of forts for defense of the area. General Washington would not have long to wait for the British to arrive.

The British fleet began arriving off New York on June 29, 1776, under the command of General William Howe. The first wave included forty-five ships and soon thereafter the number rose to at least 130 and there would be many more in the days to come. All this activity occurred before independence had been declared. Troops on board the ships were landed on Staten Island across the harbor from Long Island. Over the next several weeks, British troops continued to arrive swelling the number to over 30,000.

Near the end of the second week of July, General Howe attempted to negotiate for the surrender of George Washington and the Continental Army offering pardons. This was flatly rejected. Meanwhile both combatants prepared for the inevitable battle! Early in the morning of August 22, British troops numbering 4,000 or so landed near Gravesend Bay on the western tip of Long Island The few militia protecting this site retreated without engaging the British. This would be the beginning of more landings by British soldiers over the next four days in an effort to trap General Washington and his army. This plan was extremely effective virtually cutting off any escape route if necessary except by water.

The city of New York in 1776 covered only the southern tip of Manhattan Island with the Hudson River on the west and the East River on the east. There were no bridges connecting surrounding landmasses between the many islands including Long Island. Boats would be needed to land troops such as the British had done beginning on August 22. After four days, the British force was 15,000 and began the attack against the Continental Army occupying the high ground on Long Island known as Guan Heights. General Washington had prepared his defenses covering the south approach, but British General Howe managed to move his main force to the rear of General Washington creating panic within the Continental Army.

The British forces inflicted massive casualties on the unsuspecting defenders causing General Washington to move his Army west to Brooklyn Heights along the East River opposite Manhattan Island. The Continental Army was essentially trapped with their backs to the river. Rather than continue his attack, General Howe began a siege believing that his adversary had no option available and would suffer from entrapment. He also felt that any more British casualties were unnecessary. By luck or other fortunes, the Continental Army was able to acquire sufficient boats and escape across the East River to Manhattan Island much to the disbelief of General Howe.

By all standards, this was a decisive British victory in spite of the escape of the Continental Army that lost over 2,000 men about half that number killed and wounded the another half captured. The British Army in comparison lost less than 400. The Continental Army was badly damaged from the Battle of Long Island while the British were exuberant thinking they had delivered the knockout blow!

The British had won the day and would continue to exploit this gain. Much of the New York area would fall under British control. On November 16, 1777, the British captured Fort Washington on the north end of Manhattan Island resulted in over 150 killed and wounded and capturing nearly 3,000 of the defenders. Fort Washington was the product of General

George Washington's defensive preparations prior to the Battle of Long Island. The British renamed their conquest Fort Knyphausen after Hessian Lieutenant General Wilhelm von Knyphausen whose forces along with some British were responsible for capturing the fort.

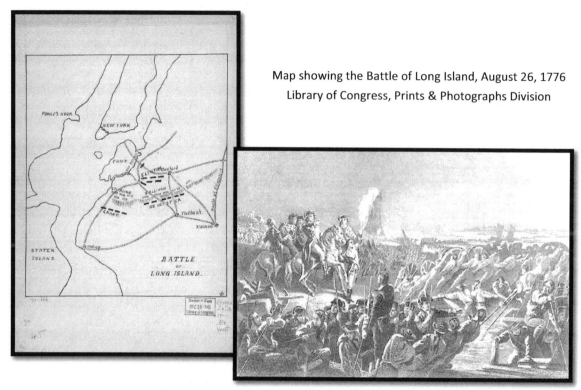

Map showing the Battle of Long Island, August 26, 1776
Library of Congress, Prints & Photographs Division

Washington's escape from Long Island August 29, 1776, showing troops in boats.
Library of Congress, Prints & Photographs Division, LC-USZ62-53982

Battle of Trenton

After the devastating defeat on Long Island, Washington and his Army eventually moved into New Jersey, then to Pennsylvania. The army needed to regroup, resupply, and enlist new recruits due to the loss. Morale was understandingly very low and General Washington needed to do all he could to change this situation. Washington himself and his beleaguered troops were in desperate need of a spark to change the current low morale and that was about to happen.

Winter was soon upon the Army and that would present the usual challenges. The Army camped near Mckonkey's Ferry not far from the Delaware River, present day town of Washington Crossing. Nearby Trenton, New Jersey, had a garrison of Hessian soldiers under the command of Colonel Johann Gottlieb Rall. Washington devised a plan to punish the Hessians for their role in defeating Washington in the Battle of Long Island and other actions.

On the evening of December 25, the Continental Army began its plan to attack the Hessians at Trenton. They would cross the Delaware River at Mckiney's Ferry a short distance north of Trenton. Then march south splitting the force into two columns, Brigadier General John Sullivan moving along the river and Brigadier Nathaniel Green to his left until they reached Trenton. The tricky part of this

US Military History – The Revolutionary War

plan was crossing the icy Delaware River at this late day in December. As it was, the weather was cold, snowy, and there was a strong wind that did little to help the poorly clad soldiers some with no shoes. In spite of these adversities, the soldiers moved on although they were behind the schedule planned by Washington.

Depiction of Washington crossing the Delaware River on the evening of December 25, 1776, prior to the attack on Hessian Troops stationed at Trenton, New Jersey
Library of Congress, Prints & Photographs Division, LC-USZ62-5012

The weather that hampered Washington also hampered the Hessians who took cover from the elements. At about 8:00 AM on December 26, Washington's troops reached the outskirts of Trenton and the Battle of Trenton began. With the element of surprise, the battle was over surprisingly soon, but not without a fierce fight in the beginning. The planning that went into the attack and the execution of that battle plan proved that the Continental Army was a force equal to its foe.

In the end, Hessian Colonel Rall was mortally wounded and died that day. None of the hessian colonels survived the attack. Of the approximate 1,200 Hessian soldiers, 22 were killed, 83 wounded, and nearly 900 captured. The captured soldiers were sent at first to Philadelphia and eventually moved to Virginia. Their fate is not known. Some Hessians soldiers were able to escape to warn the British, but their numbers were few

Washington's troops fared much better losing two to non-battle causes and five wounded during the battle. Even the treacherous crossing of the Delaware River was without loss even though some did fall into the icy water. The Battle of Trenton though not a major battle nevertheless gave a necessary boost in morale to the troops and manifested itself in battles to come. One of those would be the Battle of Princeton that would take place in just over a week's time.

Washington leading his troops in the Battle of Trenton, December 26, 1777.
Library of Congress, Prints & Photographs Division, LC-USZ62-546

Washington mounted on his horse accepts the surrender of Hessian Colonel Johann Rall at the end of the Battle of Trenton. Colonel Rall appears to be supported by two of his soldiers due to his injuries of which he would die later that day, December 26, 1777. A drum and arms lay in a pile at the bottom right of the print.
Library of Congress, Prints & Photographs Division, LC-USZ62-51811

Battle of Princeton - January 3, 1777

With the morale of the Continental Army buoyed by the victory in the *Battle of Trenton*, General Washington shifted his attention to his second goal - taking Princeton, New Jersey. Before that could happen, the *Battle of the Assunpink Creek* or the *Second Battle of Trenton* would occur.

No Continental Army victory would go unnoticed by the British. No doubt some of the Hessians soldiers who escaped from Trenton on December 26 made their way to Princeton ten miles to the north of Trenton. News of the defeat reached Lieutenant General Charles Cornwallis who set out for Princeton. Upon meeting with military commanders at Princeton, it was determined to march to Trenton. Cornwallis quickly led a force of 5,000 British troops to Trenton leaving Lieutenant Colonel Charles Mawhood at Princeton with 1,400 soldiers.

Washington on the other hand anticipated the arrival of the British troops and set up strong defenses south of the Assunpink Creek, but not before he had to plead with his troops to remain in service due to their enlistments that would expire January 1. With some convincing, nearly all agreed to stay. That was a defining moment at least for this time in the war.

Assunpink Creek flowed from the northwest into the Delaware River south of Trenton. A stone bridge spanned the creek behind which the Continental Army erected its defenses along the south side. The British troops arrived in Trenton near sunset on January 2, 1777. They immediately began their attack and were repulsed several times sustaining substantial losses while gaining no ground. Cornwallis called off the attack planning to resume the next day. However, during the night,

Washington with the majority of his army slipped away toward Princeton leaving some to give the appearance that the whole army was still in their defensive positions. Even these soldiers were gone by the time the British arrived the next morning.

Washington with his nearly 4,500 troops arrived just outside Princeton at about 8:00 AM on January 3 several hours later than planned. About the same time, two regiments of British troops were marching out of town to reinforce Cornwallis at Trenton. Spotting each other the British turned back to Princeton and the fight began. At first the engagement seemed to favor the British. Continental Army Brigadier General Hugh Mercer would be surrounded and killed resisting surrender. Other Continental troops were met with fierce fighting by the British. In the end, however, Washington's troops won the day and forced some of the British to flee while capturing about 193. Princeton belonged to Washington's Army! Casualties in this battle are the subject of discussion and disagreement. There were casualties on both sides that could number anywhere between fifty and three hundred depending on the source.

The Battles of Trenton and Princeton are considered minor victories for the Continental Army, but they were instrumental in restoring confidence in the colonial cause. Morale was up and enlistments would follow. The British military chose to abandon occupation of many posts in New Jersey as a result of the losses at Trenton, Assunpink Creek, and Princeton. On January 5, two days after the battle, Washington and his army retired to Morristown, New Jersey for winter encampment common with northern armies. This was time to rest, evaluate the military involvements, improve military skills, and prepare for the fights to come. This time was sorely needed in light of what was to come!

Scene at the Battle of Princeton showing Washington on his horse and British soldiers bayoneting Continental soldiers that may include Brigadier General Hugh Mercer.
Library of Congress, Prints & Photographs Division, LC-USZ62-469

1777 - Dark Days in the War

For much of the year 1777, the Continental Army found itself licking its wounds from one military set back after another. The few bright spots involved the victory at Princeton, a few skirmishes relating to foraging for supplies early in the year, and the defeat and surrender of British Lieutenant General Burgoyne as part of the Saratoga Campaign. Other than these few gains, the British were victorious in nineteen of the thirty-three military encounters that occurred in that year. The following are highlights of some of the military conflicts during 1777. Some of these might have been seen as large-like conflicts to the participants especially for the injured or because of comrades who were killed, but many were posturing efforts, skirmishes, raids, or chance encounters that did little to change the status of either side.

The *Battle of Millstone* occurred on January 27, 1777. It was, in fact, a skirmish or chance encounter between the New Jersey Militia and a British foraging party. The militia surprised the British resulting in several casualties and the loss of their supplies. Next was the *Battle of Punk Hill* that also involved foraging for supplies in New Jersey. The difference in this case was the size of the British foraging party numbering near 3,000. The result was the same or similar to the Battle of Millstone, but could have turned into a much larger battle under the circumstances.

The *Battle of Bound Brook* was April 13, 1777. On this date, the British turned tails on the Patriots attacking an outpost at Bound Brook, New Jersey, that was a scant seven miles northwest of a major British encampment at New Brunswick, New Jersey. The intent was to capture both the outpost and its defenders. Four thousand British and Hessian troops under the command of Lieutenant General Charles Cornwallis descended on Bound Brook at daybreak. Many of the 500 man Patriot contingent were able to escape, but anywhere from 50 to 100 were either killed or captured. The arrival of fresh Continental reinforcements deterred any plans of occupation by the British, but they managed to destroy much of what remained before returning to New Brunswick.

Another of the harassing events by the British occurred on April 27, 1777, near Ridgefield, Connecticut called the *Battle of Richfield*. Nearly 2,000 British troops under the command of Major General William Tryon, Royal Governor of the Province of New York, landed on the shores of Connecticut, attacked a small contingent of troops, and destroyed supplies of the Continental Army. Word of the attack brought out militia forces that began firing on the British troops resulting in a running battle forcing them back to their boats. The British bore the brunt of the engagement losing upwards of 150 killed and wounded and forty or so captured. In comparison, the militia saw less than 100 casualties.

Battle of Thomas Creek (Thomas Creek Massacre) involved Georgia for the first time. Military engagements in the northern colonies were limited by winter weather. The same can't be said for the south. War in the Southern Colonies especially Georgia were noticeably absent prior to 1777. Georgia was slow to involve itself in the affairs of the other twelve Colonies perhaps desiring to remain neutral, but Loyalists would force a change in thinking. A raid against Georgia by Loyalists in February 1777 prompted Georgia President, Button Gwinnett, to initiate plans to send a Patriot force against St. Augustine, the capital of British East Florida. Militia groups were organized and prepared to defend the sovereignty of the Colony against those who would cause it harm.

The plan called for both a naval and ground attack by the First and Second Georgia Regiments commanded by Colonel Samuel Elbert and a militia cavalry unit under the command of Colonel John Baker. There were approximately 300 Continentals troops and between 100 to 200 cavalry. The Georgia Regiments moved by the inter-coastal waterway and the cavalry marched overland.

The departure occurred May 1, 1777, from Sunbury, Georgia, a small town along the inter-coastal waterway approximately twenty-five miles south of Savannah. The rendezvous point was Sawpit Bluff on the southern end of Amelia Island in Florida The cavalry were the first to arrive on May 12 awaiting the arrival of the naval forces.

Word of the colonists plan to attack St. Augustine reached the British as early as April no doubt from a Loyalist spy in Georgia. Preparations were put in motion to meet the attackers before they could exercise their plan. The camp of Colonel Baker's cavalry was discovered and action was taken to have the Indians steal their horses. This was partially achieved only to have most if not all recovered by the cavalry killing one Indian in the process. On May 17, 1777, a surprise attack by British loyalists and American Indians was made against Colonel Baker's cavalry. The cavalry were overwhelmed and scattered in all directions only to be met with more firepower from the British Regulars.

Two days after the fight, May 18, Colonel Elbert arrived at the northern end of Amelia Island to discover what had taken place from cavalry members who had escaped the massacre. Considering the plight of his cavalry force and the difficulty of navigating the narrow waterways, Colonel Egbert called off the expedition and sailed back to Savannah on May 26.

This battle was a decisive victory for the British who had no losses. The number of patriot casualties varies depending on the source. After action reports from officials involved vary adding to the disparity on numbers. It is safe to say that no less than fifty cavalry troops were killed, wounded, and captured. Some of the captured were later killed by the Creek Indians in reprisal for the killing of one of their own. Attacks on Georgia by Loyalists would continue prompting another attempt by Georgia to take Florida without success.

Meigs Raid occurred on May 24, 1777, near Sag Harbor, New York. This was a raid by patriot forces on a loyalist foraging party in response to the *Battle of Richfield* in Connecticut. It resulted in the death of six loyalists and capture of 90 with no Patriot loses.

Other military conflicts followed from May through July such as the *Battle of Short Hills*, *Siege of Fort Ticonderoga*, *Battle of Hubbardton*, and the *Battle of Fort Ann* all of which were British victories. Much of August saw the same results, however, there were two battles of greater significance.

The *Battle of Oriskany* occurred on August 6, 1777, as part of the Saratoga Campaign. It is described at "one of the bloodiest battles in the Revolutionary War" in which a militia relief party numbering 700 supported by approximately 100 Oneidas Indians attempted to break the British siege on Fort Stanwix. They were attacked on their approach and suffered over 450 killed, wounded, and captured. One casualty of the battle was Militia Brigadier General Nicholas Herkimer who was severely wounded and died ten days later due to complications from surgery. The loyalists forces lost less than one hundred.

The fortunes of the Patriots would see temporary relief on August 16, 1777, in the *Battle of Bennington* that was also part of the Saratoga Campaign. The Saratoga Campaign was an attempt by the British to gain control of the Hudson River valley region that included the Highlands Department of the Continental Army. Fort Ticonderoga was in this region and was seized by the British on July 6. The *Battle of Bennington* actually occurred in New York about ten miles from Bennington that was a charter town in the New Hampshire Grant that would eventually become the State of Vermont.

British Lieutenant General John Burgoyne recently promoted after the capture of Fort Ticonderoga sent Lieutenant Colonel Friedrich Baum with a foraging party of some 1,500 Hessians to the region of Bennington in search of horses and other supplies. Neither Burgoyne nor Baum was aware that there were approximately 2,000 New Hampshire and Massachusetts' militiamen along with forces of the Green Mountain Boys camped nearby. The battle that ensued was quick and decisive leaving over two hundred Hessians dead including Lieutenant Colonel Baum and the capture of 700 more. The militia troops were not without losses of their own, but numbered well below one hundred. The militia victory was a blow to Burgoyne's attempt to seize the Hudson River valley for the British and would manifest itself with the eventual surrender of the British general and his army.

Not until October 7, 1777, would the Continental Army again become victorious. In the meantime, the following named battles belonged to the British – *Battle of Staten Island* (August 22); *Battle of Setauket* (August 22); *Battle of Cooch's Bridge* (September 3); and the *Battle of Brandywine* (September 11).

The *Battle of Brandywine* or *Battle of Brandywine Creek* deserves attention for several reasons. First, the battle involved more troops on both sides (around 15,000 each) than any other either before or after in the war. Second, the General-in-Chief for the Continental Army, George Washington, faced the General-in-Chief for the British Army, Major General Sir William Howe and his second, Lieutenant General Charles Cornwallis. Finally, the battle was the longest single day conflict lasting over eleven hours beginning before the break of dawn and ending after sunset.

The British Army set sail near the end of August 1777 from Sandy Hook Bay, New Jersey, heading for the northern end of Chesapeake Bay, a journey that took 34 days. The goal was to capture Philadelphia, the seat of the "rebellious government." Typical of many of the encounters during the Revolutionary War, the plan of the British was no secret to General Washington. It was common for the British high command to receive military intelligence from loyalists and the patriots would do the same for the Continental Army.

The *Battle of Cooch's Bridge* was one of the first encounters involving the British movement toward Philadelphia. The main thrust of the British advance would occur before dawn on September 11 meeting the forces of the Continental Army entrenched along Brandywine Creek guarding the fords that were possible crossing points for the British troops. Wave after wave of assaults caused the Continental troops to reposition time after time. The day was getting long and the British were relentless in their pursuit. By nightfall, those of Washington's men standing retreated to the safety of Chester situated on the Delaware River southwest of Philadelphia.

Philadelphia was no longer safe from British occupation. The Continental Congress moved first to Lancaster then to York, Pennsylvania. The British occupied Philadelphia on September 26 without opposition and would remain in control until June 18, 1778.

The Battle of Brandywine was a devastating loss for Washington's army with at least 300 killed, 600 wounded, and 400 captured. Further, many of the cannons of the Continental Army were captured no doubt to be used against them in future battles. The British fared somewhat better reporting 93 killed, 488 wounded, and six missing. Casualty reports for both sides are subject to question due to the sources reporting at the time. If there can be any silver lining about this battle, it would be that the Continental Army survived to fight another day!

After the British conquest of Philadelphia in the *Battle of Brandywine*, the focus shifted back to New York as part of the Saratoga Campaign. The **Battle of Freeman's Farm or First Battle of Saratoga** was fought on September 19, 1777. Lieutenant General "Gentleman Johnny" Burgoyne had planned to end patriot control of New York pinching that

army between himself from the north and a British force coming from the south. While the plan was well thought out, the southern army never materialized heading for Philadelphia instead resulting in the eventual surrender of Burgoyne.

Burgoyne's army exceeding 7,000 troops would clash with 9,000 Continental forces under the command of the cautious Major General Horatio Gates at a point along the Hudson River near Bemis Heights slightly south of the former Fort Saratoga. Supporting Gates was Major General Benjamin Lincoln and the cantankerous Major General Benedict Arnold. The American troops arriving at Bemis Heights were tasked with constructing defensive fortifications in anticipation of a British assault. Arnold was concerned that a flanking movement could threaten his position and requested of Gates to move his force forward from the heights. This request was begrudgingly granted and just in time. Mid-morning on September 19, the two forces meet and the battle began that would continue off and on for the remainder of the day.

The British Army had suffered substantial casualties in the battle that day that they could not afford showing around 550 killed and wounded. Gates troops also had casualties, but they were replenished by fresh troops that Burgoyne did not have available. By nightfall, the patriot troops had returned to the fortified works constructed on Bemis Heights awaiting the light of day and what it would bring.

Burgoyne's army suffered more than just troop loses on that day. They also were short of supplies of all types most especially ammunition and rations. The option of continuing the fight would need to be put on hold. Troop reinforcement and supplies from New York were expected, but had not arrived. Lacking the promised reinforcement and supplies, Burgoyne was faced with two choices. Either he attack his adversary or retreat back to Canada. Retreat was considered dishonorable leaving attack as the only option.

On October 7, 1777, the *Battle of Bemis Heights* or the *Second Battle of Saratoga* began. Burgoyne could not have known that Major General Gates had received substantial reinforcements outnumbering the British by at least 2,000 troops.

The British began the fight early in the afternoon on the 7th and were soon met with a barrage of fire resulting in massive losses. As the day wore on, much of the same occurred, and even Burgoyne narrowly escaped harm. One that did not escape injury was Major General Benedict Arnold who was struck in the leg and then received a broken leg when his horse fell on him that had been shot. As darkness fell, the Continental forces held the upper hand. Burgoyne retreated to his position held prior to the first battle. Surrounded by the Continental Army on October 13, Burgoyne surrendered his army on the 17th. British Lieutenant General "Gentleman Johnny" Burgoyne was allowed to return to England never to command again in the military.

Surrender of Lieutenant General Burgoyne to Major General Horatio Gates
Wikipedia

The surrender of British Lieutenant General Burgoyne had positive consequences for the colonial cause. The European adversaries of Great Britain would take notice. King Louis XVI of France began a dialogue with the American's resulting in military aid that would eventually turn the tide in the war. It would take longer than one year to make a difference, but it would show in the end.

Three days before Lieutenant General Burgoyne came to a decision on his plan of action in the Saratoga Campaign, far to the south in Pennsylvania General Washington and the Continental Army were about to embark on a campaign to take back Philadelphia that had been seized by British Major General Howe after the *Battle of Brandywine*. The *Battle of Germantown* was fought on October 4, 1777. This action was an attempt at redemption that would prove no more successful than the previous battle.

The namesake of the battle was the town of Germantown that was very near Philadelphia. For some reason, Washington could not overcome the British in spite of possessing a larger force and the element of surprise. Gains were made by Washington's men who threw everything at the British, but fog that blanketed the area caused confusion, disorientation, and lack of command and control that would spell defeat in the end. The American forces retreated with the British in pursuit for several miles. If British Major General Howe had been defeated in conjunction with the surrender of Burgoyne, the war might have taken a vastly different course. However, that did not occur and there would still be several years of conflict!

The failure of the mission at Germantown can be blamed on several outcomes. The Continental Army was to have arrived at their point of attack before dawn and did not; the fog that blanketed the area prevented coordination of the attack; and finally, the troops under the command of Brigadier General Adam Stephen engaged British troops held up in a stone house called Cliveden in violation of orders resulting in many unnecessary casualties and time lost.

Scene at Cliveden (Chew House) during the Battle of Germantown
Wikipedia

Three of the four battles ending 1777 were patriot victories though small in nature. The **Battle of Red Bank** fought on October 22 was the defense of Fort Mercer guarding the Delaware River on the New Jersey side against British Naval resupply of Philadelphia in which a Hessian force was turned back. The **Battle of Gloucester** that occurred on November 25 was a second attempt by the British to take Fort Mercer and open a supply route on the Delaware River. It too failed. The **Battle of White Marsh** in early December north of Philadelphia was an attempt by British Major General Howe to make one last attempt to defeat Washington before winter snows fell. This attempt resulted in several skirmishes rather than a full-scale battle and failed to change anything. After this last engagement, Washington and his army retired to their winter encampment at Valley Forge.

1778 - The Dark Days Continue

Changing the calendar to 1778 would make little difference to the Continental Army. The previous year had not been one of great gains nor would the next. Morale that had been high at the beginning of 1777 with victories at Trenton followed by Princeton was once again at low ebb. The winter at *Valley Forge* would not change this situation.

The winter encampment of the Continental Army at Valley Forge was anything but glamorous! Just about everything necessary for an army to survive was missing. The clothing of the men was in terrible condition to include shoes if they even had them. Sickness was rampant due to lack of adequate food, medicine, and protection from the elements. Yet, somehow the army persisted in spite of these major shortcomings albeit that some 2,500 men would die due to the effects mentioned. With the arrival of spring, there was renewed hope!

The year 1778 would see eighteen military engagements ranging from small to large. Only three would favor the Continental Army. One that deserves attention is the *Battle of Monmouth* fought on June 28, 1778. The battle itself is not as significant as those in command. Washington was still leading the Continental Army, but the British saw a change. British Major General Howe apparently disillusioned by his inability to defeat George Washington submitted his resignation as General-in-Chief of the British Army in North America. Lieutenant General Sir Henry Clinton was appointed on February 4 and replaced Howe in Philadelphia in May 1778.

With news that the French had signed a military pact with the Americans, the British made a decision to vacate Philadelphia and return to New York. Lieutenant General Clinton's orders were to move his troops on ships, but shortage of available transports forced a land march that began June 18 across New Jersey to it final destination. The Continental Army led by General Washington attacked the rear of the British column near Monmouth County in central New Jersey. Once again, poor execution foiled the attack and the British continued on their march. Both sides suffered casualties of about the same number, but fewer than could have been for the large number of troops involved on both sides.

Nearly a year and a half after the *Battle of Thomas Creek* in Florida, British forces attacked and *captured Savannah, Georgia*. This occurred on December 29, 1778. Savannah was the capital of Georgia with a population in 1778 of just under 5,000. It was also a seaport that would be of value to the British.

Georgia was defended by local militia under the authority of governor John Houston and the Southern Department of the Continental Army under the command of Major General Robert Howe headquartered at Charleston, South Carolina. News that the British were on their way to Savannah, Major General Howe marched his troops numbering around 550 in support of the militia troops. It is not certain if either the governor or Howe were aware of the number of British troops that would descend on Savannah, but that number would be over 3,000. Vastly outnumbered against a determined adversary, the patriots were forced to abandon Savannah with the loss of nearly half the force. Savannah would remain under British control until August 1781 two months before the British surrender at Yorktown.

1779 - Stalemate Year

After two years of little success, the year 1779 proved to be at least a draw that was much better than the past. There were sixteen named military engagements in the colonies of which eight were patriot victories. Similar to years past, none of these were significant enough to change the course of the war other than to prove that the British were not gaining ground.

Three of the patriot victories occurred in February one each in South Carolina, Georgia, and Quebec, Canada. The *Siege of Fort Vincennes* in Quebec in late February is notable, but not one that needs further discussion.

The *Battle of Beaufort* also known as the *Battle of Port Royal Island* fought on the third day of February in South Carolina was over control of Port Royal Island. British forces from Savannah were sent north by way of the inter-coastal waterway into South Carolina to take the town of Beaufort where a small number of Continental soldiers were garrisoned. Word of the British plan reached Major General Benjamin Lincoln commanding the Southern Department at which time a militia force under Brigadier General William Moultrie was sent to reinforce the garrison. What resulted was a skirmish involving less than 500 soldiers total on both sides that ended in less than an hour. The British failed to take Beaufort and retreated to their boats returning to Savannah.

On February 14 a more significant military conflict occurred in the interior region of Georgia some seventy miles northwest of Augusta called the *Battle of Kettle Creek*. Perhaps more significant than the outcome of the battle, is the involvement of patriotic Georgia in this battle. Recall that Georgia did not send a single delegate to the First Continental Congress and only sent delegates to the Second Congress two months after it convened. Georgia was a long way from events in the northern colonies and might have been disinterested. They may have also been unaffected by the many taxes, embargos, and other impacts by British authorities as their counterparts in the north. After repeated attacks in Georgia by loyalists, patriots were

waking to the inevitable impact of complacency and decided to take action.

British Lieutenant Colonel Archibald Campbell had seized Savannah on December 29, 1779. With Savannah under British control, Campbell marched more than a thousand troops to Augusta where an equal number of militia occupied the small town. Rather than fight, the militia forces withdrew and Campbell with Augusta in his control began recruiting Loyalists for his army. Major John Hamilton was charged with recruiting in Wilkes Country, Georgia, and Lieutenant Colonel John Boyd in the "back country" of South Carolina. After successful recruiting in South Carolina, Boyd headed back to Augusta and kept going into Georgia. This is where he was met and surrounded by militia troops at Kettle Creek and defeated. Lieutenant Colonel Boyd was mortally wounded and many of his men were killed, wounded, and captured. The outcome of this battle was two-fold. Loyalists would think twice before putting their lives on the line joining the British army, and the British would do the same trying to control the interior of Georgia! The same can't be said for South Carolina that will reveal itself in the *Battle of Camden* in 1780.

The *Battle of Stony Point* on July 16 north of New York City was a morale builder for the Continental Army. A nighttime attack by Continental troops led by Brigadier General Anthony Wayne against a British outpost at Stony Point was a total success. Nearly all of the 750 man British troops were rendered ineffective one way or another. It is unlikely that this Patriot victory changed the military balance in the war, but it did give a morale boost to the Continental Army. It also showed that General Washington was capable of contesting the British at every opportunity.

Other patriot victories occurred in the *Battle of Paulus Hook* on August 19 in New Jersey that involved a couple hundred troops in a nighttime raid on a British held fort at Paulus

Hook, and the *Battle of Newtown* August 29 on the Indian Reserve in upper New York.

This last battle was to put a stop to Indian support for the British involving 1,000 Iroquois. The battle resulted in few casualties on either side, but it did achieve its goal of ending Iroquois support for the British.

1780 – A Shimmer of Light

The war picked up steam in 1780 perhaps in anticipation of an end! The number of battles in the colonies nearly doubled over the previous year to twenty-nine of which fourteen were patriot victories though most of these occurred in the second half of the year and were of minor involvement.

The *Battle of Mobley's Meeting House* June 10-12 in South Carolina, *Battle of Ramsour's Mill* June 20 in North Carolina, *Battle of Springfield* June 23 in New Jersey, and *Huck's Defeat* July 12 in South Carolina were all patriot victories of small significance, bur victories none the less.

One battle that did not go well for the patriots was the *Battle of Camden* fought August 16 in South Carolina. Unlike the interior of Georgia that was denied to the British, South Carolina was different. In the late 1700's an area identified as Camden located at least one hundred miles northwest of Charleston was established as a trading center. It was at this site that the British established a supply depot for the southern campaign that was manned by an estimated 2,500 troops under the command of Lieutenant General Charles Cornwallis.

Patriot forces were constantly on the run in South Carolina as the British occupied all of the major population centers. In an effort to change this situation, Major General Horatio Gates with a mixed force of Continentals and militia numbering around 3,700 attempted to seize Camden from the British. The battle went terribly bad for the patriots even though the British were outnumbered. When the smoke cleared, Gates had lost half his force to all causes, all of his artillery, and a vast amount of supplies. One of Gates commanders, Major General Johann de Kalb, gave his life in the battle having been shot multiple times.

Battle of Camden depicting
the death of
Major General Johann de Kalb

Wikipedia

The defeat at Camden, South Carolina, would be softened slightly with three minor patriot victories in South Carolina. The *Battle of Musgrove Mill* August 18 followed by the *Battle of Black Mingo* August 28, and then the *Battle of Wahab's Plantation* September 20. All three encounters can be better characterized as skirmishes rather than battles without any significant change to the war effort.

The *Battle of Kings Mountain* was a Patriot victory on October 7, 1780. The battle was named for Kings Mountain in the backcountry of North Carolina, but the battle took place ten miles south in South Carolina. This was fought between Patriot militia against Loyalist militia. British Major Patrick Ferguson arrived in North Carolina the month previous for the purpose of recruiting Loyalists to help secure North Carolina for Great Britain. Patriot militia commanders were not about to let that happen.

A Patriot force in excess of 1,000 surrounded the Loyalist of equal number and totally overwhelmed them in about an hour. Major Ferguson was killed and the Loyalists still standing surrendered. The outcome of this battle changed the minds of the British in their attempt to take North Carolina.

Other battles occurred in the latter months of 1780 most of which were Patriot victories but of lesser significance. There was the *Battle of Klock's Field* October 19 in New York, *Battle of Fishdam Ford* in South Carolina on November 9, the *Battle of Blackstock's Farm* November 20 also in South Carolina, and the *Battle of Fort St. George* November 23 in New York. All four of the battles involved small number of troops and did little to change the war effort.

1781 – A Year of Significance

As busy as the fighting was in 1780, there was little change in 1771. Twenty-four named battles were fought on American soil in 1781 ten of which were Patriot victories. While the number ten might seem small compared to the total number of battles, the crowning glory was the defeat of the British at Yorktown October 19 at which time over 7,000 British soldiers surrendered to the Patriots. This Patriot victory could have ended the war, but the British were not yet convinced they had been defeated.

The military engagements in 1781 started off in South Carolina with the *Battle of Cowpens* on January 17. Cowpens of today is a short distance from Spartanburg, South Carolina, in the northwest portion of the State just south of the North Carolina Stateline. This battle was fought between Continental Army Brigadier General Daniel Morgan assigned to the Southern Department against British forces under the command of Colonel Banastre Tarleton. The number of troops on each side was around one thousand.

The outcome of the battle was a stunning victory for Morgan and his troops due largely to clever execution. The Continental Army was fully aware they were being pursued by the British and took a stand to force a fight with the Broad River at their back. Morgan's force was made up of regular and militia troops. With knowledge that some militia had run from battlefields in the past, the river at their back would deter this from happening in this battle. Also knowing that the British would be overconfident in their attack, Morgan aligned his force in three lines assigning sharpshooters in the first and the militia in the second with instructions to fire two rounds and retreat behind the third line of seasoned soldiers. This he felt would give the impression to the British that they owned the field, and that was exactly what occurred. When the smoke cleared on that January day, Colonel Tarleton's British force was nearly decimated with only he and perhaps a handful of others to limp back to the command of Lieutenant General Charles Cornwallis to report the loss.

Battle of Cowpens, January 19, 1781
Wikipedia (US-PD)

British Lieutenant General Charles, Lord Cornwallis, had ambitions to take North Carolina. The *Battle of Cowpens* was part of that endeavor that obviously failed. Four more battles would occur in North Carolina following Cowpens of which three would favor the British, but none that would prove substantial in the war. The *Battle of Cowan's Ford* on February 1 was an attempt by the Patriots to slow the British advance into North Carolina that may have delayed but did not stop it from happening. The *Battle of Haw River* fought February 25 in which a Patriot force surprised a force of British Tories with an overwhelming victory. The last two battles in North Carolina were British victories. The *Battle of Wetzell's Mill* on March 6 and *Battle of Guilford Court House* fought on March 15. These military engagements ended efforts in North Carolina until one more battle in September.

For the next six months, Virginia and South Carolina were the focus of most of the military action. Eight engagements occurred in Virginia resulting in only two Patriot victories the most significant being the *Siege of Yorktown* that led to the surrender of Lieutenant General Charles Cornwallis and his army. Five battles took place in South Carolina two of which were Patriot victories.

The *Battle of Yorktown* also known as the *Siege of Yorktown* was a Patriot victory! The British Army commanded by Cornwallis moved into Virginia in late April and established their headquarters at Yorktown. Cornwallis' move to Virginia was contrary to the wishes of the British General-in-Chief, Lieutenant General Sir Henry Clinton, who wished to focus efforts on Maryland, Delaware, and the city of Philadelphia.

Yorktown was a strategic military site with a seaport able to handle troop reinforcements and military supplies. In order for this to happen, the British Navy would need to maintain control of the waters and that would be their downfall. In July 1780 French troops began arriving in the America's in support of the Continental Army. The French Navy was not far behind that move and would aid in the defeat of the British at Yorktown a year later.

General George Washington's army along with nearly 5,500 French troops were in New York in the summer of 1781 planning to seize New York City from the British. With word that a French fleet of twenty-nine warships under the command of Admiral Francois Joseph Paul de Grasse (Comte de Grasse) was about to sail from the French West Indies for Chesapeake Bay, Washington and his French counterpart, Lieutenant General Jean-Baptiste Donatien de Rochambeau, altered their plan and began a march for Virginia. The combined American and French armies set out from New York for Virginia August 19 disguising their destination by sending false reports that would intentionally fall into British hands.

In the meantime, the British Navy received news that the French fleet was on its way to Chesapeake Bay whereby they too launched a fleet of their own from New York to intercept the French. The two navies met on September 5 in the *Battle of Chesapeake Bay* and the French drove the British back to New York spelling doom for the British headquarters at Yorktown. On September 14 the combined American and French armies reached Williamsburg, Virginia, a short distance from Yorktown. Within days the number of troops would swell to nearly 19,000 men supported with a substantial number of artillery pieces. The siege began on September 28.

In an effort to defend Yorktown, the British had constructed seven redoubts or earthen forts surrounding the town. It was these redoubts that would see the first attacks by artillery fire and occasionally by ground assault. Washington's troops occupied some of the abandoned British defenses and also constructed earthen works of their own to protect themselves from British artillery fire. The French were aligned on the left of the siege line and the Americans on the right. The French Navy had blockaded the port preventing any British reinforcements or resupply. If the British were to attempt a rescue of their comrades at Yorktown they would need to come overland and that could jeopardize the security of New York. The trap was set!

As the siege of Yorktown continued, the American and French forces moved closer to the line of the British pushing them back at every opportunity. As the troops mover closer so did the artillery that supported them. The final push took place on October 14 against heavily fortified British Redoubts 9 manned by 70 soldiers and 10 with 120 soldiers. A barrage of artillery fire was brought upon the redoubts in preparation for an all out assault. Redoubt 9 was the responsibility of the French and Redoubt 10 the Americans. Neither assault was easy, but the French had the worse due to the abatis that blocked their approach. Both redoubts were eventually captured resulting in the ability of the artillery to fire directly on Yorktown from three directions.

Cornwallis was not yet defeated and threw everything at his opponents that he had available without much success. Seeing that he could not defend Yorktown much longer, he attempted to move his troops October 16 across the York River to Gloucester Point, but that plan was scuttled when bad weather prevented further crossings. On the morning of October 17 a white flag was waved signaling an attempt at negotiation. That negotiation resulted in the surrender of the British Army! Lieutenant General Charles Cornwallis did not attend the signing of surrender on October 19 citing illness that was probably not due to anything other than total embarrassment and humiliation of his defeat at the hands of the "backward" Americans! The plunders of the siege resulted in the capture of over 8,000 British Soldiers, hundreds of artillery pieces, muskets in the thousands, twenty-four transports ships, and whatever supplies the British had left that most likely were few.

Scene of the fighting at the Battle of Yorktown
Library of Congress, Prints & Photographs Division, LC-USZ62-8233

Surrender of British Troops at the Battle of Yorktown, October 19, 1781
British Brigadier General Charles O'Hara taking the place of Lieutenant General Charles Cornwallis handing
his sword to French General Comte de Rochambeau with General George Washington standing next to him.
Library of Congress, Prints & Photographs Division, LC-USZ62-5847

1782-1783 - The End of the War?

After the defeat of a large portion of the British Army at Yorktown, the war could have come to a rapid end. This defeat and the same at the Second Battle of Saratoga in 1777 were devastating losses that apparently Great Britain dismissed as insignificant! In actuality, quite the opposite was true. The war continued to rage on for all of 1782, but fewer conflicts occurred on American soil. Much of the British anguish was taken out against both the French Army and Navy at other points on the globe although there were eight encounters between American and British forces mostly in Virginia and South Carolina with about an equal number of victories for each. One of the eight was a naval battle on April 8 called the *Battle of Delaware Bay* that was a rare Patriot victory over a superior naval force. All of the ground battles involved few combatants compared to previous battles and four involved Indians that may or may not have had British support.

The *Battle of Videau's Bridge* occurred on January 2 near Charleston, South Carolina, resulting in a British victory and the same was true for the *Battle of Wambaw* on February 24. The *Battle of the Combahee River* August 26 occurred near Beaufort, South Carolina. Here too a British victory was the result. While these few minor victories for the British may have signaled to some hope of an ultimate win in the war, actions elsewhere were in the works that spelled an entirely different outcome!

As the British tried to put on a calm face on their loss, they were at the same time involved in negotiations to end the war. Early in April 1782 the Continental Government sent Benjamin Franklin, John Jay, Henry Laurens and John Adams to Paris where they met with the British representatives Richard Oswald and Henry Strachey, advisors to the British Government. Also involved in peace negotiations were the French joined by Spain both of whom were at war with Great Britain.

All the parties involved in the peace negotiations had their own agendas. The French had been fighting Great Britain far too long and wanted a quick end to hostilities. Spain had suffered at the hands of Great Britain at every turn and wanted reprisal for the wrongs. Of course, America wanted independence from British rule.

With each country seeking their own resolution, John Jay approached the British with a peace plan between the two parties that was agreed to putting an end to what otherwise seemed like an endless endeavor. Even France and Spain solved their differences with Great Britain as did the Netherlands whose claims were vague. Although negotiations came to an end on November 30, 1782, the actual ending of hostilities were not official until the signing of the Treaty of Paris on September 3, 1783. Among the several points of the Treaty of Paris, the most significant was Britain's acceptance of the sovereignty of the United States ending all claims to territorial rights of the former colonies. It should be noted that Great Britain still held portions of North America north of the St. Lawrence River (Canada) and areas west of the Mississippi River not claimed by the United States.

The sovereign United States would take the next few years assessing their political needs. An outcome of this time resulted in the United States Constitution ratified on September 17, 1787. Peace would continue until a lack of communications would bring about the War of 1812 against the former foe, Great Britain!

Benjamin Franklin (seated center) discussing the Treaty of Peace negotiations in Paris, France.
with British representative Richard Oswald (seated front)
Library of Congress, Prints & Photographs Division, LC-USZ62-55181

Post Revolutionary War

AFTER the defeat of the British at Yorktown, the mood of those in Congress in Philadelphia was the need to disband the Continental Army or at least reduce it numbers. Some felt that a militia force was all that was needed for protection of the new country. It was clear that the transition from the Continental Army to the United States Army would not occur overnight. Quite the contrary!

The signing of the Treaty of Paris ending the Revolutionary War resulted in the disbanding of most of the Continental Army. On November 25, 1783, the British Army finally evacuated New York City allowing occupation by Washington and others. On December 23 of that year, George Washington tendered his resignation as Commander-in-Chief of the Continental Army. All that remained of the army at that time was one regiment named the First American Infantry and even that was reduced in size.

"George Washington and other Continental officers entering New York City November 25, 1783, amid a jubilant crowd"

Library of Congress, Prints & Photographs Division, LC-USZ62-128831

The United States Army would come on the heels of the Continental Army and adopted June 14, 1775, as its founding, the same date as that of the Continental Army. In some ways that date may be correct and not so in others. Actually, Congress officially established the United States Army by Resolution on June 3, 1784, such as it was with vastly reduced numbers and responsibilities. It should be recalled that there was no United States in 1775 to use the name United States Army even though the date of June 14, 1775 is used as the founding. A Resolution of the Continental Congress established the "American Army" on May 27, 1778, not the United States Army. The original two-page Resolution follows with a more readable form in actual wording after the two documents.

IN CONGRESS,

27th MAY, 1778.

ESTABLISHMENT OF THE AMERICAN ARMY.

I. INFANTRY.

RESOLVED. That each battalion of infantry shall consist of nine companies, one of which shall be of light infantry; the light infantry to be kept compleat by drafts from the battalion, and organized during the campaign into corps of light infantry:

That the battalion of infantry consist of

		Pay per month.			Pay per month.
Commissioned.	1 Colonel and Captain,	75 dollars.	1 Surgeon,		60 dollars.
	1 Lieutenant Colonel and Captain,	60	1 Surgeon's Mate,		40
	1 Major,	50	1 Serjeant-Major,		10
	6 Captains, each	40	1 Quartermaster Serjeant,		10
	1 Captain Lieutenant, each	26 2-3	27 Serjeants,	each	10
	8 Lieutenants, each	26 2-3	1 Drum Major,		9
	9 Ensigns, each	20	1 Fife Major,		9
	Paymaster, to be ta-	20 in ad-	18 Drums and Fifes,	each	7 1-3
	Adjutant, ken from	13 diti-	27 Corporals,	each	7 1-3
	Quartermaster, the line.	13 on to	477 Privates,	each	6 2-3

their pay as officers in the line.

Each of the field officers to command a company.

The Lieutenant of the Colonel's company to have the rank of Captain Lieutenant.

II. ARTILLERY.

That a battalion of artillery consist of

		Pay per month.			per month.
Commissioned.	1 Colonel,	100 dollars.	1 Surgeon's Mate,		dollars.
	1 Lieutenant Colonel,	75	1 Serjeant Major,		90ths.
	1 Major,	62 1-2	1 Quartermaster Serjeant,		90ths.
	12 Captains, each	50	1 Fife Major,		10 38-90ths.
	12 Captain Lieutenants, each	33 1-3	1 Drum Major,		10 38-90ths.
	12 First Lieutenants, each	33 1-3	72 Serjeants,	each	10
	36 Second Lieutenants, each	33 1-3	72 Bombardiers,	each	9
	Paymaster, to be ta-	25 in ad-	72 Corporals,	each	9
	Adjutant, ken from	16 diti-	72 Gunners,	each	8 2-3ds.
	Quartermaster, the line.	16 on to	24 Drums and Fifes,	each	8 2-3ds.
			336 Matrosses,	each	8 1-3d.

their pay as officers in the line.

1 Surgeon, 75

III. CAVALRY.

That a battalion of cavalry consist of

		Pay per month.			Pay per month.
Commissioned.	1 Colonel,	dol. 93 3-4ths.	1 Surgeon,		60 dollars.
	1 Lieutenant Colonel,	75	1 Surgeon's Mate,		40
	1 Major,	60	1 Sadler,		10
	6 Captains, each	50	1 Trumpet Major,		11
	12 Lieutenants, each	33 1-3d.	6 Farriers,	each	10
	6 Cornets, each	26 2-3ds.	6 Quartermaster Serjeants, each		15
	1 Riding Master,	33 1-3d.	6 Trumpeters,	each	10
	Paymaster, to be ta-	25 in ad-	12 Serjeants,	each	15
	Adjutant, ken from	15 diti-	30 Corporals,	each	10
	Quartermaster, the line.	15 on to	324 Dragoons,	each	8 1-3d.

their pay as officers in the line.

IIII. PROVOST.

RESOLVED, That a Provost be established, to consist of

	Pay per month.		
1 Captain of Provosts,	50 dollars.	2 Serjeants, each	15 dollars.
4 Lieutenants, each	33 1-3d.	5 Corporals, each	10
1 Clerk,	33 1-3d.	43 Provosts or Privates, each	8 1-3d.
1 Quartermaster Serjeant,	15	4 Executioners, each	10
2 Trumpeters, each	10		

This corps to be mounted on horse-back, and armed and accoutred as light dragoons.

RESOLVED,

Page One of the Official document of the Continental Congress showing the ESTABLISHMENT of the AMERICAN ARMY on May 27, 1778.
Library of Congress Control Number 9089050

60   US Military History- Post Revolutionary War

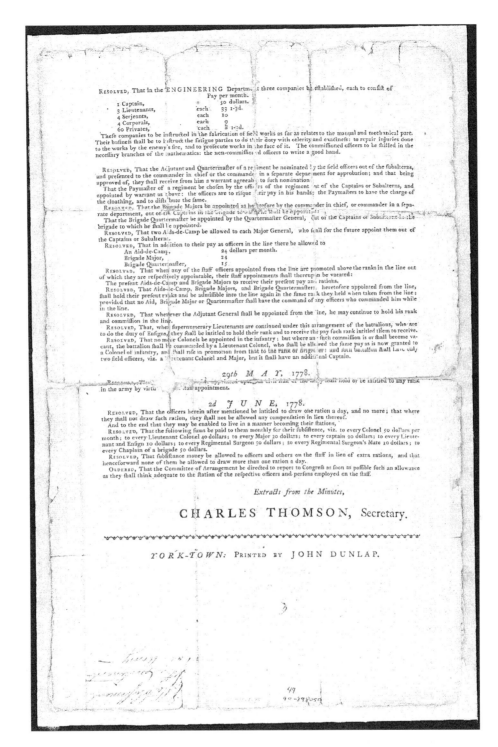

RESOLVED, That in the ENGINEERING Department three companies be established, each to consist of

	Pay per month.
1 Captain,	50 dollars.
3 Lieutenants,	each 33 1-3d.
4 Serjeants,	each 10
4 Corporals,	each 9
60 Privates,	each 8 1-3d.

These companies to be instructed in the fabrication of field works as far as relates to the manual and mechanical part. Their business shall be to instruct the fatigue parties to do their duty with celerity and exactness: to repair injuries done to the works by the enemy's fire, and to prosecute works in the face of it. The commissioned officers to be skilled in the necessary branches of the mathematics: the non-commissioned officers to write a good hand.

RESOLVED, That the Adjutant and Quartermaster of a regiment be nominated by the field officers out of the subalterns, and presented to the commander in chief or the commander in a separate department for approbation; and that being approved of, they shall receive from him a warrant agreeable to such nomination.

That the Paymaster of a regiment be chosen by the officers of the regiment out of the Captains or Subalterns, and appointed by warrant as above: the officers are to risque their pay in his hands; the Paymasters to have the charge of the cloathing, and to distribute the same.

RESOLVED, That the Brigade Majors be appointed as heretofore by the commander in chief, or commander in a separate department, out of the Captains in the brigade to which he shall be appointed:

That the Brigade Quartermaster be appointed by the Quartermaster General, out of the Captains or Subalterns in the brigade to which he shall be appointed.

RESOLVED, That two Aids-de-Camp be allowed to each Major General, who shall for the future appoint them out of the Captains or Subalterns.

RESOLVED, That in addition to their pay as officers in the line there be allowed to

An Aid-de-Camp,	24 dollars per month.
Brigade Major,	24
Brigade Quartermaster,	15

RESOLVED, That when any of the staff officers appointed from the line are promoted above the ranks in the line out of which they are respectively appointable, their staff appointments shall thereupon be vacated:

The present Aids-de-Camp and Brigade Majors to receive their present pay and rations.

RESOLVED, That Aids-de-Camp, Brigade Majors, and Brigade Quartermasters, heretofore appointed from the line, shall hold their present ranks and be admissible into the line again in the same rank they held when taken from the line; provided that no Aid, Brigade Major or Quartermaster shall have the command of any officers who commanded him while in the line.

RESOLVED, That whenever the Adjutant General shall be appointed from the line, he may continue to hold his rank and commission in the line.

RESOLVED, That, when supernumerary Lieutenants are continued under this arrangement of the battalions, who are to do the duty of Ensigns, they shall be intitled to hold their rank and to receive the pay such rank intitled them to receive.

RESOLVED, That no more Colonels be appointed in the infantry; but where any such commission is or shall become vacant, the battalion shall be commanded by a Lieutenant Colonel, who shall be allowed the same pay as is now granted to a Colonel of infantry, and shall rise in promotion from that to the rank of Brigadier: and such battalion shall have only two field officers, viz. a Lieutenant Colonel and Major, but it shall have an additional Captain.

29th M A Y, 1778.

RESOLVED, That ... appointed upon the civil staff of the army shall hold or be intitled to any rank in the army by virtue ... staff appointment.

2d J U N E, 1778.

RESOLVED, That the officers herein after mentioned be intitled to draw one ration a day, and no more; that where they shall not draw such ration, they shall not be allowed any compensation in lieu thereof.

And to the end that they may be enabled to live in a manner becoming their stations,

RESOLVED, That the following sums be paid to them monthly for their subsistence, viz. to every Colonel 50 dollars per month; to every Lieutenant Colonel 40 dollars; to every Major 30 dollars; to every captain 20 dollars; to every Lieutenant and Ensign 10 dollars; to every Regimental Surgeon 50 dollars; to every Regimental Surgeon's Mate 10 dollars; to every Chaplain of a brigade 50 dollars.

RESOLVED, That subsistence money be allowed to officers and others on the staff in lieu of extra rations, and that henceforward none of them be allowed to draw more than one ration a day.

ORDERED, That the Committee of Arrangement be directed to report to Congress as soon as possible such an allowance as they shall think adequate to the station of the respective officers and persons employed on the staff.

Extracts from the Minutes,

CHARLES THOMSON, Secretary.

YORK-TOWN: PRINTED BY JOHN DUNLAP.

Page Two of the Official document of the Continental Congress showing the ESTABLISHMENT of the AMERICAN ARMY on May 27, 1778.
Library of Congress Control Number 9089050

IN CONGRESS, 27 MAY, 1778. ESTABLISHMENT OF THE AMERICAN ARMY.

I. INFANTRY. RESOLVED, That each battalion of infantry shall consist of nine companies, one of which shall be of light infantry; the light infantry to be kept compleat by drafts from the battalion, and organized during the campaign into corps of light infantry: That the battalion of infantry consist of Pay per month. Commissioned: 1 Colonel and Captain 75 dollars. 1 Lieutenant Colonel and Captain, 60 1 Major, 50 6 Captains, each 40 1 Captain Lieutenant, 26 2-3 8 Lieutenants, each 26 2-3 9 Ensigns, each 20 to be taken from the line: Paymaster, 20 Adjutant, 13 Quartermaster, 13 in addition to their their pay as officers in the line. Pay per month. 1 Surgeon, 60 dollars. 1 Surgeon's Mate, 40 1 Serjeant Major, 10 1 Quartermaster-Serjeant, 10 27 Serjeants, each 10 1 Drum Major, 9 1 Fife Major, 9 18 Drums and Fifes, each 7 1-3 27 Corporals, each 7 1-3 477 Privates, each 6 2-3 Each of the field officers to command a company. The Lieutenant of the Colonel's company to have the rank of Captain Lieutenant.

II. ARTILLERY That a battalion of artillery consist of Pay per month. Commissioned: 1 Colonel, 100 dollars. 1 Lieutenant Colonel, 75 1 Major, 62 1-2 12 Captains, each 50 12 Captain Lieutenants, each 33 1-3 12 First Lieutenants, each 33 1-3 36 Second Lieutenants, each 33 1-3 Paymaster, Adjutant, Quartermaster, to be taken from the line. 25 16 16 in addition to their pay as officers in the line. 1 Surgeon, 75 Pay per month. 1 Surgeon's Mate, [?]dollars. 1 Serjeant Major, [?] [?]-90ths. 1 Quartermaster-Serjeant, [?] 23-90ths. 1 Fife Major, 10 38-90ths. 1 Drum Major, 10 38-90ths. 72 Serjeants, each 10 72 Bombardiers, each 9 72 Corporals, each 9 72 Gunners, each 8 2-3ds. 24 Drums and Fifes, each 8 2-3ds. 336 Matrosses, each 8 1-3d.

III. CAVALRY. That a battalion of cavalry consist of: Pay per month. dol. Commissioned: 1 Colonel, 93 3-4ths. 1 Lieutenant Colonel, 75 1 Major, 60 6 Captains, each 50 12 Lieutenants, each 33 1-3d. 6 Cornets, each 26 2-3ds. 1 Riding Master, 33 1-3d. Paymaster, Adjutant, Quartermaster, to be taken from the line. 25 15 15 their pay as officers in the line. Pay per month. 1 Surgeon, 60 dollars. 1 Surgeon's Mate, 40 1 Sadler, 10 1 Trumpet Major, 11 6 Farriers, each 10 6 Quartermaster Serjeants, each 15 6 Trumpeters, each 10 12 Serjeants, each 15 30 Corporals, each 10 324 Dragoons, each 8 1-3d.

IIII. PROVOST. RESOLVED, That a Provost be established, to consist of: Pay per month. 1 Captain of Provosts, 50 dollars. 4 Lieutenants, each 33 1-3d. 1 Clerk, 33 1-3d. 1 Quartermaster Serjeant, 15 2 Trumpeters, each 10 2 Serjeants, each 15 5 Corporals, each 10 43 Provosts or Privates, each 8 1-3d. 4 Executioners, each 10 This corps to be mounted on horse-back, and armed and accoutred as light dragoons.

RESOLVED, That in the ENGINEERING Department three companies be established, each to consist of Pay per month. 1 Captain, 50 dollars. 3 Lieutenants, each 33 1-3d. 4 Serjeants, each 10 4 Corporals, each 9 60 Privates, each 8 1-3d.

These companies to be instructed in the fabrication of field works as far as relates to the manual and mechanical part. Their business shall be to instruct the fatigue parties to do their duty with celerity and exactness: to repair injuries done to the works by the enemy's fire, and to prosecute works in the face of it. The commissioned officers to be skilled in the necessary branches of the mathematics: the non-commissioned officers to write a good hand.

RESOLVED, That the Adjutant and Quartermaster of a regiment be nominated by the field officers out of the subalterns, and presented to the commander in chief or the commander in a separate department for approbation; and that being approved of, they shall receive from him a warrant agreeable to such nomination

That the Paymaster of a regiment be chosen by the officers of the regiment out of the Captains or Subalterns, and appointed by warrant as above: the officers are to risque their pay in his hands: the Paymasters to have the charge of the cloathing, and to distribute the same.

RESOLVED, That the Brigade Majors be appointed as heretofore by the commander in chief, or commander in a separate department, out of the Captains in the Brigade to which he shall be appointed:

That the Brigade Quartermaster be appointed by the Quartermaster General, out of the Captains or Subalterns in the brigade to which he shall be appointed.

RESOLVED, That two Aids-de-Camp be allowed to each Major General, who shall for the future appoint them out of the Captains or Subalterns.

RESOLVED, That in addition to their pay as officers in the line there be allowed to An Aid-de-Camp, 24 dollars per month. Brigade Major, 24 Brigade Quartermaster, 15

RESOLVED, That when any of the staff officers appointed from the line are promoted above the ranks in the line out of which they are respectively appointable, their staff appointments shall thereupon be vacated:

The present Aids-de-Camp and Brigade Majors to receive their present pay and rations.
RESOLVED, That Aids-de-Camp, Brigade Majors, and Brigade Quartermasters, heretofore appointed from the line, shall hold their present ranks and be admissible into the line again in the same rank they held when taken from the line; provided that no Aid, Brigade Major or Quartermaster shall have the command of any officers who commanded him while in the line.

RESOLVED, That whenever the Adjutant General shall be appointed from the line, he may continue to hold his rank and commission in the line.

RESOLVED, That, when supernumerary Lieutenants are continued under this arrangement of the battalions, who are to do the duty of Ensigns, they shall be intitled to hold their rank and to receive the pay such rank intitled them to receive.

RESOLVED, That no more Colonels be appointed in the infantry; but where any such commission is or shall become vacant, the battalion shall be commanded by a Lieutenant Colonel, who shall be allowed the same pay as is now granted to a Colonel of infantry, and shall rise in promotion from that to the rank of Brigadier: and such battalion shall have only two field officers, viz. a Lieutenant Colonel and Major, but it shall have an additional Captain.

29th MAY, 1778.

RESOLVED, That [?] [?] appointed upon the civil staff of the army shall hold or be intitled to any rank in the army by virtue of [?] civilian appointment.

2d JUNE, 1778.

RESOLVED, That the officers herein after mentioned be intitled to draw one ration a day, and no more; that where they shall not draw such ration, they shall not be allowed any compensation in lieu thereof. And to the end that they may be enabled to live in a manner becoming their stations,

RESOLVED, That the following sums be paid to them monthly for their subsistence, viz. to every Colonel 50 dollars per month; to every Lieutenant Colonel 40 dollars; to every Major 30 dollars; to every captain 20 dollars; to every Lieutenant and Ensign 10 dollars; to every Regimental Surgeon 30 dollars; to every Regimental Surgeon's Mate 10 dollars; to every Chaplain of a brigade 50 dollars.

RESOLVED, That subsistance money be allowed to officers and others on the staff in lieu of extra rations, and that henceforward none of them be allowed to draw more than one ration a day.

ORDERED, That the Committee of Arrangement be directed to report to Congress as soon as possible such an allowance as they shall think adequate to the station of the respective officers and persons employed on the staff.

Extracts from the Minutes, CHARLES THOMSON, Secretary.
YORK-TOWN: PRINTED BY JOHN DUNLAP.
Establishment of the Continental Army —

On the last day of the first session of the United States Congress, September 29, 1789, Congress enacted legislation affirming the existence of the United States Army under the Constitution that had been called for in the Constitutional Convention of 1784. This may not have happened without the insistence of President George Washington who addressed Congress on August 7, 1789, with the words, *"....the national importance and necessity of which I am deeply impressed; I mean some uniform and effective system for the Militia of the United States. It is unnecessary to offer arguments in recommendation of a measure, on which the honor, safety and well-being of our country so evidently and essentially depend: But it may not be amiss to observe that I am particularly anxious it should receive an early attention as circumstances will admit; because it is now in our power to avail ourselves of the military knowledge disseminated throughout the several States by means of the many well instructed Officers and soldiers of the late Army; a resource which is daily diminishing by deaths and other causes."*

The language of the Congressional Act of September 29, 1789, did little more than affirm what already existed as a military force in the Resolution of June 3, 1784. Prior to June 3, all that remained from the end of the war were fifty-five artillerymen at West Point, New York, and twenty-five more at Fort Pitt near current

Pittsburgh. The Resolution of June 3 called for one regiment of infantry totaling about seven hundred men to come from Connecticut, New York, New Jersey, and Pennsylvania, and one additional company of artillerymen to the one already in existence. Lieutenant Colonel Josiah Harmar who would become a Brevet Brigadier General would serve as the commander of the "Regiment of Infantry" as well as the General-in-Chief of the Army as of June 3, 1784. He would continue as regimental commander until his resignation in 1792, but would be replaced as General-in-Chief in May 1791 by Major General Arthur St. Clair after repeated defeats at the hands of the Miami Indians in the Northwest Territory.

Two more companies of artillery would be added by Resolution of Congress October 20, 1786, adding to the previous two and organized into a battalion. This combined military alignment would continue to 1791 at which time a second infantry regiment would be added by Resolution of May 3, 1791. Due to the addition of a second infantry regiment, the original infantry regiment would acquire the name "First Regiment of Infantry" and the new addition the "Second Regiment of Infantry.

The *Battle of the Wabash* on November 4, 1791, in the Northwest Territory was a devastating defeat of Major General St. Clair's forces at the hands of the Confederacy of American Indians led by Chief Little Turtle of the Miami Tribe, Blue Jacket of the Shawnees, and Buckongahelas of the Delaware. The battle resulted in the worse defeat in the number of killed and wounded for any battle during the American Revolutionary War. Nearly one thousand American casualties occurred including soldiers, women, and children. Although a new regiment, the Second, was added to Major General St. Clair's military force, the number of troops available was well below that authorized. Only Major General St.

Clair and twenty-four of his men escaped unharmed from the battle of the one thousand involved. St. Clair was forced to resign prompting the appointment of Major General Anthony Wayne with a new purpose at hand.

Secretary of War, Henry Knox, proposed a reorganization of the United States Army into a legion capable of self sustained military operations involving infantry, artillery, and cavalry. Congress agreed to this proposal and by the Congressional Act of March 5, 1792, the *Legion of the United States* was formed comprised of four sub-legions, each with two battalions of infantry, one rifle battalion of light infantry, a troop of dragoons or cavalry, plus a company of artillery. A Brigadier General commanded each Sub-Legion. The Sub-Legions were recruited and trained in Pittsburgh. The first Regiment of Infantry became the First Sub-Legion and the Second Regiment of Infantry the Second Sub-Legion. The Legion of the United States continued in existence until 1796 at which time the name United States Army would return.

During the early months from June to September 1792, the Legion of the United States engaged in organizing and recruiting at Fort Lafayette in Pittsburgh. Once these efforts had been completed, the Legion moved to a site approximately fifteen miles northwest of Pittsburgh named Legionville along the Ohio River near present day Baden. At Legionville, the troops would train in all military disciplines useful against Indians in a wooded environment. They would also learn how to function as a self-sufficient force isolated from other units. With the arrival of Spring and training complete, the Legion set out on barges down the Ohio River for *Fort Washington* built in 1789 near today's Cincinnati that was used by Brevet Brigadier General Harmar during his years of fighting in the Northwest Territory.

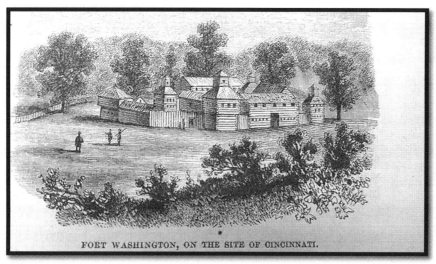

FORT WASHINGTON, ON THE SITE OF CINCINNATI.

Sketch of Fort Washington
Wikipedia

Once at Fort Washington, Major General Wayne briefly awaited orders from President Washington on what actions to be taken and then began building a series of forts along his route as he moved north. One of those was *Fort Recovery* built on the site of the defeat of Major General Arthur St. Clair in 1791. Construction began on the fort in lat 1793 and completed by springtime of the following year. Fort Recovery, Ohio, is the site today.

A supply column left the fort on June 30, 1794, and was attacked shortly thereafter by Shawnee Indians led by their Chief Blue Jacket. Part of the column was able to return to the safety of the fort although thirty-two troops were killed. Once within the protection of the fort, the skilled marksmen were able to fend off the Indians in a battle that lasted two days.

The event at Fort Recovery and others in the region would lead to the *Battle of Fallen Timbers* on August 3, 1795, ending Indian attacks in the Northwest Territory as well as British involvement in a territory claimed by the United States. The site of the battle was near present-day Toledo, Ohio. The name of the battle comes from a block of trees blown down by a storm. It was at this site that the Western Indian Confederacy would meet the Legion of the United States.

Major General Wayne and his approximately 2,000 man army would face off against approximately 1,500 Indians comprised of Miami, Wyandot, Ojibwa, Ottawa, Potawatomi, and Mingo, as well as a company of British and Canadian militia under the command of Captain Alexander McKillop. The Legion troops were trained to attack with vigor, charge with bayonets, and give no ground. Employing these tactics, the battle was over quickly forcing the Indians to retreat to Fort Miami where their entry was blocked by the British occupying the fort.

The outcome of the battle would lead to the *Treaty of Greenville* in 1795 between Major General Wayne and Chief Little Turtle that would end British occupation of the Northwest Territory and grant the region to Ohio and that of the Great Lakes to the United States. Before ending the military campaign of Major General Wayne, a number of new forts would be built. One of these was Fort Wayne named after the General. Fort Wayne, Indiana, derives its name from the fort built nearby along the Maumee River.

US Military History– Post Revolutionary War

Major General Anthony Wayne defeating the Western Indian Confederacy at the Battle of Fallen Timbers, August 3, 1795

Library of Congress,
Prints & Photographs Division,
LC-USZ62-110274

Major General Anthony Wayne

Library of Congress,
Prints & Photographs Division,
LC-USZ62-5644

With the work of securing the Northwest Territory for the United States completed, the Legion of the United States could end its involvement. The Congressional Act of May 30, 1796, called for a reorganization of the military structure thereby returning the name United States Army ending the four-year reign of the Legion of the United States. The reorganization became effective November 1 of that year and specified: *Section 1. Be it enacted by the Senate and House of Representatives of the United States of America in Congress assembled, That the military establishment of the United States, from and after the last day of October next, be composed of the corps of artillerists and engineers, as established by the act, entitled "An act providing for raising and organizing a corps of artillerists and engineers;" two companies of light dragoons, who shall do duty on horse or foot, at the discretion of the President of the United States; and four regiments of infantry, of eight companies each;*

the company of dragoons shall consist of one captain, two lieutenants, one cornet, four sergeants, four corporals, one farrier, one saddler, one trumpeter, and fifty-two privates; and shall be armed and accoutred in such manner as the President of the United States may direct. The Act continued with more details listing the ranks and positions for each military component, pay for each, clothing and rations to be received not just in type but amounts all contained in a total of twenty-three sections.

Changes to the military organizations of the United States Army would be an ongoing measure for the years leading up to the War of 1812. Some organizations would see consolidations while others would be discontinued only to resurface as events deemed them necessary. The years from 1796 to 1812 would involve the use of the army on the frontier. Indian hostilities were a constant threat as greater number of settlers moved west into uncharted territories.

Settlers moving westward
Library of Congress,
Prints & Photographs Division,
LC-USZ62-126267

US Military History– Post Revolutionary War

The War of 1812

IF there was ever a war that should never have happened, the War of 1812 would come to the top of the list. The lack of global communications in 1812 can be partially blamed for the war. The War of 1812 was between the United States and Great Britain resulting to a large part by trade issues prompted by Great Britain's war with France. Much of the growth of the United States after the Revolutionary War resulted from trade with other countries. The United States was rich in goods that other countries did not have such as cotton, lumber, tobacco, rice, etc. Both Great Britain and France sought these goods and took steps to deny each other from acquiring them. France enacted the *Berlin and Milan Decrees* of 1806-1807 in an attempt to prevent trade by other countries with Great Britain. In turn, Great Britain retaliated with a series of *Orders in Council* that called for a blockade of French ports and other ports that would support France. Both these trade restrictions had unintended consequences on U. S. trade that angered many in this country who relied on the revenue from selling their goods.

The British Royal Navy Controlled the Seas with enormous number of ships of all kinds from schooners to warships. To avoid the consequences of defying British demands, U. S. ships were required to stop at British ports for inspection before venturing to other ports where they could unload their goods. This action was, of course, to prevent the French from receiving support for their war effort. To complicate matters, the British Navy would stop ships at sea and search for British sailors on board. Those they found would be impressed into the Royal Navy to bolster their numbers. On some occasions, Americans and men of other nationalities were impressed that resulted in strong objections!

An incident on June 22, 1807, was the very kind just mentioned and did little to endear the standing of the British Royal Navy with the United States. The *USS Chesapeake* was about to set sail for the Mediterranean to relieve the *USS Constitution*. On board among the crew were three British seamen who had deserted from the British Royal Navy not uncommon at the time. Requests from the British Ambassador to return the three men were rejected by Commodore James Baron of the *Chesapeake*

USS *Chesapeake*
Wikipedia

News of the departure of the *USS Chesapeake* from Norfolk alerted three nearby British ships one of which was the *HMS Leopard*. The *Leopard* followed the *Chesapeake* for some distance before signaling a request to board that was granted. Commodore Baron was given an order to search his ship for British seamen that was refused. Soon after the refusal, the *Leopard* fired shots on the *Chesapeake* causing it to strike its colors indicating its willingness to allow a search. The British then removed four men from the *Chesapeake*. The firing on the Chesapeake resulted in the death of three sailors and the wounding of eighteen others including Commodore Baron.

The result of the *Chesapeake* incident caused much anger among Americans who took action against the British by damaging provisions waiting to be loaded on British ships. Further, President Thomas Jefferson ordered all ports closed to British ships and those present to leave immediately. The path to war was still five years off, but the over-powering actions of the British Royal Navy would pave the way for the eventual conflict. Americans were in no mood for Great Britain to bully the United States as they had prior to the Revolutionary War.

In an effort to counter the trade embargos that faced the United States as well as impressment of sailors, a series of Acts were passed beginning in 1806. The first was the *Non-Importation Act* of April 28, 1806, forbidding certain British goods from coming into the United States in hopes of getting Great Britain to cease actions taken on the high seas. Some of the banned items were important to the life of Americans while others seemed silly. Woolen items, glass and glassware, leather, silver items, paper, nails and spikes were useful. Playing cards, pictures and prints, hats, and beer products were non-essential. This Act failed to achieve its desired intent, and was replaced over a year later by the *Embargo Act*

of December 22, 1807. This latest Act placed restrictions on both Great Britain and France for their unfair treatment of U. S. shipping, but also placed restrictions on American shipping. Unfortunately, the embargo caused more harm to the United States than to the countries it intended to punish! New England suffered the most by the Embargo Act because a large part of shipping took place in that part of the country. The unpopular Embargo Act acquired the name O-Grab-Me, embargo spelled backwards. The Act was repealed in March 1809 and replaced at that time by the *Non-Intercourse Act*.

The Non-Intercourse Act lifted all restrictions on American shipping except that destined for Great Britain and France. Most U. S. goods were shipped to the very two countries on which restrictions were placed that would result in a loss of revenue for American producers. For that reason and not unlike those Acts that had gone before, the Non-Intercourse Act failed. It was replaced May 14, 1810, by the *Mason Bill No. 2.* that allowed both Great Britain and France the opportunity to suspend hostilities against American shipping. The country that agreed would receive favor while the opposite would be true for the other. At first, Napoleon took advantage of the offer believing that he could cripple the economy of Britain. Great Britain took offense to this offer and threatened military action that would soon after result in the United States declaring war against their former foe, GREAT BRITAIN!

A Declaration of War against Great Britain was called for in the United States Congress on June 1, 1812. On June 18, 1812, President James Madison signed the declaration. The House of Representatives voted seventy-nine to forty-nine in favor of the Declaration while the Senate voted in favor nineteen to thirteen. Most of the members of Congress who voted in favor of war were from the South and the West where trade and shipping concerns were of lesser importance. Members from New England opposed the war for the opposite reasons. Henry Clay, Speaker of the House of Representatives from Kentucky, was a vocal supporter of the Declaration of War. Senator James Lloyd of Massachusetts, a merchant and businessman before becoming a Senator, was opposed.

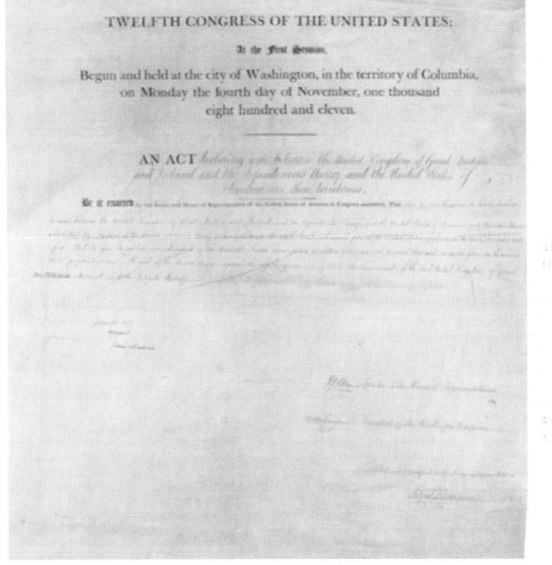

This primary source comes from the General Records of the United States Government.
National Archives Identifier: 299950

Full Citation: Act of June 18, 1812, 2 STAT 755, Declaration of War with Great Britain, War of 1812.; 6/18/1812; General Records of the United States Government, Record Group 11. [Online Version, https://www.docsteach.org/documents/document/act-of-june-18-1812-2-stat-755-declaration-of-war-with-great-britain-war-of-1812, November 15, 2016]

The Declaration of War document shown previous may be confusing listing at the top the words, *"Begun and held at the city of Washington, in the territory of Columbia, on Monday the fourth day of November, one thousand eight hundred and eleven."* That date was the beginning of the First Session of the Twelfth Congress and does not refer to The Act itself dated June 18, 1812, with the actual wording of the Declaration provided next.

"AN ACT declaring war between the United Kingdom of Great Britain and Ireland and the dependencies thereof, and the United States of America and their territories."

"Be it enacted by the Senate and House of Representatives of the United States of America in Congress assembled, That war be, and the same is hereby declared to exist between the United Kingdom of Great Britain and Ireland, and the dependencies thereof, and the United States of America and their territories: And that the President of the United States is hereby authorized to use the whole land and naval force of the United States ,, ,, ,, ,, ,, ,, ,, to carry the same into effect; And to issue to private armed vessels of the United States Commissions or Letters of Marque and General Reprisal, in such form as he shall think proper, and under the seal of the United States, against the vessels, goods and effects of the Government of the Said United Kingdom of Great Britain and Ireland, and the subjects thereof."

[signed] June 18. 1812

approved

James Madison

[signed] H Clay, Speaker of the House of Representatives.

[signed] Wm H. Crawford, President of the Senate, pro tempore.

[signed]I certify that this act did originate in the House of Representatives

[signed] Patrick Magruder, Clerk

Conflicts of the War of 1812

1812 (Major battles in bold)

First Battle of Sackett's Harbor – July 19
Battle of Brownstown – August 4
Battle of Maguaga – August 9
Battle of Fort Detroit – August 15-16
Battle of Queenston Heights – October 12
First Battle of Locolle River – November 20

1813

Battles of Frenchtown – January 18-22
Battle of York – April 27
Battle of Fort Meigs, OH – May 5
Battle of Fort George – May 25-27
Second Battle of Sacket's Harbor May 28-29
Battle of Stoney Creek – June 6

Battle of Craney Island – June 22
Battle of Beaver Dams – June 24
Battle of Fort Stephenson – August 2
Battle of Lake Erie – September 10
Battle of Thames River – October 5
Battle of Chateauguay – October 26
Battle of Chrysler's Farm (Field) – November 11
Battle of Fort Niagara – December 18

1814

Battle of Locolle Mills – March 30
Battle of Oswego, NY – May 5-6
Battle of Sandy Creek – May 29-30
Battle of Chippewa – July 5
Battle of Lundy's Lane (Niagara)– July 25
Battle for Fort Erie – August 4 to September 21
Battle of Bladensburg – August 24
Battle of Plattsburgh – September 6-11
Battle of Lake Champlain - September 11
Battle of North Point – September 12
Battle of Chesapeake Bay – September 13
Battle of Fort McHenry – September 13
Battle of Malcolm's Mills – November 6
Battle of Lake Borgne – December 14

1815

Battle of New Orleans – January 8, 1815

1812 – The War Begins

The War of 1812 was both a land and sea war with major emphasis on the word sea. There were twelve major conflicts in the war divided almost equally between land and sea and twenty minor engagements. The number of naval battles may not enlist much discussion except the United States was far from a naval power with only seventeen ships in its inventory. Great Britain on the other hand had in excess of a thousand ships and a Navy that dominated the seas everywhere in the world. Because shipping trade ruled the day, it seems only fitting that the War of 1812 should involve ships as the center of the conflict.

The total troop strength of the U. S. military in 1812 numbered around ten thousand and that included both ground and naval forces. Many of that number were not yet trained in the tactics of war.

The Congressional Act of June 26, 1812 (2 Stat. 764) called for a total of twenty-five regiments of infantry, four regiments of artillery, two of dragoons (cavalry), one regiment of light infantry (riflemen) engineers and artificers. Once this was achieved, the authorized strength of the army would rise to 36,700. Those numbers were changed again by the Act of January 29, 1813 (2 Stat. 794-797) that authorized an additional twenty regiments of all types calling for enlistment service of one year. It is a guess as to the strength of the military of Great Britain that was most likely much greater than the U. S. even with the increases authorized by the Congressional Acts.

It wasn't necessary for a declaration of war to get the war movement underway. Early in 1812, William Hull, Governor of the Michigan Territory, asked President James Madison to consider military action against the British who were creating unrest in the region inciting Indians against American outposts. Hull got his wish, but not the way he expected. William Hull was a veteran of the Revolutionary War and lacking anyone of equal standing available in the territory, President Madison appointed him a brigadier general in the army with instructions to take the necessary actions against the British and their Indian allies. On May 25, 1812, Brigadier General Hull assembled an army of three regiments of Ohio militia along with the Fourth U. S. Infantry. This gathering took place in west central Ohio west of Columbus. On June 10, Hull and his army marched north arriving at Fort Detroit on July 5. At Fort Detroit Hull's forces were joined by the Michigan Militia.

Sketch of Fort Detroit of 1710 built by the French along the Detroit River
Wikipedia {USPD}

Brigadier General Hull marched his forces into Canada July 12 crossing the Detroit River heading for Amherstburg some sixteen miles southeast at the mouth of the Detroit River. This was the site of British Fort Amherstburg (Malden) that was defended by a small force of about three hundred. Hull on the other hand had a Regular regiment of infantry just under 600 and militia numbering over 1,600. What he didn't have was adequate supplies and artillery due to broken carriages. Realizing that an assault on the fort with these deficiencies would be pointless, the attack was called off to the disappointment of Hull's officer corps and the army returned to Fort Detroit.

Not long after Hull's army moved into Canada, the first battle of the war that happened to be a naval battle occurred on July 19, 1812. This was called the *First Battle of Sacket's Harbor* that involved United States and British naval forces on Lake Ontario. Sacket's Harbor is located in northern New York State along Lake Ontario. It was a ship

building port for the United States. On the day in question, Five British ships mounted with a variety of guns sailed into Sacket's Harbor area with apparent intent to capture the *USS Oneida* and merchant ship *Lord Nelson*. A surrender demand was refused and a fight ensued. Some of the guns of the *USS Oneida* were brought to shore where a land battery was established. Between the guns on the *USS Oneida* and those in the shore battery, the U. S. forces were able to inflict damage on the British ships causing them to retreat from the harbor ending the battle. Sacket's Harbor would see a second naval battle ten months later.

With the first battle of the war at an end, the focus shifted back to the Michigan Territory and the plight of Fort Detroit. The **Battle of Brownstown** was fought on August 5, 1812. This was a minor skirmish just south of Fort Detroit involving an American force of some two hundred men attempting to secure supplies for Brigadier General Hulls' army and return them to Fort Detroit. As the

U. S. troops were about to cross Brownstown Creek they were attacked by two dozen Indians under the leadership of Shawnee Chief Tecumseh. The U. S. troops bore the brunt of the attack with eighteen killed, twelve wounded, and seventy momentarily missing that eventually returned to Fort Detroit. The Indians were virtually unscathed.

Another minor engagement called the *Battle of Maguaga* took place on August 9 very near the Battle of Brownstown. American forces of Regulars and militia were sent to retrieve the supplies that failed to reach Fort Detroit during the previous battle. Opposing forces included British Regulars, militia, and Native American Indians. This engagement was a comedy of errors on both sides except for the casualties that occurred. Whether or not the supplies made it to Fort Detroit is unknown.

With Brigadier General Hull's forces holed up at Fort Detroit, British Major General Isaac Brock gathered his forces and set up camp on the Canadian side of the Detroit River where he prepared to starve the U. S. garrison into submission. The siege began on August 15, 1812. After receiving captured documents indicating that Hull's army was badly in need of supplies and morale was low, Brock changed his tactics. What followed instead was trickery by the British that would ultimately lead to the capture of Fort Detroit and all American troops less the few who were able to escape.

To trick Hull into believing that the number of both British forces and Indian allies were greater than actually present, excess uniforms of British Regulars were worn by the militia giving the impression that many more Regulars were present in camp. Brock also ordered that single campfires be lit rather than one large fire for a unit giving again the illusion a very large force. Further, troops would show their presence and then sneak back only to show themselves again giving the impression they were new troops and the chow lines would do the same trick all in view of Brigadier General

Hull and his much larger force watching from Fort Detroit. The Indians were also involved in the trickery doing much the same as the British plus whooping up war cries to scare the unsuspecting American troops. After a volley of artillery fire into Fort Detroit landed in the officer mess killing several officers, Brigadier General Hull displayed a white flag ending the siege of Fort Detroit. It took only two days for the British to totally embarrass and deflate the American attempt to rid them from Canada. There would be more attempts later by American forces with better results.

Due to the belligerence of the British Royal Navy against United States shipping, the first major battle in the war was initiated by the United States. That conflict was the *Battle of Queenston Heights* on October 13, 1812, in Ontario, Canada. The battle was fought between United States Army Regulars supported by a complement of New York militia all under the command of Major General Stephen Van Rensselaer against British Regulars and Mohawk Indians led by Major General Isaac Brock. The purpose of the battle was to gain control of a portion of Canada and remove the British from the region that had failed under Brigadier General Hull. Another U. S. officer involved in this battle was Lieutenant Colonel Winfield Scott commanding the artillery assets, but not the Second Artillery Regiment as some report because the regiment was not formed until 1821. The significance of Lieutenant Colonel Scott is his future role as General-in-Chief of the United States Army in 1841 where he served in that capacity until his retirement November 1, 1861.

Despite superiority in numbers, the Americans failed to achieve their goal in this latest battle due to a number of blunders involving a lack of military training and failure to take advantage when the opportunity was ripe. The large U. S. force consisting of 900 Regulars and 2,650 Militia were not near enough to defeat one-third that number in opposition. Once again the militia failed to carry their weight in the battle. When the smoke cleared after the battle, Major General Van Rensselaer's forces suffered over 1,100 killed, wounded, and captured. The British and their Mohawk allies lost just over one hundred in all categories. While the British won the day, their commander Major General Brock was killed in the battle and replaced by Major General Roger Hale Sheaffe.

The last engagement of 1812 was the *First Battle of Locolle River* on November 20. This was a quick skirmish of American troops rousting a small garrison of British militia and Kahnawake Mohawk warriors defending a blockhouse near Locolle, Quebec. The American victory would be brief as a British counterattack reversed the outcome. There would be a second battle in 1814.

1813 – The War in Full Swing

The third major battle of the war was a land battle like the second with the purpose of retaking Fort Detroit from the British after the failure of Brigadier General Hull at the Siege of Fort Detroit August 16, 1812. This new battle was the *Battles of Frenchtown, Battle of the Raisin River*, or the *River Raisin Massacre* that involved a series of engagements from January 18-22, 1813. The *Battle of the Raisin River* was actually two battles named *First Battle of Raisin River on January 18* and *Second Battle of Raisin River on January 22*. The outcome of these two battles led to the *River Raisin Massacre*. Like the previous battle, these engagements were a devastating loss for the United States, and, in fact, that which occurred on January 22 accounted for the highest number of casualties for any battle in the war. The River Raisin Massacre resulted in the brutal death of many of the American captives massacred at the hands of the Indians. The battles took place in the Michigan Territory near present-day Monroe, Michigan in the far

Southeast part of the State not far from Lake Erie.

Naval activity on the Great Lakes was a frequent scene during the War of 1812. Both the U. S. and Great Britain were involved in naval engagements such as that of the First Battle of Sacket's Harbor. In an attempt to deny the British any hold in Canada, an American naval force of fourteen ships transported ground troops to the vicinity of York, the provincial capital of Upper Canada at that time and present-day Toronto. Once there they captured the town and all its holdings forcing the small garrison to retreat to Kingston in the eastern portion of Ontario. This was called the *Battle of York* fought on April 27. The battle was not without losses on both sides. The commander of the expedition, American Brigadier General Zebulon Pike was killed as were fifty-five other Americans most of whom died when the retreating British blew up the ammunition magazine at the fort. The British forces suffered just as many casualties from the battle along with nearly three hundred captured soldiers. After achieving the goal of capturing York, the American force abandoned their conquest and sailed for Fort Niagara to prepare for whatever would come next.

The loss of Fort Detroit in August 1812 prompted the United States to establish a series of forts in the Northwest Territory under the military control of the Army of the Northwest commanded first by Brigadier General James Winchester followed by Major General William Henry Harrison, future President of the United States. Fort Meigs was one of the forts situated along the Maumee River on which construction began February 1, 1813, and completed before being attacked April 28 by Major General Henry Proctor the commander of British held Fort Detroit. The attack turned into a siege that lasted to May 9 with a number of engagements outside the fort during that time. Feelings between Proctor and Indian Chief

Tecumseh were less than cordial resulting in words that caused each to go their separate ways. The Americans suffered substantial casualties in killed and wounded and the number of captured exceeded five hundred. The British and their Indian allies had far fewer casualties, but Fort Meigs was never taken.

Shortly after the Battle of York came the *Battle of Fort George* that occurred from May 25-27. Fort George was a British held fort on the west bank of the Niagara River a short distance south of the American held Fort Niagara on the opposite side of the river. This battle involved American forces conducting a joint naval and ground assault consisting of fourteen ships, ten infantry regiments, and three artillery regiments totaling around four thousand troops. The infantry regiments were the Fifth, Sixth, Ninth, Thirteenth, Fourteenth, Fifteenth, Sixteenth, Twenty-first, and Twenty-fifth plus the First U. S. Riflemen. The artillery regiments were the Second, and Third along with the U. S. Light Artillery. The order of battle involved the Headquarters and three brigades. Opposing the Americans were about one thousand British Regulars and three hundred militia troops.

The naval flotilla sailed from Fort Niagara landing the American ground forces on the shore of Lake Ontario not the Niagara River where the British had established their primary defenses. British shore batteries were engaged and silenced by naval gunfire under the direction of Commodore Oliver Hazard Perry allowing a somewhat secure landing although there were initial engagements by the British ground forces that were pushed back with success. British Brigadier General John Vincent in command at Fort George recognized the futility of further resistance and ordered a withdrawal of his troops from the fort after first spiking the cannons and exploding the ammunition magazines. The hasty withdrawal allowed only one magazine to be exploded causing little damage.

Colonel Winfield Scott leading the attack in the Battle of Fort George, May 27, 1813
Library of Congress, Prints & Photographs Division, LC-USZ62-48156

Fort George was taken by the Americans with losses, but fewer than those of the British. Half of the original British force at Fort George was killed, wounded, or captured. Vincent and those troops that escaped reached a site approximately ten miles south where they regrouped and would eventually engage the American force in a surprise attack in the Battle of Stoney Creek. The naval forces used in the Battle of Fort George left unprotected Sackets Harbor that would also see conflict.

Fort George remained in control of the American forces until early December when it was learned that a British force threatened the small number of defenders at the fort. A decision was made to abandon the fort along with burning the nearby village of Niagara that is present-day Niagara-on-the-Lake. This action took place on December 10 forcing hundreds of residents out into the cold. The American forces took refuge in Fort Niagara across the Niagara River in New York. The British arrived at Fort George and the burning village on December 10 horrified at the scene. In retaliation, six days later the British crossed the Niagara River into New York attacking and capturing Fort Niagara resulting in the death of sixty-five Americans, sixteen wounded, and three hundred forty-four captured. The British held Fort Niagara for the remainder of the war.

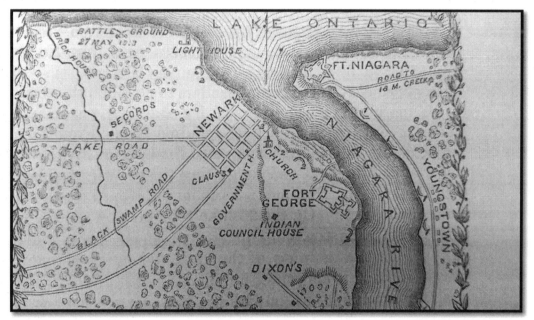

Map showing the location of British Fort George in comparison to American Fort Niagara
Wikipedia

May 28-29, 1813, was the *Second Battle of Sackets Harbor,* a major battle between American and British forces. This time the British goal was two-fold: seize the town thereby bringing an end to ship building that was a major activity at Sackets Harbor and end the use of the harbor by American Naval ships. Six British ships sailed from Kingston May 27 with around 1,400 ground troops heading for Sackets Harbor arriving the next morning. Kingston, Canada, was about twenty-five miles to the north across Lake Ontario from Sackets Harbor in New York.

Before any attempt could be made on the intended target, the British encountered a series of bateaux (flat-bottomed boats) ferrying

U. S. recruits of the Ninth and Twenty-first Infantry Regiments. The two regiments had different paths of establishment. The Ninth was originally established in 1798, deactivated and reactivated by the Act of January 11, 1812. The Twenty-first was formed for the first time by the Act of June 26, 1812, calling for twenty-five regiments of infantry and other regiment types for the War of 1812.

Sighting the bateaux with the American soldiers, the British with their Indian allies attacked resulting soon after in their surrender, but not before some thirty-five Americans were killed. Several Americans escaped reaching Sackets Harbor to give warning of the approaching British allowing time to prepare for the imminent attack. Sackets Harbor was well defended with several forts, blockhouses, and defensive barriers such as abatis (pointed stakes facing the enemy). In addition there were around four hundred Regular troops supported by two hundred and fifty militia plus an additional five hundred who rushed to the scene. Only two U. S. naval ships were present at the time, both armed schooners. The Regular troops were made up of two detachments of the First Light Dragoons and two detachments each of the First and Second U. S. Artillery. The entire Ninth U. S. Infantry arrived after the battle had ended.

On the morning of May 29, the British landed ground troops to begin the assault. From the moment they landed on shore they were met with both cannon and rifle fire stalling any attempt to achieve their goal. When it was clear that little good would come of the attack it was called off and the British returned to their ships. The casualty count on both sides was about the same with slight favor to the British, but the British were unable to achieve their goal and retreated from Sackets Harbor.

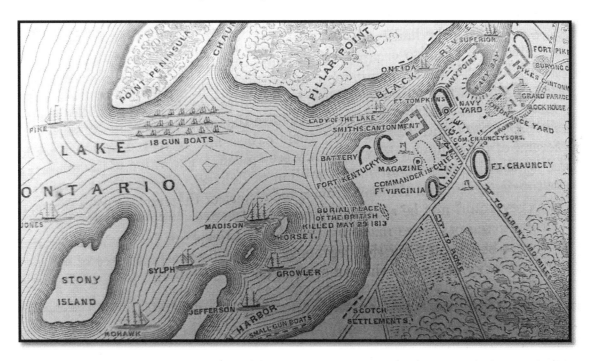

Map of Sackets Harbor and the American defenses during the Second Battle of Sackets Harbor in War of 1812. The burial site of British soldiers killed in the battle is just below the words "Fort Kentucky."

Wikipedia

The second attack on Sackets Harbor by the British was far from the last naval engagement in the Great Lakes region nor the last ground battle. The *Battle of Stoney Creek*, Ontario, Canada was a land battle fought June 6 involving British Brigadier General John Vincent's troops that had been defeated in the Battle of Fort George just over a week earlier. The American pursuit of the British after winning at Fort George was lackluster giving way to a defeat of their own when a surprise attack was made on their camp near Stoney Creek. A British force of about seven hundred attacked the poorly organized Americans at twice their number in a night attack.

American units involved in the battle were the Fifth, Twenty-third, and Twenty-fifth Infantry Regiments, and the Second Artillery Regiment. The Fifth Regiment of Infantry was initially established in 1798, discontinued in 1800 only to be reestablished in 1808 due to hostilities caused by British on American shipping, especially the USS *Chesapeake* affair. The Twenty-third and Twenty-fifth Regiments were established by the Act of June 26, 1812.

The Americans were caught totally off guard and suffered immediate casualties followed by a series of blunders that changed the course of action in slight favor of the British. After less than an hour the battle seemed to be a stand off even though the British claimed victory and had suffered just as many casualties to include their commander Brigadier General John Vincent who was apparently thrown from his horse causing him to lose memory of what had taken place and where he was when the battle ended. After the battle, the American forces abandoned their camp marching some distance closer to Fort Niagara in New York allowing the British to occupy the ground that was vacated.

An anomaly in the War of 1812 was a conflict that occurred near Norfolk, Virginia, June 22, 1813. That anomaly is that few military engagements took place in that part of

the country at least at that time of the war. This was the *Battle of Craney Island* fought against a British Naval shore party that quickly ended in an American victory.

A minor engagement titled the **Battle of Beaver Dams** took place on June 24 that occurred after the successful capture by Americans of Fort George. Some six hundred American Regular troops attempted to capture a British outpost at Beaver Dams that failed to happen. Nearly the entire American force was killed, wounded, or captured.

August 2, 1813, was the date of the minor *Battle of Fort Stephenson* along the Sandusky River near Sandusky, Ohio. Fort Stephenson was occupied by a contingent of U. S. Regulars of the Seventeenth Infantry Regiment numbering about one hundred-sixty and commanded by Major George Croghan. British Major General Henry Proctor's failure to take Fort Meigs in April apparently wore on his character and decided to make amends for his shortcomings by attacking Fort Stephenson. Proctor had more troops than necessary to capture the fort at 1,600 Regulars plus Indian allies, but was unable to do so due to the tenacity of Major Crogan who artfully positioned his troops within the fort and easily defended it on several assaults. The American casualties amounted to one killed and seven wounded. The British on the other hand had twenty-six killed, forty-one wounded and twenty-nine missing. Although this was a minor engagement, it was a decisive American victory and British Major General Proctor was again denied his claim to fame!

One of the largest naval battles of the War of 1812 was fought on September 10, 1812. This was the *Battle of Lake Erie* also called the *Battle of Put-In-Bay* that involved nine American ships under the command of Commodore Perry against six British ships led by Commander Robert Heriot Barclay. The Americans had three brigs (USS *Lawrence, Caledonia, & Niagara*), five schooners (USS

Scorpion, Ariel, Sommers, Porcupine, & Tigress), and one sloop USS *Trippe*. The British had one schooner, one sloop, two brig, and two large vessels identified as ships.

Naval dominance of Lake Ontario in 1812-1813 belonged to the U. S. Navy while Lake Erie was under the control of the British after the capture of Fort Detroit in August 1812. In an effort to change this scenario, the U. S. Navy established a shipbuilding yard at Presque Isle, Pennsylvania, complete with a protected but shallow harbor. Presque Isle is situated along the shore of Lake Erie in western Pennsylvania very near present-day Erie. Shipbuilding began at Presque Isle sometime in late 1812.

In early 1813 a decision was made to build two 20-gun brigs that would eventually become the *USS Lawrence* and *USS Niagara*. The task of supervising construction of these vessels was that of Master Commandant Oliver H. Perry

Examples of the three types of ships involved in the Battle of Lake Erie.
Brig on the left, Schooner center, and Sloop right.

In the meantime, the British were doing much the same as the Americans, building ships at the Royal Navy Dockyard in Amherstburg, Ontario. Commander Barclay needed more ships to transports supplies to and from the various British outposts around Lake Erie. Under construction was the *HMS Detroit* that Barclay was anxious to have completed. Aware that Presque Isle was doing the same for the Americans and assured that the *Detroit* was in capable hands, he sailed from Amherstburg to Presque Isla and established a blockade of the harbor on July 20 preventing American ships from leaving the port. Here he stayed for nine days until his supplies ran low. The British ships left on July 29 opening the way for Perry to move his yet to be completed ships out of the harbor. In order to achieve this feat, the heavy cannons had to be removed to allow the ships to cross the shallow water over the sand bar. This was achieved with a great deal of effort and once in the open water the two ships were refitted with their weapons.

British Commander Barclay's return a few days later to discover the U. S. Navy ships had made their escape, but took no action at that time awaiting the completion of the *HMS Detroit*. Meanwhile, Perry and his new ships sailed to Sandusky, Ohio, where new crews were added and the U. S. Navy was ready to take control of Lake Erie disrupting the British supply efforts. Put-in-Bay near South Bass Island was the staging area for Perry and his fleet of nine ships.

Construction on Barclay's *Detroit* was completed in August 1813 and he was ready to take on the American ships that were disrupting his supply efforts. The British fleet of six ships set sail from Amherstburg in early September arriving off Put-in-Bay on the morning of September 10 and the battle began. Perry's flagship, *USS Lawrence* was flying a flag with the words *"Don't Give Up the Ship"* that were the dying words of his friend Captain James Lawrence of the frigate *USS Chesapeake*. The wind favored the British in the beginning then soon after shifted in favor of the Americans. However, the long guns on all the British ships could reach much further than those on the nine U. S. Navy ships and the first shot of the battle came from the Detroit striking the *Lawrence*.

As the naval battle raged on the *Lawrence* was virtually disabled resulting in heavy casualties at which time Perry transferred himself and his flag to the *Niagara* where he continued the fight. The British also suffered heavy casualties including many officers to include Barclay himself who was wounded. The *Detroit* and *Queen Charlotte* of the British fleet collided causing their lines to become entangled. Perry took advantage of this situation attacking both with massive firepower resulting in their surrender ending the battle. All six British ships were captured on that day ending British control of Lake Erie and opening the way to retaking Fort Detroit from the British!

Commodore Perry preparing his crew for battle

Library of Congress, Prints & Photographs Division, LC-USZ62-8503

Ships engaged in the Battle of Lake Erie, September 10, 1813

Library of Congress, Prints & Photographs Division, LC-USZ62-2775

Commodore Perry being rowed from the disabled flagship *USS Lawrence*
to the *USS Niagara* in order to continue the battle and victory.
Library of Congress, Prints & Photographs Division, LC-USZ62-2159

The American naval victory in the Battle of Lake Erie opened the way for the return of Fort Detroit from British occupancy and other gains in Upper Canada. The **Battle of the Thames** that also went by the name **Battle of Moraviantown** occurred on October 5, 1813, in Upper Canada approximately seventy miles east of Detroit near the present-day city of Chatham, Ontario. British Major General Henry Proctor who was in command of Fort Detroit and involved but failed in the Siege of Fort Meigs and the attack on Fort Stephenson was forced to abandon the fort after supremacy of Lake Erie was in the hands of the United States Navy. Proctor's force of around fifteen hundred and the Indians under Chief Tecumseh retreated to Moraviantown where they were engaged by the Army of the Northwest under the command of Major General William Henry Harrison.

Harrison's force made up mostly of militia troops numbered just under four thousand to include naval assets vastly out numbered the enemy. The battle that ensued was primarily a ground affair and the beleaguered and half starved British were no match for the men under Major General Harrison. The British put up a half-hearted fight with many surrendering after the first engagement leaving the Indians to pick up where they could, but that too would prove unsuccessful. The Americans had won the day and equally important was the death of Chief Tecumseh. Even the Chief of the Wyandot's, Roundtree, was killed in the battle. Although the casualty numbers in killed and wounded on both sides including Indians were relatively small for the type of battle, all the British left standing were made prisoners that accounted for the entire force.

The fight for Upper Canada was not over by the Battle of the Thames even though this was a feather in the hats of the American forces. Another battle would occur near the end of October that would not prove equal to the last.

The Death of Chief Tecumseh at the Battle of the Thames, October 5, 1813
Library of Congress, Prints & Photographs Division, LC-USZ62-26050

The desire to take Canada for the United States and ultimately drive Great Britain from North America was evidenced in the *Battle of Chateauguay* October 26, 1813, in Lower Canada or more accurately that portion of land east of Lake Ontario along the St. Lawrence River from Montreal to Quebec. This battle involved an attempt by roughly four thousand American troops, two-thirds of which were Regulars and the remainder militia, to take Montreal from the British and their Mohawk allies at less than half in number.

The American forces involved two avenues of approach led by two major generals. Major General Wade Hampton began his move on Lake Champlain to Plattsburgh, New York, and then moved northwest following the Chateauguay River while Major General James Wilkinson started from Sackets Harbor. The move of the Americans was no secret to the British who sent reinforcements to Montreal and prepared defenses at the same time to meet the enemy.

The engagement that followed fits the scenario of many of past conflicts in which errors of judgment or just plain blunders lost the day. Hampton's force never reached Montreal and instead was forced to engage the British along the Chateauguay River in New York where the British had placed their defensive barriers. After a half-hearted attempt, the American forces retreated to the point of their original beginning ending the second to final attempt to take Canada. Casualties for the Americans were slightly less than one hundred while the British suffered less than twenty-five.

Major General Wilkinson's troops never made it to the battle scene, but would soon be engaged next in the *Battle of Crysler's Farm* on November 11. Meanwhile, Major General Hampton's troops returned to Plattsburgh but not before he submitted his resignation from the military that took effect April 6, 1814, ending his military involvement.

Scene from the Battle of Chateauguay, October 26, 1813

Wikipedia

The ***Battle of Crysler's Farm*** or ***Crysler's Field*** (sometimes named Chrysler) November 11 would be the last American attempt to take Canada away from British control, but like the Battle of Chateauguay, it too would fail. Both battles were part of the St. Lawrence Campaign. When American Major General James Wilkinson failed to arrive in support of Major General Hampton's action in the Battle of Chateauguay, he would try to take Montreal on his own. With a force of eight thousand men half of whom were involved in the battle, Wilkinson would fail to achieve his objective as Hampton had failed before him.

Major General Wilkinson was supported with eleven infantry regiments and one squadron of dragoons taking bateaux (flat-bottomed boats) from Sackets Harbor, New York, along Lake Ontario down the St. Lawrence River toward Montreal. The total American force was divided into four brigades.

The First Brigade included the Twelfth and Thirteenth Regiments of Infantry along with a squadron of the Second Dragoons. The Second Brigade had the Sixth, Fifteenth and Twenty-second all of which became the Advance Guard. The Third Brigade included the Ninth, Sixteenth, and Twenty-fifth Regiments while the Fourth Brigade had the Eleventh, Fourteenth, and Twenty-first Regiments. Only about half of the troops would take part in the upcoming battle and only some of the regiments.

From the very start Wilkinson would have shortcomings much the same as Hampton in his endeavor. Troops were poorly trained, ill equipped, and there was a shortage of supplies. Although the eventual target was to be Montreal, even that was in doubt as the large force moved down the St. Lawrence River. Further, many populated areas would need to be passed that meant disembarking the boats to secretly bypass on foot while the boats would need to do the same on the river. Wilkinson departed Sackets Harbor on October 17 and only arrived at Prescott, Ontario, on November 7 still some one hundred twenty-five miles from Montreal. It was during this time period that Wilkinson learned the fate of Hampton's failure at Chateauguay. The army disembarked their boats on the north side of the river and marched around Ogdenburg on the opposite side of the river. Once passed, they re-embarked the majority of the command leaving a small shore party to prevent any attack along the route and continued down the river three more days to November 10.

The presence of the British was no secret to Major General Wilkinson. There had been sporadic encounters along the route prompting the need to include troops along the riverbank as well as those in the bateaux. The American army camped for the night on November 10 on the north side of the St. Lawrence River not far from Cornwall, Ontario, across the river from St. Regis, New York

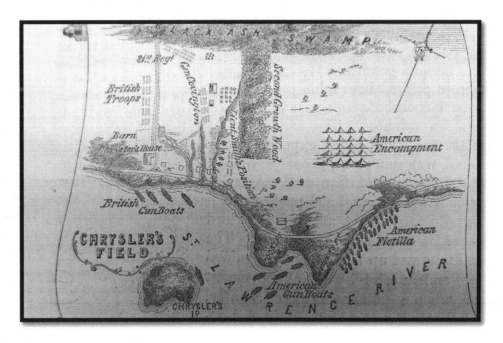

Disposition of troops prior to the Battle of Chrysler's Farm (Field) near Cornwall, Ontario, November 11, 1813

Wikipedia

A mile or two from the American camp was that of the British forces numbering less than a thousand. The morning of November 11 was a cold rainy greeting for both forces, but that would make little difference in the battle to take place that started slow and progressed as the hours passed. Each side had their gains only to fall back and start over. This scenario continued to late afternoon when it was apparently determined that the American force would not be able to go further and made their retreat to their boats and the safety of the south side of the St. Lawrence River into New York. Perhaps the British were of the same mindset as the Americans as they too ceased any aggression, or perhaps the weather that had become unsettled was the cause for their breaking off the engagement.

Major General Wilkinson's troops bore the brunt of the battle with over one hundred killed, nearly two hundred fifty wounded, and over one hundred captured. The British reported thirty-one killed, one hundred forty-eight wounded, and thirteen missing. Of course the Americans had more troops involved in the conflict than their British counterparts that may have accounted for the greater loss.

The American force far superior in numbers was unable to complete the task of expelling the British from Lower Canada and this battle would spell the end of such attempts for the remainder of the war. Major General Wilkinson declared the campaign over and winter quartered his army at French Mills the present-day Fort Covington, New York, a short distance south of the St. Lawrence River. He would eventually move to Plattsburgh, New York, along Lake Champlain.

1814 – The End In Sight!

The year 1814 would see the end of the war except for one unfortunate episode due to a lack of communication resulting in one more battle early in 1815. The year 1814 would also see other significant events. The Peninsular War as part of the Napoleonic Wars pitting France against Great Britain and other nations would come to an end in April 1814 with the defeat of Napoleon's army. Great Britain could now focus all its assets on defeating the Americans. One battle after another was the theme of 1814 that saw the burning of Washington and the attack on Fort McHenry from which the Star Bangled Banner song resulted. Before all that could happen one American general would make an attempt to salvage his career.

Near the end of January 1814 four thousand troops of the beleaguered army of Major General Wilkinson at French Mills were ordered to move to Plattsburgh, New York. At Plattsburg they were to receive much needed supplies, treatment for the sick and wounded, and rest from the ravages of war. At the same time two thousand of Wilkinson's troops were ordered back to Sackets Harbor under the command of Brigadier General Jacob Brown. Once at Plattsburgh, Wilkinson began plotting to redeem himself for the crushing defeat at Crysler's Field anticipating that his military career was about to end. After deliberation, he settled on a small British outpost defended by less than one hundred men while his force numbered four thousand.

The engagement that ensued was the *Battle of Locolle Mills* that occurred March 30, 1814. Locolle Mill consisted of a blockhouse and a stone building used as a mill just north of New York into Canada. The name came from the Locolle River that was more a stream than a river. March was still winter in northern New York and southern Quebec, Canada. Any military action would face the harsh elements of that date. Nevertheless, Wilkinson marched his large army approximately twenty-five miles north in an effort to prove his worthiness that resulted in exactly the opposite. The small British garrison literally humiliated the American forces inflicting more casualties than they themselves received. Major General Wilkinson called off further action and retreated back to Plattsburgh. Wilkinson received word on April 11 from Secretary of War, John Armstrong, Jr., of his removal from command not entirely unexpected.

Naval supremacy of Lakes Erie and Ontario fluctuated between the United States and Great Britain during the War of 1812. The British Navy held Lake Erie until the Battle of Lake Erie relinquished control to the Americans. Lake Ontario was a different situation with the British Navy in control of the northern half of the lake with strong assets at Kingston and the United States Navy the southern portion at Sackets Harbor. Both countries maintained ship building yards in their respective areas and the winter of 1813-14 saw construction of ships by each.

The British were ready with their new ships before the Americans had completed theirs. As soon as Lake Ontario was clear of ice the British planned to strike the American fleet, but the target of Sackets Harbor was considered too risky with the few troops available to the British. Instead, Fort Ontario near Oswego, New York, would become the target. Oswego was a supply point for Sackets Harbor and it was thought that the guns for the new ships under construction would be supplied through Oswego.

British Commodore James Lucas Yeo set sail with his fleet of eight warships with nearly a thousand soldiers and marines on board from Kingston on May 3 heading for Fort Ontario and Oswego a distance of approximately fifty miles. The ships arrived off the shores of Oswego on the morning of May 5 with intent to land the troops, but adverse weather conditions prevented a landing at least for the moment to the advantage of the American who took this time to prepare for what would follow.

The next morning, May 6, the weather was calm and the landing took place. Opposing the British were nearly two hundred-fifty men of the Third Regiment of Artillery supported with two hundred New York militia and two-dozen U. S. Navy sailors. The overwhelming number of British soldiers and the cannon fire from the ships pushed the Americans away from the fort. In the aftermath, the British were able to capture vast supplies and several of the cannons destined for the new ships in Sackets Harbor. Fort Ontario was totally destroyed by fire set by the British and the attack was declared a total success. Casualties on both sides numbered around one hundred each of all classes, but the major story was the capture of supplies and the cannons. It is doubtful if the British were aware that twenty-one more cannons were still on the supply route some miles from Oswego. These guns would make their way to Sackets Harbor, but not before another engagement at the end of May.

British troops disembarking for a landing at Oswego, New York, May 6, 1814

Library of Congress, Prints & Photographs Division – LC-DIG-ppmsca-23090

The guns and supplies destined for Sackets Harbor that had not arrived by the time of the Battle of Oswego were under the watchful eye of Lieutenant Melacthon Taylor Woolsey. Woolley set out May 28 on Lake Ontario with nineteen small boats loaded with items for the navy yard at Sackets Harbor. His departure point was the Oswego River at the site of the battle on May 6. In addition to the supplies, Woolsey was accompanied by 150 soldiers for protection. The expedition had traveled about fifteen miles to the mouth of the Big Salmon River when it was discovered that one of the boats was missing. It was at this point that Woolsey met up with over one hundred Oneida Indians who would guard the shoreline as the boats moved further on their journey.

Capture of Fort Oswego on Lake Ontario May 6, 1814
Library of Congress, Prints & Photographs Division, LC-USZ62-137155

Sensing that the missing boat fell into the hands of the British thereby exposing the rest to the same fate, Woolsey continued five miles further to a protected harbor at the mouth of Sandy Creek. Here he sent the riflemen ashore to hide amongst the trees and the boats further up the creek. Soon several British ships were sighted confirming Woolsey's suspicion. Along the creek the Americans waited the arrival of the British forces. On the morning of May 30 the Americans would have their opportunity surprising the British with a volley of fire completely catching them off-guard and forcing their surrender. This became known as the *Battle of Sandy Creek* that was an American victory. The American casualties were two wounded while the British suffered thirteen killed, thirty wounded, and 140 captured. In addition six British ships were captured. Needless to say, the supplies reached Sackets Harbor to the satisfaction of U. S. Navy Commodore Isaac Chauncey who was able to mount the guns in his new ships that allowed the U. S. Navy control Lake Ontario from July 1814 to late in the war.

Much of the war to this time occurred in the region of Lakes Erie and Ontario in both ground and naval battles. Another of the same in Upper Canada (Ontario) was the *Battle of Chippawa* July 5, 1814. This battle like the previous was an American victory, but involved large armies on both sides. This time the Americans brought the war to the British who occupied the west side of the Niagara River (Canada) with a large contingent of troops and several forts.

Kingston held by the British on the northern side of Lake Ontario in Upper Canada (Ontario) was the main target desired by the War Department. This could be achieved if the U. S. Navy would participate, but the new ships were not yet ready and Commodore Isaac Chauncey was not able to provide any support until later in July. American Major General Jacob Brown who was successful in defeating the British in the Battle of Sackets Harbor was tasked with leading the American forces in this new endeavor that would take place not at Kingston, but along the Niagara River to the south of Lake Ontario near Lake Erie.

With a combined military force around 3,500, Brown marched his army with Brigadier General Winfield Scott in command from Buffalo, New York, across the Niagara River and captured the sparsely defended garrison at British Fort Erie on the opposite shore. This occurred on July 3. With this easy victory under their belt, the Americans began a march north up the left bank of the Niagara River to near Chippawa River. It was here that the large American force under Scott would meet up with just over two thousand British troops. The battle that ensued was largely a stand off as each army fired volley after volley at the lines of each other. In the end, it was the British who withdrew from the battlefield and Scott did not pursue further, but did so two days later reaching close to British Fort George that was too heavily defended to undertake at least at that time

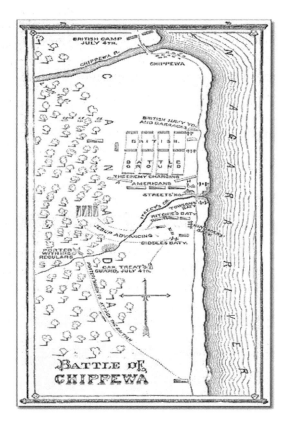

Map showing the location of troops in the Battle of Chippawa July 5, 1814.

(Note: The Chippawa River (spelled correctly) today is called the Welland River in Niagara Falls, Ontario, Canada)

Wikipedia

Casualties were high for both sides though the British count was higher. The British listed 108 killed, 319 wounded, 75 wounded prisoners, 15 prisoners, and 18 missing. The Americans on the other hand had 60 killed, 249 wounded, and 19 missing. The casualty count was high as indicated, but the more important outcome of the battle was that the Americans stood their ground matching skills with what was supposed to be a much superior army. Morale for the Americans improved and just the opposite occurred for the British.

On the heels of the Battle of Chippawa would come a major battle ranking second to the Battle of Frenchtown in the number of casualties during the War of 1812. This was the *Battle of Lundy's Lane* or the *Battle of Niagara Falls* that occurred July 25. American Major General Jacob Brown along with his two Brigadier Generals Winfield Scott and Eleazer Ripley remained in the same region of Canada after the Battle of Chippawa. The U. S. Navy at Sackets Harbor still was not able to come to the aid of Brown thereby nullifying any attempt to attack Fort George.

Both Fort George in Canada and Fort Niagara in New York were in the hands of the British since the middle of December 1813 (see Battle of Fort George May 27, 1813). British Lieutenant General Gordon Hammond, Lieutenant Governor of Upper Canada, had arrived at Fort George and began plans to expel Major General Brown's American forces from Canada. Troops from Fort George moved south while British Troops at Fort Niagara did the same along the east side of the Niagara River hoping to trap the Americans. Meanwhile, Brown began moving his forces north from his position south of the Chippawa River unaware of the strength of the British Army. The two armies would clash on July 25 at Lundy's Lane, an east west route today identified as Route 20. This engagement became the *Battle of Lundy's Lane*.

The American Army had a total strength of 2,500 consisting of seven infantry regiments including the First, Ninth, Nineteenth, Twenty-first, Twenty-second, Twenty-third, and Twenty-fifth plus some militia troops. The British forces numbered a thousand more than the Americans. The Battle commenced late in the afternoon of July 25 and almost immediately tore into the American troops only to see a reversal shortly thereafter. This scene would continue for the remainder of the day to midnight. There was much confusion experienced by both sides resulting in friendly fire on ones own troops. Eventually, neither side could muster enough able-bodied men to carry on the fight. Casualties were high and supplies short. Both Major General Jacob Brown and Brigadier General Winfield Scoot were wounded requiring Scott to retire from the battle area. Brown's order to retreat met with objections from his officer corps, but they did as ordered ending up at Fort Erie in the days to follow. British Lieutenant General Drummond was in no shape to pursue the Americans at that moment, but did remain along the battle line until he too withdrew to Queenston to regroup and resupply.

The casualty count was staggering though the total numbers vary by source. The British may have experienced 84 killed, 539 wounded, 169 captured, and 55 missing. The American's suffered 171 killed, 572 wounded, and 117 missing. In spite of the vast number of casualties, the British gave credit to the tenacity of the American troops who steadfastly met the challenge of the British Army and survived to fight another day. That day would come in August when Drummond once again moved to drive the Americans out of Canada arriving near Fort Erie occupied by the remnants of the seven infantry regiments involved in the Battle of Lundy's Lane plus the addition of the Eleventh Regiment.

What followed next was the longest single engagement (siege) of the war lasting nearly a month and a half that was essentially a continuation of the previous battle fought with many of the same commands on both sides.

The British would eventually achieve their goal of removing the Americans from Upper Canada (Ontario), but would pay a hefty price in manpower and not the victory they expected.

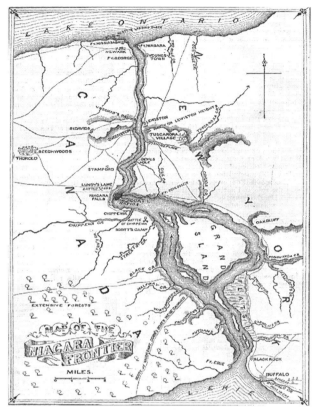

Map of the Niagara River complexes of Canada and New York. Lundy's Lane is located to the right of the letter "N" in the word Canada. The Chippawa River is located halfway between the letter "N" and "A" in Canada.

Wikipedia

Scene at the Battle of Lundy's Lane showing the close combat involved between the armies.

The *Siege of Fort Erie* began August 4 with the arrival of the British forces under the command of Lieutenant General Gordon Hammond. Fort Erie was built by the British in 1764 and saw action in the Revolutionary War.

Upon the arrival of the American forces at Fort Erie after the Battle of Lundy's Lane July 25, improvements were made for the defense of the fort that was already a substantial fort.

Sketch of Fort Erie along the shore of Lake Erie, Ontario.
Wikipedia

The siege began slow and built as the days passed. An attack August 3 into New York by the British with the intent of disrupting supplies destined for the American forces in Fort Erie was a failure. The British were building three artillery batteries from which they could fire on the fort. Three U. S. Navy ships were active against the British activities firing from locations on the Niagara River until

they were attacked and two destroyed by British ships. The weather played a major role in the events of the siege. Rain was frequent and some storms were intense enough to change the outcome of actions.

The British opened fire on the fort August 13 with their artillery from two of the completed batteries that proved largely ineffective. The third battery would not be completed until September 15. The artillery barrage was followed by a ground assault late August 15 that lasted into the next day. With each assault the attackers were repelled with deadly results. At one point, the British had managed to take a bastion only to have a powder magazine explode beneath their feet killing as many as two hundred fifty men in an instant. Fearing that the entire area was mined, the British resorted to a siege rather than subject themselves to further losses.

A siege may have been in place by the British, but the Americans were not about to throw up their hands and surrender. Instead, they were making plans of their own to send the British packing. A small force was sent out September 4 to attack British Battery No. 2. The battery was subdued after several hours of fighting when a violent storm ended the attack The same scenario occurred September 17, this time for the Battery No. 3 that ended with capture of the battery. While this action was occurring, Battery No. 2 was attacked for the second time succeeding in its capture. Before the Americans could cause the same result in Battery No. 1, the British counterattacked driving the Americans out of each of the captured batteries resulting in large number of casualties on both sides.

The American attacks on the batteries could have been avoided had they known that Drummond was prepared a day earlier to remove all the cannons from his batteries and return to Fort George. The bloody result could have been prevented. Nevertheless, the British forces did withdraw from the siege and moved north to the vicinity of Chippawa Creek. In the meantime, American Major General George Izard with his army from Plattsburgh, New York, arrived September 17 on the east side of the Niagara River and marched to the fort to support the American troops. The arrival of Izard's troops swelled the number of Americans to over 6,500 that was far greater than the 2,500 the British had available to fight.

Major General Izard was senior to Major General Brown and assumed command of the American forces. Some efforts were undertaken to follow the British north, but it was a half-hearted attempt. The winter season was approaching and supply lines were becoming difficult. Izard made the decision to vacate Fort Erie for New York, but before doing so it was mined and destroyed. Major General Brown upon his request moved with his troops to the defense of Sackets Harbor.

Casualties from the Siege of Fort Erie for the British numbered half their original force of 3,000. For the Americans, slightly less than half the initial 2,500 troops were counted as casualties. Many of these could have been avoided except for the effort to seize the British batteries on September 17. Thus, ended the fight for Upper Canada. Fort Erie was later occupied by the British, but never rebuilt.

Nearly the entire war effort to the time of the Siege of Fort Erie had been conducted around Lakes Erie and Ontario as pointed out earlier. Just after the siege began, a battle occurred in the region of Maryland unusual for the war at that time. The defeat of Napoleon in April 1814 released the British from their commitments in that war enabling them to send troops and ships to North America. Both Upper and Lower Canada were reinforced with additional troops thereby lessening the chance for claiming the region for America. British Naval ships were active along the Atlantic coastline of the United States as early as 1813 conducting raids against vital American assets of all kinds. The Battle of Craney Island June 22, 1813, was one such raid that failed to accomplish its objective. These raids could have been more productive if the British had a sufficient number of troops. With the defeat of Napoleon in Europe more ships and more troops sailed to this coastal area. The *Battle of Bladensburg* fought on August 24, 1814, resulted from this new effort.

The American military commanders of both ground and naval forces in and around New York had mastered the techniques of fighting against the British, but that could not be said for their counterparts to the south such as Maryland and more particular, Washington, D. C. Brigadier General William H. Winder, a paroled officer captured in the Battle of Stoney Creek was charged with defending Washington and Baltimore in the event of an attack by the British. Available to Winder were over 6,000 militia and less than 500 Regulars, but little preparation had taken place should such an attack occur. A two-prong attack would take place that involved a joint ground and naval effort by the British first on Bladensburg, Maryland, followed by Washington, D. C. All efforts by Winder and his unprepared force to stop the attack were unsuccessful. Bladensburg would fall and the path to Washington was open to the British.

Near the end of the day, Wednesday, August 24, the British had reached Washington, D. C., and set fire to many of the buildings including the White House and the Capitol. This marked a dark day in the history of the United States. Whether poetic justice or Divine intervention, a storm the next day put out the fires and damaged many of the British ships anchored on the Potomac River. This storm may have been a hurricane due to the degree of damage, but whatever it was, it apparently convinced the British to leave the area. Once the British were gone, Washington, D. C., came back to life!

Scene of the burning of Washington, August 24, 1814
Library of Congress, Prints & Photographs Division, LC-USZ62-117176

The British departure from Washington after burning many of the government buildings returned to the vicinity of Baltimore nineteen days later that did not end well for them. Meanwhile, the British in the north would stage a ground and naval attack on Plattsburg, New York, situated along the upper region of Lake Champlain.

The *Battle of Plattsburg* also known as the *Battle of Lake Champlain* began September 6, 1814, as the second of two possible objectives for the British plan to inflict harm on America now that the Peninsular War in Europe had ended and sufficient troops were available for the war. The first objective was to have been Sackets Harbor, but the British high command had reservations on its success thus opting for Plattsburg. British Lieutenant General Sir George Prevost, Commander-in-Chief and Governor General of Canada organized an effective force of some 8,000 men under the command of Major General Sir Francis de Rottenburg and began the march south August 31. Word of the British movement allowed American commander Brigadier General Alexander Macomb to dispatch troops to harass the British as they advanced, falling back as the need arose. This action continued to September 6 when the British arrived near Plattsburg. The Americans crossed to the east side of the Saranac River removing the planks on the bridge and prepared for engagement. At the same time, the naval forces of both sides were about to engage one another though the British Navy had three more ships (16) with 95 guns, some with long range capability, while the U. S. Navy ships were equipped with 85 guns.

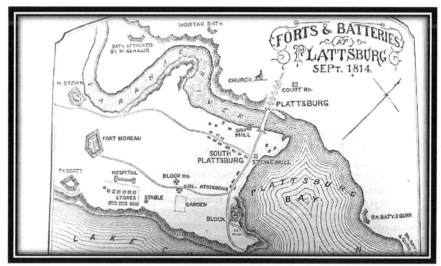

Sketch of Plattsburg, New York
Wikipediia

The British battle plan was to conduct a coordinated ground and naval attack against Brigadier General Macomb's army and the U. S. Navy commanded by Captain Thomas Macdonough. The U. S. Navy ships had moved to Plattsburg Bay off Lake Champlain hoping to draw the British Navy into close combat reducing the advantage of the long guns on the British ships. This move proved extremely effective causing heavy damage to several of the British ships and soon after the surrender of four while the remaining gunboats withdrew from the battle. The U. S. Navy suffered 52 sailors killed and 58 wounded. The British had 84 killed and 110 wounded. British Navy Captain George Downie was killed in the battle.

The British ground attack was to begin at the same time as the naval battle, but started late and hardly moved before word came that the British Navy had been defeated. Without the support of the navy, Lieutenant General

Prevost determined that any attempt to continue the ground plan would be pointless. He called off the effort to the objection of some of his commanders and the entire army marched back to Canada departing late that evening, September 11. The United States Navy proved superior to that of the world power British Royal Navy and saved the day!

The total British losses were 168 killed, 220 wounded, 317 captured, four ships, and more important the loss of the battle. This ended all British efforts in the United States for the duration of the war. One ironic fact surrounding the timing of this battle was the meeting at the same time of British and American officials in Ghent, Netherlands, attempting to negotiate a peaceful end to the war. This meeting would result in the Treaty of Ghent, December 24, 1814.

Battle scene at Plattsburg, New York, September 11, 1814
Library of Congress, Prints & Photographs Division, LC-USZ62-49655

"McDonough's victory on Lake Champlain" during the Battle of Lake Champlain
also called the Battle of Plattsburg, September 11, 1814
Library of Congress, Prints & Photographs Division, LC-USZ62-2353

The day after the Battle of Plattsburg was the first day of the **Battle of Baltimore** fought September 12-15 that was actually two battles named the **Battle of North Point** and the **Bombardment of Fort McHenry**. There were substantial British ground and naval assets of 5,000 infantry and 19 warships faced off against a much larger American ground force of 11,000 with the same outcome as that at Plattsburg.

On September 12, 1814, the British infantry led by Major General Robert Ross disembarked his forces on North Point peninsula from ships on Chesapeake Bay. Their objective was Baltimore. This landing was no secret to the American commander, Major General Samuel Smith, who dispatched Brigadier General John Stricker with a force to meet the attackers. The terrain favored Stricker who used delaying tactics while inflicting lethal fire on the British resulting in the death of Major General Ross. The death of Ross demoralized the British troops and delayed any present movement. Colonel Arthur Brooke took command of the British troops. He regrouped and began moving against the Americans. The American troops began an organized withdrawal all the while continuing to fire on the British causing even more casualties. Colonel Brooke halted his command as dark approached on that first day assessing his losses and anticipating the silencing of Fort McHenry. Stricker moved his forces to Baltimore where more troops were preparing the defense of the city. British casualties on this first day of battle were 44 killed and 295 wounded while Stricker's troops suffered 24 killed, 139 wounded, and about 50 captured.

The next day, Tuesday, September 13, British Colonel Brooke began a march toward Baltimore without interference from Brigadier General Stricker who had withdrawn to the entrenchments surrounding Baltimore. Brooke planned to attack the American line late that evening, but several set backs coupled with what appeared to be a massive American force in front of him changed his plans and conducted a withdrawal to the ships in the bay.

The **Bombardment of Fort McHenry**, the second objective of the Battle of Baltimore, began on the morning of September 13 and continued for an entire day. Fort McHenry was an obstacle to the British ships entering Baltimore Harbor and using their guns on the city. Inflicting only minor damage on the fort and the Americans doing the same to the British ships, the bombardment ended. The British had run out of ammunition. The result of the day-long bombardment was one wounded British sailor and four Americans killed and 24 wounded. The naval bombardment had failed and so had the ground attack. The British sailed out of Chesapeake Bay, but would again see action in the very last battle of the war at New Orleans, Louisiana, after the war had supposedly ended.

Sketch of Fort McHenry

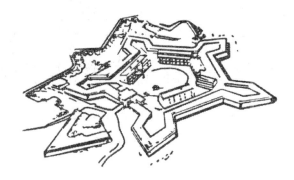

The Battle of Baltimore was a military victory for the United States, but there was one non-military outcome that lives with this country to this day. American Francis Scott Key, a thirty-five year old lawyer was a guest aboard the *HMS Tonnant*, a British ship in Chesapeake Bay, when Fort McHenry was bombarded. Key was on board to secure the release of prisoners one of whom was Dr. William Beans who had been held by the British for arresting British soldiers who were looting local farms. Key was not allowed to go ashore until after the battle had ended. On the night of September 13 Francis Scott Key witnessed the bombardment of Fort McHenry from his place on the *HMS Tonnant* and at first light the next morning seeing the American flag still waving was inspired to write a poem titled "Defense of Fort McHenry." Later, the poem was set to music to the tune of a British song, "To Anacreon in Heaven" that was the official song of the Anacereontic Society, a gentlemen's club of amateur musicians in London, England, in the 18th Century. The society acquired its name from the Greek poet, Anacreon.

The poem was renamed at some point to the Star Spangled Banner with the same tune as before. The United States Navy was the first to officially use the song in 1889. A Congressional Act of 1931 officially recognized the Star Spangled Banner as the National Anthem replacing other songs such as "Hail Columbia" and "My Country, Tis of Thee" to name just two at that time. The original poem included four stanzas and the singing of the National Anthem usually includes only the first of the four.

Scene showing the bombardment of Fort McHenry on the night of September 13, 1814, that inspired Francis Scott Key to write the "Defense of Fort McHenry."
Library of Congress, Prints & Photographs Division, LC-USZ62-61

DEFENCE OF FORT M^cHENRY.

The annexed song was composed under the following circumstances—
A gentleman had left Baltimore, in a flag of truce for the purpose of getting released from the British fleet, a friend of his who had been captured
at Marlborough.—He went as far as the mouth of the Patuxent, and was
not permitted to return lest the intended attack on Baltimore should be
disclosed. He was therefore brought up the Bay to the mouth of the Pa-
tapsco, where the flag vessel was kept under the guns of a frigate, and
he was compelled to witness the bombardment of Fort M'Henry, which
the Admiral had boasted that he would carry in a few hours, and
that the city must fall. He watched the flag at the Fort through the
whole day with an anxiety that can be better felt than described, until
the night prevented him from seeing it. In the night he watched the Bomb
Shells, and at early dawn his eye was again greeted by the proudly waving
flag of his country.

Tune—Anacreon in Heaven.

O ! say can you see by the dawn's early light,
   What so proudly we hailed at the twilight's last gleaming,
Whose broad stripes and bright stars through the perilous fight,
   O'er the ramparts we watch'd, were so gallantly streaming?
And the Rockets' red glare, the Bombs bursting in air,
Gave proof through the night that our Flag was still there;
     O ! say does that star-spangled Banner yet wave,
     O'er the Land of the free, and the home of the brave ?

On the shore dimly seen through the mists of the deep,
   Where the foe's haughty host in dread silence reposes,
What is that which the breeze, o'er the towering steep,
   As it fitfully blows, half conceals, half discloses ?
Now it catches the gleam of the morning's first beam,
In full glory reflected now shines in the stream,
     'Tis the star spangled banner, O ! long may it wave
     O'er the land of the free and the home of the brave.

And where is that band who so vauntingly swore
   That the havoc of war and the battle's confusion,
A home and a country, shall leave us no more ?
   Their blood has washed out their foul footsteps pollution.
No refuge could save the hireling and slave,
From the terror of flight or the gloom of the grave,
     And the star-spangled banner in triumph doth wave,
     O'er the Land of the Free, and the Home of the Brave.

O ! thus be it ever when freemen shall stand,
   Between their lov'd home, and the war's desolation,
Blest with vict'ry and peace, may the Heav'n rescued land,
   Praise the Power that hath made and preserv'd us a nation !
Then conquer we must, when our cause it is just,
And this be our motto—" In God is our Trust ;"
     And the star-spangled Banner in triumph shall wave,
     O'er the Land of the Free, and the Home of the Brave.

Francis Scott Key's Poem, Defense of Fort McHenry
Wikipedia

The Battles of Plattsburg and Baltimore were defeats for the British that may have been a window into ending the war between Great Britain and the United States. Talks were underway in Ghent, The Netherlands, on just that subject. The British may not have the heart to continue the fight, but that was not the same for the Americans. What some identify as the last battle of the War of 1812 may be true in one sense and not in another. The *Battle of Malcolm's Mills* on November 6 initiated by American forces to disrupt British supply lines in Upper Canada was the last battle before the signing of a peace treaty, but slow communications prompted one later battle that should never have happened.

Canada was a prime location for military action during the War of 1812. If it wasn't American forces attacking the British, it was British attacking the Americans. The Battle of Malcolm's Mills was the former situation that was not exactly a battle, but a series of raids hoping to seize and destroy vital supplies necessary for the British to survive. American Brigadier General Duncan McArthur with a force of 750 mounted infantry troops from Ohio and Kentucky left Detroit October 22 for the eastern region of Upper Canada (Ontario). Upon reaching an area forty-five miles west of Lake Ontario along the Grand River on November 4, they surprised and totally scattered British militia forces without as yet destroying any of the supplies. At this venture, the Americans turned south focusing their attention on several locations where mills would be found closer to the north shore of Lake Erie.

With news of McArthur's advance into the region, Canadian militia forces assembled at Malcolm's Mills near present-day Oakland some thirty miles north of Lake Erie. On November 6 the two forces engaged one another that resulted in a decisive victory for the Americans after which the mills were burned to the ground. American casualties were reported as one killed and six wounded. The Canadian militia fared much worse suffering eighteen killed, nine wounded, and 126 captured. The captured were most likely freed since there was no purpose in the captivity and it would prevent the rapid movement of the mounted infantry. Brigadier General McArthur moved his forces further south to Port Dover along Lake Erie capturing and destroying other mills along the route. Having successfully achieved much if not all of the intended objectives of the campaign, the American troops headed back to Detroit arriving on November 17, 1814.

The Treaty of Ghent –

A war that began as an offshoot to the Peninsular War in Europe and perpetuated by aggressive British Royal Navy interference in American trade was about to end. United States and British officials had participated in peace talks from August 1814 while the war raged on in America. The British desire to keep a trade embargo against France and impressment of British sailors off ships of other flags was no longer necessary due to the defeat of Napoleon and end of the Peninsular War.

Five Americans, John Quincy Adams, Henry Clay, James A. Bayard, Sr., Jonathan Russell, and Albert Gallatin had been meeting with officials from Great Britain on the issue of peace. At first, the negotiations were one-sided offered by the British under the impression that their military campaigns in America would be successful forcing a capitulation by the American envoys. Just the opposite occurred evidenced in the Battles of Plattsburg and Baltimore. The British were now more conciliatory in their demands.

Great Britain's demand for territorial gains in North America and control of the Great Lakes would not happen. Neither would their demands for an Indian State in the Northwest Territory. In the end all gains of land, ships, and even prisoners would be returned by both sides. The treaty was signed on December 24 by the negotiating participants and formally agreed to by the Prince Regent, the future King George IV, on December 30, 1814, followed by the United States on February 17, 1815. News of the treaty agreement did not reach the United States until a month after the signing. This delay would result in the LAST battle of the war and another devastating defeat for Great Britain.

Painting by A. Forestier showing the signing by the participants in the Treaty of Ghent with the British on the left and the Americans on the right.
Wikipedia

Unbeknown to both the British and Americans that a treaty had been agreed upon to end the War of 1812, a British fleet of sixty ships and nearly 15,000 troops arrived in the waters of the Gulf of Mexico on December 12, 1814, not far from the recently acquired Louisiana Territory. The British Navy was under the command of Admiral Sir Alexander Cochrane and the Army under Major General Sir Edward Michael Pakenham. The British would be opposed by Major General Andrew Jackson and less than 5,000 troops consisting of Regulars from the Army, Marines, and Navy; State militia, Indian allies; and civilians. There were several U. S. Navy ships available to Jackson to block advance of the British.

The first engagement of this campaign occurred on December 14 at which time about 1,200 British sailors and marines using small boats attacked a small number of the U. S. Navy ships in the *Battle of Lake Borgne*. The British were able to capture all the American ships and inflict casualties totaling six killed, 35 wounded, and the capture of 86. The British were victorious, but they too suffered losses. Seventeen sailors were killed and 77 wounded. Nine days later on the morning of Friday, December 23, another British force of nearly 2,000 reached a point along the Mississippi River approximately nine miles south of New Orleans. Here they camped for the day waiting upon the arrival of reinforcements. The presence of the British so close to New Orleans alerted Major General Jackson who set in motion plans for a night attack.

With a military force equal in number to the British, the Americans attacked the unsuspecting British that evening that did little to dislodge them from their camp, but did give them reason to question their intent. The attack was no small engagement in the number of casualties on both sides. The Americans reported 24 killed, 115 wounded, and 74 missing. The British numbers were 46 killed, 167 wounded, and 64 missing. Once the Americans had completed their mission, they withdrew several miles closer to New Orleans anticipating further encounters with British forces that would happen January 1, 1815.

The defense of New Orleans included the construction of several earthen batteries holding twelve guns. On January 1 part of British Major General Pakenham's army approached the fortifications and began an artillery barrage damaging several of the American guns. This may have doomed the Americans except that Pakenham ran out of ammunition and had to call off the attack. Still not organized, the British waited several days for the remainder of the troops to arrive from the ships.

On January 8, the British began their full scale attack on Major General Jackson and New Orleans. The Americans had prepared well establishing three defensive lines with barriers to impede any assault. The British were walking into a lethal killing field and that is exactly what happened. Major General Pakenham and his second in command Major General Samuel Gibbs were mortally wounded. Some accounts of the battle put the British number of killed at 700, wounded at 1,400, and 500 captured. Others show the number of killed closer to 300 and the other two categories remaining about the same. Regardless of which numbers are correct, in comparison to the Americans casualties they are astounding. The Americans list 11-13 killed and 23-30 wounded. Needless to say, this was a major victory for Major General Andrew Jackson and the United States troops.

Major General Andrew Jackson and his troops firing on the
British forces in the Battle of New Orleans, January 8, 1815
Library of Congress, Prints & Photographs Division, LC-USZ62-7809

The day after the crushing defeat of the British forces near New Orleans, there would be a futile attempt to capture Fort St. Philip along the Mississippi river leading to New Orleans. This too ended in failure. The British were not going to achieve any of their goals and made plans to withdraw from Louisiana which they accomplished January 19, 1815. Apparently not satisfied that British control of the region was over, the naval fleet with what remained of the troops set sail for Mobile Bay in today's Alabama where they attacked and captured an earthen complex called Fort Bowyer that would be the precursor to the present-day Fort Morgan. An interesting note is that Fort Bowyer had been attacked by the British on September 14-16, 1814, without success that cost the lives of 34 British Royal Marines. More British attacks would have occurred if word of the Treaty of Ghent had not arrived as it did on February 13, 1815. The British cancelled all further military plans. The war had ended!

Summary

The War of 1812 was costly not just in dollars, but also men that paid the ultimate price with their lives and those wounded that carried their disabilities with them after the war. Estimates of dollar amounts were about the same for both the United States and Great Britain at a number slightly more than one million dollars. These numbers will vary from one source to another the same as casualty count.

If the battle summaries are correct, the American losses show 1,839 killed, 3,312 wounded, 5,790 captured with an additional 150 wounded that were captured. In comparison, British numbers reflect 1,694 killed, 4,879 wounded, 3,100 captured with an additional 326 captured that were wounded, and 145 missing in action. There may have been over 3,000 British deaths due to other causes during the war. The number of non-battle losses due to disease and other causes is unknown.

Each side in the war may claim victory, but in essence both sides lost men and material that need not have happened. This all began over trying to prevent American trade with two countries that were at war with each other, Great Britain and France. France did not wage war with the United States as did Great Britain even though they too took issue with the Americans trading with their adversary. Perhaps, Great Britain had not gotten over the outcome of the Revolutionary War and this war was a means of retaliation. This fact may be supported by the desire of some English people to condemn the Treaty of Ghent hoping to continue the war. If there could be one positive outcome of the War of 1812, it would be that from the last battle of the war in 1815, the United States and Great Britain have maintained a mutual relationship supporting one another in world events to the present.

U. S. flag during the War of 1812

Native American Indian Wars

(1513 – 1865)

FROM the moment European explorers set foot in North America, contact was made with native American Indians. Sometimes these encounters were friendly, more often not! It must have been frightening and sometimes threatening for the Indians to see a people unlike themselves with ideas, beliefs, and ways much different to what they had been accustomed. The Europeans came from a civilized culture and spoke a different language. Clothing was made in many different materials and colors. Transportation was with wagon wheeled carriages on wide and cleared roadways. Dwellings were constructed with lumber, brick, or stone and would be the same in the new world. Domestic animals both worked the land and became food sources. Each of these areas were foreign to the American Indians and may have caused many of the conflicts that would occur from the first European landing as early as 1513 with the arrival of Spanish explorer Juan Ponce de Leon in present-day St. Augustine, Florida. Of course the loss of Indian land to the settlers also contributed to conflicts.

North America was home to vast numbers of Native American Indian tribes spanning the continent from coast to coast before the arrival of the first European explorers followed by the settlers. Indians in the eastern regions close to the Atlantic coast were the first to encounter the new arrivals. As time passed, all of the North America Indians would encounter settlers in their domain and conflicts were commonplace both large and small. Encounters that involved large numbers of combatants have been recorded in history and small episodes involving single families or individuals of both settlers and Indians are lost forever or may be told as folklore of that time.

Indian conflicts with Europeans date back to the time of Juan Ponce de Leon and continued into the Twentieth Century. There are over one hundred-fifty documented Indian Wars or conflicts that occurred during that time. For this writing, some conflicts will have brief mention and others with historical significance more detailed description. Those that involve the U. S. Military will be covered as much as possible. Further, only those Indian Wars that occurred toward the end of the American Civil War in 1865 will be covered in this work. Recalling the French and Indian War, Revolutionary War, and even the War of 1812, American Indians were allied with one side or the other in many of the conflicts. Those occurrences will be briefly mentioned during the time they happened, but the detail will be left to that covered previously.

The range of conflicts spans every conceivable type. There were chance encounters, horrific massacres, retaliations for previous conflicts, and outright wars lasting days and sometimes years. Individuals and local militia groups were the only recourse against Indian hostilities in the years before the establishment of the United States. This task was undertaken by the Spanish, French, and British during their tenure in North America. The United States military would take on the responsibility for the new nation upon its founding, but that would not stop civilians or even groups of civilians from taking up arms if a threat was perceived.

"Nez Perce" oil painting by Everett Russell

Major Native American Indian Conflicts

Jamestown Massacre – March 22, 1622
Mystic Massacre - May 26, 1637
King Philip's War – 1675-1676
King William's War – 1689-1697
French and Indian War – 1689-1763
Fort William Henry Massacre – August 1757
Lord Dunmore's War – 1774
Gnadenhutten Massacre – March 8, 1782
Battle of Tippecanoe – November 6, 1811
Battle of Fort Dearborn – August 15, 1812
Battle of Frenchtown – January 22, 1813
Fort Mims Massacre – August 30, 1813
Peoria War – September 19- October 21, 1813
Battle of Horseshoe Bend – March 27, 1814
First Seminole War -1816-1818
Arikara War –June 2, 1823
Winnebago War – 1827
Black Hawk War - 1832
Battle of Wisconsin Heights – July 21, 1832
Battle of Bad Axe – August 1, 1832

Second Seminole War - 1835-1842
Comanche Wars – 1836-1875
Cherokee War – 1839
    Battle of the Neches – July 1839
Council House Fight – March 19, 1840
    Battle of Plum Creek – August 11, 1840
Whitman Massacre – November 29, 1847
Cayuse War – 1848-1855
Navajo Conflicts – 1849-1863
Bloody Island massacre – Spring 1850
Sioux Indian Wars – 1854-1890
Third Seminole War – 1855-1858
Grattan Fight – August 17, 1855
Battle of Seattle – January 26, 1856
Antelope Hills Expedition – January – May 1858
Coeur d'Alene – 1858
Battle of Four Lakes – September 1, 1858
Battle of Pease River – December 18, 1860
Battle of Apache Pass – March 1862
Bear River Massacre – January 29, 1863

Battle of Canyon de Chelly – January 1864
Sand Creek Massacre – November 29, 1864
Colorado War – 1864-1865
Snake War – 1864-1868
Battle of Killdeer Mountain – July 28, 1864
Battle of Rush Creek – February 8-9, 1865
Powder River Expedition – Aug – Sep 1865
First Battle of Adobe Walls – Nov 25-26, 1864
Battle of Platte Bridge Station – July 26, 1865
Battle of Red Butte – July 26, 1865
Battle of Tongue River – August 29, 1865

Indians Wars to 1800 -

At the time Spanish explorer Juan Ponce de Leon arrived off the coast of north central Florida around April 1513, a land that did not have a name at that time, he and his shipmates did not encounter Native American Indians, but that would change in early June of that year when the expedition reached the western side of the peninsula. Here a band of Calusa Indians who at first were interested in trade suddenly became hostile and a fight ensued. This may have been the very first conflict between Europeans and Native American Indians in North America.

A second early encounter of Europeans with American Indians occurred around 1571 in an area thought to be along the north shore of the York River off Chesapeake Bay in the future State of Virginia. A Spanish Jesuit priest and six Jesuit brothers from Cuba established a mission by the name of *Ajacan* in this area in September 1570. This was an attempt to bring Christianity to the local Indians. A Native American Indian who may have come from the Kiskiack tribe was taken from the same area in 1561 by Spanish explorers. He became a convert to the Jesuit faith and returned to the area from which he was taken with the Jesuits in 1570.

For whatever reason, that Indian who may have had help from tribal Indians in the area

turned on the Jesuits within months of establishing the mission and killed them all except one young boy named Alonso de Olmos. A Spanish ship from St. Augustine carrying supplies arrived at the mission site in 1572 and was attacked by Indians that may have been the same Kiskiack. The Spaniards killed a number of the Indians and captured others from whom they learned the fate of the Jesuits and the young boy. The Indian captives were exchanged for Alonso de Olmos and the ship and crew returned to St. Augustine ending the mission effort in Virginia.

Jamestown in the Colony of Virginia was the first permanent English establishment in North America after the failed Roanoke Colony known as Sir Walter Raleigh's Lost Colony of Roanoke. The founding of Jamestown was May 14, 1607, on the current Jamestown Island in the James River. The Powhatan Indians and in particular the Paspahegh tribe were friendly in the first years of contact, but that peaceful arrangement turned to hostilities and the near total elimination of the tribe by 1610. This was the first conflict with the native Indians of the Colony of Virginia. Another would occur in 1622

The *Indian Massacre of 1622* occurred around Jamestown, Colony of Virginia, by Indians of the Powhatan Confederacy. This was the beginning of the Powhatan Wars that lasted to 1644. Indian Chief Opechancanough used deception to attack unsuspecting settlers who had angered the Indians over the acquisition of Indian land. There were nearly 350 settlers massacred in the attacks, but Jamestown itself was spared due to early warning. The only thing uncertain about the massacre is the exact date due to a difference in which calendar was in use at that time. The attack may have occurred on March 22, 1621, instead of 1622, but that doesn't change the outcome.

Woodcut of the Indian Massacre of 1622 in the Colony of Virginia
Wikipedia

Following the Indian Massacre of 1622, twenty-two years of conflict occurred resulting in the death of many more Indians and as well as settlers. The colonists took action against the Powhatan tribes in every way possible destroying crops, canoes, entire villages, whatever they could get their hands on, and confiscating more Indian land. The situation in the Colony of Virginia would play out in other regions in North America. The *Pequot War* occurred in 1636-1637 between the Pequot Indians and English colonists from New England made up of the Massachusetts Bay Colony, Plymouth Bay Colony, and Saybrook Colony in the future State of Connecticut. This war also pitted Indians from one tribe against another. The Narragansett and Mohegan tribes allied with the colonists against the Pequot's.

The Pequot Indians attempted to exercise control over other Indians tribes from the region. This effort spilled over to the killing of Europeans prompting actions by the various colonies and their Indian allies. Several raids were conducted by the Massachusetts Bay Colony militia against the Pequot villages burning then to the ground and destroying crops that were intended to carry them through the winter. In turn, the Pequots brought revenge upon the Saybrook Colony killing several men and women and taking hostage of young girls. This prompted the Saybrook Colony to raise their own militia force and undertake an attack of their own against the Pequot.

Early Tuesday morning, May 26, 1637, the Saybrook militia conducted an attack on a Pequot village identified as Mistick Fort. The attack would be called the *Mystic Massacre* for the nearly 500 men, women, and children who would be killed on that day. Those killed were not by muskets but by fire that engulfed the village. The few that escaped the blaze were struck down by the militia troops waiting outside the inferno.

Attack on the Pequot Indians resulting in the Massacre of 1622
Library of Congress Wood Engraving

A nearby village of Pequot sprang into action harassing the Saybrook militia as they returned to the boats that had ferried them to the attack site. This did little good as more Pequot were killed. Rather than remain in the same region where so many had been lost, the Pequot people decided to move further west. Several weeks after the attack on Mistick Fort a second militia group set out to put a stop to the Pequot once and for all! The Pequot were surrounded resulting in the capture of several hundred mostly women and children while the leader, Sassacus. escaped along with nearly a hundred warriors. Sassacus sought refuge with the Mohawk tribe only to be killed by them ending the Pequot War. The result of this war was the virtual elimination of the Pequot people.

A conflict called *King Philip's War* began June 20, 1675, and lasted nearly eleven months. This war was fought between the once peaceful Wampanoag tribe and colonists of New England. King Philip was not a monarch as the name might indicate. Instead, he was Metacomet, chief of the Wampanoag having replaced both his father and older brother. Metacomet acquired the name Philip during the peaceful time his father was chief. Whether the name was given to him by the colonists or at the hand of his father is not known. After succeeding his older brother as chief, Metacomet initiated war against the New England colonists that may have been a long time coming due to a number of festering issues one of which was infringement on Indian land. Another issue was the execution of three Wampanoags accused of killing one John Sassamon, an Indian convert to Christianity.

An attack on colonial villages and killing of the inhabitants resulted in a response of like manner by militia from Massachusetts and Plymouth Colonies against the people and villages of the Wampanoag, Nipmuck, Podunk,

Narragansett, and Nashaway tribes. This back and forth conflict resulted in no less than eleven named conflicts until the defeat and death of Metacomet and many of his Indian allies on August 12, 1676. One of the well-known incidents was The *Great Swamp Fight* that occurred on November 2, 1675. When King Philip's War finally ended, Indian casualties were as many as 3,000 and one-third that number of colonists from the causes of war and disease. Peace was restored in New England!

Engraving of The Great Swamp Fight, November 2, 1675, during King Philip's War
Wikipedia

King William's War occurred during the French and Indian War from 1689 to 1697 and was covered under the French and Indian War chapter on page 7. This war involved Native American Indians aligned with the French against the British.

The years of the French and Indian Wars saw a number of Indian hostilities against the English colonists. The *Schenectady Massacre* occurred on February 8, 1690, when Algonquin Indians destroyed the village by that name killing around sixty colonists, nearly half of whom were women and children. The *Deerfield Massacre* followed on February 29, 1704, at which time Deerfield, Massachusetts, was attacked by four different Indian tribes killing nearly sixty colonists and taking many more of the inhabitants as prisoners.

Seven years later the *Tuscarora War* named after the Tuscarora Indians took place in 1711 in North Carolina. Settlements were raided killing hundreds of the inhabitants and destroying property. The North Carolina militia defeated the Tuscarora's in 1713. Ironically, the Yamasee Indians who were allied with the colonists in the Tuscarora War waged war themselves against the colonists in the *Yamasee War* that began in 1715 and continued to 1718. The Yamasee Indians conducted attacks in South Carolina duplicating the carnage of the Tuscarora War nearly wiping out the settlers. The cost of the war to the Yamasee's was even more devastating than that of the colonists. Those Yamasee that survived lost their identity and joined other tribes.

A period of calm followed the Yamasee War to 1757 when the French and Indian War saw the *Fort William Henry Massacre*. This event is covered in this work under the French and Indians Wars beginning on page 14. In brief, this massacre involved the *Abenaki* and perhaps as many as seventeen other tribes who attacked a paroled British column after surrendering Fort William Henry to the French.

With little time for peace, the next seven years saw at least five more Indian conflicts connected in one way or another to the French and Indian Wars. The first was the *Cherokee Uprising* from 1758-1761. The Cherokee Indians were allied with the British against the French in the early years of the war. Tensions grew between the two over minor incidents that led to a parting of ways for at least some of the young Cherokee warriors. What followed were Indian raids against the British that were met with retaliation by the British further escalating the conflict. In short, a large colonial militia force finally put down the uprising leading to a number of peace treaties between the Indians and each of the various colonial states.

The next Indian war began in May 1763 as the French and Indian War ended. It involved the British against fourteen Indian tribes led by the chief of the Ottawas, Pontiac or Obwandlyag. The war took on the name

Pontiac's War or *Pontiac's Rebellion* after the Indian leader, and was fought over resentment of British decrees against the Indians in the Great Lakes region. The Indians drove the British from nearly all their outposts killing many colonists and British soldiers in the process, but could not take Fort Detroit even after a several month long siege. A change in British policy toward the Indians resulted in a fragile peace in 1764, but it was by no means the end to the conflict. Indian raids continued until July 1766 at which time Pontiac himself agreed to end all hostilities.

An offshoot of the Pontiac War resulted in four named incidents. The *Battle of Bushy Run* was fought on August 5, 1763, when a relief column of British soldiers headed to break the Indian siege of Fort Pitt were attacked by those same Indians. The attack failed to drive off the reinforcements. On September 14, Indians attacked a British supply train resulting in the death of more than seventy soldiers and teamsters. This episode is called the *Devil's Hole Massacre*.

As was often the case in colonial America, Indian atrocities were countered with retaliation when military efforts did not provide a satisfactory response. A group of men from the village of Paxton, Pennsylvania, took it upon themselves to meet aggression with their own medicine. About fifty armed men of the village attacked and killed six Susquehannock Indians on December 14, 1763. Those Indians had nothing to do with the events in the Pontiac War. Other Susquehannocks who escaped the slaughter were placed in protective custody only to suffer the same fate as the previous six when the Paxton men broke into their safe location. The *Paxton Boys* continued their attacks on peaceful Indians until Benjamin Franklin negotiated and end to the killing in January 1764.

Scene of the "Paxton Boys" in the murder of Susquehannock Indians, December 14, 1763
Wikipedia

The actions of the Paxton Boys may be overshadowed by the *Enoch Brown School Massacre* July 26, 1764. A log schoolhouse near present-day Greencastle, Pennsylvania, with school in session was entered by four Delaware Indians who proceeded to kill and scalp the schoolmaster, Enoch Brown, and eleven of the children, two of whom survived the scalping, Four children were taken as captives. Returning to their village, the four Indians were excoriated by the chiefs for killing children.

For the next ten years, a relative peace prevailed between the colonists and Native American Indians. However, as would be the case, peace would come to an end as settlers moved westward into Indian lands that had not been breached to that point. Trust between colonists and Indians was fragile at best. An incident by one party would easily prompt a response by the other. On April 30, 1774, just such an incident occurred when settlers killed several Mingo Indians in what is called the *Yellow Creek Massacre*. The unprovoked incident prompted Indian attacks against settlers moving westward in the Colony of Virginia resulting in Lord *Dunmore's War* named after John Murry, Earl of Dunmore. Andrew Lewis and his colonists defeated the Shawnee Indians in the *Battle of Point Pleasant* in the Colony of Virginia (now West Virginia) on October 10, 1774. This action put to rest the Indian attacks in that part of the Colony of Virginia.

The years leading up to and beyond the American Revolutionary War saw several Indian conflicts. The *Chickamauga Wars* extended from 1775-1794 fought over land acquisitions in Virginia, Kentucky, Tennessee, North and South Carolina, and Georgia. The *Battle of Wyoming* also called the **Wyoming Valley Massacre** occurred July 3, 1778, near present-day Wyoming, Pennsylvania, between United States Patriots and British Loyalists supported

US Military History – Native American Indian Wars

by Iroquois Indians. This could have been covered in the section on the Revolutionary War except that the massacre was attributed to the Indians who killed and scalped well over 200 of the patriots. The *Cherry Valley Massacre* on November 11, 1778, mirrored the Wyoming Valley Massacre in many ways. There was indiscriminate killing of at least thirty non-combatant civilians from the village along with sixteen militia troops of the Seventh Massachusetts militia including the commander Colonel Ichabod Alden. Many of the civilians who escaped the carnage were taken captive and ransomed later for their release. The Wells family did not escape the carnage. Jane Wells, sister of Robert Wells was one of those killed by the Seneca Indians depicted in the artist's rendition next. The village was destroyed, but the fort held by the Seventh Massachusetts militia was never breached.

No matter the attempts by colonists and Indians to form a peaceful existence, something always crept into the mix to change the outcome. There were those on both sides that would never accept peace due to the differences in life styles, beliefs, and previous events that soured their feelings. Proof of this is the *Gnadenhutten Massacre* on March 8, 1782, that resulted in the mass murder of ninety-six men, women, and children of the Delaware tribe at the hands of some Pennsylvania militia who had experienced the wrath of Indian atrocities at an earlier date or to relatives of theirs. The Indians were captured harvesting their crops, accused of supporting the British, tried by militia justice, and convicted of the crimes! They were sentenced to death that was carried out to the dismay of some and supported by others. This incident was a black mark on colonial America.

"Incident at Cherry Valley – fate of Jane Wells"
Library of Congress,
Prints & Photographs Division,
LC-USZ62-111117

Indian Wars in the first half of 1800 -

Indian wars in the first half of 1800 were impacted somewhat by the War of 1812 and later by the American Civil War, but both of these wars pale in comparison to the impact of settlers expanding their reach to the regions west of the original colonies. Proof of this last fact is the *Battle of Tippecanoe* fought on November 7, 1811, between U. S. forces under the leadership of the Territorial Governor of Indiana, William Henry Harrison, and the Shawnee tribe led by Tenskwatawa, brother of Tecumseh.

The battle occurred after repeated talks failed to resolve issues related to treaties with other Indian tribes, and, of course, the taking of Indian land. Major General Harrison launched an expedition of 1,000 troops in an effort to convince the Shawnees that they did not speak for other tribes. At his disposal were elements of the Fourth and Seventh U. S. Infantry, militia from Indiana and Kentucky, Light Dragoons from Indiana, and several Rifle companies. As the column approached its objective on November 6 near Prophetstown present-day Lafayette, Indiana, they were met by an Indian with a message from Tenskwatawa calling for talks the next day. This was an apparent ruse and delaying action by the Indians who attacked the encamped troops November 7 with around 500 to 700 warriors. The attack proved only partially effective causing heavy casualties for Harrison's troops, but the Indians eventually withdrew from the battle and left the region giving Americans the victory. American troop casualty counts revealed sixty-two killed either instantly or mortally wounded, and around 126 injured. Indian casualties were never actually known, but estimates range around fifty killed and slightly less than one hundred wounded.

Fighting scene at the Battle of Tippecanoe, November 7, 1811
Library of Congress, Prints & Photographs Division, LC-USZ62-5338

The year 1812 saw the second war with Great Britain in the Americas. The War of 1812 also involved Indians allied with Great Britain most likely thinking that the alliance might put a stop to Americans seizing Indian land. Two months after the Declaration of War against Great Britain, the *Fort Dearborn Massacre* occurred on August 15, 1812.

Fort Dearborn was built in 1803 by U. S. troops in what is now downtown Chicago, Illinois. At that time it was in the Illinois Territory under the overall jurisdiction of Brigadier General William Hull, Army of the Northwest. Word of the British capture of forts in the Michigan Territory prompted Hull to order the evacuation of Fort Dearborn. The troops along with their families were attacked along the evacuation route by a large force of nearly five hundred Potawatomi Indians. The attack was a massacre killing and capturing all of the sixty-six troops and the twenty-seven dependents including a number of children. Some of the Americans died in captivity and the rest were ransomed for their freedom. Fort Dearborn was burned to the ground but would be reconstructed in 1816.

Another Indian war as part of the War of 1812 was the *Battles of Frenchtown* covered on page 76. As written, this involved other named battles such as the First and Second Battles of Raisin River and the Raisin River Massacre. These battles occurred January 18-22, 1812. Many of the Indian Wars involved the word massacre and such was the case August 30, 1813, in the *Fort Mims Massacre* that was part of the Creek War.

Creek War 1812-1813

The Creek War began with unrest between two factions of the Muscogee people also known as Creek Indians, namely the Red Stick Creeks of the Upper Towns and the Lower Creeks identified by their location primarily in Alabama. The Red Sticks were opposed to any and all settlers on their land and fought with both their Creek brothers to the south who had assimilated with American ways and the settlers. The Red Sticks viciously attacked and killed the southern Creek Indians and burned their villages then turned their attention to American settlements resulting in much the same outcomes.

Fort Mims was a log stockade built in late summer 1813 surrounding the plantation home of Samuel Mims in Alabama located approximately thirty-five miles north of current Mobile. The stockade was built in response to a potential threat of Indian reprisals after militia forces attacked a group of Red Stick Indians at Burnt Corn Creek earlier that summer. The site of Fort Mims was home to a substantial community of settlers equal in number to the nearly three hundred militia troops. In spite of early warnings, nearly 1,000 Red Stick Creek descended on Fort Mims as the settlement was about to enjoy their noon meal. The people of the settlement had lowered their guard as time had passed without incident from the Burnt Corn Creek episode. The gate to the fort was open and sentries were not on alert. That situation was their undoing. Nearly the entire settlement of militia and civilians were killed or captured with only a few escaping the carnage. The impact of this attack would receive harsh reprisal in seven months from Major General Andrew Jackson, but not before another Indian attack to the north in the Illinois Territory.

Red Stick
Chief Menawa
Wikipedia
(US-PD)

Print depicting Indians massacring the inhabitants at Fort Mims August 30, 1813, near soon to be incorporated Mobile, Alabama, as part of the Creek Indian War.

Wikipedia

After the Fort Dearborn Massacre August 1812, a number of retaliatory raids were conducted against the Potawatomi Indians and their Kickapoo allies in the Illinois Territory that did little to resolve anything except cause more unrest. The Illinois Territory included the eventual States of Illinois, Wisconsin, parts of Minnesota and Upper Michigan. A year after the Fort Dearborn Massacre a fort was built in the same territory near Peoria, established in 1691 by the French, and named for the Peoria Indians. The fort was named Fort Clark and may have been for William Clark of the famous "Lewis and Clark Expedition." At that time American influence in the territory was countered both by the British and Native American Indians.

The fort was attacked by Potawatomi Indians on September 19 and repelled. A month later on October 21, a second attack was launched by a combined force of Potawatomi and Kickapoo Indians that was soundly defeated due the arrival of nearly one thousand reinforcements of mounted Roger's Rangers. The Indians were scattered, their villages burned, ending further encounters by these tribes. This conflict was called the *Peoria War*.

The Peoria War was a later response to the Fort Dearborn Massacre as was the *Battle of Horseshoe Bend* a later response to the Fort Mims Massacre. Other names are attributed to this battle such as Tehopeka, Tohopeka, Cholocco Litabixbee, and The Horseshoe. Whatever name is used doesn't change the battle on March 27, 1814, involving American forces under Major General Andrew Jackson against the Red Stick Creek Indians who were responsible for the Fort Mims Massacre August 30, 1813.

Recall that the Red Stick Creeks of the Upper Towns in Alabama were opposed to the American settlers in every way just the opposite to that of their fellow Creeks of the Lower Towns. Conflicts took place culminating in the Fort Mims Massacre by the Red Sticks. Tiring of attacks on American settlements the call went out for a full-scale response ending the Indian hostilities that had caused so much unrest in Alabama. Brigadier General Andrew Jackson answered that call with 2,600 infantry including the U. S. Thirty-ninth Regiment and militia as well as 600 allied Cherokee and Lower Creek Indians. Together they marched from Fort Williams in lower Alabama arriving March 27, 1814, at a site near Horseshoe Bend in the Tallapoosa River of east central Alabama near the current Alexander City.

Jackson prepared his forces for battle against the Red Sticks who had fortified their encampment, but the outcome against the smaller number of Indian warriors around 1,000 was over after a brief but hotly contested fight. The Red Stick Creek suffered as many as 800 killed in the battle, far more than the fifty or so American soldiers. Chief Menawa of the Red Stick was wounded, but survived with the remaining members of his tribe to join with the Seminole Indians in Spanish Florida. They would fight again against U. S. soldiers in the First Seminole War. Jackson would be promoted to major general and distinguish himself in the Seminole Wars and the last battle of the War of 1812 – The Battle of New Orleans.

Scene at the Battle of Horseshoe Bend showing the United States troop, perhaps the Thirty-ninth Infantry Regiment, encountering the Red Sticks at their fortified site on March 27, 1814.
Wikipedia

The First Seminole War –

There were many Indian wars in North America, but the First, Second, and Third Seminole Wars thrust this nation into protracted and violent conflicts over many years unlike any of the other Indian wars. The Seminole Wars started in Spanish Florida in 1816 and ended in American Florida in 1858.

After a successful campaign against the Red Stick Creek Indians in the Battle of Horseshoe Bend in Alabama, Major General Andrew Jackson would lead his troops into west Florida where the Red Stick Chief Menawa and the remainder of his warriors had fled after the battle. West Florida was Seminole land and Menawa joined up with the Seminole nation. West Florida was also safe haven to runaway slaves who joined the same. The word Seminole that comes from the Spanish *cimarron* meaning "wild people" or "runaway" does not refer to a tribe, but a nation of tribes and was given to those Indians of north and central Florida. The Creek Indians were the predominate group that formed the Seminole nation (Alachua, Miccosukee, and Muscogee Bands) and Calusa tribe native to southwest Florida.

The War of 1812 was still in progress in 1814 and Great Britain would do anything to disrupt the United States military even in Florida. The first action by the British was to supply weapons to the Indians followed by construction of a fort along the Apalachicola River simply called British Fort. At the conclusion of the War of 1812, the British abandoned the intact fort in the spring of 1815 leaving it to the fugitive slaves and those Indians who remained. The fort took on a new name as "Negro Fort" and would play a role in the First Seminole War. Word spread about the "Negro Fort" prompting other fugitive slaves to seek safety near its location.

The existence of the fort caused great concern not only for Georgia slave owners but others such as Georgia native and Secretary of War, William Crawford. Crawford instructed Major General Andrew Jackson to convey to the Spanish Florida governor of Pensacola that the fort should be destroyed by Spain. If the Spanish were not able to accomplish this action, the U. S. would do it for them. This message was delivered to the governor on April 23, 1816. The Spanish governor claimed not to have the means nor the authority to destroy the fort leaving that up to Jackson. Steps were put in motion to achieve that end.

In early 1816, Brevet Major General Edmund Pendleton Gaines received orders to establish a fort along the Georgia side of the Chattahoochee River. It became Fort Gaines named after the general that is the site of the present-day town of the same name. In the first week of June 1816 Gaines sent Lieutenant Colonel Duncan Lamont Clinch with a battalion of the Fourth U. S. Infantry to establish a defensible position further south along the Flint River near the confluence of the Chattahoochee River just above Spanish Florida. The site was expected to be temporary and only minimal work was accomplished. The site was named Camp Crawford. The plan was to supply both the fort and camp using the Apalachicola River from the Gulf of Mexico. In order to accomplish this task, ships would need to pass the Negro Fort that may give reason for its destruction.

A coordinated plan was instituted calling for Lieutenant Colonel Clinch to march south with a force from Camp Crawford arriving near the Negro Fort as supply ships arrived in Apalachicola Bay. Clinch marched his force south as planned, but the ships were the first to arrive and received word to wait for the arrival of the ground troops. Having need for fresh water aboard the ships, a shore party was dispatched in search of the needed water. Once on shore the sailors were immediately attacked by the inhabitants of the fort and all but one were killed. This killing occurred around July 17, 1816, and named *The Watering Hole Massacre* that gave the Americans all they needed to institute their plan to destroy the fort.

Ten days after the Watering Hole Massacre, both ground and naval forces were in place on July 27 ready to attack the fort. Lieutenant Colonel Clinch with his soldiers from the Fourth U. S. Infantry surrounded the fort and naval Gunboats #149 and #154 closed within firing range of the fort. The first shots came from the fort and soon after the Gunboats responded. The fifth shot fired from the Gunboat #154 was a "hot shot" (a cannonball heated to glowing red) that was a direct hit on the powder magazine in the fort resulting in an extensive explosion obliterating the fort and killing nearly all the defenders including women and children. When a casualty count was made, it was estimated that 270 inhabitants of the fort were killed instantly and many of the wounded would not survive their injuries. This episode ended the use of that part of Spanish Florida by fugitive slaves, but would lead to the actual First Seminole War engagement.

In the spring of 1818 Major General Andrew Jackson arrived at the former site of the British Fort later called Negro Fort. Here he ordered Army engineer Lieutenant James Gadsden to build a new fort that would take on the name Fort Gadsden. Fort Gadsden would play an important role in prosecuting the Seminole Wars and later in the American Civil War.

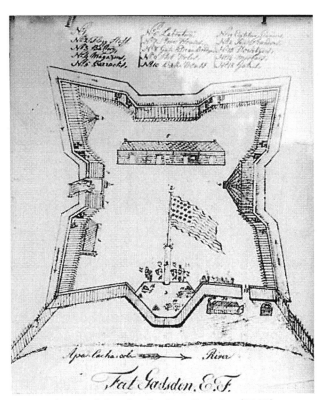

Sketch of the plan for Fort Gadsden (2009)
The writing at the top of the sketch identifies the buildings by number and purpose. The direction of the Apalachicola River is shown by the arrow above the name of the fort at the bottom. (2009)

Front and back of a plaque at the site of the former Fort Gadsden, Florida. (2009)

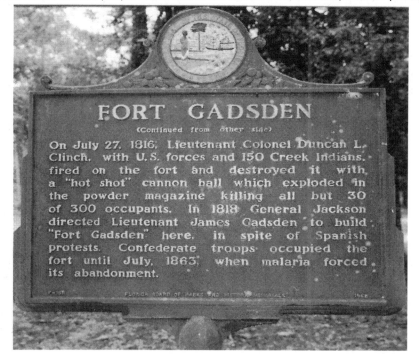

The destruction of the Negro Fort on July 27, 1816, was not directly involved in the First Seminole War, but it was a sign of things to come. The region was a powder keg waiting to explode between settlers and Seminole Indians exchanging assaults at every turn. Camp Crawford became a permanent military site after the destruction of the Negro Fort where buildings were constructed and a name change to Fort Scott. Some miles to the east of the fort was a Mikasuki Indian village called Fowltown. The Mikasukis were part of the Seminole nation and their chief, Neamathla, strongly objected to the encroachment of settlers onto Mikasuki land. Chief Neamathla did not honor the Treaty of Fort Jackson that had ceded southern land in Georgia, his land, to the United States.

This dispute prompted Brevet Major General Gaines to authorize an attack on Fowltown that may have been the first battle of the Seminole War. On November 21, 1817, approximately 250 troops were sent to remove Neamathla and his people from the village. That attempt failed, but a second try the next day was successful resulting in the death of some inhabitants of Fowltown. With the impact of Fowltown fresh in their minds, an array of Indian tribes including Seminole, Red Stick Creek, and some Black Seminole warriors staged a surprise attack on a supply mission for Fort Scott traveling the Apalachicola River.

Lieutenant Richard W. Scott of the Seventh U. S. Infantry was in charge of transporting supplies to Fort Scott by way of the Apalachicola River. With Scott were thirty-nine troops many of whom were ill, seven women, and four children. Laying in wait to ambush were several hundred Indians who had chosen a position along the river where the current would most likely take the boats. That position was on the east side of the river a short distance south of the current Lake Seminole. As the supply boats approached the area on November 30, 1817, the attack occurred known as *The Scott Massacre of 1817*. Lieutenant Scott and thirty-two men were killed along with six of the women and all four of the children. Five men escaped the carnage four of whom were wounded and one woman was taken captive. The woman was rescued the next spring when American led forces under Major General Andrew Jackson invaded Spanish Florida.

The Scott Massacre of 1817 did little to enhance the standing of the Seminole and Creek Indians in the minds of both the American people and the government. In fact, the response from President James Monroe was to throw the full weight of the United States Army against those responsible and their people. Spanish Florida was off limits to the forces of the United States military until this episode. Brevet Major General Edmund Pendleton Gaines would have been called upon to supervise the response, but was on assignment in East Florida. The task fell to Major General Andrew Jackson. His orders were punish the rebellious Indians, but not to attack or destroy Spanish sites. Jackson assembled his force at Fort Scott near the border with Spanish Florida in early March 1818. The troops included 800 U. S. Infantry members most likely from the Fourth Infantry, 2,000 militia troops divided equally between Tennessee and Georgia, and nearly 1,500 Lower Creek Indians who were friendly toward the United States. This army marched into Florida on March 15 and arrived at the site of the former Negro Fort along the Apalachicola River where Jackson authorized the construction of Fort Gadsden mentioned previously (see p. 119).

Fort Gadsden was built on Spanish controlled territory, but that meant little to Major General Jackson. He was intent on punishing the Spanish for not supporting the United States just as much as the Seminole and

Red Stick Creek Indians. Leaving the construction of the fort in hands of Lieutenant Gadsden, Jackson began his mission against his adversaries marching northeast where he attacked and burned the Indian village of Tallahassee on March 31 and the village of Miccosukee a short distance east the following day. Next he turned his attention south to St. Marks along the Gulf of Mexico and seized the Spanish fort by the name of San Marcos de Apalache. Using the seized fort as a headquarters, Major General Jackson continued his efforts further east along the Suwannee River. Here he encountered several villages that had been occupied mostly by fugitive slaves along with at least one Red Stick Creek village. At this last village, a number of the Indians were killed and women and children captured. It was at this same village that Elizabeth Stewart was found who had been captured in the Scott Massacre of 1817.

Having accomplished all that he thought necessary, Major General Jackson returned to Fort Gadsden. Once there, he learned that more Indians were gathering supplied by the Spanish. With a force of 1,000 he marched toward Pensacola on May 7, 1818, the location of the Spanish Florida governor. Pensacola was defended by a small number of Spanish soldiers. Word of Jackson's approach sent the government and soldiers to the safety of nearby Fort San Carols de Barrancas (Fort Barrancas) leaving the town to Jackson. Cannon fire was exchanged for a couple of days after which the fort was surrendered to the Americans. This attack on Spanish sovereignty caused international repercussions calling for the dismissal of Major General Jackson. After cooler heads prevailed, the matter was put to rest whereby Spain ceded Florida to the United States July 10, 1821. Ironic perhaps, Andrew Jackson would become the military governor of Florida in March 1821, but resigned that role after three months and returned to his home in Tennessee. He would be elected to the U. S.

Senate for Tennessee in 1823 and President of the United States in 1829.

The First Seminole War was not solved by the efforts of Major General Andrew Jackson in 1818. Florida as a territory of the United States was popular to settlers and they arrived in large numbers. The more settlers there were, the less Indian land there would be and the more likely there would be conflicts. The U. S Government took steps to establish a reservation in middle Florida for the Seminole and other Indian tribes. The Treaty of Moultrie Creek was to be the agreement between the U. S. Government and the designated chiefs. The terms of the treaty were gradually accepted by the various Indian tribes, but there were problems from the beginning. Government promises made were not kept and mistrust festered to the time of the Second Seminole War beginning in 1835.

Interim to the Seminole Wars –

In the years between the First and Second Seminole Wars, other parts of the country saw Indian conflicts. One of those conflicts was the *Arikara War* of August 9, 1823, near the Missouri River in present-day South Dakota. The first contact with the Arikara Indians occurred in 1804 during the Lewis and Clark expedition. That contact was peaceful, but changed a year later when Arikara Chief Ankedoucharo died during a visit to Washington. D. C. Blame for the death was placed on the Americans and the peace soured over the ensuing years perpetuated by growing discontent with fur traders who populated the land of the Arikara. This situation came to a head on June 2, 1823, when a band of Arikara warriors attacked and killed fifteen trappers.

Here as in the case of most if not all Indians attacks there was a military response. This, however, was different in that this was the first Indian conflict between the United States and the western Indians. Under the command of

Lieutenant Colonel Henry Leavenworth, future namesake of Fort Leavenworth, Kansas, a force of soldiers of the Sixth U. S. Infantry, Sioux Indians, and a number of trappers from the Rocky Mountain Fur Company assembled to attack the warriors of the Arikara tribe who were responsible for the incident on June 2. The combined military force exceeded 1,000 men against an estimated 600 warriors.

Lieutenant Colonel Leavenworth began his attack on August 9 using the Sioux in the first wave that accomplished little. The next day he employed his artillery followed by an infantry assault neither of which could penetrate the Indian defenses. In a last ditch effort, Leavenworth offered a peaceful solution that was accepted by the warriors though they had little faith that it would be honored. The Arikara left their village under cover of night and Leavenworth with his army left the site on August 15 but not before burning the village.

Another named war that never really materialized was the **Winnebago War** of 1827. A small group of Ho-Chunk Indians of the Winnebago tribe attacked and killed several civilians in the Michigan Territory (Wisconsin) who were there seeking to mine lead. Those of the Ho-Chuck who were responsible for the killings were quickly identified and placed under arrest ending the episode. The events surrounding the Winnebago War exemplify the tenuous relationship between Americans and Indian tribes of this region and regions to come in the west. It should be noted that there were also intertribal conflicts occurring at the same time across this country.

Many of the Indian conflicts involved white settlers occupying land of the Indian tribes; however, the **Black Hawk War** in 1832 was unique in that the opposite occurred. This war was named for Chief Black Hawk of the Sauk Indian tribe who led his people and those of the Fox, Ho-Chuck, Kickapoo, Meskwakis, and Potawatomi from their land in Iowa into the new State of Illinois in violation of the 1804 Treaty of St. Louis. The Treaty of St. Louis resulted in Black Hawk relinquishing much of the Indian land in the western half of Illinois to the United States. This group of six tribes was known as the *British Band* for their support of the British during the War of 1812. Why Black Hawk chose to return to the very land he gave up in 1804 is uncertain, but that move concerned Governor John Reynolds of Illinois and the U. S. Government. It could mean only one thing – War!

To counter the possibility of war, Brevet Brigadier General Henry Atkinson was appointed to command a force of First U. S. Infantry and militia troops from the State of Illinois commanded by Brigadier General Samuel Whiteside. Initial attempts to negotiate a peaceful solution to the Indian incursion onto Federal land met with confusion and misunderstanding that ultimately led to the first battle. The Black Hawk War was actually eight individually named battles and some without names. The first was the **Battle of Stillman's Run** fought May 14, 1832, by a militia force of around 250 men commanded by Major Isaiah Stillman, namesake of the battle. What was to have been a mission to monitor Black Hawk and his band escalated into a confrontation that could have been avoided by more seasoned soldiers. Black Hawk claimed to have sent a delegation under a flag of truce to negotiate, but they were taken prisoners and other Indians were fired on without warning. Black Hawk fought back. In the end, Stillman and his militia were routed by Black Hawk resulting in eleven militia killed. If Black Hawk had come to Illinois for peaceful reasons, the events of the Battle of Stillman's Run changed that thought.

The outcome of the Battle of Stillman's Run resulted in a series of Indian raids against small groups of individuals in northern Illinois followed by settlements primarily in the

Michigan Territory or southern Wisconsin of today. Black Hawk and his warrior band were now in a war against the U. S. Government without support from other Indian tribes who wanted no part in the conflict and even supported the U. S.

After the defeat at Stillman's Run, the militia under Brigadier General Whiteside lost confidence in their role and left the ranks. At the same time Indian raids instilled fear in the inhabitants of the region calling for new measures against Chief Black Hawk. It was necessary for Brevet Brigadier General Atkinson to reorganize his force that he accomplished by recruiting new militia supported by regular army troops into what Atkinson called the *Army of the Frontier*. This was a large force of some 600 regular infantry and over 3,000 new militia troops. Other individuals formed militia organizations not part of the Army of the Frontier. Notables in this latter group was Colonel Henry Dodge of the Michigan Mounted Volunteers whose organization would progress by Congressional Act to the *Battalion of Mounted Rangers*, then to the *United States Regiment of Dragoons*, and finally the *First U. S. Cavalry*. Another notable member at this time was Private Abraham Lincoln, future President of the United States.

News of the newly organized *Army of the Frontier* prompted Black Hawk to conduct more raids in a futile attempt to draw the army away from his main campsite near Lake Koshkonong in south central Michigan Territory (Wisconsin). Colonel Dodge responded by tracking down eleven of the raiding party who were involved in the most recent raid cornering them near the Pecatonica River in the southern Michigan Territory on June 16. This action resultied in the *Battle of Pecatonica* also known as the *Battle of Horseshoe Bend* that is different from the battle of the same name in Alabama on March 27, 1814. All eleven of the raiding party were killed in this action that would be followed that day and the next couple of days by similar outcomes.

On the same day Colonel Dodge and his men were involved in the Battle of Pecatonica, the *First Battle of Kellogg's Grove* took place in the far northwest portion of the State of Illinois. Black Hawk was apparently determined to spread his raids over a wide area far from his main camp in the Michigan Territory. Illinois militia troops commanded by Captain Adam W. Snyder pursued a raiding party of some thirty warriors killing six while suffering the lost of three militia. Members of the same raiding party may have been involved in the *Battle of Waddens Grove* two days later. Major James W. Stevenson and his Illinois militia fought a hand-to-hand battle against this band of Indians. Three militiamen were killed in this battle and Stevenson himself was severely wounded. There may have been as many as six of the Indian band killed in this encounter.

An unnamed conflict occurred June 20, 1832, near *Fort Blue Mound* in the Michigan Territory involving an estimated one hundred Sauk Indians who attacked two militiamen killing one immediately and the other a short time later as he made a dash for the fort. On June 24 the Apple River Fort approximately fifteen miles south of the Wisconsin border came under attack by an estimated two hundred of Black Hawk's Sauk and Fox Indians. This became known as the *Battle of Apple River Fort* that lasted less than an hour resulting in the loss of several of the Black Hawk's Indians and only one member from the fort. Captain Clark Stone and about thirty of his Illinois militia garrisoned the fort. A warning to the nearby population gave them time to seek safety inside the fort before the arrival of the raiding party. Unable to defeat the fort's defenders, the Indians raided the nearby homes taking everything they could lay their hands on.

When the sun rose the day after the Battle of Apple River fort, the next Indian conflict would occur in the same place as nine days earlier. This was the *Second Battle of Kellogg's Grove* that involved Black Hawk against a battalion of 170 Illinois militiamen commanded by Major John Dement. The initial engagement took place in the open, but the militia force was able to take cover in the fort and held off the assault. Black Hawk lost nine of his warriors and ended the attack returning to his main camp at Lake Koshkonong. Militia casualties from the battle resulted in five killed and three wounded.

Black Hawk may have tired of the war losing many of his warriors, or he was finding difficulty in supporting the woman, children, and elderly men at his camp; whatever the reason he decided to return to his safe area west of the Mississippi River. The retreat of Black Hawk's beleaguered band was able to stay unnoticed until mid July when word of their whereabouts was made known to Colonel Dodge. A pursuit began July 15, 1832.

Black Hawk had arrived in Illinois with around five hundred warriors and six hundred women, children, and elderly men. He was leaving the Michigan Territory with fewer than six hundred total due to warrior losses and death from disease and other causes. That number would fall even further as the days of the march continued. On July 21 the pursuing militia caught up with Black Hawk near present-day Sauk City, Wisconsin, along the Wisconsin River. Here Black Hawk and Neapope of the Kickapoo tribe established a delaying action allowing the Indian non-combatants to cross the river. There were fewer than 120 Indian warriors facing 750 militiamen and over half the Indians would be killed in this defense. This engagement was the *Battle of Wisconsin Heights*. The battle was successful in allowing those Indians not involved in the conflict to reach the west

shore of the river; however, the militia eventually crossed the river and continued the pursuit.

The Black Hawk War was about to come to a close, but there would be one last battle to fight. Black Hawk and his followers were in worse shape than when they started their trek. They were starving, sick, and there were wounded that slowed them down. They wished for no more than to be allowed to return to their former land. They were a defeated people who longed for an end to the misery that would not be granted.

Black Hawk and what was left of his people reached the mouth of the Bad Axe River planning to cross the Mississippi River to freedom. This would not happen at least for the majority of the band nor for Black Hawk. An armed steamboat, the *Warrior* paroled the Mississippi River alerted to the likelihood of the Indians crossing the river. The crew of the *Warrior* sighted Black Hawk's people on August 1. An attempt to surrender was either ignored or misunderstood. The crew opened fire killing twenty-three of the warriors.

Black Hawk decided to head north leaving most of his people who had enough of the situation and could no longer flee. In the meantime, the army caught up to those who remained and the last engagement of the war began on the morning of Thursday, August 2, 1832. This was the *Battle of Bad Axe* fought between 1,300 U. S. regular and militia troops against roughly 150 Indian warriors. The U. S. First Infantry troops were Companies A, B. G, and K under the command of Major Bliss. The battle could best be described as a bloodbath wherein all or nearly all of the warriors were killed costing the lives of fourteen Americans. In addition, over one hundred Indians drowned while trying to cross the Mississippi River.

This was the end of the Black Hawk war, but it was not the end of the killing. The few of the *British Band* who managed to cross the

Mississippi River were hunted down by members of the Menominee and Dakota tribes and killed or captured. Chief Black Hawk and others who had gone north before the Battle of Bad Axe were captured and imprisoned for a time only to be released and treated like great Indian chiefs!

Scene at the Battle of Bad Axe, August 2, 1832, during the Black Hawk War showing Indians at the center right between the trees firing at the American troops (not seen), and non-combatants at the center bottom fleeing for the river.   Wikipedia

Second Seminole War – Beginning

The Second Seminole War did not officially begin until 1835, but the years from the end of the first war in 1819 to 1835 were not years of total peace between the United States and the Seminole people. Unable to maintain the necessary authority or support the needs of Florida, Spain ceded Florida to the United States in 1819 under the Adams-Onis Treaty. Florida's Indian situation was now totally in the hands of the United States. The Treaty of Moultrie Creek was ambitious, but not all Indians were satisfied with the terms.

The treaty agreed to September 18, 1823, called for a four million acre reservation in the middle of Florida. The United States would be responsible for protecting those on the reservation as long as they remained peaceful. Farming equipment along with cattle, hogs, and rations would be provided until the Seminoles were able to plant and harvest their own crops. Compensation of $5,000 a year for twenty years would be paid in addition to providing a school and blacksmith if roads were allowed to be built across the reservation, and finally, runaway slaves were to be turned over to the United States.

The hesitation of the Indians to accept the conditions of the treaty prompted the construction of Fort Brooke in 1824 near Tampa of today. Four companies of the Fourth

U. S. Infantry garrisoned the fort as early as January 1824 one of which was Company B. Around this time Company H, Second U. S. Artillery, was stationed at Fort Brooke followed soon after by Companies A, B, C, and G. This move was intended to persuade the Indians of the Seminole Nation to accept the conditions of the Treaty of Moultrie Creek. It would take more than building a fort to convince the Indians to accept the terms of the treaty. In July 1824 the Territorial Governor of Florida, William Pope DuVal, called for a meeting at St. Marks with the chiefs of the Miccosukee (Arpiucki) and Seminole (Neamathla) to discuss the necessity of moving to the new reservation. Duval gave the chiefs until October 1, 1824, to make the move. Prior to the meeting, Duval had mobilized the militia if force was necessary to carry out his order!

Fort Brooke c. 1835
Library of Congress, Prints & Photographs Division, LC-USZ62-16519

The Miccosukee as part of the Seminole nation gradually moved to the reservation, but not by October 1. Some members moved within a year only to move back to their previous areas. By 1826 nearly all Indians were finally on the reservation, but their lives were not as they were before. Promised rations were not forthcoming. Planted crops suffered due to drought conditions. Life on the reservation was not working but the Indians endured! Early in 1832 life on the reservation would change. A meeting was called for the Seminole chiefs to meet at Payne's Landing near the Ocklawaha River on reservation land.

At that meeting it was declared that the Indians on the reservation were to be moved west to the Indian Territory, present-day Oklahoma. The move was the result of the *Indian Removal Act* passed by Congress in 1830 under President Andrew Jackson. At first the Indian chiefs agreed to the move only to refute the same a short time later. This hotly contested situation was a lead up to the Second Seminole War.

The outcome of the 1832 meeting produced the *Treaty of Payne's Landing* signed May 9 and enacted by Congress April 1834 calling for the removal of all of Florida's Seminole Indians to an area west of the Mississippi River within three years retroactive to the original meeting date. What followed was outright rejection of the treaty by a group of vocal chiefs refusing to leave the reservation. More complacent Indians agreed to leave and were harassed and even killed by their counterparts. Seminole attacks began on settlers and on military units. This prompted the appointment of Brigadier General Duncan Lamont Clinch as commander of Florida military forces. The Second Seminole War had begun!

The events of the Second Seminole War are best described in the words of the Fourth U. S. Infantry who were placed in the forefront of the war. *"Rarely, if ever, have troops been called upon for service under such trying circumstances as in this war. The region in which troops were compelled to operate consisted of swamps, overflowed thickets, and dense tropical forests of unknown extent. Poisonous insects and serpents under foot and an atmosphere reeking with fevers and disease overhead. The enemy to be subdued was cunning and active as he was cruel and treacherous. For days at a time the troops waded in the swamps or patrolled the streams in search of an enemy who only showed himself when in sufficient numbers to massacre isolated detachments. Treachery and deceit resulted from every conference with the Indians...."* [1] The severity of this description was manifested on December 28, 1835, in an attack on a U. S. Army column described as the *Dade Massacre*.

Brevet Major Francis Langhorne Dade, Company B, Fourth U. S. Infantry, was charged with leading a column of troops numbering one hundred-ten men from Fort Brooke to Fort King a distance over one hundred miles. The reinforcement column left Fort Brooke on December 23, 1835, consisting of Company C, Second U. S. Artillery, Company B, Third Artillery, and eleven soldiers of Brevet Major Dade's own Company. Already stationed at Fort King was Company F, Second U. S. Artillery. Approximately half way to Fort King, the column was surprised by a large band of Seminole Indians numbering around 300 led by their Chief Micanopy who killed all but two soldiers who managed to escape and return to Fort Brooke alerting the command to the massacre. The attack lasted from that Monday morning to early afternoon and exemplifies the brutality of the Fourth Infantry's words cited previously.

Map of the "Dade Massacre" site.

Florida Center for Instructional Technology, College of Education, University of South Florida

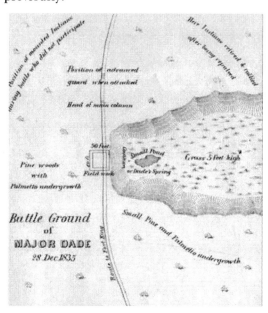

The impact of the massacre sent more troops to Florida including Brevet Major General Winfield Scott as commander of U. S. forces in the area. On February 20, 1836, Brevet Major General Edmund P. Gaines and over 1,000 troops reached the Dade Massacre site for the first time. Once there the task of identifying and burying the dead took place. Those 108 men would remain buried at the site until the end of the Second Seminole War when they were disinterred and reburied in the St. Augustine Post Cemetery that would become a National Cemetery in 1881.

The site of the attack is marked today as the Dade Battlefield Historic Memorial and listed on the U. S. National Register of Historic Places and as a U. S. National Historic Landmark. Each year the week after Christmas a reenactment is held as close to the date of occurrence as possible.

The Dade Massacre was just the beginning of the atrocities that would occur during the Second Seminole War. On the same day as the Dade Massacre, Fort King in the center of the territory was attacked by a Seminole band under upstart Osceola who turned on his Indian agent friend Wiley Thompson killing him and Lieutenant Constantine Smith before attacking the fort. Osceola would commit other atrocities before his capture by deceit in October 1837 that caused further conflicts to occur during the war. Fort King was built in 1827 near present-day Ocala and named for Colonel William King, former commander of the U. S. Fourth Infantry Regiment. The fort was built near the Indian agency that would play an active role during the Second Seminole War

On December 31, Brevet Brigadier General Duncan Lamont Clinch unaware of the massacre arrived at the Withlacoochee River from Fort Drane a distance of approximately thirty miles. Fort Drane was established on the sugar plantation of Brevet Brigadier General Clinch in 1835 by Captain Gustavus Savage Drane assigned to the Second U. S. Artillery. With Clinch were 250 regular troops from Companies D and F, Second U. S. Artillery, and Companies C and H of the Third U. S. Artillery. There were an additional 500 Florida militia troops commanded by Brigadier General Richard Keith Call all heading for the Seminole stronghold at the Cove of the Withlacoochee.

Burial site (Three Pyramids) of the Dade Massacre victims and other soldiers killed during the Second Seminole War located at the St. Augustine National Cemetery (2017)

Arriving at the river, Clinch failed to locate a fordable crossing point and was forced to send small numbers of his command across the river at a time using a single canoe that had been found. Hiding on the opposite shore were the very Indians he planned to attack. When one hundred and ninety-five regular troop and twenty-seven militia had crossed the river, the Indians led by Osceola and Alligator began to attack that was fended off by bayonets and the help of militia troops firing from the opposite side of the river. Four soldiers were killed in the attack and fifty-nine wounded. Some reports list only forty wounded. The Second U. S. Artillery suffered one man killed and twelve of the wounded. The Third Artillery may have accounted for the other casualties, but that information is not available. Indian casualties may have been five killed and unknown number of wounded.

Some reports called this a victory for Brevet Brigadier General Clinch, but this was most likely a draw when it comes to the failure of completing the attack on the Seminole village. After the engagement, Clinch and his troops returned to Fort Drane, but would see action again in March 1836 as part of Major General Winfield Scott's three-prong campaign against the Seminoles near the same location at the Withlacoochee River.

Second Seminole War in 1836

Meanwhile the Seminole Indians were making their own attacks most often on defenseless men, women, and children. The region along the Atlantic coast was under attack. The New River area was the scene of such attacks on civilians as was St. Augustine to the east. The *Battle of Dunlawton* near St. Augustine occurred on January 17, 1836, whereby local civilian volunteers known as the Mosquito Roarers led by Major Benjamin Putnam fought against Seminoles who attacked

and burned the sugar plantation. Four men were killed and thirteen to nineteen wounded.

It didn't take long for Washington to act after the hostilities in Florida of late 1835 and early 1836. Congress appropriated $600,000 for the war cause, the War Department authorized the appointment of Major General Winfield Scott to assume command of the Florida troops on January 22, and more Federal troops were sent to the region. Brevet Major General Winfield Scott would be the first in a parade of generals who experienced varied and sometimes questionable success as commanders of U. S. forces during the years of the Second Seminole War.

Meanwhile in New Orleans, Major General Edmund Pendleton Gaines organized a force of 1,100 men including six companies of the Fourth Infantry led by Lieutenant Colonel David Emanuel Twiggs, a Regiment of Louisiana volunteers commanded by Brigadier General Persifor Frazer Smith, two companies of Artillery armed as infantry, and set sail February 3 for Fort Brooke in Florida. One of those who joined Major General Gaines was First Lieutenant James Farley Izard of the First U. S. Dragoons who had heard of the Dade Massacre and volunteered to go with Gaines to Florida. The significance of Lieutenant Izard's action will soon become clear.

Upon arriving at Fort Brooke February 10, General Gaines found there was little intelligence regarding the situation of Brigadier General Clinch who he thought to be at Fort King. Horses were in short supply but rations were adequate. In order to meet his goal of punishing the Indians for the attack on the Dade party, ten days rations were issued to the troops and the command set out for Fort King on February 13. Included in the command were seven companies of the Fourth Infantry; Companies A, B, D, F, G, and H of the Second U. S. Artillery Regiment. and Louisiana volunteers. Gaines took the same route as the

Dade party and found the remains of the men on February 20. Completing the identification and burial of the fallen, attention turned to reaching Fort King and ascertaining the situation of General Clinch.

Fort King was forty miles march and the number of provisions was a concern. There were enough rations if the command turned back to Fort Brooke at this point, but that might jeopardize the position of General Clinch. Receiving encouragement from his staff that Fort King should have received sufficient supplies to serve the command, they marched on reaching the fort two days later on February 22.

To General Gaines dismay, General Clinch was instead at Fort Drane twenty-two miles to the north and the anticipated provisions had not arrived at Fort King. The troops of General Gaines had two days of rations remaining. Waiting for the supplies to arrive was deemed impractical and a decision was made to return to Fort Brooke. General Clinch was able to provide General Gaines with a few supplies for the return march.

With minimal supplies in hand, Gaines immediately headed back to Fort Brooke by a different and shorter route hoping to engage the Seminoles along the way. This route brought the column to the same site of General Clinch's encounter with the Seminoles on December 31 and the same problem of finding a suitable ford in the Withlacoochee River.

While attempting to find a crossing site in the river, gunfire erupted from the opposite side of the river by the Indians resulting in the loss of one soldier killed and seven wounded. The troops camped for the night and the next day began to search for a suitable crossing. Lieutenant James F. Izard took on the responsibility of finding the best point to cross the river when he was struck near his left eye by a bullet fired by an Indian. "He fell, but called out while falling, *Lie still men, and maintain your positions.*"[2] Lieutenant Izard died of his wound March 5, 1836, seven days after being hit.

Major General Gaines was faced with a dilemma. He was not able to cross the river, and did not think he could return to Fort King due to his supply situation. Instead, he instructed his troops to construct a temporary fortification as best they could that was named Camp Izard for the fallen officer. Word was sent to General Clinch at Fort Drane to come to his aid. Perhaps due to petty differences, Major General Scott who was now overall commander of troops in Florida refused to give permission for General Clinch to assist Gaines until in defiance of such orders relief came on March 6, eight days after the initial attempt to cross the river.

Ironically, on the day the relief forces under General Clinch arrived, General Gaines was in conference with the very Indians who had been attacking him The Indians had tired of the fight losing many warriors and sought a peaceful solution. This might have occurred, but Clinch's troops mistook the conference as other than peaceful and fired on the Indians scattering them in all directions.

This episode might have gone better if everything had gone according to plan but it didn't! The anticipated relief by General Clinch trapping the Indians between the two American forces never happened because Major General Scott refused permission for such action. The supplies that would have been adequate for a few days were used up causing extreme hardship on the troops because it took eight days for the relief. And then, there was constant harassment by Seminoles that cost the lives of four killed and forty-six wounded. For these reasons, it may not be fair to second guess General Gaines decision to remain at his location believing that a relief column would soon arrive, but one can only speculate how this situation might have changed if General Gaines had decided instead to return to Fort King in the first place!

As it was, General Clinch brought all the provisions he could handle including forty head of beef cattle for the beleaguered troops. For the next three days the Seminole honored their commitment to end hostilities allowing the troops to swim and fish in the river unmolested. Chief Micanopy was to have met with General Gaines to finalize the agreement, but he did not show. On March 9, 1836, General Gaines placed his troops under the command of General Clinch and the entire force began the march to Fort Drane on March 10 arriving a day later. On March 11, Major General Edmund P. Gaines left for New Orleans by way of Tallahassee and Pensacola.

It was now Major General Winfield Scott's turn to implement his military plan. He devised a three-prong attack plan involving 5,000 troops to converge on the main Seminole encampment known as the *Cove of the Withlacoochee* (River). This was the same site that earlier had proved troublesome for Generals Clinch and Gaines. One column would move north from Fort Brooke under Colonel William Lindsey of the Second U. S. Artillery supported by Companies A, B, G, and H; another southwest from Volusia led by Brevet Brigadier General Abraham Eustis (Fourth U. S. Artillery?) that may have included Companies C and E of the Second Artillery; and a third moving south from Fort Drane commanded by Brevet Brigadier General Duncan Lamont Clinch with Companies C, H, and I of the Third Artillery and most likely Companies D and F of the Second Artillery accompanied by Major General Scott. Moving through undeveloped Florida at that time in history was no easy task. Delays were encountered along the three routes so that by the time the three columns approached the objective, the Indians had vanished.

Florida was not a hospitable region as noted by the words of the Fourth U. S. Infantry.

Many men on Scott's expedition could go no further due to sickness and some wounded from minor skirmishes with Seminoles along the march. Major Mark Anthony Cooper was tasked with establishing a temporary camp for those in need of rest allowing Brevet Major General Scott to continue on to Fort Brooke to regroup and resupply. Major Cooper commanded the First Battalion Georgia Foot Infantry. He along with the men of his battalion constructed a log stockade on the west side of Lake Holathlikaha for the protection of the men left under his charge. The site acquired the name of Camp or Fort Cooper. Fortunately for those protected by the improvised fort, an attack by Osceola and his Seminole warriors were driven off several times before Major General Scott returned April 18, 1836, with more men and necessary supplies allowing removal of the sick and wounded ending the need for Fort Cooper. Today, the area is the Fort Cooper State Park near Inverness, Florida.

Major General Winfield Scott's failure in his three-prong attack plan in March 1836 did not please his superiors at the War Department. Shortly after returning from Fort Cooper with the wounded and sick, he was recalled to Washington and replaced temporarily by Brigadier General Edmund Meredith Shackelford awaiting the arrival of the newly assigned commander in the Seminole War, Brevet Major General Thomas Sindey Jesup.

General Jesup did not assume command until December 9, 1836. In the interim between Major General Scott's departure and Major General Jesup's arrival, there were a number of actions and conflicts that impacted the war effort.

Fort Alabama upriver from Fort Brooke on the Hillsborough River was abandoned in late April 1836 that would be replaced in December of that same year under the name Fort Foster. Fort Alabama was built in early 1836 by men serving in the Alabama Battalion of Mounted volunteers led by Major David Caulfield and named for the State of the men who were responsible for its construction. Colonel William Lindsey of the Second U. S. Artillery supervised the construction. Captain Elmore's South Carolina Volunteers of the Corps of Columbia and Richland Riflemen built Fort Barnwell in 1836 along the east shore of the St. Johns River in eastern Florida. Major William Gates of the First U. S. Artillery was in command at the fort at the time it came under attack April 14, 1836, but was easily defended.

Print of Fort Barnwell aka Camp Volusia along the banks of the St. Johns River c.1836
Library of Congress, Prints & Photographs Divison, LC-USZ62-16518

Fort King to the west of Fort Barnwell was abandoned May 17 and burned in July by Seminoles, rebuilt in 1837 and remained an important site to the end of the war. A blockhouse occupied by American soldiers near the mouth of the Withlacoochee River saw relief from a lengthy siege by Seminole Indians. Some reports indicate the blockhouse was freed from the siege in December 1835 and others show June 1836. There is no way to know which date is correct. Fort Drane built on the plantation of General Clinch was abandoned July 17 due to sickness that plagued many of the Florida forts that resulted in similar outcome. The regular army troops from Fort Drane were reassigned to Fort Gilleland thirty miles to the north. Fort Gilleland was established in 1835 by Brevet Major James A. Ashby, Second U. S. Dragoons, and named for Captain Lewellen Gilleland, U. S. Army. Fort Drane became a casualty of the war. The Seminoles burned the fort and occupied the plantation until they were driven off in early October by Tennessee militia as part of the late 1836 campaign of Brigadier General Call.

Scene showing Seminole Indians attacking the blockhouse controlled by American Soldiers that may have occurred as early as December 1835 to as late as June 1836.
Library of Congress, Prints & Photographs Division, LC-USZ62-11463

On June 9, 1836, Seminoles attacked near the community of Micanopy where Fort Defiance was located. Fort Defiance was established some time in 1835 as a U. S. Army post. The location was a strategic crossroads in central Florida. Many of the roads to and from other forts established during the Second Seminole War connected to Fort Defiance. The fort was commanded by Major Julius Heileman, Second U. S. Artillery, and defended by Companies D and E of the Second, Companies C, H, and I of the Third Artillery, and Company D of the Second Dragoons. The attack took place outside the community and was met by the troops under Major Heileman's command. The Indians were driven off ending the episode. One private from Company D, Second Dragoons, was mortally wounded, Major Heileman died a few days later due to reported stress, and First Lieutenant Thompson B. Wheelock of the Second Dragoons died six days later from a fever. Company D, Second Dragoons was again involved on July 19 near Welika Pond while escorting a supply train from Fort Drane to Fort Defiance. Captain James A. Ashby and twenty-six of his dragoons

were attacked near their destination. Although severely wounded, Captain Ashby continued to lead his dragoons until reinforcements arrived from Fort Defiance. The Indians numbering at best guess two hundred-fifty attacked the column resulting in two privates mortally wounded and nine others with wounds of varying degree including Captain Ashby. Fort Defiance did not remain long as it was burned in August due to sickness of the soldiers stationed there; however, it was rebuilt a year later and named Fort Micanopy.

August 21, 1836, saw another Indian engagement near the former Fort Drane involving Companies A, C, H, and I, Third U. S. Artillery, as well as Company C, Fourth Artillery. The extent of this conflict is not known, but may have been an attempt to drive the Seminoles off the plantation land where Fort Drane had been located before being burned by the Indians. Other actions undertaken in 1836 included additional funding for the war effort. The United States recognized that the war in Florida was not going to end anytime soon. As a result, Congress voted to allocate an additional $1.5

million over the previous $600,000 that it offered earlier in the year. Little did they know that much more would be needed before the war would end!

Very few areas of Florida aside from the Panhandle were free from Indian hostilities in 1836 and that was especially true for the central part of the territory. September 18 saw the *Battle of San Felasco Hammock* in north central Florida that involved a combined force of regular military and militia numbering around one hundred fifty against a larger band of Indians estimated at three hundred led by John Jumper also known as Hemha Micco. The U. S. troops were from Fort Gilleland in current Alachua County that came into existence after the abandonment of Fort Drane to the south. Colonel John Warren commanded the militia troops and, Captain D. D. Tompkins was in command of Company B, First U. S. Artillery. The Indians were driven off with a great number of killed and wounded. One militia man was killed.

Territorial Governor Richard Keith Call tried his hand at what others had failed to achieve. Governor Call had previous military experience under Major General Andrew Jackson and again under Brevet Brigadier General Clinch in the December 31, 1835, action against the Seminole Indians. Governor Call was adamant that he could accomplish what other military commanders had failed to achieve. Call's persistence won him approval from the War Department on May 25, 1836, to initiate his plan using volunteers and militia with a few Federal troops in the very same effort against the Seminole stronghold at the Cove of the Withlacoochee. In this endeavor, Governor Call would also wear the hat of military commander of the militia in the rank of brigadier general.

The campaign was to have started during the summer months, but delays in enlistment of 1,000 men pushed the operation into September. General Call's attempt to recruit from Florida resulted in few enlistments. The majority of the militia force came instead from Tennessee. President Andrew Jackson called on Tennessee to mobilize a militia force to fight against the Creek Indians in Alabama. Several thousand men responded to this call, but found the need to fight in Alabama had ended. Instead, the Tennessee troops moved to Tallahassee where they joined Governor Call in his plan to fight the Seminoles. The Tennessee force was under the command of Brigadier General Robert Armstrong and consisted of the First and Second Regiments of Tennessee Mounted Volunteers.

The military force moved from Tallahassee to Suwanee Old Town a distance of one hundred miles in the first leg of the campaign. Suwanee Old Town was along the Suwanee River near present-day Fanning Springs, Florida, about thirty miles from the Gulf of Mexico. On September 20 Governor as well as Brigadier General Call began the next leg of the movement with his mounted troops from Suwanee Old Town to the abandoned Fort Drane a distance of nearly fifty miles. The Tennessee troops drove the Seminole occupiers away from the abandoned Fort Drane and were joined there by Company C and part of Company A, Fourth U. S. Artillery Regiment. This combined army marched the thirty or so miles to the Withlacoochee River arriving October 12 where they were involved in the first skirmish with Indians. As in past attempts to attack the Indian stronghold at the Cove of the Withlacoochee, the river was once again too high to allow the troops the opportunity to cross nullifying the mission.

Supply shortages had plagued prior military missions that General Call had hoped to avoid. In his planning he sent supply ships to the mouth of the Withlacoochee River with instructions to establish a depot. One supply ship, the steamboat *Izard* ran aground in the river and overturned in the current losing the supplies preventing a depot from being established. This was just the beginning of supply shortages that prevented both men and animals from fulfilling their mission responsibilities. The lack of forage resulted in the loss of hundreds of horses prompting the mounted troops to become ground infantry causing a great deal of unrest among the men.

Unable to cross the river and supplies all but gone, General Call was forced to abandon his attack plan and search instead for sources of food to feed the men and forage for what few horses remained. Where this source of supplies came from is speculation, but it was achieved and Call was determined to make good on his claim that he could do better than the Federal Army commanders. On Sunday, November 13, 1836, Brigadier General Call's forces were back at the Withlacoochee River and finally made a successful crossing. Added to the original Tennessee troops and the two companies of the Fourth U. S. Artillery were Companies D, E, F, G and H also of the Fourth Artillery. The Seminole stronghold Cove of the Withlacoochee was found vacated, but four days later contact was made with Seminole Indians. A day later, November 18, after periodic engagements the Seminoles were pushed further south into an area known as the Wahoo Swamp.

The *First Battle of Wahoo Swamp* took place on November 21, 1836, between some 2,500 American troops and an unknown number of Seminole Indians led by two chiefs, Osuchee and Yaholooche. The result of the battle was an American victory primarily because the Seminoles retreated from the battle to fight another day as they had done in many of the previous engagements! This battle would end General Call's duty as military commander.

After the battle, General Call marched his command to Fort Florida, a U. S. Army supply depot situated along the St, Johns River near present-day DeBary, Florida. Major General Winfield Scott had established the fort early in 1836. Time at Fort Florida was spent resting, enjoying rations that had been in short supply during the months of active service, and preparing to return to life before the call-up. The Tennessee troops were soon on the march to Fort Brooke near Tampa where they would board ships for home by way of New Orleans. They embarked from Fort Brooke December 26 and arrived in New Orleans on January 6, 1837. From New Orleans they marched back to Tennessee.

On December 9, 1836, General Call received word that Major General Thomas Jesup had arrived in the territory and assumed command of the Florida operations ending Call's duel responsibilities. Although President Andrew Jackson expressed his disappointment in Call, the governor did achieve what no other officer had been able to do – find and attack the Seminoles on their ground causing them to flee.

As General Call's expedition was coming to an end in early December 1836, across the territory to the west a new fort was under construction. This fort would take on the name Fort Foster for Lieutenant Colonel William S. Foster, Fourth U. S. Infantry. Fort Foster was built on the former site of Fort Alabama that had been abandoned and destroyed earlier in the year. In addition to the fort, a bridge was built over the Hillsboro (Hillsborough) River that had also been destroyed about the time of the fort. Fort Foster consisted of two blockhouses as part of a log stockade With construction work well underway, Lieutenant Colonel Foster left the site with part of his command heading for Fort Armstrong with a number of supply wagons loaded with provisions for the men and forage for horses.

During Lieutenant Colonel Foster's absence from the fort on his supply mission, U. S. Navy Lieutenant Thomas J. Leib was placed in command of the fort. Lieutenant Leib was assigned to the *USS Concord*, a wooden-hulled, three-masted sloop-of-war placed in service in 1828. The defenders of the fort were fifty U. S. sailors and twenty artillerymen to man the two mounted cannons Several Indian attacks were made on the fort and the nearby bridge over the Hillsboro River without success. Fort Foster was abandoned in early summer 1837 typical of many of the Florida forts due to sickness of the troops. It would be reactivated in the fall and remain active until the summer of 1838. The site of Fort Foster today is on the U. S. Register of Historic Places. A replica of the fort has been constructed on the site.

Replica of the original Fort Foster
Wikipedia

The site of Lieutenant Colonel Foster's supply mission, Fort Armstrong, was built in November 1836 by members of the Tennessee militia in support of Brigadier General Call's military action against the Seminole Indians in the First Battle of Wahoo Swamp. Fort Armstrong was named for the Tennessee commander, Brigadier General Robert Armstrong. The fort was built a short distance north of the site of the Dade Massacre of December 28, 1835, along the Fort King trail.

The year 1836 did not go well for the military efforts against the Seminole Indians in the Florida Territory. Four general officers (Clinch, Gaines, Scott, and Call) each had a hand in military operations that fell short of victory with only General Call coming the closest to success. Much of this failure was due to the cunning actions of the Indians who would fade into the hammocks and swamps at the first sight of a military force. Whether the troops could not or would not pursue their adversaries is unknown, but it did not happen at least in 1836.

The arrival of Major General Thomas Jesup at the end of 1836 brought a new approach to fighting the Seminoles that would be implemented early in 1837. General Jesup's plan involved a massive military force of at least 9,000 men from all branches of the military (army, navy, and marines) as well as militia troops in a coordinated effort to cut off every possible source of supply for the Seminoles. Small troop forces would keep the Seminoles on the constant move thereby preventing time to grow and harvest crops needed for sustainment. Planted crops would be destroyed whenever and wherever they could be found. This effort essentially starved some of the Seminoles into submission. Chief Micanopy and his followers would eventually agree to a truce, but others like Osceola (William Powell) and Ar-pi-uck-I (Sam Jones) defied any attempt to be subdued and moved south to the region of the Everglades.

Second Seminole War in 1837

While General Jesup's plan was in the implementation stage, conflicts took place as they had in the past. The first recorded conflict of 1837 occurred on January 23 near Lake Ahapopka (Apopka) the site of a Seminole village. A skirmish took place between U. S. military forces involving at least Company E, Fourth U. S. Artillery along with Alabama mounted volunteers commanded by Lieutenant Colonel David Caulfield against Seminole Indians and runaway slaves. Seventeen of the village inhabitants were captured and Chief Osuchee (Cooper) and a number of his warriors were killed. Four days later the *Battle of Hatchee-Lustee* occurred near the present Disney World in Orlando.

The military units involved in the battle may have been the same as that at Lake Ahapopka. It is known that Company E, Fourth Artillery, along with Companies B, C, D, F, G, H, and I, were involved. Also present were Marines under the command of the Commandant of the Marine Corps, Colonel Archibald Henderson; the Third Artillery commanded by Brevet Brigadier General Walker Keith Armistead; and no doubt the Alabama militia troops. The site of this engagement was a Seminole village the same as Lake Ahapopka. Thirty to forty Seminoles were found at the village mostly women and children, but that number may have been higher. Also at the village were a large number of pack- horses laden with supplies and nearly 1,500 cattle ready to move elsewhere. The attack on the village resulted in a number of captives again mostly women and children. Those not captured fled into the swamp. Indian casualties may have been eight, but the American troops suffered at least three killed, two of the Marines and one soldier from Company I., Fourth Artillery, and four Marines wounded.

The result of these last two engagements put some of the Seminole Indians and their Black Seminole allies in a difficult position. The loss of their supplies and equipment at Hatchee Lustee forced them to reconsider their decision to wage war. Aware of the predicament facing the Seminole Indians, General Jesup sent a captured Seminole with a message to the chiefs offering to discuss solutions to ending the war. A positive response to that message was received on January 29 and two days later a black Seminole named Abraham (Holatoochee), a spokesman for Chief Micanopy, met with Jesup. Abraham stated that the Miccosukee Seminole band were responsible for the hostilities and Micanopy and his band of Alachua were ready for peace, but wished to remain in Florida. February 3, Seminole leader Jumper (Otee Emathlar), Alligator (Halpatter Tustenuggee), and Hapatophe met with General Jesup reaffirming that the Miccosukee band were responsible for starting the war and offered to bring those of Micanopy's band to a meeting with Jesup. That meeting occurred on February 23 and involved Davey (Holatoochee), Cloud (Yaholoochee), Alligator and other Seminole leaders. The outcome of this gathering produced a truce for those followers of Micanopy that would last until June.

"The Seminole players in the negotiations to end the war."
Abraham (left) – Wikipedia (US-PD)
Chief Jumper (center) Library of Congress, Prints & Photographs Division, LC-USZ62-74420
Chief Micanopy (right) Library of Congress, Prints & Photographs Division, LC-DIG-ds-03377 (chg B/W)

While Micanopy's Alachua Seminoles were in the process of making concessions for peace, other bands were doing just the opposite. On February 8, King Philip (Emathla) of the Mikasuki band along with his son, Coacoochee (Wildcat), and several hundred of his followers attacked Camp Monroe located near Lake Monroe in an area of present-day Sanford. King Philip was well known for his hostile exploits during the Second Seminole War having connections to the Red Stick Creeks of Alabama.

Camp Monroe was established by Lieutenant Colonel Alexander C. W. Fanning, Second U. S. Artillery, in December 1836 with the aid of several companies of artillery and perhaps Dragoons. Lieutenant Colonel Fanning was in command of the camp at the time of the February attack that was repelled, but at a cost of the life of Captain Charles Mellon and the wounding of fourteen others. Soon after the attack, the camp was renamed Fort Mellon in honor of the fallen officer. Fort Mellon was abandoned in June of that same year due to sickness like so many of the Florida forts. Seminoles were quick to burn the fort, but it would be rebuilt and occupied November 4, 1837, as a U. S. Army supply depot and remained until the end of hostilities in 1842.

In the days and weeks following the attack on the newly named Fort Mellon, there was a concerted effort by many of the Seminole chiefs to talk peace. General Jesup met with some of the chiefs and agreed to allow certain demands, but as time passed there was little proof that peace would occur! Trust was lacking by both parties, but on March 18, 1837, Chief Micanopy agreed in principle to the *Articles of Capitulation* calling for his followers to relocate to the Indian Territory. The Indians were to surrender at Fort Brooke awaiting transportation to their new home. Micanopy and many of his followers did, in fact, arrive at Fort Brooke, but their stay was short. On June 2, Osceola and Abiaka (Sam Jones), two leaders who did not agree to peace, arrived near Fort

Brooke with a large force for the purpose of freeing all the Seminoles who had turned themselves in for relocation. Micanopy and those who followed him to Fort Brooke for whatever reason left the fort ending the intent of the *Articles of Capitulation*!

Major General Jesup was angered by the dishonesty of the Seminole Indians and promised consequences would follow in due time. Summer was approaching and that was not a good time to conduct military operations evidenced by the sickness that plagued many of the soldiers during that time of year.

Instead, minor efforts were employed to keep pressure on the various Indian bands until the end of the summer season. Further, any large scale military effort would require more Federal and militia troops that had changed assignments or were released from duty after it was believed a peace had been agreed upon. It did help that Congress appropriated an additional $1.6 million for the war effort

A major breakthrough occurred on September 9, 1837! King Philip (Emanthla) was captured with eleven of his Mikasuki band by Florida militia troops commanded by Brigadier General Joseph Marion Hernandez and three companies of Second Dragoons. This event took place south of Fort Peyton and St. Augustine, Florida. A day later, Uchee Billy, and his brother, Uchee Jack, and twenty of his band of Yuchis were also captured in the *Battle of Mosquito Inlet*. One militia casualty, Lieutenant John Winfield Scott McNeil, resulted from this last capture. Uchee Billy died at Fort Marion November 25, 1837.

After King Philip's capture, he sent a message to his son, Coacoochee (Wild Cat), that he wanted to talk with him. Coacoochee agreed if he could come under a flag of truce. King Philip was sixty-one years of age at the time and may have expressed his desire to end the fighting encouraging his son to do the same.

Coacoochee under a flag of truce met with General Hernandez offering to bring in his followers. He was either captured at that time, October 17, or three days later, and sent to Fort Marion in St. Augustine where he was held prisoner. A day after the possible capture of Coacoochee, October 20, Osceola and Coe-Hajo were offered the same opportunity to talk with General Hernandez about a peace settlement when they were seized, shackled, and sent to Fort Marion the same as Coacoochee. Osceola remained at Fort Marion only a few weeks when he was transported to Fort Moultrie at Charleston, South Carolina. Here he would die on January 30, 1838, at the age of thirty-four. King Philip would also die the same year in the Indian Territory.

The arrest of many of the popular chiefs angered the Seminole people who vowed to continue the fight. Before the death of Osceola, Coacoochee and nineteen other Seminole captives escaped from Fort Marion on the night of November 29 heading south to warn others of the perceived treachery of General Jesup. It should be noted that Jesup had lost total trust in the Seminoles who went back on their word to surrender as early as March. He would no longer tolerate their deception, thus ordering Brigadier Hernandez to make the arrest.

All efforts of Major General Jesup to end the war had fizzled. Chief Ar-pi-uck-I (Sam Jones) whose name has many variations such as Aripeka, Aripeika, and Abiaka was about to make surrender preparations when the escaped Ocacoochee met with him and changed his mind. What followed was the *Battle of Lake Okeechobee* December 25, 1837. This battle involved Colonel Zachary Taylor, First U. S. Infantry, who left Fort Brooke on December 14 with a force of over 1,000 men against several Seminole chiefs and four hundred Indian. The battleground was a dense hammock surrounded by a cypress swamp.

Depiction of the seizure of Seminole Chief Osceola October 21, 1838

Wikipedia

Colonel Taylor's troops consisted of the First Infantry Regiment commanded by Lieutenant Colonel Davenport minus Company C, six companies of the Fourth Infantry led by Lieutenant Colonel William S. Foster (no companies identified), seven companies of the Sixth Infantry under Lieutenant Colonel Alexander R. Thompson (A, B, F, G, H, I & K), four companies of the Fourth Artillery led by Captain Munroe (A, B, D, & H), Colonel Richard Gentry's First Regiment Missouri Mounted volunteers, Major Morgan's Missouri volunteer Spy Battalion, thirty pioneers, thirteen pontoneers, and seventy Delaware Indians.

The Indian chiefs facing Colonel Taylor's forces included Ar-pi-uck-I (Sam Jones), Otulke Thloco (The Prophet), Halpatter Tustenaggee (Alligator), Coacoochee (Wild Cat) and Holata Micco (Billy Bowlegs II). The site of the Indian position was selected because it could be easily defended against any attacker. This would be proven when Colonel Gentry's Missouri volunteers began a frontal assault and were cut

down almost immediately. Gentry was mortally wounded and died of his wounds that day. The Missouri volunteers who survived the initial assault scattered to the rear prompting the Sixth Infantry to move into the fray. They too would receive intense fire from the Indians hidden in the tall sawgrass and trees of the hammock. The Sixth Infantry commander, Lieutenant Colonel Thompson, would suffer the same fate as Colonel Gentry and many of his officers and non-commissioned officers were either killed or wounded

After inflicting severe casualties on the Federal attackers, the Seminoles once again disappeared into the swamps and the troops did not follow. Colonel Taylor assessed the outcome of the battle apparently calling it a success, but it may have been the worst battle of the war. The casualty count for Federal troops was twenty-seven killed and one hundred-eleven wounded. The Regimental breakdown for the First Infantry included four wounded, Fourth Infantry had three enlisted men killed and one officer and nineteen enlisted wounded, Sixth Infantry had four officers and sixteen enlisted men killed and two officers and 53 enlisted wounded. The Missouri troops had four killed and thirty-two wounded. The First Regiment of Mounted volunteers listed two killed and twenty-five wounded. The Spy Battalion had two killed and 7 wounded. Indian casualty estimates list eleven killed and fourteen wounded.

The low casualty count for the First Infantry is due to having the role as Reserve. They were not called upon to fight until much of the action had ended. The Fourth Artillery did not participate at all in the battle. Instead, they were given a mission to construct a fort along the west bank of the Kissimmee River that had been nearly completed when Colonel Taylor returned to the location on December 28. The name Fort Basinger was given to the stockade fort in recognition of Lieutenant William E. Basinger, 2nd U.S. Artillery, who was killed at the Dade Massacre December 28, 1835. The fort was constructed with two blockhouses on adjacent corners. It was to be used as a depot for further military missions in the region of Lake Okeechobee and remained until it was abandoned in 1850. In spite of not capturing the Seminoles in the Battle of Lake Okeechobee, Colonel Taylor was commended for his effort and promoted in the rank of Brevet Brigadier General. He would go on to engage the Seminoles in other actions.

Second Seminole War in 1838

The New Year began with a bang in the form of another battle. The *Battle of Jupiter Inlet* was fought on January 15, 1838. The same Jupiter Inlet of today along the Atlantic Coast due east of Lake Okeechobee. The battle also went by the name *First Battle of the Loxahatchee River* for the river of that name where the battle took place. Navy Lieutenant Levin Minn Powell was in command of a combined force of sailors, soldiers, and marines on a mission to search out potential Indian activities. These men were part of the *Waterborne Everglades Expeditionary Unit.* Arriving near the Jupiter Inlet, signs were spotted that indicated possible Indian activity. Lieutenant Powell went ashore to investigate with fifty-five sailors and twenty-five soldiers of his command . As they approached the site they were ambushed and overwhelmed by perhaps 300 Indians led by Chiefs Halleck-Hajo and Tuskegee. The troops suffered four killed and twenty-two wounded. Lieutenant Powell was among the wounded. The remainder of the force was able to retreat to the safety of their small boats along the river.

This battle would bring Major General Thomas Jesup to march on the site with a much larger army nine days later in what would become the *Second Battle of the Loxahatchee River*. The force of 1,500 troops was comprised of part or all of the Second Dragoons led by Lieutenant Colonel William Selby Harney; Companies B, D, and H of the Fourth Artillery; a Battalion of Tennessee volunteers under Major William Lauderdale; and an Alabama Battalion of Mounted Volunteers commanded by Lieutenant Colonel David Caulfield. This force descended on the camp along the Loxahatchee River forcing the Indians to take flight into the swamp to prevent being overwhelmed. The outcome of this battle was reason for the Indian chiefs to once again listen to peace talks.

After the campaign along the Loxahatchee River, General Jesup established Fort Jupiter on January 24, one day after the end of the battle. From here he sent word to the chiefs offering to talk peace. Chief Halleck-Hajo along with Toskegee agreed to a meeting. The talks included the possibility of leaving the Seminole and their allies on Florida land and suggested that their followers could show faith by assembling near the fort. Many of the Indians and Blacks arrived at the fort, but Washington would not change the policy of relocation

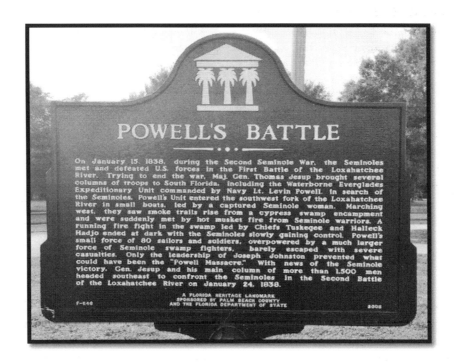

Marker above for the Battle of Jupiter Inlet or First Battle of the Loxahatchee River, January 15, 1838.
Marker below for the Second Battle of the Loxahatchee River, January 24, 1838

Fearing that news of Washington's refusal to change their relocation policy would send the Indians back into the swamps, General Jesup had Colonel David E. Twiggs and his Second Dragoons arrest the nearly seven hundred assembled near Fort Jupiter. A handful of Indians did escape including Passac-Micco whose involvement in the Seminole War is known but vague. The Indians and Blacks captured were promptly marched to Fort Brooke and sent west out of Florida.

After the last two battles in south Florida involving large military forces against a dwindling number of Seminoles and their allies largely due to captures, conflicts became fewer and with less combatants. The Indians were less likely to attack the troops unless they were in need of supplies to survive, but attacks did occur and sometime on civilians. Most of the Indian crops had been destroyed by troops in an effort to force their surrender and they had been driven to the swampy regions of the Everglades where efforts to follow were difficult but not impossible.

On March 22, 1838, Major William Lauderdale leading his Tennessee volunteers in addition to one company of the Third Artillery surprised a group of Seminoles led by Chief Ar-pi-uck-i at a site called Pine Island Ridge that was an island in the Everglades. Companies D and G, Fourth Artillery, led by Lieutenant Colonel James Monroe Bankhead are also reported to have participated in the battle. This action is labeled the *Battle of Pine Island Ridge* and may have been in response to the New River or Cooley Massacre that occurred nearly three months earlier on January 6. Seminole Indians killed the wife and children of William Cooley on that January day near their New River home perhaps without cause. The New River originates in the Everglades and flows to the Atlantic Ocean at Fort Lauderdale. The massacre site was about eight miles from the Pine island Ridge that today is Davie, Florida.

Although Major Lauderdale and his troops are said to have driven the Indians from the island, other accounts point to the Indians leaving before contact was made. No casualty count is reported for the conflict, but Ar-i-uck-i and his small band escaped once again and were pursued south to the region of Key Biscayne where Lieutenant Colonel Harney and his Second Dragoons caught up only to be denied capture of the band. Conflicts for the reminder of 1838 point only to an engagement of Company I, Fourth Artillery, at Tuscawilla Pond near Ocala on April 29. Whatever occurred has not been documented other than the involvement of the lone company of the Fourth Artillery.

At some point after the Second Battle of Loxahatchee River, Major General Jesup returned to Fort Brooke at Tampa with intentions to take up the fight against those Indians near the Withlachochee that played a role early in the war. That did not happen! Instead, General Jesup was relieved of command on May 15, 1838, and replaced by Brevet Brigadier General Zachary Taylor.

During the year and a half tenure of Major General Thomas Jesup's command in Florida, nearly two thousand Seminole Nation Indians and Blacks either surrendered or were taken captive, and some four hundred killed. Those surrendered and captured were sent to Fort Brooke for removal to the Indian Territory. The first removal was May 1837 involving more than 1,200 and an additional three hundred were sent in June.

Due to the stifling summer heat and danger of sickness, General Taylor concentrated his efforts along the more seasonable coast areas. When the season permitted, construction began on a number of forts linked together by road networks with the intent of maintaining the Seminoles to the southern regions. The cost of building forts meant that Congress would once again need to pour money into the war effort. The actions of the military did not mean that Indian attacks ended! There were isolated encounters often against civilian targets while avoiding contact with military troops as much as possible. However, much of the year 1838 saw less military activity than past years.

Second Seminole War in 1839

The year 1839 began much the same as the previous year had ended. Militarily it was quiet except for the forts and roads that were built, but little if any reason to fight. Along the southeastern coast of the Atlantic Ocean there were several skirmishes. One skirmish occurred on February 11 near the New River inlet, another February 20 near Fort Lauderdale that involved a detachment from Company K, Third Artillery, resulting in two privates killed. Near the Miami River February 28, a detachment of Company I of the Second Infantry was involved resulting in the death of Captain Samuel L. Russell and wounding of another unnamed soldier. On March 20 near Miami, a detachment of Company H, Second Infantry, met Indians who killed one corporal.

To the northwest close to the Gulf of Mexico near Fort Frank Brooke in the present Taylor County, a skirmish occurred May 2 involving Company F, Sixth Infantry, resulting in the death of one private. Some distance South of Fort Frank Brooke between Fort No. 3 and No. 4 another skirmish took place on May 20. This involved a detachment of Company K, Seventh Infantry. One sergeant was reported killed.

Early in May, Major General Alexander Macomb, Commanding General of the United States Army, arrived in Florida in an attempt to forge a final peace agreement with the Seminole Nation. The nation was tired of the war and Congress was tired of pouring money into what seemed an endless endeavor. Peace efforts had been on the table in the past and, not surprisingly, the Seminole were cautious of such talks having been tricked on previous occasions. On May 19 an agreement was reached that called for a cessation of fighting by the Indians in exchange for land on which to live in southern Florida. This peace arrangement worked for two months!

That peace was shattered on July 21 when a Detachment of Company F, Sixth Infantry, was attacked while on the march between Fort Frank Brooke and Fort Andrews. Due to the fact this region was in the northern part of the territory, the peace effort may not have been known. At any rate, one soldier was killed in the incident. There was a major violation of the peace agreement much closer to General Macomb's effort that surely was known to the Indians.

Lieutenant Colonel William S. Harney, Second U. S. Dragoons, had established an outpost near a civilian trading post along the Caloosahatchee River of present-day Fort Myers where a future Fort Harvie would be established November 4, 1841. The military command numbered twenty-eight dragoons. For whatever reason and perhaps no reason at all, the trading post was attacked early on Tuesday morning, July 23, 1839, by around one hundred fifty Indians resulting in civilian casualties and anywhere from eight to thirteen soldiers killed and one wounded. Lieutenant Colonel Harney and the remainder of his command were able to escape to safety using boats to cross the river or hid in the area. Those killed were enlisted soldiers from Companies A, C. D. E, and F. Spanish Indians led by Chekika and Hospetarke were responsible for the attack. Both Indians leaders were connected to Chief Micanopy causing concern that the all the Seminoles were responsible for the attack. At any rate, the peace agreement was off!

While these several episodes in 1839 might seem like major involvements, they were actually small engagements except that of Dragoons. Other sporadic incidents occurred throughout the territory after the attack of July 23. One incident took place near Fort Andrews on August 29 whereby a detachment of Company I, Sixth Infantry, engaged Indians resulting in one sergeant and one private killed. Another skirmish took place September 10 near Fort Fanning in which a military escort of Company D, First Infantry, was attacked. One private was killed and one wounded. In none of these incidents are the Indian casualties known. Often times the Indians would carry off their killed and wounded before any count could be made.

Fort Lauderdale had a second skirmish on September 27 involving Company K, Third Artillery. Two privates were killed. Tampa Bay across the territory was the site of another encounter. The Florida militia would encounter Seminoles on November 9 in which one soldier was killed and two wounded. Indian casualties are unknown as was commonly reported. After a lackluster 1839, military involvement would pick up in 1840.

Historical plaque marking the site of Lieutenant Colonel Harney's outpost along the Calooshatchee River that came under attack July 23, 1839, ending the peace arrangement with the Seminole Indians established by Major General Macomb.

Second Seminole War in 1840

The year 1840 saw a number of skirmishes and at least five named battles. There were two skirmishes that occurred on January 24 both around lesser known forts. The first was near either Fort New Smyrna or a camp of the same name. Company B, Third Artillery, saw action against an unknown band of Indians resulting in four artillerymen wounded. The second on the same day was connected to the supply of provisions for Fort Preston near present-day Bristol in Gadsden County. A detachment of three soldiers from Company E, Second Dragoons, were in charge of the supply wagon when they were attacked by twenty to thirty Creek Indians who drove off the men wounding one. A few days later, Captain Erasmus D. Bullock, Second Dragoons, came upon the same Indians and chased them away dropping all the supplies they had taken.

The Seventh U. S. Infantry was active during 1840. Company C was involved in a conflict on February 1 near Fort No. 5 situated close to the present-day Ocala National Forest in central Florida. The skirmish resulted in one sergeant killed and two soldiers wounded. On March 15, Company B saw action near Fort Drane wounding one soldier. Company A saw three engagements at or near Fort King on March 24, April 14 and 28 when two privates were killed in each of the first two skirmishes and one in the last. These conflicts are referred to as the *Battle of Fort King* at least by the Seventh Infantry who only recently arrived in the Florida Territory and may not have been accustomed to the level of fighting.[3] Each incident was more like skirmishes involving small number of combatants on either side. The engagement on April 28 involved sixteen troops under the command of Captain Gabriel James Rains who were on a scouting mission when attacked by an unknown number of Indians. The soldiers were able to fight their way back to the fort even though Captain Raines was severely wounded yet survived. Two of Captain Rains' privates were not as lucky as they were killed in the attack.

A more significant conflict involving the Seventh Infantry occurred on May 19 identified as the *Battle of Bridgewater*. While the outcome of the "battle" is recorded in history, the name does not share the same. Second Lieutenant James S. Sanderson, Company C, Seventh U. S. Infantry, and five soldiers were killed on May 19, 1840, ambushed by forty to fifty Indians while pursuing the enemy who earlier that day attacked Lieutenant J. W. Martin and three of his men from Company K of the Second Infantry who were couriers carrying messages from Fort Waccahootee (Wacahoota)

to Fort Micanopy both in present Alachua County. Lieutenant Martin was wounded and two others, one sergeant and one private, were killed while the fourth soldier escaped to Fort Micanopy alerting Lieutenant Sanderson and his seventeen troops. The Attack on Sanderson and his men is an area known as Levy's Prairie.

Attacks by Indians on military couriers was not all that uncommon during the war, but It seems unlikely that such a large force of Indians would engage four soldiers for that purpose unless they came upon them while preparing for other action. A small Indian party was more likely to be involved in attacking small numbers of soldiers. Perhaps the Indians were planning to attack Fort Micanopy that was close to where Lieutenant Sanderson and his troops were engaged. If an attack on Fort Micanopy was the original goal of the Indian band, the plan was foiled when they met the couriers and subsequently the eighteen soldiers from Fort Micanopy! We will never know the real purpose of such a large band of Indians at that time.

Other commands saw action in the early months of 1840. Company I, Second Dragoons was involved in action on April 10 near Fort Wool wounding one soldier. Fort Wool was established in 1835 in present-day Dixie County. Two days later, April 12, Companies C and I, Sixth Infantry, were engaged while on the march between Fort Griffin and Fort Fanning approximately thirty miles apart in the northwest part of the territory causing the wounding of one soldier. On the opposite side of the territory near Fort Lauderdale, Company K, Third Artillery, commanded by Captain W. D. Davidson, fought with Indians resulting in four wounded men. A day later, April 25, the action shifted again to the northwest near Fort Barker in current Lafayette County. It was here that Company I, First infantry, was involved in action resulting in the death of one sergeant. It should be apparent that shifting of the military action all over the territory meant that measures were necessary to bring this war under control.

On May 6, 1840, Brevet Brigadier General Walker Keith Armistead, Third Artillery, replaced Brevet Brigadier General Zachary Taylor as commander of the Florida troops. This change in command was at the request of General Taylor. General Armistead at once began operations during the summer months that had not happened during the tenure of previous commanders. This action took a toll on the health of the soldiers, but it also caused the Seminoles the use of their summer growing season resulting in the destruction of crops and their dwellings wherever possible. This time period also introduced the Eighth Infantry into the Florida military family to go along with the First, Second, Third, Sixth, and Seventh Infantry , the Second Dragoon; and the Third Artillery.

Later Portrait of Major General Zachary Taylor
Library of Congress, Prints & Photographs Division, LC-USZ62-38086

The month of July 1840 saw several engagements. Company B, Second U. S. Infantry, was engaged on July 12 near the Cow Creek Hammock that cost the lives of one sergeant and one corporal. The Cow Creek Hammock may be near the Farmton Wildlife Management Area slightly west of I-95 close to Osceola, Florida. A day later near Fort Pleasant in current Taylor County a distance of nearly one hundred seventy-five miles northwest of the Cow Creek Hammock, detachments from Companies B and D, Sixth U. S. Infantry, saw Indian activity resulting in the loss of one private from each company and another soldier wounded. Then again, one hundred ten miles back to the southeast just east of Orange Lake there was an attack near Fort Russell July 16 that involved Company I, Second Dragoons, under the command of Captain Benjamin Lloyd. Beall. One soldier was wounded in the skirmish.

On July 24, 1840, sixteen soldiers from Companies A and F, Second Dragoons, led by Sergeant C. O. Willis were guarding horses when attacked by Indians near the Wekiva River. Neither the exact location near the Wekiva River nor the circumstances surrounding the events of this conflict have been revealed, but it is plausible that Sergeant Willis was charged with a detail of dragoons who were attacked when either guarding the horses of the command or were attempting to water the horses at the river. The outcome resulted in the loss of Private Isaac Childs from Company A killed in the action. To the south along the Atlantic coast, a detachment of Company K, Third Artillery, was engaged by an unknown number of Indians near the New River Inlet without the loss of any troops.

An incident of major proportions occurred on August 7, 1840, that is important due to the devastation that resulted, but had little military involvement. Spanish Indian Chief Chakaika or Chekika who was responsible for the attack on the dragoons near Charlotte Harbor on July 23, 1839, attacked the civilian population in the settlement on Indian Key in the present-day Florida Keys. Chakaika's reputation was one of a ruthless killer who would stop at nothing to take out his hostilities on anyone anywhere! The population on Indian Key on August 7 numbered between 50 and 70 inhabitants. Of that number Chakaika and his band killed thirteen and destroyed the settlement looting all they could before burning the buildings. There was a brief military response from nearby Tea Table Key where the Navy had a small base consisting mostly of a hospital, but the few sailors present were unable to change the outcome. Chakaika and his band would not escape for long.

The Seventh U. S. Infantry was busy from the middle of August to the same timeframe in September. On the 13th of August detachments from Companies A and C were in conflict with Indians near Fort Wheelock located at the south end of Orange Lake. Two privates were killed and one soldier was wounded. On the 30th of the month Companies E and I of the Seventh Infantry were engaged near Fort Micanopy resulting in the death of three privates. A week later on September 6 two more detachments from the Seventh Infantry, B and H, led by Lieutenant W. K. Hansen skirmished with Indians near Fort Wacahoota (Waccahootee). This conflict resulted in the death of Private Michal Hefferman assigned to Company H and the wounding of three soldiers one of whom was Private Augustus Eckart of Company B.

A new command was introduced into the war effort in Florida. The Eighth U. S. Infantry left Jefferson Barracks in St. Louis on September 24 for a four-year tour in the Florida Territory. This tour would extend beyond the end of the Second Seminole War. Eight companies under the command of Lieutenant Colonel Newman S. Clarke traveled by steamboat down the Mississippi River eventually arriving at Tampa Bay. The regimental commander, Colonel William J. Worth, and two more companies, E and H. joined the regiment at Tampa Bay. From here the ten companies of the regiment marched to Fort King arriving November 5 and remained about a month at which time they returned to Fort Brooke on December 2, 1840. The Eighth Infantry would see action against the Seminole Nation in 1841 and 1842.

There was an apparent lull in conflicts from the episode of September 6 to November 1, 1840, but one skirmish occurred on the 1st that would be the last until December. Company G, Third Artillery, commanded by Captain Hezekiah Garner, had an encounter with Indians near Picolata along the St. Johns River approximately ten miles west of St. Augustine, Florida. The St. Johns River was used as a major supply route for military involvement in the Florida Territory. Whether this encounter was related to the movement of supplies is not known nor are the Indian band or how many. One sergeant and one private were killed in the action.

A major offensive took place from December 3-24, 1840, against the Seminole in the Everglades where they had taken refuge. Lieutenant Colonel Harney assisted by Major Thomas T. Fauntleroy both of the Second Dragoons departed Fort Dallas near Miami December 3 with two hundred thirteen troops made up of portions of Company A, B, D, F, H, and K of the Second Dragoons along with Company D, H, I, and K, Third Artillery. Using boats requisitioned from the Navy, the command navigated the waters of the Everglades searching island by island for the enemy. The troops were disguised in Seminole clothing in order not to raise an alarm if spotted. On December 9, the soldiers came upon a village where they captured a number of Indians and hung some of the warriors. The next day, Thursday, the camp of the Spanish Indian Chakaika was discovered. Caught completely by surprise, Chakaika is killed trying to escape and the rest of his warriors are executed! No sympathy is shown those Indians who had created hostile actions without cause. Lieutenant Colonel Harney had gotten his revenge for the unprovoked attack on him and his men July 23, 1839! One soldier, Private William N. Aller, Company H, Second Dragoons, was killed during the three-week operation and another soldier wounded.

One last major incident took place on December 28, 1840, known as the *Martin's Point Hammock* affair. Lieutenant Walter Sherwood, Seventh U. S. Infantry, and Lieutenant N. Hopson were in charge of a detail of ten men from Company C, E, and I, Seventh Infantry, escorting the wife of Lieutenant Alexander Montgomery from Fort Micanopy ten miles to Fort Wacahootee (Waccahootee) Four miles from Fort Micanopy, the detail was attacked by an estimated thirty Indians led by Halleck Tustenuggee and Coosa Tustenuggee. Two privates, one from Company C and the other Company I, were killed immediately. Lieutenant Sherwood called for Mrs. Montgomery to take cover in the wagon, but in doing so was struck by a bullet and killed. Vastly outnumbered and exposed to rifle fire from the hammock, the troops did their best to protect themselves. Meanwhile, Lieutenant Hopson was able to mount his horse and galloped back to Fort Micanopy for reinforcements and returned to the attack site finding Lieutenant Sherwood and Sergeant Major Francis Carroll both dead. Two soldiers of the escort team were wounded. The Indians were driven off, but the damage was done!

Halleck Tustenuggee had been a nemesis for the military from the start of the war. He was cunning, treacherous, and would not stop his hostile actions until his capture at the end of the war. Coosa Tustenuggee on the other hand was more pragmatic recognizing that the attack that killed the wife of an officer would result in a response like no other. Fearing that response, Coosa Tustenuggee soon after deliberately ran into a detachment of dragoons and surrendered himself, thirty-two warriors, and sixty women and children. All were sent to the Indian Territory not long after.

Second Seminole War in 1841

At the start of 1841 there had been an estimated 2,980 Seminole Indians relocated west. These numbers are largely estimates based on the sometimes inaccurate reporting. There may have been an equal number of Indians still remaining in Florida. Halleck Tustenuggee, Coacoochee (Wild Cat), Holata Micco (Billy Bowlegs II), Thlocklo Tustenuggee (Tiger Tail), Apreika (Sam Jones), Otulke Thloco (The Prophet), Hospetarke, and no doubt some upstarts were still causing unrest.

The first conflict of 1841 occurred on January 7 near Fort Lauderdale involving Company I, Third Artillery, commanded by Captain Martin Burke. All that is reported is the death of one soldier. Fort Russell to the east of Orange Lake was attacked March 2 by an estimated seventy to one hundred Indians led by Halleck Tustenuggee. This engagement is known as the *Orange Creek Bridge* affair. Lieutenant William Alburtis, Company K, Second Infantry, led a small force from the fort charging and scattering the Indians from the area. One corporal and two privates were killed as well as seven wounded. Casualties were inflicted on the attackers, but those numbers are not known. A day later, March 3, a skirmish took place near Fort MacKay some twenty miles southeast of Fort Micanopy. The significance of this skirmish came to light two days later when the camp of the Indians involved in the skirmish was found and there was clothing belonging to Lieutenant Sherwood and Mrs. Montgomery who were killed December 28, 1840. This camp must have been that of Halleck Tustenuggee and his followers.

Two days after the Orange Creek Bridge affair, March 4, the Second Infantry was again involved in a skirmish with no doubt Halleck Tustenuggee. Company D led by Captain Ephraim K. Barnum was involved with Indians near the Ocklawaha River. The Orange Creek that flowed from Orange Lake emptied into the Ocklawaha River. This might indicate that Company D was stationed at Fort Wheelock or Fort MacKay both in the vicinity of the river.

Efforts to entice the Seminoles to surrender had met with varied success. Often times the chiefs would agree to peace talks only to acquire supplies and then sneak off in the night having achieved their only purpose. On March 5 that scheme once again manifested itself when Coacoochee (Wild Cat) appeared at Fort Cummings dressed as Hamlet. The costume

was taken from a theatrical troupe the year before in which several of the actors were killed. Two others with Coacoochee were dressed as Richard III and Horatio. Coacoochee met with General Armistead over the next five days and agreed to talk with his followers and return with his answer. The next meeting was on March 22 at Fort Brooke at which time Coacoochee agreed to surrender after the June Green Corn Dance.

May 1, 1841, Lieutenant William Tecumseh Sherman escorted Cooacoochee to Fort Pierce the same as present-day Ft. Pierce, Florida. While at the fort the chief met with Major Thomas Childs, Third Artillery, in command at the fort who agreed to allow the chief one month to bring his followers in for relocation to the Indian Territory. During the month of May, Coacoochee's people freely moved in and around Fort Pierce again taking advantage of supplies. Suspicions were immediately raised that surrender may never happen and that Coacoochee was only interested in supplying his followers. Upon arrival at the fort on June 4, Coacooche, his younger brother Otulke, his uncle the brother of Emaltha (King Philip), and thirteen warriors were arrested. This group was moved to Fort Brooke, readied for transport west, and got as far as New Orleans when word was received to return to Fort Brooke. Colonel Worth had other plans for Coacoochee and ordered his return.

One day before the arrest of Coacooche and his fellow Indians, Brevet Brigadier General Walker Keith Armistead was relieved of command of the Florida troops on May 31, 1841, and replaced by Colonel William Jenkins Worth, Eighth U. S. Infantry. Colonel Worth was the eighth Florida troop commander and a no nonsense officer who would bring an end to the war!

On July 4 with Coacoochee in irons on board a transport in Tampa Bay having been returned from New Orleans, met with Colonel

Worth who made him an offere that reads: *"Coacoochee, I am your friend; so is your Great Father in Washington. What I say to you is true. My tongue is not forked like a snake's. My word is for the happiness of the red man. You are a great warrior; the Indians throughout the country look to you as a leader by your counsels they have been governed. This war has lasted five years; much blood has been shed, much innocent blood. You have made your hands and the ground red with the blood of women and children. This war must now end. You are the man to do it; you must and shall accomplish it. I sent for you that through the exertions of yourself and your men you might induce your entire band to emigrate. I wish for you to state how many days it will require to effect an interview with the Indians in the woods. You can select three or five of these men to carry your talk; name the time, it shall be granted; but I tell you, as I wish your relatives and friends told, that unless they fulfill your demands, yourself and these warriors now seated before us shall be hung to the yards of this vessel when the sun sets on the day appointed, with the irons upon your hands and feet. I tell you this that we may well understand each other. I do not wish to frighten you; you are too brave a man for that; but I say what I mean, and I will do it. It is for the benefit of the white and red man. This war must end, and you must end it…"*

Sketch of Coacoochee (Wild Cat)
Wikipedia

To this arrangement Coacoochee agreed selecting five of his band to carry the message to the members of his following who had forty days to turn themselves in or the hangings would take place. In ten days six warriors and a number of women and children arrived at the departure site. This pattern continued to the last day of the month when seventy-eight warriors, sixty-four women, and forty-seven children arrived giving a total of one hundred eight-nine for the forty day period.

Colonel Worth's methods were having a profound impact on bringing other Indians in for relocation all with the help of Coacoochee. In August, Hospetarke was enticed by Coacoochee to participate in what he thought were peace negotiations at Camp Ogden near the Peace River when he was seized along with eighteen warriors and eventually his entire band totaling one hundred twenty-seven. This effort using Coacoochee would continue until October 12, 1841, at which time Coacoochee along with two hundred plus Indians and Blacks would depart on board ships for New Orleans and eventually the Indian Territory.

During the month of July while Colonel Worth was implementing his plan with Coacoochee, other conflicts were taking place elsewhere in the territory. Soldiers attacked a Seminole camp near the Ocklawaha River on July 16 that involved detachments from Company C, Seventh Infantry, and Company D, Eighth Infantry. Sergeant Abraham Bridges, Company C, was killed rushing the camp, the only casualty of the attack. Company H, Eighth Infantry, under the command of Lieutenant G. H. Hansen was involved in a skirmish on July 17 at Camp Ogden along the Peace River. Captain Thomas P. Gwynne established Camp Ogden in 1841 that today is the town of Fort Ogden in DeSoto County of south central Florida. The attack on July 17 resulted in the death of one private. The Indians involved were not identified.

The role of some of the Second Dragoons would change on October 17, 1841. Companies A, D, E, F, and G were ordered to Fort Jesup in Louisiana and Fort Towson in Arkansas. The remaining companies would remain in Florida until May 29, 1842, at which time they were ordered to Baton Rouge, Louisiana. The Second Dragoons had served well in their role in the Second Seminole War and had lost two officers and twenty enlisted men killed in action. The number of non-combat deaths was five officers and one hundred ninety-two enlisted soldiers. These last numbers point out the harsh conditions under which the United States military was required to operate!

The region of central Florida was plagued by Seminole Halleck Tustenuggee and would stretch further north as soon will be described. On September 29, a detachment of Company B, Second Dragoons, was involved in a skirmish twelve miles north of Fort Russell resulting in the wounding of Private Edward Hood. The soldiers were detailed to escort a supply wagon and had camped for the night when attacked.

Although Halleck Tustenuggee was not identified in the skirmish, either he or members of his band are believed to have participated. Nearly two months later on December 20, the settlement of Mandarin on the east side of the St. Johns River approximately twelve miles north of present-day Jacksonville was attacked by Indians and burned. Accounts by residents are clear. *"In December 1841 the Seminole Indians attacked and burnt the town and massacred the inhabitants. The incident occurred on December 20 by chiefs Powis-fixico (Short Grass) and Halleck-Tustenugee and his band."*

At the same time Halleck Tustenuggee was terrorizing the inhabitants of the Mandarin Settlement far to the north in Florida, Major William Goldsmith Belknap conducted a sweep of the Big Cypress Swamp in the Everglades in search of Thlocklo Tustenuggee (Tiger Tail) and Holata Micco (Billy Bowlegs II). Major Belknap utilized detachments from Company D, Fourth Infantry, recently returned to Florida, and Company I, Eighth Infantry. The operation was only marginally successful capturing some Indians, but not their intended goal. Two soldiers were killed in this action, Private William Foster, Company D, and Sergeant John Doane from Company I. This military objective ended the year 1841.

Second Seminole War in 1842

After the attack on the Mandarin Settlement by Halleck Tustenuggee, Colonel Worth was more than ready to put an end to the Indian who had done so much harm to both civilians and the military. Colonel Worth was equally determined to do the same to Thlocklo Tustenuggee (Tiger Tail), Holata Micco (Billy Bowlegs II), Otulke Thloco (The Prophet), and Areipka (Sam Jones). Some of these efforts would become successful while others would come up short.

At times, multiple companies of infantry and dragoons were sent in search of these Seminole Indians. Major Joseph Plympton, Second Infantry, commanded one of the searches with Company B, K, and a detachment of Company G totaling one hundred and two soldiers. They were looking for Halleck Tastenuggee in the area of Dunn's Lake present-day Crescent Lake in Putnam County. On January 25, 1842, the command located the Indian band and an attack was made in what was called the *Haw Creek* Affair near the Wahoo Swamp area. The Indians scattered in all directions and once again Halleck Tustenuggee escaped, but two of his band were captured. Second Infantry losses included Private Edward Carnes who was killed in the action and two others soldiers wounded. Far too many times this same scenario was played out where a frontal attack allowed the Indians to escape into the swamps or hammocks. This was discerning to Colonel Worth who vowed to put a stop to this practice if he could. That would soon change, but not before one more smaller engagement.

On February 12, Company H, Eighth Infantry, led by First Lieutenant P. Smirsh, would see action in the Wahoo Swamp area. The exact location is not provided, but one soldier, Sergeant Harvey Seward, was killed, and another soldier was wounded. A better opportunity would come on April 19, 1842. On that date, a large military force of some two hundred soldiers would advance on the *Big Hammock of the Palaklikaha Swamp* some thirty miles south of Fort King in the vicinity of Fort Armstrong. This force consisted of Company K, Second Dragoons; Company C, Second Infantry; Companies C, D, F, and I, Fourth Infantry; and Company B, Eighth Infantry. Captain Croghan Ker, Second Dragoons led this force assisted by First Lieutenant George A. McCall, Fourth Infantry.

As the troops approached the site surrounded by water, they fired into the hammock and received return fire from the Indians. Company K, Second Dragoons, attacked from the rear cutting off the retreat that had been the case in so many previous conflicts. The Indians were in a disarray scattering in small bands in any direction they could. Many Indians escaped as did Halleck Tustenuggee, but all their supplies were left behind. Indian casualties may have been small with one killed, two wounded and one captured. The captured Indian may have been the father-in-law of Halleck Tustenuggee, Osane Micco. This was a devastating loss for Halleck Tustenuggee's band and would soon lead to a desire to once again talk peace. For this conflict, one soldier was killed, Private Augustus R. Wandell, Company K, Second Dragoons, and three from the same Company K were wounded.

Whether Halleck Tustenuggee was willing to talk peace or Osane Micco encouraged him is uncertain, but the "thorn" in Colonel Worth's side did eventually appear at Fort King where he and many of his warriors were seized. The date may have been April 29, 1842. The event at Fort King was planned as a feast, but it was a ploy to end the reign of Halleck Tustenuggee once and for all! The captured were transported to Cedar Key for confinement, the headquarters for Colonel Worth, and subsequently all were relocated to Fort Gibson beginning July 14 and arriving September 5, 1842. While this action was taking place, other conflicts were occurring with other Seminoles one of whom was Thlocklo Tustenuggee (Tiger Tail).

Soldiers from Company D and E, Seventh U. S. Infantry, assigned to Fort Wacahoota (Waccahootee or Watkahootee) in present Alachua County were involved in a skirmish May 17, 1842, most likely with Thlocklo Tustenuggee who had been on a killing rampage of recent. Many of the engagements at this time in the war were not reported in detail as previous. All that is known is one soldier from Company D, Private Daniel

McNeil, was killed as was Private Christopher Duff, from Company E. On the same date of this last action, Company F, Seventh Infantry, commanded by First Lieutenant F. Britton was involved in a skirmish near Clay's Landing along the Suwannee River. Here too, the events of the skirmish are lacking other than the loss of one soldier killed and two wounded.

The Second Seminole War was basically over for the most part as the month of June 1842 approached. By General Order No. 28 issued by Colonel William Jenkins Worth on August 14, 1842, it was declared as such. By no means would this mean that no more hostilities would occur; quite the contrary! Several Seminole chiefs were still holdouts among them Thlocklo Tustenuggee (Tiger Tail), Octiarche, Holata Micco (Billy Bowlegs II), Otulke Thiocco (The Prophet), and Arpekia (Sam Jones). The first of this group to be seized was Octiarche followed by Thlocklo Tustenuggee both in the November timeframe. They and their followers were shipped to New Orleans in late December, but Thlocklo Tustenuggee (Tiger Tail) would go no further. He died in New Orleans awaiting transfer to the Indian Territory. The remaining three chiefs would never leave Florida and were allowed to remain with their followers in the Great Swamp of the Everglades and other reservations as their ancestors do today.

Colonel William Jenkins Worth
Commander, Eighth United States Infantry
Library of Congress, Prints & Photographs Division, LC-USZ62-77231

The cost of the war has been estimated to be thirty to forty million dollars and resulted in an estimated 1,466 lives lost from combat, disease, and other causes. The sad realization is that the Second Seminole War only partially resolved the situation in Florida. A third war would be necessary beginning in 1855. Before that war could occur, however, other Indian wars would take place around the western territories during the Texas War for Independence as well as the United States War with Mexico.

Indian Wars in Texas

In the years following the Texas Revolution that ended April 21, 1836, Native American Indian conflicts occurred in the new Republic initiated by both Indians and government officials. The Indian tribes of Cherokee, Kickapoo, and Shawnee of Northeast Texas became embroiled in conflict with the Texas authorities over land rights. This conflict kicked off the *Cherokee War* of 1839 and would lead to the *Battle of Neches* on July 15, 1839.

In February 1836, Sam Houston made a promise of land in Northeast Texas to Cherokee Indians and other tribes in return for neutrality in the region. A year and a half later, the ruling government denied this agreement over the objection of Sam Houston creating uncertainty on all sides. Also around this time, information came to light the Mexican Government was trying to interfere in the fragile stability of the new Republic by supplying weapons and ammunition to the Indians in a plot to overthrow the government of Texas. The discovery of this plan prompted the government to send a five-member commission to speak with Chief Bowles of the Cherokee tribe about moving his people and other tribes out of Texas. Chief Bowles was given no option other than move or be forced to move.

What happed next is cloudy not by the events but why they occurred! Chief Bowles agreed to move his followers and was in the process of doing so when the Indians were attacked by Texan troops July 15. What precipitated this attack is lacking. Might the attack have been for supporting Mexico against the Texas Republic? The answer is unclear, but the *Battle of Neches* continued the next day, July 16, and ended with the death of Chief Bowles and about one hundred of his followers. Those Indians that were able to escape made their way to the Indian Territory. The Texans lost five killed and twenty-eight wounded.

Less than a year later, peace negotiations were held between Texas authorities and some Comanche Indians in San Antonio March 19, 1840. The Comanche had created havoc in Texas for some time taking substantial captives that were never released. The many wars had taken a heavy toll on the number of Indians as an earlier smallpox epidemic had done. Three Comanche delegates arrived in San Antonio January 10 indicating a desire for peace. Peace talks were agreed to on the condition that all captives would need to be released at the time of the meeting. Twelve Comanche chiefs arrived in San Antonio on March 19 with many of their warriors, women, and children, but only two captives. This action brought indignation from the Texan authorities and all eleven chiefs were told that they would be jailed until they fulfilled the release of all the captives. Armed soldiers were brought into the meeting hall to enforce this announcement at which time the chiefs attempted to force their way out of the hall. Shots rang out from the soldiers and total chaos ensued both inside and out. This became the *Council Hall Fight*. Soon after all twelve chiefs lay dead as did twenty-three other Indians including three women and two children. Twenty-nine Comanche were taken prisoner and held as ransom until the white captives were released.

One Indian squaw was sent as a messenger to the Comanche camp with word that those Indians jailed would be released when all the white captives were returned to San Antonio. The Comanche were not the only ones to suffer casualties in the fray. Some unsuspecting civilians would be caught in the crossfire between soldiers and Indians. Seven inhabitants were killed one of whom was a soldier, and perhaps ten more wounded of unknown description.

What happened next was a slaughter by the Comanche of thirteen captives including children in the most inhumane manner possible. On the other hand, the Comanche held at San Antonio were eventually moved to other locations and all would eventually escape alive unlike their captives! The Comanche were not done. Chief Buffalo Hump began a vicious retribution on the inhabitants of settlements in the Republic of Texas that is known as the *Great Raid of 1840*. Before this action was finished, as many as twenty-five settlers would be killed, the settlement of Victoria rampaged, Linnville plundered and destroyed, other white captives taken and murdered, and goods of all kinds stolen if not destroyed.

Chief Buffalo Hump gathered Comanche from all over Texas to form a raiding party numbering four hundred. The first raid was on Victoria, Texas, on August 6. Victoria would record at least half of those killed during the Great Raid of 1840. The next attack occurred on August 8, 1840, on Linnville along the Texas coast. Linnville was completely caught off guard and suffered immediately casualties before the inhabitants could take refuge in boats offshore where the Indians could not follow. From the boats the people could see their town at first looted then burned. When the raiders finally left Linnville, they took with them many pack animals loaded with the contraband from the settlement that included silver bullion recently arrived at the port from New Orleans.

While the Comanche were celebrating their successes, the Texas Rangers were closing fast on the marauders who were slowed by the many pack animals. The slow pace allowed the Texas Rangers to make contact on August 12 and the *Battle of Plum Creek* ensued. Captain Matthew Caldwell led the hundred or so Gonzales and Seguin Rangers and Colonel Edward Burleson led an equal number of Rangers from Bastrop. Interestingly, Captain Caldwell was one of those wounded at the Council House Fight March 19. When the Battle of Plum Creek began near Lockhart, Texas,, there was an immediate exchange of gunfire after which the Indians mounted their horses and sped away leaving most of the pack animals with their plunder. The Rangers chased after in like fashion killing some and scattering the rest of the Indians in all directions. Many of the Comanche were able to escape along with a sufficient number of pack animals, but the immediate danger of additional raids had come to an end. The same can't be said for future Comanche attacks as Chief Buffalo Hump continued his atrocities until the middle of the 1850's.

Indian Wars Shift North and West

Texas would see more hostilities as noted, but named conflicts shifted north and west in the late 1840's and into the 1850's. The Oregon Territory in the late 1840's included the land of Washington. As settlers moved west along the Oregon Trail, they came to places inhabited by Indian tribes not accustomed to people unfamiliar to them much the same as the first settlers in the east. Missionaries made up some of these new people who were accepted at first by the Native Americans. As was true in the east, these settlers brought not only new ways of life, but also disease to which the Indians had not developed immunity.

Dr. Marcus Whitman was a Presbyterian mission doctor who befriended the Cayuse Indians near Walla Walla located in the southeastern part of present Washington State. Dr. Whitman along with the Reverend Henry Spalding, their wives, and some supporters established a mission in the region in 1836. While Reverend Spaulding tended to the spiritual support of the Cayuse from the time of the group's arrival, Dr. Whitman was involved in treating their physical needs along with the spiritual ones. As the years passed, attitudes and cooperation would wane blaming Dr. Whitman for causing the death of some two hundred of the Cayuse people due to measles. The Indians believed that the measles sickness was the fault of the missionaries and took out their anger on those at the mission leading to the *Whitman Massacre* on November 29, 1847. The massacre was the killing of all fourteen members of the mission including Dr. Marcus Whitman for whom the massacre is named. The massacre led to the *Cayuse War* lasting from 1847-1855 whereby the Oregon Rifles were organized by the Oregon Territorial Government to combat the Indians. The five Cayuse Indians involved in the massacre were eventually captured and convicted in 1850 of their involvement and hanged. The Cayuse War raged for a few more years, but much reduced from its inception.

Indian Wars Shift Back to the Southwest

An incident involving Comanche and Apache Indians took place June 17, 1848, at a point along the Santa Fe Trail that acquired the name **Battle of Coon Creek**. A supply train under the command of Lieutenant William Bedford Royall, Second Regiment Missouri Mounted Volunteers, came under attack on that date by some two hundred Indians. Lieutenant Royall had previously linked up

with First Lieutenant Phillip Stremmel and sixty-five officers and enlisted men of Company C, Battalion of Missouri Mounted Volunteers. Between the two commands, the Indian attack was thwarted and the supply train was allowed to continue to its objective of Fort Mann in Kansas. Many of the troops involved in this confrontation were headed to join American forces in the Mexican War. It is worthy to note that Lieutenant Royall would continue to serve in the military with the Union Army during the American Civil War achieving the rank of Brevet Colonel

In the years following the Mexican War in 1848, Indian conflicts dominated the scene before, during, and even after the American Civil War. In 1849 the **Navajo Conflicts** against U. S. Army troops flared up in Arizona and New Mexico. These conflicts continued until 1863. The **Mariposa War** in California took place from 1850-1851 and involved the Paiute and Yokut Indians who reacted to gold miners who flooded the region disrupting the lives of their people and forcing them off their lands in search of gold.

As Mormon settlers moved into the region of present-day Utah, conflicts would eventually occur as was true in many similar situations. The period of 1851 to early 1854 was a time of conflict between Mormons and the native Ute Indians. The culmination of these conflicts was the **Walker War** named for the Ute Indian Chief Walkara who also went by the names Wakara, Wahkara and Walker. Chief Walkara warred against the Mormons until a fragile peace was negotiated May 1854.

A Flood of Indians Wars

The years following the Mexican War saw constant conflicts with Native American Indians in the western territories. Many of these conflicts were due to settlers moving into the new regions gained from Mexico. When Indians would kill settlers, settlers would retaliate by killing Indians. This scenario took place in the **Gunnison Massacre** October 21, 1853, when a Pacific Railroad survey party of seven men were killed by Ute Indians; the **Sioux Wars** in Minnesota and Dakota Territory that lasted from 1854 to 1890; the Kaibai Creek Massacre August 17, 1854, in California where Indian men, women and children were killed by settlers; and the **Ward Massacre** August 20, 1854, in which some twenty members of the Alexander Ward party traveling the Oregon Trail were killed by Shoshone Indians. These types of conflicts would not stop in 1854, but continue for the years to come. A major conflict in Florida, however, would shift attention from the back and forth involvement in the western regions.

The Third Seminole War

Two Seminole Wars were apparently not enough! When the Second Seminole War officially ended August 14, 1842, not all Seminole Indians had been moved to the Indian Territory. Two of the most defiant, Sam Jones (Arpiucki) a powerful medicine man and Billy Bowlegs II (Holata Micco) with a small band of Seminole supporters found refuge in the swamps of the Everglades until 1855 at which time confrontations would occur once again between themselves and Regular Army troops. This kicked off the **Third Seminole War** that began in late 1855 and continued to May 8, 1858.

Seminole Indian Billy Bowlegs (Holata Micco)
Wikipedia (US-PD)

Following the Mexican War, U. S. Army units were scattered across the western territories at new and existing forts that dominated the region. Their mission was to provide protection to the many settlers who might fall prey to Indian attacks and lawless men who had little regard for the peaceful citizens. One of these U. S. Army units was the Second U. S. Artillery who initially was sent back east before splitting up in different directions west and south. In 1849, Companies E, F, H, I, and K were sent to Florida. In 1850, four of these companies were sent to Charleston, South Carolina, in response to talk of secession. They returned to Florida in 1852. The Second U. S. Artillery except the light batteries and Company H were stationed in Florida in November 1853, first to Pensacola then to Fort Brooke near present-day Tampa. Major John Munroe commanded the northern portion of Florida from Fort Brooke and Major Harvey Brown the southern region near the Caloosahatchie River and Fort Myers.

The Second U. S. Artillery's mission in Florida was two-fold. First, they were to build roads and perform scouting duty, and second, to do what they could to force the remaining Seminole Indians to the Indian Territory. One soldier that would play a significant role in this endeavor was First Lieutenant George Lucas Hartsuff. Lieutenant Hartsuff was assigned to the Topographical Engineers responsible for surveying thus far unexplored lands. In this capacity, new sites were selected for the establishment of forts such as Forts Simon Drum and Shackleford. He along with his team would have the first encounter with Seminole Indians on December 20, 1855, that began the Third Seminole War.

A detachment of ten soldiers from Companies E, G, I, K L departed from Fort Myers on December 7, 1855, as part of Lieutenant Hartrsuff mapping mission. This was one of several similar missions that had been undertaken by Lieutenant Hartsuff since his arrival in Florida in July 1854. Due to the hot summer months, surveying was conducted in the cooler winter months as it was in this situation. As the troops were breaking camp on Thursday morning of December 20 in the area of the Big Cypress Swamp, they were attacked by a band of Seminole Indians. In the fight, Lieutenant Hartsuff was severely wounded while two soldiers and two teamsters were instantly killed. Three other soldiers were wounded along with two uninjured all of whom managed to make their way back to Fort Myers some sixty-five miles away. Lieutenant Hartsuff was severely wounded and hid from the Indians until he too was able to return to the fort where his wounds were treated. The lieutenant quickly recovered and undaunted soon led another scouting party to the area in which he had been attacked.

The number of Seminole Indians in 1855 numbered three hundred at most including women and children. There may have been forty to fifty warriors total. Much of the Third Seminole War revolved around small engagements in which the Indians would attack individuals or small groups of inhabitants and the U. S. Army or Florida militia would respond. Named battles such as that in the first two Seminole wars did not happen.

The event of December 20 was far from the only action of the Second U. S. Artillery in the Third Seminole War. On January 18, six soldiers from Companies C and L on wood cutting detail were attacked near Fort Denaud (Deynaud) along the Caloosahatchee River in present-day Hendry County. Five soldiers were killed and one escaped. On March 29 Companies E and G with Captain Arnold Elzey in command were engaged at Chocaliska (Chokoolskee) Key resulting in the death of two and wounding of one soldier, and April 7 a combined force of one hundred eleven men from Company L of the First U. S. Artillery and Companies C and L from the Second U. S. Artillery were attacked in the vicinity of the Big

Cypress Swamp. This conflict resulted in one soldier killed and the wounding of three. One last engagement of the Second U. S. Artillery occurred August 2 that again involved Company E. commanded by Lieutenant Henry Benson. This latest action took place near Punta Rassa and resulted in one soldier killed. These conflicts ended the Second U. S. Artillery role in Florida. In December 1856 the regiment would take stations in New York and Virginia replaced in Florida shortly thereafter by the Fifth U. S. Infantry that would made its headquarters at Fort Myers.

Not all Seminole attacks involved the U. S. Army. Civilians were also the target of Indian attacks in which homes were burned and men, women, and even children were indiscriminately killed. Unlike such killings by Indians, the U. S. Army did not condone actions against Indian women and children, but that is not to say that some did not occur as collateral results during battle. One Seminole who was known to take part in attacking civilian settlements was Ocsen Tustenuggee who himself would pay the ultimate price on June 16, 1856, when he and other Seminoles were caught in a surprise attack by militiamen near the Peace River. Before this incident and perhaps at the hands of Ocsen Tustenuggee's band, an attack occurred near Sarasota Bayou in which a home was burned and one man killed, and another attack on the Braden Plantation along the Manatee River that proved too strong to overcome except that slaves and cattle were led away only to be retaken by a pursuing militia force.

The month of May 1856 saw at least three incidents. On May 2, U. S. Army troops most likely the Second U. S. Artillery joined by Florida militia troops found abandoned villages in the Everglades that they burned. One Seminole attack that surprised military officials was on the home of a family by the name of Bradley who lived in Pasco County well north of Fort Brooke. This area was far from the territory of the Seminoles in the Big Cypress Swamp. Ocsen Tustenuggee may have been involved in this attack as well in which Mrs. Bradley and two children were killed. Another attack in central Florida on May 17 was on a military supply train traveling from Fort Brooke to Fort Fraser (Frazer) in Polk County. Three men accompanying the supply train were killed, one survived. The end of 1856 saw an attack December 17 on a home near New Smyrna in which the occupants were killed. After this attack, more homes were burned in the vicinity of Dunlawton Sugar Mills near today's Daytona Beach.

Third Seminole War in 1857

The arrival of the Fifth U. S. Infantry in Florida changed very little other than who would pick up the action against the Seminole Indians and where they would be garrisoned. Colonel Gustavus Loomis was in command of the regiment performing duty out of Fort Myers. Colonel Loomis was a seasoned officer who served in the War of 1812, Black Hawk War, Second Seminole War, Mexican War, and now in the Third Seminole War. When part of the regiment took part in an expedition to Utah in June 1857, Colonel Loomis remained in Florida and became the commander of the Department of Florida until the end the last Seminole War.

Military involvement during 1857 against Seminole Indians mirrored much the same from the previous year. The Fifth U. S. Infantry saw action March 5, 1857, while on reconnoitering detail in the Big Cypress Swamp. This endeavor was part of a larger force consisting of Company M, Fourth U. S. Artillery, and Companies A, B, D, E, F, G, H, and I of the Fifth Infantry that spanned from March 4 to April 23. On March 5 elements of the Fifth Infantry were attacked in which one man was killed and three soldiers under the command of Lieutenant Edmund Freeman and the lieutenant himself were severely wounded. If reports are correct, Captain Carter L. Stevenson stationed at Fort Keais some twenty miles away came to the rescue and drove the attackers away.

Not long after the March 5 incident, Company M, Fourth U. S. Artillery, came under attack March 13 at which time it was reported that a Private King was wounded. No other information about this attack was recorded, and, in fact, much of the information about the Third Seminole War is sketchy at best. Another reported incident with very little information is an Indian attack on an Army detachment at Palm Hammock near Pavillion Key at some time in May.

It is known that at least some companies of the Fifth U. S. Infantry left Florida around June 1857 for duty in the expedition to Utah. This left Colonel Loomis with the Fourth U. S. Artillery and the addition of the newly organized First Regiment Mounted Florida Volunteers under the command of Colonel Samuel St. George Rogers. The War Department authorized the volunteers for the purpose of taking up the slack in Florida as regular troops were shifted elsewhere. The regiment of ten companies was established July 27, 1857, for a period of six months.

Colonel Loomis at this time in the war resorted to the use of "alligator boats" with low draft to access the water routes into the Seminole strongholds. This endeavor was partly successful, but largely resulted in the capture of Seminole women and children. More incursions into the swamps took place in November when Seminole villages were discovered and burned. On November 26, Florida volunteers under Colonel Samuel St. George Rogers' First Regiment destroyed a "large Seminole village" in the Big Cypress Swamp. These acts received an expected response from Billy Bowlegs and his warriors

who killed several horses before attacking and killing several of the soldiers.

End of the Third Seminole War

The events at the end of 1857 and the same in the beginning of 1858 may have been the straw that broke the camel's back. Without the villages and crops necessary for Seminole life, there wasn't much reason to keep up the fight! A Seminole delegation from the Indian Territory reached Florida in an effort to convince Billy Bowlegs and his warriors to end their hold out and leave for the west. On March 15 Seminole Chief Billy Bowlegs and his father-in-law Assinwar agreed to accept removal. On May 4, 1858, the steamship *Grey Cloud* departed for the west with anywhere from 161 to 171 Indians. Arpiucki (Sam Jones) was not among those on board the Grey Cloud. His age was near 100 and chose to live out his life in the swamps of Florida along with perhaps one hundred or so other Seminole Indians. Arpiucki died in 1860. Billy Bowlegs also died shortly after arriving in the Indian Territory. Colonel Gustavus Loomis declared the end of the Third Seminole War on May 8, 1858, ending all Indian Wars east of the Mississippi River.

No Stoppage to Indians Wars

As already pointed out, an Indian war in one part of the country didn't mean all others ceased for that time period. In fact, Indian conflicts were taking place in the western territories at the same time as the Texas War for Independence and during the Mexican War just as they were during all the Seminole wars. Wherever there were white men of all persuasions on Indians lands including settlers, there would be conflicts sooner or later. For that reason, militia groups at first followed by U. S. Army soldiers took up stations on Indian lands.

There are many small conflicts between settlers and Indians some of which have already been discussed, but the larger conflicts especially those involving U. S. Army troops on full time duty now that other major wars had ended will be the primary focus to the end of 1865.

One such incident is the **Grattan Fight** or **Grattan Massacre** that took place August 18, 1854, long before the start of the Third Seminole War. The Grattan Massacre is named for Lieutenant John Lawrence Grattan, a recent West Point graduate assigned temporarily with the Sixth U. S. Infantry at Fort Laramie in the Nebraska Territory, now the State of Wyoming. This incident resulted from a Lakota Sioux Indian who butchered a cow that belonged to a Mormon traveling on the Oregon Trail. Lieutenant Grattan, a sergeant, one corporal,

twenty-seven privates, and one interpreter entered the Sioux camp of an estimated 4,800 Indians in an attempt to arrest the Indian who was believed responsible for killing the cow. Things quickly got out of hand and Lieutenant Grattan along with his entire party were killed by the Indians.

This incident did little to help the cause of peace between Lakota Sioux Indians and the military plus settlers in the region. A burial party was sent to the massacre and found mutilated bodies of the soldiers making identity difficult. The bodies were transported back to Fort Laramie and interned for a period before removing them to other locations. Lieutenant Grattan was reburied at Fort Leavenworth, Kansas, and the other soldiers now lie in the Fort McPherson National Cemetery south of Maxwell, Nebraska.

Fort McPherson National Cemetery (2001)

Public outcry called for retribution, but it would take a year to get underway. Colonel William S. Harney, Second U. S. Dragoon, assembled a large force of some six hundred men consisting of the Sixth and Tenth U. S.

Infantry Regiments, and the Fourth U. S. Artillery as well as his own command. This army began its march August 24, 1855, from Fort Kearny, Nebraska Territory.

Aware that the U. S. Military was about to enact revenge for the killing of their soldiers, nearly half the Lakota Sioux took refuge at Fort Laramie while the others prepared for a fight that would occur September 3, 1855, known as the **Battle of Ash Hollow** or **Battle of Bluewater Creek** in which there were casualties on both sides, but the victory was that of Colonel Harney and his forces. Twenty-seven soldiers are recorded as killed in the battle compared to eighty-six Indians and the capture of seventy or so women and children who were transported to Fort Laramie. For the time being, this quieted the Indian unrest in that region of the west.

Entrance marker to
Fort Laramie
(2001)

Fort Laramie
Barracks Row
(2001)

Washington and Oregon Territory Conflicts

The Whitman Massacre in 1847 was a window of things to come in the far northwest territories of Washington and Oregon. Both territories and the surrounding region saw Indian conflicts over a multitude of causes beginning in the middle 1850's. The discovery of gold in the Columbia River basin brought an influx of miners who occupied lands that had been granted to the Indians under various treaties. Settlers following the Oregon Trail resulted in similar occupation of Indian lands. Conflicts with Indians were not limited to one tribe, but included the Yakama, Cayuse, Nisqually, Spokane, Umitilla, Palouse, Coeur d'Alene (Schitsu'umsh), Walla Walla, Northern Paiute, and others.

Unrest between Indians and settlers in the Rogue River region of southern Oregon sparked the last of several **Rouge River Wars** that occurred in the same region. The indiscriminate killing by settlers of twenty-seven Rouge River Indians in October 1855 resulted in the killing of a like number of settlers. On October 25 Rogue River Indians surprised a detachment of twelve soldiers from the Third U. S. Artillery on a reconnaissance mission in southern Oregon resulting in the death of two soldiers. The soldiers were apparently unaware of the earlier incident resulting in the killing of Indian men, women, and children by settlers. A war was born!

Another engagement began six days later, October 31, near the same vicinity as the last that saw U. S. troops responding to what happened to the twelve Third U. S. Artillery soldiers and other killings. This incident became known as the **Battle of Hungry Hill** involving one hundred five U. S. soldiers from Company E and a detachment from Company C of the First U. S. Dragoons; detachments from Companies D and H, Third U. S. Artillery; detachments from Companies D and E, Fourth U. S. Infantry; as well as one hundred forty-five Oregon militia against some five hundred men, women, and children of the Rogue River Indian band of Umpquas, Rogues, Shastas, and Klamaths

The outcome of this last battle did not go well for the troops whose presence was discovered before any attempt to attack could be undertaken. The terrain favored the Indians that resulted in the death of four regulars and the wounding of seven. The Oregon militia suffered a like number of killed and twenty wounded. The Indians themselves may have lost a total twenty warriors killed and wounded.

Several conflicts involving only Oregon militia spanned the timeframe from the last battle with U. S. regulars to March 1856 at which time U. S. troops were once again in the forefront. From March 20 to March 26, 1856, several encounters were made against the Rogue River Indians.

March 20, Captain Edward O. C. Ord, Company B, Third U. S. Artillery, engaged Indians near the mouth of the Rogue River at which time eight Indians were killed and eight more wounded at a cost of two enlisted soldiers wounded. On March 26, Major Robert C. Buchanan, Fourth U. S. Infantry, led a force of one hundred twelve soldiers also near the mouth of the Rogue River where they burned an abandoned Indian village and fought some lingering Indians killing five while several more drowned in their attempt to escape by way of the river.

Forty miles to the southeast of the previous action near the Illinois River, Company C, First U. S. Dragoons and a detachment from Company E of the Fourth U. S. Infantry were involved against Rogue River Indians March 24. Two soldiers would be killed in this engagement and four wounded. No Indian casualties were reported.

Captain Edward O. C. Ord in command of Company B, Third U. S. Artillery was again involved in action against Indians on April 29. Captain Ord's soldiers were escorting wagons down the Oregon coastline when attacked by Chetco Indians as they were crossing the Chetco River. This conflict resulted in one soldier mortally wounded and one other whose wounds were not life threatening. Two Indians may have been killed as well as several wounded.

One last major conflict would bring the Rogue River War to an end! This took place on May 27-28, 1856, known as the **Battle of Big Bend** or **Big Meadows** that was inland along the Rogue River.

Captain Andrew Jackson Smith commanded fifty soldiers of the First U. S. Dragoons and Lieutenant Nelson B. Switzer's Company G, Fourth U. S. Infantry. The U. S. soldiers were present for a scheduled peace conference with Tecumtum ("Elk Killer"), also known as Chief John of the Etch-ka-taw-wah, band of Athabaskan Indians, Chief Cholcultah (George), and Chief Limpy of the Umpqua (Illinois River Haw-quo-e-hav-took band).

Word came to Captain Smith that Chief Tecumtum was not about to talk peace, but planned to attack the U. S. soldiers. Captain Smith immediately established a defensive position that would take them through to dark. The fight continued the next morning putting the soldiers in grave harm with many wounded, ammunition running low, and little water.

At this time, Captain Christopher C. Auger arrived at the battle with his Company G, Fourth U. S. Infantry, and drove off the Indians. Within a quarter hour the battle was over, the Indians having fled the battleground. Two days later, Chiefs George and Limpy agreed to surrender, and Chief John would do the same but not until late in June.

This last battle was costly in lives lost at eleven soldiers and another twenty wounded.

It is safe to say that Indian casualties were also significant, but no numbers are reported. By the end of June 1856, hostilities ended and the Rogue River Indians soon after were relocated to reservations. This put an end to the Rogue River War!

The Washington Territory itself would see Indian conflicts many of which were part of the **Yakima War** in the Yakima Valley east of the Cascade Mountains spilling into the **Puget Sound War** in the area of present-day Seattle west of the Cascade Mountains. It may be hard to distinguish one war from the other except for the Indians who took part.

Indians involved in the Yakima War included the Yakama, Walla Walla, Umatilla, Nez Perce, and Cayuse. The Nisqually Indians along with Muckleshoot, Puyallup, and Klickitat were involved in the Puget Sound War. There were other Indian tribes in both regions that remained neutral and even supported the territorial governments and the U. S. Military. Both wars resulted from dissatisfaction with treaties that called for the many Native Indian tribes of the region to give up their lands and be placed on a reservation.

Under the Yakama Chief Kamiakin and Nisqually Chief Leschi, tribes rebelled against relocation and conflicts occurred for about a year in the case of the Puget Sound War and three years for the Yakima War before the U. S. Army and Washington militia troops forced Kamiakin and his followers onto the reservations. Chief Leschi would suffer a less fortunate outcome soon to be revealed!

Fourth U. S. Army Takes Action

Aware that trouble was brewing among the Indians, the Fourth U. S. Infantry in garrison at many of the forts in the region was called upon to put down the unrest. Major Granville Owen Haller marched to the central Washington Territory in late September from Fort Dalles in the Oregon Territory situated along the

Columbia River approximately seventy-five miles east of present-day Portland. Major Haller led a force of eight-four mounted soldiers. First Lieutenant William A. Slaughter did the same on September 27 from Fort Steilacoom along Puget Sound forty-five north of Seattle with forty-eight soldiers from Companies A and C, Fourth U S. Infantry. The plan was to trap the Indians between the two forces that would be coming from two different directions.

Colonel Granville O. Haller, c. 1890
Wikipedia

The first conflict in the Washington Territory began October 6, 1855, in which Companies I and K and a Detachment of Company H all of the Fourth U. S. Infantry under the command of Major Haller were engaged against Yakama Indians numbering around 1,500. This conflict carries the name **Battle of Toppenish Creek** that took place about ten miles southwest of current Yakima, Washington. In this conflict five soldiers were killed and seventeen wounded. The Yakama Indians may have had twenty or so killed and wounded, but their success gave them and other Indian tribes reason to further resist efforts to relocate.

This last battle proved that more troops would be necessary to quell the unrest. This prompted District Commander Major Gabriel J. Rains, Fourth U. S. Infantry, stationed at Fort Vancouver, Washington Territory, to order more troops in the field and requested of the Territorial Governor the organization of two companies of volunteers.

In response to Major Rains call for more troops, Captain Maurice Maloney, Fourth U. S. Infantry, commander at Fort Steilacoom, departed October 22 with a force of 238 men consisting of 115 soldiers from Companies A and C, Fourth U. S. Infantry; eighty-seven militia of Company B, Puget Sound Mounted Volunteers under the command of Captain Gilmore Hays; five officers; and thirty-one teamsters. During the course of this movement a series of Indian attacks by Muckleshoot's under the guidance of Nisqually Chief Leschi took place against settlers in the region of the

White River resulting in the death of nineteen men, women, and children. These attacks became the **White River Massacre** that took place October 28, 1855.

Captain Maloney's forces would see action against Indians on November 3 near Connell's Prairie thirty miles south southeast of Seattle. Captain Hays and First Lieutenant Slaughter engaged Indians after one soldier was shot and killed while cutting down a tree to cross the White River. A battle known as the **Battle of White River** ensued for some six hours that left only one soldier wounded and anywhere from twenty-five to thirty Indians killed.[4]

Captain Hays and Lieutenant Slaughter were further engaged November 6 pursuing Indians from their encounter three days earlier. This action occurred near the Puyallup River to the west of the previous action resulting in one soldier assigned to the Fourth U. S. Infantry who was killed and four others wounded all four of whom it was thought would recover from their wounds.[5] Apparently, Captain Maloney called off any further pursuit at this point and returned with his force to Fort Steilacoom.

Meanwhile, on the east side of the Cascade Mountains, the **Battle of Union Gap** also called the **Battle of Twin Buttes** began

November 9 and continued for one more day. Major Gabriel J. Rains with a force of some seven hundred soldiers discovered the village of Yakama Chief Kamiakin and approximately three hundred braves along with some women and children. Largely outnumbered, Chief Kamiakin began a delaying action against his foe while the women and children escaped to safety. In the end, Major Rains called off the pursuit due to the condition of his troops who were exhausted. No casualties were reported by the military and only one Indian was killed.

The new year of 1856 was not much different from the previous year. A conflict with Indians took place January 26 called the **Battle of Seattle** that was quickly put to rest with the help of artillery fire supported by Marines from the U. S. Navy Sloop-of-war *Decatur* anchored in Puget Sound. With Indian attacks on the rise, the settlers from the White River as well as locals flocked to the safety of the blockhouse along Puget Sound in anticipation of an attack. That attack came on January 26 as noted and could have been much worse except for the artillery fire. As it was, two settlers were killed in the brief attack, but Indian casualties may have been as high as twenty-eight.

Settlers seen rushing to the safety of the blockhouse along Puget Sound January 1856 with perhaps the USS Decatur in the waters to the right

Wikipedia

All this activity was cause for more troops to be brought into the fight. The Fourth Infantry added several more companies from Fort Vancouver plus two companies from the newly arrived Ninth U. S. Infantry who joined with the Fourth. The Ninth U. S. Infantry had fought in the Mexican War, but was disbanded in August 1848 only to be reorganized March 3, 1855. After completion of its organization, the regiment moved to Fort Vancouver in the Washington Territory arriving in late January 1856. From here Companies D and H were sent at Fort Steilacoom and soon were involved in fighting Indians.

On March 1, the two companies from the Ninth were joined by a detachment from Company M of the Third U. S. Artillery along with Company A of the Fourth U. S. Infantry against Indians near the White River in the area of Muckleshoot Prairie not far from other conflicts that had previously occurred in the region of the White River. One or two soldiers were killed in this action and six to eight others wounded. No Indian casualties were reported. No name was given to this conflict.

Frequent small conflicts occurred at various times in 1856 without significant outcomes, but that does not mean that all engagements were of the same caliber. On March 10, 1856, Captain Gilmore Hays and approximately one hundred of his Company B Puget Sound Mounted Volunteers were in the process of building a blockhouse and ferry for crossing the White River in a region called Connell's Prairie near present-day Buckley, Washington. Here they were attacked by about one hundred-fifty Klickitata Indians as part of Nisqually Chief Leschi's warring party again dissatisfied with treaty violations forcing the Indians off their lands. The Indian attack went poorly causing as many as thirty Indian losses while the volunteers suffered only four men wounded. The outcome of this conflict was the straw that broke the camel's back for Chief

Leschi and his followers. From here Leschi and his people retreated over the Cascade Mountains into eastern Washington Territory where Leschi was captured in November 1856 and hanged for his actions February 19, 1858. All that was left of the Indian conflicts in the Washington Territory was the Yakima War.

One of those conflicts was called the **Cascades Massacre** that occurred March 26, 1856, in which an attack by Yakama, Klickitat, and Cascade Indians resulted in the killing of fourteen settlers and three soldiers in an area along the Middle Cascades of the Columbia River. The unit of the three soldiers may have been Company H, Fourth U. S. Infantry, commanded by Captain Henry D. Wallen. Settlers took refuge in nearby buildings some of which were unoccupied and burned by the Indians. A sergeant and eight enlisted men from the Ninth U. S. Infantry found safety in a nearby blockhouse that came under siege.

Word of this latest attack brought relief troops from two different directions. Lieutenant Philip Henry Sheridan, Fourth U. S. Infantry, left Fort Vancouver on March 27 with forty soldiers on a steamboat and steamed up the Columbia River as far as the rapids. The relief party may have then used smaller boats that were pulled beyond the rapids before once again using them to reach the area of the blockhouse and chase off the Indians. At Fort Dalles to the east along the Columbia River, Major Edward Jenner Steptoe, Ninth U. S. Infantry, gathered a force of two hundred men from the First U. S. Dragoons; Companies A, E, F, and I of the Ninth U. S. Infantry and Company L of the Third U. S. Artillery and steamed down river to the rapids, then marched overland to the relief of the troops at the blockhouse arriving at about the same time as Lieutenant Sheridan's force.

The Indians that fled on the arrival of the U. S. forces were pursued and many captured. A number of these warriors were tried for their participation in the attacks that took the lives of both settlers and soldiers and eight were found guilty and hanged. The action of March 27-28 resulted in the loss of three soldiers and the wounding of four. Other minor incidents would occur in the months following in 1856, but things seemed to be quiet for the most part. The Ninth U. S. Infantry was responsible for the surrender of five hundred hostile Indians in July and no other engagements are recorded for all of 1857.

The Coeur d'Alene War in 1858

Why there are no recorded Indian incidents in 1857 seems strange, but such as it is that would change in 1858. An extension of the Yakima war was the **Coeur d' Alene War** involving Indians of the Coeur d'Alene, Spokane, Palouse and Northern Paiute tribes. The first battle of this was the **Battle of Pine Creek** that took place May 17, 1858, in which one hundred sixty-four soldiers from Companies C, E, and H of the First U. S. Dragoons, and Company E of the Ninth U. S. Infantry under Brevet Colonel Edward Jenner Steptoe left Fort Walla Walla, Washington Territory, in search of Indians who had murdered two miners. Brevet Colonel Steptoe found the Indians numbering about one thousand who may have been led by Chief Kamiakin who was apparently in no mood to hear what Colonel Steptoe had to say.

Recognizing that the U. S. troops were vastly outnumbered and the Indians were showing signs of hostility, Colonel Steptoe broke off the meeting and withdrew, but prepared for a fight that he would soon experience. The Indians attacked on the morning of May 17 and the U. S. troops were faced with more than they could handle. By nightfall it was clear that any further resistance would be fatal for all the troops. A quiet and hasty retreat was the only measure to prevent total disaster and that was what took place.

Burying their dead of five enlisted and two officers, the remainder managed to slip away unnoticed and eventually returned to Fort Walla Walla only slightly less for their dilemma.

The impact of Brevet Colonel Steptoe's involvement with Indians brought the call for more troops to inflict punishment on those Indians responsible just as it had been done in the past. That effort would see Major Robert Selden Garnett, Ninth U. S. Infantry, command a force of Companies C, G, and I of the Ninth U. S. Infantry and Company D of the Fourth U. S. Infantry led by Lieutenant George Crook to find, attack, and punish those Indians involved against Colonel Steptoe in May.

Major Garnett's troops found their foe August 15 near the Yakima River in present-day Ellensburg, Washington, and quickly overran the Palouse Indians resulting in the surrender of seventy. During this early morning engagement, Lieutenant Jesse K. Allen was accidently shot by his own men the only U. S. casualty for the conflict. Justice was swift for the Indians who were believed responsible for the killings of Brevet Lieutenant Colonel Steptoe's men on May 17. Major Garnett had five Palouse Indians hanged.

Not long after this last action, the **Battle of Four Lakes** occurring September 1 would be a decisive victory against the Indians and bring an end to the Yakima and Coeur d'Alene Wars. Colonel George Wright commanding the Ninth U. S. Infantry received word that the same Indian tribes (Yakama, Palouse, Spokane, and Coeur d'Alene) that faced Brevet Lieutenant Colonel Steptoe and Major Garnett had gathered at an area known as Four Lakes that lay southwest of present-day Spokane, Washington, and were ready for a fight!

Colonel Wright organized a military force of around six hundred men from Companies C, E, H, I, and a detachment of D all of the First U. S. Dragoons plus Companies A, B, G, K, and M of the Third U. S. Artillery, and finally Companies C and E of the Ninth U. S. Infantry. In addition there were thirty Nez Perce Indians acting as scouts and perhaps as many as two hundred teamsters handling the wagons and two each 12-pounder and 6-pounder cannons.

The battle began early on September 1 and was over by 2 P. M. that same day. Not a single man of Colonel Wright's command was killed or wounded. The Indians on the other hand lost many warriors largely due to the new Springfield Model 1855 rifle-musket that could fire accurately up to 1,000 yards. The Indians were driven from the field and pursued for a distance before giving up the chase. For all practical purposes, the Indians had met their match yet there would be one more engagement that spelled the end.

After a three-day rest, Colonel Wright resumed the pursuit catching the fleeing Indians on the Spokane Plain September 5. A similar scenario took place as it did at the last battle inflicting more casualties on the Indians. Yakama Chief Kamiakin himself was severely wounded by artillery fire and two days later the entire Indian force surrendered! Here again justice was swift. A number of unrelenting Indians were hanged as was the nephew of Chief Kamiskin called Qualchin who were responsible for many deaths of innocent settlers. On September 23, Colonel Wright declared a treaty with the Indians that forced them onto a reservation that was the root of the Yakima War in the first place. The war may have been over, but that did not mean that there would not be other conflicts with individual Indians in the territory in the months and years to come!

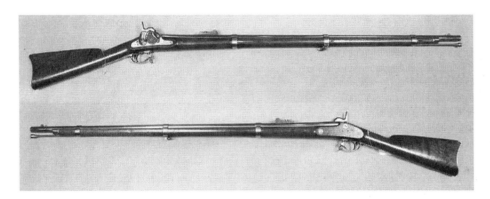

The Springfield Model 1855 Rifle-Musket that saved the day for Colonel Wright's soldiers
on September 1 and 5, 1858
Wikipedia

Indian Conflicts from 1858-1865

There were many Indian conflicts between the years 1859 to 1865 some of which were minor and some not so! The remainder on this topic will focus on select conflicts that are of greater importance in name and outcomes. The first of these took place during the American Civil War involving volunteer units from California as they marched to free the Arizona Territory from Confederate control. The **Battle of Apache Pass** occurred July 15-16, 1862, in which Captain Thomas L. Roberts of Company E, First California Infantry and Company B, Second California Volunteer Cavalry commanded by Captain John C. Cremony came under attack by as many as five hundred Apache Indians led by Mangas Coloradas and Cochise.

The California troops were attempting to determine if a water source called Dragoon Springs was suitable to provide sufficient water for the 2,500 men of Colonel James Henry Carleton's California command waiting to enter New Mexico. To reach the Dragoon Springs, Captain Roberts troops would take a route through Apache Pass that was then and today a mountain pass over 5,000 feet twenty miles south of Bowie, Arizona, in Cochise County. Dragoon Springs may today be called Apache Springs.

As the troops were nearing the Pass, Apache Indians attacked as if they knew the soldiers were coming. The Apaches had constructed defensive positions behind stone barriers and hid behind every possible obstruction available to them. What saved the day for the soldiers was the two 12-pounder howitzers they brought with them. Opening fire on the attackers with the howitzers gave the soldiers room to maneuver into better positions. Once this was achieved, the Apaches fled and Captain Robert's men were able to reach the spring that they desperately needed.

The Apaches returned the next day, but the howitzers again pounded their positions ending the attack once and for all. Two soldiers were killed in the Battle of Apache Pass and three wounded, but Indian losses were speculated to be much greater. A short time later, Fort Bowie was established near the Pass to protect others using the spring. On July 4, the California Column reached Mesilla, New Mexico Territory, and what Confederate troops that had remained in the territory withdrew to Texas.

The California Volunteers were again in action against Indians on January 29, 1863, this time in the far southeastern portion of Idaho that was Washington Territory at that time. This became the **Bear River Massacre** or **Battle of Bear River** resulting from years of Shoshone Indian conflicts with area settlers. Colonel Patrick Edward Connor in command of the Third California Infantry conducted an assault using Company K on a Shoshone camp along the Bear River. The Shoshoni men, women, and children were caught unaware and unmercifully slaughtered resulting in upwards of two hundred fifty men, women, and children killed and over one hundred fifty wounded and captured. The U. S. troops were not without losses themselves. Twenty-one or so soldiers were killed and perhaps forty-six wounded out of the two hundred or so that took part in the attack. After this engagement, Colonel Connor was promoted to Brigadier General and would again see involvement in the **Powder River Expedition of 1865** that was part of the Sioux Wars soon to be covered.

On September 18, 1862, Colonel James Henry Carleton commanding the California Column was promoted to the rank of Brigadier General and became the commander of the Department of New Mexico. He would direct military activities in the New Mexico Territory until the department was disbanded June 27, 1865. One military action that occurred was the **Battle of Canyon de Chelly** January 12-14, 1864, in the northeast region of Arizona within the New Mexico Territory.

Colonel Christopher Houston "Kit" Carson commanding the First New Mexico Cavalry was tasked by Brigadier General Carleton to end the Navajo Indian holdout of relocating to a reservation called Bosque Redondo near Fort Sumner in east central New Mexico. Colonel Carson departed Fort Defiance (Fort Canby) January 6, 1864, with three hundred eighty-nine troops of the First New Mexico Cavalry heading for the Canyon de Chelly to the west. The plan was to divide the troops and approach the canyon from both ends to achieve the ultimate goal of capturing the Navajo people under the leadership of Manuelito, Barboncito, and his brother Delgado. This effort is labeled as a battle, but it can hardly be called such by what took place. As the troops moved through the canyon there was only sporadic contact with small bands of Indians and anything and everything that could be useful to the Navajo people was destroyed preventing any likely return.

The Canyon de Chelly was Navajo land and they knew it well virtually hiding from the cavalry troops who searched for them. With plenty of current provisions on hand, this situation might have continued except for the fact that next winter's crops had been destroyed and there would be suffering to come. Many of the Navajo people decided to accept reservation life as the best outcome under the circumstances. By Summer 1864, as many as 8,000 Navajo's prepared for a march of three hundred miles across nearly all of New Mexico to the Bosque Redondo Reservation near Fort Sumner. This effort is called the **Long Walk of the Navajo** that took eighteen days and cost the lives of two hundred or more Navajo who were too weak to make the trek. The Indian reservation policy proved ineffective and within four years the Navajo returned to their ancestral lands without opposition.

Christopher Houston "Kit" Carson c. 1860
Frontiersman, Indian Agent, and Army Officer
Wikipedia

The American Civil War that began in 1861 pulled most of the Federal troops to the campaigns in the east leaving much of the west under the protection of local and State militia troops. This was the case with the Battle of Canyon de Chelly and those mentioned before during this time period. The **Colorado War** occurred from 1863-1865 and was fought by the various Colorado Volunteer units in the area of Colorado, Wyoming, and Nebraska. A significant event of this war was the **Sand Creek Massacre** of November 29, 1864, in which the District of Colorado commander, Colonel John Milton Chivington, led a force of some seven hundred men of the First and Third Colorado Cavalry and First New Mexico Volunteer Infantry in a raid against what might have been peaceful Cheyenne and Arapaho Indians.

The outcome of this raid was the slaughtering of as many as one hundred thirty-seven Indians of which there might have been one hundred five who were women and children. This attack was at first hailed as a victory over hostile Indians, but time would show that the mutilation of the bodies was anything but humane especially the women and children. Colonel Chivington was investigated for his actions and admonished, but since he had resigned from the military no action could be taken against him. Regardless, the Sand Creek Massacre was a black mark against many who took part and remains the same today!

The largest military force ever assembled against Native American Indians occurred July 28-29, 1864, in the Dakota Territory of that time, North Dakota of today. Brigadier General Alfred Sully received orders from Major General John Pope in command of the Department of the Northwest to establish a number of forts along the Missouri River in an effort to maintain lines of communication in the region. Gold had been discovered in Montana and Idaho and it was important to keep the flow of gold moving to the government in Washington that was involved in the American Civil War.

General Sully had at his disposal over 2,300 troops organized into two brigades. The First Brigade was commanded by Lieutenant Colonel Samuel McLean Pollock and consisted of the Sixth Iowa Cavalry and three companies of the Seventh Iowa Cavalry, Major Alfred Bruce Brackett's Minnesota Cavalry Battalion, Companies A and B of the First Dakota Cavalry Battalion, and one company of Indian Scouts. Colonel Minor T. Thomas had the Second Brigade made up of the Eighth Minnesota Infantry Mounted, six companies of the Second Minnesota Cavalry, Major C. Powell Adams commanding four companies of Hatch's Independent Minnesota Cavalry Battalion, Third Minnesota Battery under Captain Jones, and four companies of the Thirteenth Wisconsin Infantry.[6]

The first of the forts established by General Sully was Fort Rice on July 7, 1864. The fort was named for Brigadier General James Clay Rice who was mortally wounded May 10, 1864, at the Battle of Spotsylvania Court House during the Wilderness Campaign of the American Civil War. General Sully's force departed from Fort Rice on July 19 in search of Sioux Indians. That search ended on July 28 when the Sioux encampment was located near Killdeer Mountain close to the Dakota Badlands and the **Battle of Killdeer Mountain** or **Battle of Tahkahokuty Mountain** began.

General Sully's troops faced nearly the same number of Sioux Indians as his force. The arrival of the U. S. troops was no surprise to the Sioux whose weapons were mostly bow and arrow. The U. S. troops on the other hand had a number of artillery pieces that would prove extremely useful in the rugged terrain that meant that cavalry charges would be difficult if not impossible to undertake. The Federal troops began a slow ground movement toward the encampment as the two sides engaged in a running battle on that Thursday in July. During this time, the Sioux were able to remove their old, women, and children to the safety of the badlands. The approach to the encampment by General Sully's force came around dark on the first day. Here the troops halted for the night while the artillery kept a constant barrage of the Sioux camp. By daylight, the camp had been virtually abandoned by the Indians leaving just about everything as it had been.

The next order of business called for the troops to destroy everything left in the camp to include tipis (tepees) and all food sources that was achieved on Friday. Taking account of the casualties from the battle on the previous day, there were three killed and ten wounded of Sully's troops and the Sioux may have suffered anywhere from thirty-one to one hundred-fifty killed and wounded. There would be conflicts and casualties to come as a pursuit of the Indians into the badlands was undertaken several days after the initial battle.

Three months after the Battle of Killdeer Mountain, the **First Battle of Adobe Walls** would occur November 25, 1864, along the Canadian River near the current Stinnett, Texas, about forty-five miles northeast of Amarillo, Texas. This was the first of two such battles with the same name occurring ten years apart. Two hundred soldiers of the First New Mexico Cavalry Volunteers, seventy-five unidentified Infantry soldiers, and a substantial number of Indian scouts left Fort Bascom in the New Mexico Territory November 10, 1864, under the command of Colonel Christopher Houston "Kit" Carson with the mission of punishing the Kiowa, Comanche, and Apache Indians who had made attacks against settlers. This effort was part of the Apache Wars that began in 1864 at the time the Navajo were forced onto the Bosque Redondo Reservation near Fort Sumner in the New Mexico Territory.

Alerted to the whereabouts of the Indian tribes by his Indian scouts, Colonel Carson set about with his dismounted cavalry to the site of the first Indian encampment belonging to the Kiowa. The troops arrived early in the morning of Friday, November 25, and attacked the village. This action alerted the nearby encampments of the Comanche and Apaches who came to the rescue of their Indian allies while the women and children were rushed to safety. Colonel Carson's force now faced upwards of 1,500 Indians and a battle raged throughout the day. Due to the overwhelming number of Indians, the outcome could have been much worse for the U. S. soldiers except for the two mountain howitzers that were used effectively against the Indians.

With artillery ammunition running low and no advantage of gaining ground, Colonel Carson determined that it would be best to regroup to safer ground and examine the situation. After some thought and input from his trusted Indian scouts, it was determined to call off the mission and return to Fort Bascom. The First Battle of Adobe Walls was essentially a draw although military heads declared it a victory. Casualty count for the Americans was six killed and twenty-five wounded. Indian estimates were put at a total of sixty killed and wounded.

After the Sand Creek Massacre November 29, 1864, the various tribes of Cheyenne, Lakota Sioux, and Arapaho began a movement northward to a more secluded area heading for the Powder River region in today's Wyoming and Montana. This was a large group of Indians numbering 4,000 to 5,000 of which around 1,000 were warriors. During the process of the move, punitive raids were conducted against any and all settlers in the region and the settlement of Julesburg in the Colorado Territory was burned February 2. Another attack was made against the **Mud Springs Stagecoach and Telegraph Station** in southwestern Nebraska Territory near present-day Dalton, Nebraska, staffed by five civilians and nine soldiers. The telegraph operator was able to alert the military at Fort Mitchell some fifty plus miles to the east as well as Fort Laramie over one hundred miles to the west. This action prompted the usual response from military sources. This resulted in the **Battle of Mud Springs** February 4-6, 1865.

Lieutenant William Ellsworth and thirty-six soldiers of his Company H, Eleventh Ohio

Cavalry, responded from Fort Mitchell arriving February 5 after an all night ride. They were engaged shortly thereafter by most likely the same group of Indians who had attacked the Station the day before, but were able to drive off the Indians by releasing their horses from the corral. Early the next morning, February 6, Lieutenant Colonel William Oliver Collins with Company C of the Eleventh Ohio Cavalry arrived from Fort Laramie swelling the total force to around one hundred seventy. Again the Indians attacked, but were driven off as before. That evening an additional fifty soldiers arrived with a 12-pounder mountain howitzer. The plan was to take the offensive the next morning, but the Indians apparently decided to end their attack and move north rather than further engage the soldiers. This battle resulted in the death of one soldier and the wounding of eight others. Indians casualties are unknown.

Following the Battle of Mud Springs, Lieutenant Colonel Collins began a pursuit of the Indians to their surprise knowing the small number of troops compared to their own. He would catch up to them February 8 at the North Platte River near present-day Broadwater, Nebraska, a short distance north of the Battle of Mud Springs. Early morning Wednesday, February 8, the troops reached the encampment of the Indians and dug in for a battle. Shortly thereafter the **Battle of Rush Creek** began that lasted into the next day. The large number of Indian warriors could have spelled disaster for the outnumbered soldiers except for the use of the howitzer that kept the Indians at a distance and on the defensive. The day ended without gains by either side.

The next morning there was another attack by the Indians without success and the engagement broke off, the tribes returning to their northward trek. This time Colonel Collins declined to pursue declaring that it would prove no useful purpose! Casualty counts for the soldiers were two killed, nine wounded, and perhaps ten men suffering from frostbite. On February 10, Lieutenant Colonel Collins with his troops began the movement back to Fort Laramie. This ended present action against the three Indian tribes who continued their way to the Powder River region, but there would be further military response beginning in August 1865.

More Effects of the Sand Creek Massacre

If Colonel John M. Chivington could have envisioned the consequences of his actions against Indians at Sand Creek on November 29, 1864, perhaps he might have done things differently. And then, he might have had good reason to take the action he did that is not known. Regardless, the Sand Creek Massacre began a period of major unrest in the region of the Nebraska, Colorado, and Dakota Territories.

The Indian tribes of the Cheyenne, Lakota Sioux, and Arapaho who moved into the Powder River region of present northeast Wyoming and southeast Montana were intent on keeping this area free of any whites regardless of their purpose. This included travel along the Bozeman, Oregon, and Overland Trails. Frequent attacks by small and large groups of Indians occurred in these regions soon after the arrival of the spring season of 1865. Military volunteer units were assigned to the various stations in the west providing protection for those who settled in the region as well as wagon trains moving west. There was nothing glamorous about this duty and many of the soldiers were "Galvanized Yankees" or Confederate soldiers who volunteered for such duty rather than face prison terms.

An area along the North Platte River near present-day Casper, Wyoming, was an important crossing point for wagon trains for both the Oregon and Bozeman Trails. This was known as the Platte Bridge Station that included a military stockade manned by about one hundred soldiers under the command of Major Martin Anderson of the Eleventh Kansas Volunteer Infantry. This crossing point meant more whites to the region that the Indians vowed to shut down and would eventually occur, but there would be a number of conflicts prior to achieving that end.

On May 20, the **Deer Creek Station** near present Glenrock, Wyoming, manned by one hundred soldiers from Companies D and L of the Eleventh Kansas Volunteer Cavalry was attacked by an equal number of Cheyenne Indians. After a brief encounter, the Indians broke off the attack taking twenty-six horses. One soldier was killed in the attack. Additional Indian raids took place at the **Sweetwater Station** May 26 some eighty miles west of Casper, Wyoming, manned by a unit of the Eleventh Ohio Volunteer Cavalry, and on Saturday, May 27, at **St. Mary's Station** also called **Rocky Ridge Station** further west where a detachment of five soldiers of the Eleventh Ohio Volunteer Cavalry were assigned. This later station was attacked and burned by approximately one hundred fifty Indians and burned, but the soldiers were able to escape to safety and with the use of a "relay sounder" report the attack.[7][8] These two raids resulted in the closing of the Oregon Trail that fit into the plan of the Indians.

With the closing of the Oregon Trail, the Indians shifted their focus to the more southern Overland Trail. The Overland Trail was primarily a stagecoach route that traversed across present-day Wyoming essentially following south of the current Interstate 80 route with stations about every ten to fifteen miles. Word reached Captain Jacob L. Humfreville in command of Company K of the Eleventh Ohio Cavalry at Fort Halleck near Elk Mountain that various stagecoach stations had

been attacked by Indians. Captain Humfreville immediately sent out a patrol of thirty-one soldiers from Company K under command of First Lieutenant James A. Brown who found three stations to the west (Sage Creek, Pine Grove, and Bridger Pass) deserted. Upon reaching the fourth station of **Sulfur Springs** located about eighty miles west of Elk Mountain, the civilian personnel from the three deserted stations were found gathered at that point. Believing that the attacks had gone no further west, Lieutenant Brown began his return to Fort Halleck leaving five soldiers to protect Sulfur Springs stopping at each of the three deserted stations returning the respective civilians as well as a corporal and four men at each for protection.[9]

On June 3, the Eleventh Kansas Cavalry was engaged in another fight near **Dry Creek** close to Platte Bridge Station. This incident resulted from Indians attempting to draw the soldiers from the protection of their stockade that was partially successful. Lieutenant Colonel Preston B. Plumb, Eleventh Kansas Cavalry, stationed at Camp Dodge immediately began a pursuit of the attackers with ten men from Company B of the Eleventh Kansas Cavalry and word to have twenty more soldiers from Companies A and F of the same command to follow as promptly as possible. Once at Platte Bridge Station, Colonel Plumb gathered ten men from Company G of the Eleventh Ohio Cavalry to assist in the pursuit.

According to Colonel Plumb, "A hard chase of five miles brought me up within shooting distance of the Indians, and a running fight ensued, which resulted in 1 Indian pony killed and 2 Indians wounded. Over half of the detachment had fallen behind on account of their horses not being able to keep up, and the Indians made an effort to turn the scale by suddenly wheeling about and charging upon us, but failing to induce a corresponding movement on our part they scattered and ran off at a rate of speed that showed that their previously comparatively lagging gait had some ulterior purpose in view.[10] A further pursuit was undertaken that was unsuccessful and resulted in the loss of two privates, one from Company F, Eleventh Kansas Cavalry and the other from Company G, Eleventh Ohio Cavalry.

Frequent Indian attacks similar to those already covered occurred into July. On June 8, the **Sage Creek Station** near present-day Saratoga, Wyoming, manned by five soldiers and two civilians came under attack by as many as one hundred Lakota Sioux and Cheyenne Indians. This was the same Sage Creek Station that had been deserted earlier and re-garrisoned with five soldiers by First Lieutenant James. A. Brown about June 5 on his return to Fort Halleck from the Sulfur Springs Station. The five soldiers quickly ran low of ammunition and decided to make an escape along with the two station keepers. Pursued and outnumbered by the Indians, they had little chance. Only two soldiers, although wounded, managed to reach Pine Grove Station to the west. Once at Pine Grove, the decision was made to evacuate the soldiers and civilians once again to Sulfur Springs Station collecting the detachment at Bridger Pass Station as they moved. A patrol a day later found the Sage Creek Station had been burned.

Incidents like that at the Sage Creek Station were daily occurrences during this time of year all over the Nebraska, Colorado, and Idaho Territories. Military patrols would be sent out to combat the Indian raids most of which accomplished little. The Lakota, Cheyenne, and Arapaho planned one last major push to end the Platte Bridge Station and the use of the bridge. A large Indian force of some 3,000 warriors moved south over one hundred miles from the Powder River region arriving July 24 within a few miles of the Platte Bridge Station. Again the Indians tried to entice the soldiers from their stockade as they had done June 3. This attempt failed just as it had earlier.

The one hundred-man garrison at Platte Bridger Station was under the overall command of Major Martin Anderson, Eleventh Kansas Cavalry. The arrival of some twenty soldiers from the Third U. S. Volunteer Infantry and Company G, Eleventh Ohio Cavalry, boosted the total strength at the station to one hundred twenty. Regardless of this number, the troops were vastly outnumbered for whatever action was to be taken! Adding to this discrepancy in troop numbers was mistrust between several of the officers and Major Anderson.

Informed that four freight wagons with a military escort led by Sergeant Amos Custard would soon be passing the Platte Bridge Station on their way to Fort Laramie from Sweetwater, some officers expressed concern that a relief force should be sent out to protect it in view of the hostile Indians in the vicinity. Major Anderson declined to take action at that time and to add insult to the situation, Anderson's officers declined to lead the relief force some placing themselves on the sick list to avoid the duty. First Lieutenant Henry C. Bretney, Company G, Eleventh Ohio Cavalry, was at odds with Major Anderson over his removal from command at the Platte Bridge Station earlier in July, and the refusal to provide a relief force for the soldiers escorting the freight wagons caused further resentment.

Second Lieutenant Caspar W. Collins, Eleventh Ohio Cavalry, son of Lieutenant Colonel William O. Collins of the same command, had arrived at Platte Bridge Station from Fort Laramie July 25 with eleven of his men on their way to join their unit at Sweetwater Station. With Major Anderson's officers refusing to form a relief party, Lieutenant Collins volunteered to undertake the mission if provided with sufficient men from the Eleventh Kansas Cavalry. What followed became known as the **Battle of Platte Bridge** that cost the life of Lieutenant Collins and four soldiers from the Eleventh Kansas Cavalry.

Lieutenant Collins and his meager force had little chance of providing relief to Sergeant Custard and his escort detail outnumbered by hundreds of Indian warriors who sprang up from every possible position once the soldiers crossed the bridge. Lieutenant Bretney protested to Major Anderson for not providing further support and was arrested. Meanwhile, Sergeant Custard had started his move to Platte Bridge Station unbeknown of the effort to provide relief for him. Five miles from the station, the Indians sighted the freight wagons and an attack ensued named the **Battle of Red Butte** for the location of the fighting.

Sergeant Custard and his small force were overwhelmed by hundreds of Indians and in the end twenty-two soldiers including Sergeant Custard were killed. Two soldiers managed to reach the safety of Platte Bridge Station. Indian casualties were at least eight killed and many wounded from the Spencer rifles used by the soldiers. Platte Bridge Station was renamed Fort Casper in honor of Second Lieutenant Caspar Collins. The name Fort Collins was already used in recognition of Lieutenant Colonel William O. Collins that is the namesake today of Fort Collins, Colorado.

Platte Bridge Station guarding the upper crossing of the North Platte River
Wikipedia

Powder River Expedition

Before the Battle of Platte Bridge, efforts were in the works to punish the Lakota, Cheyenne, and Arapaho Indians for their many raids and destruction undertaken after the Sand Creek incident. Major General Grenville Mellen Dodge commanding the Department of the Missouri placed Brigadier General Patrick E. Connor in charge of this effort titled the **Powder River Expedition**. Before the

expedition could be undertaken, Major General Dodge relinquished command of the Department of the Missouri on June 27, 1865, to Major General John Pope that changed little in the mission. Initially the expedition force was to have been over 10,000 men, but the end of the American Civil War resulted in many units that were mustered out of Federal service. Instead, General Connor organized a smaller force into three columns consisting of 2,300 soldiers, nearly two hundred Indians

Scouts, and an equal number of civilian teamsters to transport supplies.

The Left or Western Column was under the command of Colonel James Harvey Kidd. Colonel Kidd's command included Companies L and M from the Second California Volunteer Cavalry Regiment, six companies from the Sixth Michigan Volunteer Cavalry (Colonel Kidd's command), Company F from the Seventh Iowa Volunteer Cavalry Regiment, Companies E and F from the Eleventh Ohio Volunteer Cavalry Regiment, a detachment from the Second Missouri Volunteer Light Artillery Regiment, a detachment from the U. S. Army Signal Corps, Pawnee Scouts, Omaha and Winnebago Scouts, wagon train teamsters, and frontiersman Jim Bridger as a guide. The total strength was around 925 men.

Lieutenant Colonel Samuel Walker commanded the Central or Middle Column totaling six hundred men. This included eight companies from the Sixteenth Kansas Volunteer Cavalry Regiment (Colonel Walker's command), Company H from the Fifteenth Kansas Volunteer Cavalry Regiment, and a mountain howitzer section of two cannons. The last column was the Right or Eastern Column under the command of Colonel Nelson D. Cole. Colonel Cole had the largest force at over 1,100 men made up of twelve companies from the Twelfth Missouri Volunteer Cavalry Regiment, seven batteries from the Second Missouri Volunteer Light Artillery Regiment (Colonel Cole's command), a detachment from the U. S. Army Signal Corps, and an Ordnance Rifle Section.

The Western Column left Fort Laramie July 30, 1865, (some accounts show August 1 or 2) accompanied by Brigadier General Connor. The plan was to march to the Powder River region and establish a fort at which the remaining columns would meet. Construction on the fort began August 11 and named Fort Connor to be renamed Fort Reno that November. The fort was located near the Powder River along the Bozeman Trail some fifty-five miles north of the Platte Bridge Station. Part of the force was involved in construction of the fort while the remainder headed north in search of Indians. It wouldn't take long before the first engagement of the Powder River Expedition occurred on August 13 at a point called Crazy Women's Fork.

The **Battle of Crazy Women's Fork** was s brief encounter between Pawnee Scouts associated with General Connor's expedition and a small group of Cheyenne Indians that ended with neither side achieving more than flexing their muscles. Crazy Woman's Fork was a small tributary creek to the west of the Powder River not far from the new fort under construction. This incident would be one of many similar occurrences associated with the Powder River Expedition. On August 16, a second incident occurred called the **Powder River Massacre** in which the same Pawnee Scouts involved in the Battle of Crazy Woman's Fork caught up with and surprised perhaps the same group of Cheyenne encountered earlier. The outcome this time was devastating for the Indians killing all twenty-seven men and women of the Cheyenne party.

A much larger battle took place August 29, 1865, along the Tongue River at a point as far north as one can go in the central portion of present-day Wyoming without entering Montana. This was named the **Battle of Tongue River** that involved Brigadier General Connor and two hundred troops along with seventy Omaha, Winnebago, and Pawnee Scouts as well as guide, Jim Bridger, and two mountain howitzers. These forces were against approximately five hundred Arapaho Indians led by their Chief Black Bear who had established an encampment along the Tongue River.

Guide Jim Bridger it is said spotted smoke rising from the encampment and alerted General Conner still some distance from the camp. After a nighttime march, General

Connor's men reached the site of the camp early in the morning of August 29 and the attack began. Chief Black Bear and many of his warriors were away fighting against the Crow Indians leaving a few warriors to protect the women, children, and old men. Regardless of the gender of the Indians, a fierce fight ensued with women said to have fought as hard as the warriors. In the end, General Connor's men won the day killing a total of sixty-four Arapaho including fifty-four warriors and the remainder women and children. Fewer than twenty women and children were captured and released later. The Arapaho encampment was totally destroyed by the troops. The Arapaho survivors managed to flee, but the warriors would harass the troops as the days wore on. Brigadier General Connor's casualties included two soldiers killed and seven wounded, and three Indians Scouts were also killed.

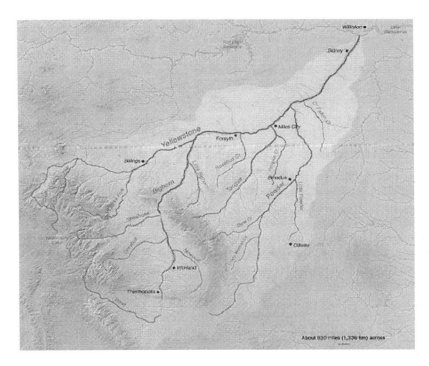

Map of the Powder River Expedition area
Wikipedia

Prior to the action of the Western Column during the Powder River Expedition, Colonel Nelson D. Cole and his Right or Eastern Column departed from Omaha, Nebraska Territory, July 1, 1865. By the time the troops reached Bear Butte in the Black Hills region on August 13, nearly a six hundred mile march, neither men nor animal were in any condition to engage in fighting. Meanwhile, Lieutenant Colonel Samuel Walker with his Central or Middle Column departed from Fort Laramie August 6 and met up with Colonel Cole in the Black Hills August 19, 1865. This march was much shorter, but that did not diminish the suffering any more than that for Colonel Cole's troops.

With the two columns now near each other, they began their movement to the Powder River region in an effort to link up with Brigadier General Connor. It would not take long for Colonel Cole's forces to come in contact with hostile Indians as they did on the morning of September 1 near Alkali Creek in the east central portion of present-day Custer County, Montana. This encounter was not at the hands of Colonel Cole's troop, but rather an attack by Indians bent on capturing as many horses as they could.

The capture of horses was a frequent action by Indians for two reasons. First, horses allowed the various tribes to move effectively for both hunting and attacks against their enemies. Second, the capture of horses denied the cavalry the opportunity to conduct warfare against the Indians. Cavalry on foot was of little value in the vast regions of the west. In the encounter on September 1 and throughout the day, Colonel Cole's forces suffered the loss of four killed and two wounded. Indian losses are believed to be four killed and an equal number wounded.

Contact with mainly Sioux Indians continued over the next several days with no significant outcomes. Marching south on September 8, the military column was detected by Indians approaching their large village of over 2,500 Sioux, Cheyenne, and Arapaho Indians. Rather than wait for the column to come in sight and attack, the Indians took the fight to the soldiers. This activity continued over the next several days with only sporadic results. At no time did the two military columns inflict much more than a few casualties nor did the Indians result in the same for the soldiers who were tattered and worn at this time in their effort.

It was not until September 13 that the Eastern and Central Columns made contact with Scouts of Brigadier General Connor. Only then were they informed of the establishment and location of Fort Connor where they proceeded arriving a week later on September 20, 1865. The men of both Colonel Cole's and Lieutenant Walker's commands were in such terrible condition, Brigadier General Connor declared them unworthy of further service and sent them to Fort Laramie to be mustered out of military service!

Having achieved only partial success, the Powder River Expedition was essentially over September 25, 1865. The casualty count from contact with Indians was minimal, but the loss of men to the elements and the arduous duty were far greater. The Bozeman Trail was still controlled by the three Indian tribes virtually shutting it down to settlers and explorers. More wars were to come to end the Indians hostilities in the Powder River region, but for now Brigadier General Patrick Edward Connor would be reassigned to duty in Utah.

---

[1] The Army of the United States, Historical Sketches of Staff and Line, Center of Military History, Edited by Theophilus Frances Rodenbough, Bvt. Brigadier General, U. S. A., and William L. Haskin, Major, First Artillery, New York Maynard, Merrill, & Co., 1896. Fourth Regiment of Infantry, Lieutenant James A. Leyden, p. 457.

[2] Ibid, First Regiment of Cavalry, Captain R. P. Wainwright, p. 154.

[3] Ibid, Seventh Regiment of Infantry, Lieutenant A. B. Johnson, p. 498.

[4] The Official History of the Washington National Guard, Volume 2, Washington Territorial Militia in the Indian Wars of 1855-56; p. 9.

[5] Ibid; p. 10

[6] The War of the Rebellion: a compilation of the official records of the Union and Confederate armies. ; Series 1 – Volume 41 (Part II), p. 30-31.

[7] Ibid, Vol. 48, (Part II), p. 724-725

[8] Ibid, Vol. 48, (Part I), p. 294

[9] Ibid, p. 295-296

[10] Ibid, p. 305-306

Texas War of Independence

andwiched between the Native American Indian Wars up to 1835 and the Second Seminole War from 1835-1842 was the *Texas War of Independence from Mexico* also known as the *Texas Revolution* that began October 2, 1835, and ended April 21, 1836. For a war, this was about as short as they come although no less costly!

Texas became a province of Mexico in 1821 after Mexico won its independence from Spain. It was the same year Spain transferred control of Florida to the United States.

In the years prior to 1821, settlers poured into the Texas region upsetting the balance of power. The non-Hispanic population out numbered Hispanics three to one. Mexico's government imposed regulations on the Texian population that was inconsistent with the desires of those who made the territory their home. This balance came to a head in 1835 when control by Mexico was deemed oppressive to the majority of non-Mexican inhabitants. Inhabitants of Mexican Texas were known as Texians.

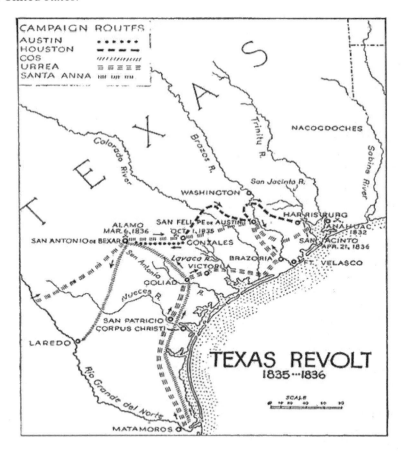

Battle Map of the Texas Revolution

Wikipedia

Battles of Texas Revolution

Pre Battles –

Battle of Velasco – June 25-26, 1832

Battle of Nacogdoches – August 2, 1832

Current Battles –

Battle of Gonzales – October 2, 1835

Battle of Goliad – October 10, 1835

Battle of Concepcion – October 28, 1835

Siege of Bexar – November 1-14, 1835

Goliad Campaign – Feb 18 – Mar 27, 1836

Battle of the Alamo – Feb 23 – Mar 6, 1836

Battle of San Patricio – February 27, 1836

Battle of Agua Dulce – March 2, 1836

Battle of Refugio – March 12-15, 1836

Battle of Coleto – March 19-20, 1836

Battle of Copano – March 21, 1836

Goliad Massacre – March 27, 1836

Battle of San Jacinto – April 21, 1836

Prior to the official outbreak of the war, Texian militia fought the Mexican Army in the *Battle of Velasco* June 25-26, 1832. One cause of this battle was the cancellation by the Mexican government of immigration rights of United States citizens to settle in the province of Texas. Mexico feared that too many U. S. citizens were settling in their province that might lead to annexation by the United States. A second cause was the enactment of custom duties that were considered punitive on goods necessary for the livelihood of the settlers. A third cause was the arrest of several settlers for various reasons by Mexican military leader Colonel Juan Davis Bradburn.

The Mexican government established three garrisons in the southern region of Texas to collect the duties that the law authorized. The first post was called Anahuac along Trinity Bay at the mouth of the Trinity River. A second was Velasco to the west that was a settlement along the Gulf of Mexico at the time of 1832 that is present-day Surfside Beach. It controlled commerce activity to the Brazos River. The third was Fort Teran to the east of Anahuac that controlled the Neches River where it emptied into the Gulf of Mexico near current Port Arthur, Texas. The site of the battle was Fort Velasco.

Before the Battle of Velasco, Frank W. Johnson and militia under his command attempted to seize the post at Anahuac on June 10. After a brief encounter with Mexican soldiers, the militia withdrew calling instead for a siege of the post. This encounter led to the Battle of Velasco that began on June 25, 1832, that became a two day affair involving approximately one hundred Mexican soldiers led by Colonel Domingo de Ugartechea against a slightly larger militia force under the command of John Austin, a settler but of no known relation to Stephen Fuller Austin. Austin and his militia forced the surrender of the fort's garrison that resulted in the death of five Mexican soldiers and the wounding of sixteen others. Austin's men reported seven killed and fourteen wounded. No further action was taken at this time with news that those previously arrested had been released and that situation would remain at least until the government enacted more regulations in August against the settlers that would result in a full blown battle.

The *Battle of Nacogdoches* was a brief but deadly battle that began August 2, 1832. After the Battle of Velasco, the Mexican commander at Nacogdoches, Colonel Jose de las Piedras, issued a proclamation calling for all Texians to surrender their arms. A delegation of those called to surrender their arms met with Colonel Piedras demanding a retraction of the order that Piedras refused to change.

Apparently undaunted by the refusal, the delegation returned that evening only to be fired upon by Mexican cavalry. The fight began! Soon large groups of Texians were involved in the conflict forcing the Mexican soldiers to retreat to the protection of whatever could provide them cover. During the night, Colonel Piedras and his soldiers evacuated Nacogdoches. A small group of Texians caught up with the retreating column August 3 and a battle ensued. When all was said and done, Colonel Piedras fled leaving his command in the hands of his second, Captain Francisco Medina, who surrendered the troops. The Battle of Nacogdoches was over. Mexican casualties numbered forty-seven killed, forty wounded, and three hundred captured. Those captured were paroled back to Mexico. Texian casualties were few showing three killed, four wounded one of whom died later.

The Battle of Nacogdoches was a window into what was coming in Texas. The election of Antonio Lopez de Santa Anna on April 1, 1833, did little to settle the unrest in the Providence of Texas and even created unrest in Mexico. The entire region was in arms waiting to explode. The first incident occurred on September 1 as the armed schooner *San Felipe* sailed from New Orleans with supplies and munitions arriving near Brazoria, Texas, and was in the process of transferring supplies onto the steamer *Laura*. On board the San Felipe was Stephen F. Austin recently released from a Mexican prison where he had been held on suspicion of treason. As the supply transfer was nearing completion, the Mexican Navy schooner *Correo de Majica* approached the two ships and a cannon engagement began lasting nearly an hour. The *Correo de Malica* received the brunt of the cannon fire and was forced to withdraw only to be pursued and captured the next day. The captured crew were placed in chains and transported to New Orleans for a later trial that turned into a circus and the eventual release of the crew.

The first shots of the Texas Revolution may have been that of the previous naval battle, but the first real battle was the **Battle of Gonzales** that took place on October 2, 1835. Mexican Colonel Domingo de Ugartechea, commander of all Mexican troops in Texas, sent a six man detail to Gonzales to retrieve a cannon provided by Mexico and used by the inhabitants to protect against Indian attacks. Colonel Ugartechea was concerned that the cannon might be used against his troops due to the unrest at that time. The population of Gonzales was not about to give up their cannon and stood firm against its removal. Soon after, Colonel Ugartechea dispatched one hundred dragoons from San Antonio de Bexar under the command of Lieutenant Francisco de Castaneda and a stand off ensued between the Texians numbering one hundred fifty. Eventually a skirmish did occur in which the dragoons took the brunt of the conflict losing two soldiers after several hours of fighting and then withdrew. The Texians had zero casualties. The impact of this battle was noted in the United States as well as Mexico. Mexican President Santa Anna responded by sending more Mexican troops to Texas!

In addition to the issues pointed out earlier for the unrest in Texas, the problem was compounded in early 1835 when Mexico and more particularly President Santa Anna adopted a centralized form of government over the previous Federalists rule. This caused problems not only in Texas, but also Mexico that required control before the Texas problem could be addressed. Once Mexico was stabilized, President Antonio Lopez de Santa Anna responded by sending his brother-in-law, General Martin Perfecto de Cos to Texas with approximately five hundred troops that would add to some two hundred that had been sent earlier under the command of Colonel Nicolas Condelle. General de Cos landed with his troops on September 20 at Copano Bay that served as a main supply port, marched north first to Refugio that was manned by a small garrison of Mexican troops, and then to the Presidio La Bahia at Goliad arriving on October 2, 1835. Receiving word of the Battle of Gonzales, General de Cos made a rapid departure from Goliad on October 5 for San Antonio de Bexar. Lacking adequate wagons to transport his supplies at the time of his departure, General de Cos left them at the Presidio La Bahia.

The Texians were aware of the arrival of General Cos in Texas and made plans to kidnap him at Copano and what was thought to be a large sum of money and vast supplies. This plan could not be implemented because General de Cos moved from one place to another before the Texians could muster their forces. An alternate plan included an attack on the Presidio La Bahia in Goliad in hopes of securing the supplies that were left at that place. This would be known as the *Battle of Goliad*. Captain George Collinsworth in command of approximately one hundred twenty-five Texians conducted a pre-dawn attack on the presidio surprising the small garrison of around fifty soldiers commanded by Colonel Juan Lopes Sandoval. Within thirty minutes the Texians controlled the fight causing the Mexicans to surrender. The captives were temporarily detained and then released by Stephen F. Austin on the condition they return to Mexico. Mexican losses were one soldier killed, the sentry on watch, and three wounded. The Texians suffered one man wounded. This ended the Battle of Goliad at this time, but Goliad would see further involvement later in the war.

About this time in the revolution, Texians may have regarded their accomplishments as a sign that they were invincible. Empresario Stephen F. Austin in command of the Texian Army put in place plans to take on the Mexican stronghold at San Antonio de Bexar. On October 22, James Bowie was appointed as colonel and James Walker Fannin, Jr., as captain over a militia force of ninety men designated as the First Battalion. Together these officers set up a camp near Mission San Francisco de la Espada where the rest of the Texian Army joined them on October 27. Colonel Bowie and Captain Fannin were sent to locate a strong defensive position that was found at Mission Concepcion approximately two miles south of San Antonio de Bexar. In the early morning of October 28, Mexican General Martin Perfecto de Cos, overall commander of Mexican forces in Texas stationed at San Antonio de Bexar dispatched Colonel Domingo Ugartechea with two hundred seventy-five cavalry and infantry soldiers to Mission Concepcion to meet the Texian troops. The *Battle of Concepcion* would occur on October 28, 1835.

The defensive position selected by Colonel Bowie and Captain Fannin provided a distinct advantage to the Texian force. Colonel Ugartechea was unable to push the Texians from their position after three assaults in a battle that lasted around thirty minutes. After the last failed assault, the Mexican troops withdrew. Mexican casualties were once again much greater than that of the Texians even though reports on the number of the fallen Mexicans varies greatly from a low of fourteen killed to as many as seventy-six. There were also a substantial number of wounded. Regardless of what number of killed is correct, only one Texian was killed and another wounded. This battle was a decisive victory for the Texians and produced a *Siege of San Antonio de Bexar* that would be the next major focus in the revolution.

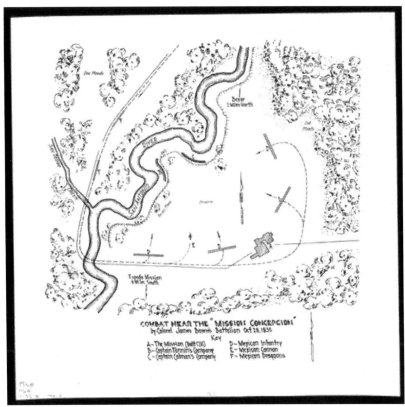

Battle Site of Mission Concepcion
Wikipedia

Before the siege of San Antonio de Bexar could gain strength, Fort Lipantitlan along the Nueces River near present-day San Patricio, Texas, would be attacked and captured November 4, 1835, by Texian forces under the command of Captain Ira Westover. Fort Lipantitlan was one of only two forts in Texas garrisoned by Mexican troops at that time in the revolution now that the Presidio La Bahia at Goliad had been captured The only other fort was Bexar about to come under siege. Mexican Captain Nicolas Rodriquez commanded Fort Lipantitlan with slightly less than one hundred men.

The details of the *Battle of Lipantitlan* also known as the *Battle of Nueces Crossing* reveal that favor was on the side of the Texians! Captain Rodriquez received orders to harass the Texians at Goliad and marched with the majority of his troops arriving October 31 only to find that the Texians had left the day before. Meanwhile, Captain Westover was preparing his troops to attack Fort Lipantitlan when it was learned that most of the garrison had left for Goliad. With the use of a captured local, Captain Westover had the man convince the garrison to surrender which was accomplished without firing a shot. The next day the Texians began securing supplies and munitions from the fort before dismantling the structure and burning nearby huts. By that afternoon, the Mexican troops returned and a brief battle ensued lasting about thirty minutes. It would take one more day before Captain Rodriquez and his beleaguered troops withdrew south to the safety of Matamoros, Mexico. The loss of Fort Lipantitlan to the Texians cut off all lines of communication to San Antonio de Bexar that would help in the pending siege by Stephen F. Austin and others..

The months of November and December 1835 involved a number of personnel changes affecting those Texians connected to the revolution. November 14 saw a number of changes. American born Henry Smith becomes governor of the Mexican territory of Texas; Stephen F. Austin, William H. Wharton, and Branch T. Archer are selected to serve as commissioners to the United States; Colonel Edward Burleson is appointed commander-in-chief replacing Austin; and Sam Houston is appointed commander-in-chief of the regular Texas Army with the rank of major general and with no authority over the Burelson's militia. All these changes at the time the siege was underway. November 18 saw the introduction of the first independent military organization into the Texas Revolution from the United States. The New Orleans Greys was a volunteer group of one hundred twenty men who organized to fight for Texians against Mexico. They would see battle throughout the conflict resulting in the death of forty-five from their ranks.

On the morning of November 26 word was received at the Texian siege camp of a pack train nearing San Antonio de Bexar for the relief of General de Cos. Colonels James Bowie and William Jack were dispatched with one hundred men to intercept the train that was believed to be carrying gold and silver to pay the troops and to purchase supplies. This episode was called the *Grass Fight* Affair that took place on November 26, 1835. The pack train was intercepted and the Mexican escort driven off, but the pack animals were not carrying gold and silver only grass feed for horses. From this discovery, it was determined that General de Cos and his command must be in a demoralizing situation of which a dialogue could end the siege, but not yet due to discontent in the Texain camp.

The winter months were upon the troops and many tired of the fight and wished to return to their homes and families. One who was not of the same mind was Colonel Ben Milam who wanted to take the fight to the Mexicans. He convinced others to join him and an attack was launched on December 5 into the confines of San Antonio de Bexar. This assault achieved limited success and stalled. A second assault was undertaken two days later, December 7, at which time Colonel Milan was killed, but General de Cos's men were driven into the interior of Bexar and ultimately into the Alamo. With nowhere to go and no chance of further reinforcements, a standoff occurred for the next two days. On December 9 the Mexicans presented a flag of truce that resulted in a suspension of military action followed with the ultimate surrender of General Martin Perfecto de Cos. The surrender was signed on December 10, 1835. The general and his army marched out of the Alamo on December 14, 1835, on their way back to Mexico. The siege in no way was only a siege. Casualties occurred during this time on both sides most likely during the two assaults of December 5 and 7. For some reason, casualty counts were not very accurate for the Texas Revolution and this conflict is no exception. For the Texians, those killed range from four to six and wounded from fourteen to thirty-five. Numbers for the Mexican troops show even more disparity listing anywhere from one hundred fifty to three hundred killed and/or wounded. Colonel Burleson resigned his commission on December 15 and many of his militia troops returned home. Colonel Frank W. Johnson assumed command of the remaining militia

At the time the Siege of San Antonio de Bexar was in progress, General Santa Anna who was also the President departed Mexico City on November 28, 1835, marching north with a 6,000-man army for Texas. This move would eventually have a dramatic impact on the Texas

Revolution. Around the same time, the Mexican Congress enacted the *Tornel Decree* that essentially gave the Mexican Army the authority to execute any prisoners captured during the Revolution and that is precisely what occurred.

At the end of December 1835 the Mexican Army had been expelled from the Mexican province of Texas. General Santa Anna with his large army was moving north to reclaim San Antonio de Brexar and General Jose de Urrea was moving north from Matamoros in what would become the *Goliad Campaign* covering the period of February 18 to March 27, 1836. This campaign was an effort to reclaim the Texas gulf coast region extending from San Patircio north to Goliad. Four named battles would occur from February 27 to March 20 as part of this campaign

In late December 1835, Federalists supporters in Mexico devised a plan to attack the Centralist government in the Mexican city of Matamoros. The Texas General Council was in favor of this plan and ordered Major General Sam Houston and the Regular Army to assist in its execution. General Houston was persuaded by Governor Henry Smith to ignore the order of the General Council and he did. Undaunted by General Houston's withdrawal from the plan, Colonel Frank White Johnson in command of the volunteers and James Grant took up the call and began efforts to attack Matamoros. For the next month or so, these two men organized a fighting force and devised their plan of attack.

Little did they know that Mexican General Jose de Urrea was about to march from Matamoros with an army of five hundred fifty troops well aware of the plan to attack Matamoros. General Urrea left Matamoros on February 18 and met up with Johnson on February 27 in the *Battle of San Patricio*. This encounter was no battle at all, but a total rout of Johnson and his forty-three men who were caught totally unaware of the Mexican

troops until it was too late. Within about fifteen minutes the Texians were overwhelmed losing around sixteen killed and the remainder captured except for six including Johnson who escaped to Refugio where they sent word to Goliad of the attack.

At the time General Jose de Urrea was making his approach to San Patricio, General Santa Anna was continuing his march north to San Antonio de Bexar and arrived February 23, 1836, and immediately began the siege of the Texian occupied Alamo. To the south General Urrea's forces were looking for James Grant known to be somewhere in the vicinity of present-day Kingsville herding a large number of horses. The events that follow are named the *Battle of Agua Dulce Creek* at which place the Mexican troops numbering around one hundred fifty surprised the fifty or so Texians on March 2. This encounter was more a skirmish than a full blown battle, but the outcome was much the same as the Battle of San Patricio. Upwards of fifteen Texians were killed and a half dozen captured. The remainder managed to escape as did James Grant only to be tracked down and killed. Needless to say, the expedition to attack Matamoros was dealt a severe blow by the last two conflicts and not surprisingly would never take place.

The date of March 2, 1836, was not only the date of the Battle of Ague Dulce Creek, it was also the date of the Texas Declaration of independence from Mexico. The Republic of Texas is born! Also on this date, General Martin Perfecto de Cos, brother-in-law, of President Santa Anna, returned to San Antonio de Bexar where he had been defeated in December 1835. General Cos would obviously play a role in the siege and ultimate destruction of the Texan forces at the Alamo in four days of his arrival.

Perhaps the most well known event of the Texas Revolution is the *Battle of the Alamo* that only an alien invader from another planet would not have heard about unless our current education system has hid this historical event from students! Colonel James Bowie and Lieutenant Colonel William Barret Travis along with volunteer Davy Crockett and two hundred plus defenders of the Alamo would come under attack on March 6, 1836, by ten times that many Mexican soldiers led by General Santa Anna that has memorialized the phase "Remember the Alamo."

What exactly is the Alamo and where did its name come from? There is no one answer to these two questions. First of all, the Alamo was a Spanish Mission with its beginnings in 1718 that looked nothing like the Alamo of 1836 nor today. Even its name was different, San Antonio de Valero. This new mission was the idea of the new Spanish governor of Texas, Martin de Alarcon, who himself led an expedition to the current site. In addition to the mission, Alarcon also erected a presidio (fort) named the Presidio San Antonio de Bexar and a settlement with a similar name, San Antonio de Bexar. The mission itself was moved from its original location within a year of its establishment to the opposite side of the San Antonio River and would need to be rebuilt after a 1724 hurricane destroyed the structure. The rebuilt mission was located on its present site on the opposite side of the San Antonio River from San Antonio de Bexar. As the years pasted, the mission complex grew in size and defense. Larger more permanent buildings were constructed enclosed by a wall for protection. Spanish Texas was plagued by Indian attacks from Apache and Comanche. The walls were obviously meant to protect those at the mission and nearby inhabitants of San Antonio de Bexar.

A Spanish Mission would require a chapel for religious purposes. The Spanish were bringing Christianity to the New World and many of the inhabitants in this area were converts to the faith. The new complex, however, would never see the completion of the chapel under Spanish control. Over time, the mission would house the first hospital in Texas, serve as a convent for religious women, and become a walled fortress covering several acres. Its role as a Christian mission would fade away in the late 1700's and become a fortress occupied by armed men. Even the name Mission San Antonio de Valero would gradually fade away and acquire the name Alamo. The word Alamo may have come not from the building complex, but from a Spanish military company of colonial lancers by the name La Compania de Alamo de Parras. Correspondence in the early days of 1800 shortened the name of the military unit using only the name "Alamo" that apparently stuck from that time to the present.

It is doubtful that the Alamo would have much distinction today if it weren't for the Battle of the Alamo that took place on that early Sunday morning, March 6, 1836. The defenders were lulled into complacency the night before by the quiet that had evaded them for so many nights since the siege began on February 23. General Santa Anna had suspended the constant cannon fire on the Alamo that had the impact he apparently had hoped for before launching his daylight assault.

The two thousand Mexican soldiers quietly approached the outer walls of the Alamo undetected. The sentries outside the Alamo had fallen asleep and were quickly silenced. Mexican General Martin Perfecto de Cos and Colonels Francisco Duque, Jose Maria Romero, and Juan Morales moved their forces around the perimeter of the Alamo while the defenders were asleep. The battle began with shouts from the Mexican soldiers rousing to action all behind the walls.

The first assault by the Mexican troops was repulsed by both musket and rifle fire from within the Alamo. Many Mexicans were killed and wounded. A second assault a few minutes later ended in much the same way. On the third assault, the attackers found gaps in the walls and took immediate advantage pushing the Texians into the interior portion of the Alamo where hand-to-hand fighting occurred. Some Texians managed to escape outside the compound only to be struck down by waiting dragoons. The vast number of Mexican soldiers quickly overwhelmed those on the inside and no one was spared . Anyone who was alive was either shot or impaled on a lance. Those who offered surrender were executed by firing squad. All this carnage was the Mexican Government and President Santa Anna's fulfillment of the *Tornel Decree* calling for the execution of all persons involved in the Texas Revolution. The few women and children of the Alamo defenders were freed, and one Texian defender, Henry Warnell, may have escaped the carnage of the Alamo only to die later of unknown cause.

Battle scene of fighting inside the Alamo occurring March 6, 1836 Library of Congress, Prints & Photographs Division, LC-USCZ4-2133 (chg to B/W)

Sketch of the Chapel Ruins of the Alamo Library of Congress, Prints & Photographs Division, LC-USZ61-292

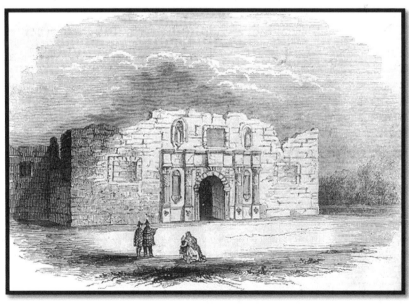

The Battle of the Alamo momentarily derailed the Goliad Campaign meant to restore the supply line from the Texas gulf coast all the way to San Antonio de Bexar. Previously two battles had been fought during the campaign that began February 18 both of which were Mexican victories. The Texians attempt to attack Matamoros had been put to rest by both battles and there would be two more battles between Texians and Mexicans that would further devastate efforts to achieve Texas independence.

Mexican General Jose de Urrea was the leader of the Goliad Campaign leading an army of 1,500 men from Matamoros into southern Texas. This large force was no match for the meager number of Texian who were charged with defending the territorial gains they had achieved at the end of 1835. One site after another would fall to General Urrea and the next loss was March 12 in the *Battle of Refugio*.

Refugio was a town twenty-seven miles south of Goliad with no fortification other than the Mission Nuestra Señora del Refugio. Mexicans loyal to the centrist Mexican government had ravaged the town sometime around the first of March causing those opposed to the government to fear for their lives. Word of this situation reached Colonel James Walker Fannin Jr. at Goliad who had improved the defenses at the Presidio La Bahia and renamed it Fort Defiance. Colonel Fannin agreed to send relief to Refugio as soon as there were wagons available to transport the families back to Goliad. Those wagons became available on March 10 and twenty-eight volunteers under Captain Amon B. King left Fort Defiance the next day for Refugio.

On Friday March 11, Captain King began to gather the families for transport, but got sidetracked engaging locals who were continuing to loot other homes. This delay allowed General Urrea's troops to arrive at Refugio forcing Captain King to gather the families and take refuge in the Refugio Mission. King sent a messenger to Colonel Fannin requesting reinforcement that was accomplished by the arrival March 13 of Lieutenant Colonel William Ward and eighty men from his Georgia Battalion. Interestingly, the Georgia Battalion was formed with volunteers from Columbus, Macon, and Milledgeville, Georgia, who would fight along side Texians in their war for independence.

The arrival of Lieutenant Colonel Ward provided only short term relief from the siege at the mission as arguments over command authority caused Captain King to go one way and Lieutenant Colonel Ward another. This decision would lead to the capture of Captain King and his men of which King and fourteen of his men would be executed soon after. Lieutenant Colonel Ward with many of his men managed to extricate themselves from the area making their way first to Copano and then to Victoria only to fall victim to capture on March 22 as many of Mexican General Urrea's men had surrounded much of the coastal area and beyond. The Battle of Refugio was costly for both the victor and the loser. Mexican casualties are estimated at one hundred fifty killed and fifty wounded. The Texians and American supporters list sixteen killed, fifteen executed, and over one hundred captured of which many would be executed in the Goliad Massacre on March 27, 1836.

Colonel James W. Fannin at Fort Defiance received orders from Major General Sam Houston to evacuate Goliad once news was received of the Alamo defeat. Colonel Fannin delayed his departure from the fort waiting for word on the fate of both Captain King and Lieutenant Colonel Ward. That delay was ill advised as General Urrea's forces were closing fast on Goliad. With little time to spare, Colonel Fannin marched from Fort Defiance around 9 A. M. on March 19 with nearly three hundred men consisting of the San Antonio (New Orleans) Greys, Alabama Red Rovers,

Burr H. Duval's Kentucky Mustangs, Hugh McDonald Frazer's Refugio militia, Texian regulars under the command of Captain Ira Westover, and Mobile Greys led by Albert C. Horton.

Due to constant delays along the march from Fort Defiance, the column had only gone half the twenty-five miles to their intended objective at Victoria when beset by the Mexican forces of General Urrea.around 1:30 P. M. The area was near Coleto Creek and became the *Battle of Coleto Creek* or the *Battle of the Prairie* or the *Batalla del encinal del Perdido* by the Mexicans.

Colonel Fannin was in the open and quickly formed his command in a square defensive configuration amongst the tall prairie grass. General Jose de Urrea wasted no time in attacking the position three times that went on until nightfall. During the night, sharpshooters engaged each other causing some casualties adding to those from the daytime encounter. When Colonel Fannin left Fort Defiance he

took wagon loads of munitions of all kinds, but failed to include extra food and water perhaps thinking that twenty-five miles was not far enough to worry about these items. Now that the column was surrounded in the open the items of food and water loomed large. The wounded could not be treated and water was essential for cooling the cannons once fired.

On the morning of March 20, the Mexicans resumed artillery fire into the square prompting Fannin and his officers to seek a surrender agreement. Mexican General Urrea was agreeable to the surrender, but cautioned that General Santa Anna had the ultimate authority on the outcome. That outcome would be no amnesty that would play out seven days later when many captured Texians and Americans in this battle and others would be executed in the *Goliad Massacre*. The Battle of Coleto Creek was not kind to the Mexicans either who lost between one and two hundred men among the killed, wounded, and missing

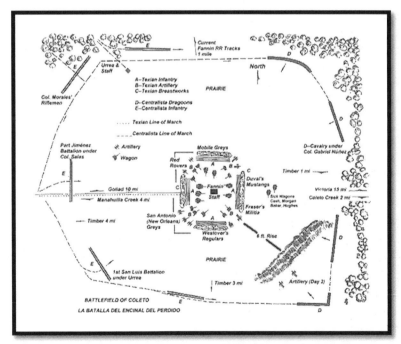

The battle plan of Colonel Fannin and his troops at the Battle of Coleto Creek, March 19-20, 1836

SONS OF DEWITT COLONY TEXAS

After the surrender of Colonel Fannin and his forces in the Battle of Coleto Creek, the Mexican Goliad Campaign was about to end. What took place next was no doubt a grave mistake by the Mexican Government and its President (General) Antonio Lopez de Santa Anna and would soon lead to the end of Mexican control over Texas! This event would be known as the *Goliad Massacre*!

The *Tornel Decree* of taking no prisoners was carried out on Palm Sunday, March 27, 1836. At that time all but a few prisoners held by the Mexicans at Goliad were marched out of the fort between two rows of Mexican soldiers and executed as they passed. Those captives unable to walk were shot where they lay. Colonel Fannin unable to stand was seated in a chair and shot. The bodies of those executed were piled and burned. The number executed was around four hundred. Mexican Lieutenant Colonel Jose Nicolas de la Portilla had fulfilled the order issued by President Santa Anna himself!

Some men were able to survive this carnage for various reasons. There were some who feigned death that were able to give insight later about what happened. A few men were spared who had special skills needed by the Mexicans, and seventy-five members of the Nashville Battalion were spared perhaps because they were unarmed at the time of their surrender. Needless to say, the result of the Goliad Massacre numbered the days of General Santa Anna and his large army.

Portrait of Colonel James W. Fannin
Second in command to Major General Sam Houston
Wikipedia

The events of March in Texas gave concern to it inhabitants that their establishments would be next to fall to the Mexican Army. People fled to safety in a hurry taking little with them except what they could carry. The Texas Army under Major General Sam Houston was making the same withdrawal to the chagrin of many of his officers and men who were determined to stand and fight. General Houston was called a coward, but whether by luck or design he would own the day very soon. As the Texas Army moved east, so did the Mexican Army all the while moving further from their supply lines and reinforcements if needed. It is unknown if this is what General Houston had in mind, but it did work to his advantage.

General Santa Anna had remained at San Antonio de Bexar until March 29 at which time he marched east to link up with General Joaquin Ramirez y Sesma. The first week of April, Santa Anna marched with a force of some seven hundred troops to a location near present-day Houston and an eventual encounter with the Texan Army near Lynch's Ferry on the Jacinto River. At this place the two armies would camp on April 20 close to each other, but out of sight of one another. Mexican General Martin Perfecto de Cos arrived on the morning of April 21 with over five hundred reinforcements adding to the seven hundred already present. General Houston's army was now outnumbered by nearly three hundred. Little did that matter for what was in the works!

It is safe to say that General Santa Anna was no doubt over-confident that his army was superior to that of Major General Houston, but he failed to recognize the will of the Texians who would "Remember the Alamo" and "Remember Goliad." Minor skirmishes took place on Wednesday April 20 between small groups from each army, but they had little impact on events to follow. General Houston's army was hidden from view and General Santa Anna had no idea of the strength. The early part of Thursday passed with no action by either side that stretched into early afternoon. Santa Anna was lulled into thinking that the Texians would not take any action and allowed his troops to rest many falling asleep that had been deprived for some time. Around 4 P. M., General Houston's army began a quiet movement upon the sleeping Mexican Army catching them in total surprise. After the minute hand on a clock had move fifteen times, the Mexicans were running for their lives with the Texians right behind. The *Battle of San Jacinto* was underway!

The action that followed was more a rout than a battle; the Mexican soldiers were running without their weapons that they left as they ran. The Texians gave no mercy to their enemy killing anyone they could without concern. Efforts by the command to stop the bloodshed went without acknowledgement. There was retribution to be paid and it was delivered. Meanwhile General Santa Anna fled the scene only to be captured the next day found hiding in a marsh. There was an immediate call for his execution, but Major General Sam Houston would have no part of it. No Mexican escaped the rout with as many as six hundred thirty killed, over two hundred wounded, and about three hundred captured. The Texians suffered nine killed and thirty wounded. The day belonged to the Republic of Texas and that was enough!

The Battle of Jacinto was the last battle of the Texas Revolution, but there were thousands of Mexican troops still on Texas soil that had to be resolved. With the capture of Santa Anna, command of the Mexican Army in Texas fell upon the second in command, General Vicente Filisola. General Filisola was instructed by Santa Anna to prepare a withdrawal to Mexico of all Mexican forces in Texas. General Jose de Urrea was opposed to this order but unable to change the mind of General Fisisola. The withdrawal of Mexican troops from Texas began in mid-May and reached Matamoros, Mexico, June 15. General Filisola soon after resigned his commission turning over his command to General Juan Jose Andrade who had been left in charge of the Alamo when General Santa Anna began his ultimate defeat.

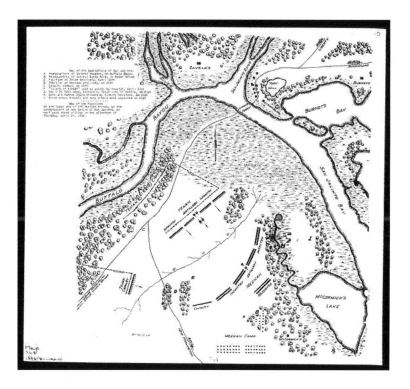

Battlefield layout for the Battle of San Jacinto, April 21, 1836
Wikipedia

Authority for the withdrawal of Mexican forces from Texas was called for under the *Treaties of Velasco* signed by President (General) Antonio Lopez de Santa Anna on May 14, 1836, at Velasco, (Surfside Beach), Texas. There were two treaties, one public and one secret, neither of which were ratified by the Mexican Government. The public treaty contained ten Articles with each one addressing the usual remarks involved in ending a war: All hostilities would cease, the Mexican Army would leave Texas, private property taken in the war would be returned, etc. The Secret Treaty of Velasco contained four Articles, but referred to what Antonio Lopez de Santa Anna would do personally as opposed to the Public Treaty that addressed what he would do as President of the Mexican Government. The wording of the Secret Treaty was not that revealing. Antonio Lopex de Santa Anna would eventually return to Mexico, but was deposed as President and disgraced for his defeat only to reclaim his stature at a later time.

The site of the Battle of San Jacinto is memorialized today by a monument towering over five hundred sixty-seven feet high honoring those men who died fighting for the Texas Independence from Mexico. The monument is located on the Houston Ship Channel near the City of Houston, Texas.

U. S. - Mexican War
1846 - 1848

FOLLOWING the defeat of Mexico in the Texas Revolution of 1835-1836, Mexico made several attempts to disrupt the stability of the new Republic of Texas. There were attempts to arm the Native American Indian tribes against the Republic and Mexican loyalists residing in Texas organized in an attempt do the same such as the Cordova Rebellion. Needless to say, Mexico was not about to give up ground in Texas without a fight. This situation came to a head in 1846 shortly after the Republic of Texas willingly became the twenty-eight State of the United States on December 29, 1845. Mexico reacted by ending diplomatic relations with the United States and war was not far behind.

Prior to Texas joining the Union, newly elected US President James Knox Polk offered to purchase disputed land in Texas lying between the Nueces River north from Corpus Christi then westward to the Rio Grande in the territory of Coahuila that today is the southern portion of the State of Texas. This offer was rejected. Land claims and disputes were common as settlers of the United States moved westward. Mexico lay claim to much of what would eventually become the southwestern United States. The region of Texas was no exception. The Treaty of Velasco signed after the Texas Revolution transferring land from Mexico to the Republic of Texas was never honored by the Mexican Government. Mexico claimed that the land from the Nueces River to the west was theirs as was all of Texas!

Undaunted by the rejection to purchase the disputed territory and concerned that Mexico was flexing its military muscles, President Polk in early July 1845 placed Brigadier General Zachary Taylor in command of U. S. troops with instructions to prepare to march to Texas to secure the area. This army would be known as the *"Army of Occupation"* with the words "of Texas" added later. General Taylor assembled his army in and around Fort Jesup, Louisiana, and most departed from New Orleans by ship for Corpus Christi, Texas, around July 25, 1845, arriving in early August 1845.

The *"Army of Occupation"* at that time consisted of the Third and Fourth Regiments of Infantry; Companies B, C, D, E, F, H & K of the Second Dragoons, Companies A, C, E & I, Third Regiment of Artillery, and four companies from the Second U. S. Artillery (Heavy). Soon to join was the Fifth, Seventh, and Eighth Regiments of Infantry; and Companies A, C, E, & I of the Second Artillery (Light). This force numbered around 3,500 men by October 1845 and would eventually be involved in several battles in southern Texas and northern Mexico. General Taylor's army remained at Corpus Christie until March 1846 at which time it marched to the area of the Rio Grande opposite of Matamoros, Mexico, in preparation for whatever was to come.

Not to be outdone, the arrival of U. S. military forces in the disputed territory resulted in Mexican General Antonio Lopez de Santa Anna to respond with his own army. Mexico was the first to declare war on April 23, 1846, and the first to draw blood on April 25, 1846, in the Thornton Affair. Because of the Thornton Affair, General Taylor called upon President Polk and Congress to declare war against Mexico that was accomplished on May 13, 1846.

Major General Zachary Taylor, "Old Rough and Ready"
Commander of Northern U. S. forces in the Mexican War of 1846-48
Library of Congress Prints & Photographs Division, LC-USZ62-38086

The United States war against Mexico would be fought in two regions of Mexico at different times. General Taylor's forces would concentrate on the northern portion of Mexico, and later, Major General Winfield Scott with a large army would focus on the central and southern areas of Mexico.

United States force under the command of Major General Winfield Scott would land off Vera Cruz, Mexico, in early March 1847 with its attention on southern Mexico and the ultimate objective of Mexico City. This force would be comprised of some of Major General Taylor's troops and eight new regiments of infantry authorized by an Act of Congress February 11, 1847, calling for one year service. This Act would result in the formation of the Ninth, Tenth, Eleventh, Twelfth, Thirteen, Fourteenth, Fifteenth, and Sixteenth Regiments of Infantry. Also organized was the Regiment of Voltigers and Foot Riflemen. These new Federal organizations along with troops garnered from General Taylor's forces and ninety-nine military units from twenty-four States consisting of brigades, regiments, battalions, and independent companies brought this large fighting force to at least 9,000 men and perhaps more. In addition to the ground forces, the U. S. Navy was also represented. Forty-seven naval ships were involved in the Gulf of Mexico that was identified as the "Home Squadron." Nineteen ships were engaged in action along the California coastline that was identified as the "Pacific Squadron." This war was by no means some small affair. It was, in fact, the largest military force thus far in the existence of the United States of America!

Battles of the Mexican War 1846-1848

Thornton Affair – April 25, 1846

Siege of Fort Texas – May 3-9, 1846

Battle of Palo Alto - May 8, 1846

Battle of Resaca de Parma – May 9, 1846

Battle of Monterey – July 7, 1846

Battle of Yerba Buena – July 9, 1846

Battle of Canoncito – early August 1846

Battle of Santa Fe – August 18, 1846

Siege of Los Angles – September 22-30, 1846

Battle of Monterrey – September 21-23, 1846

Battle of Chino – September 26-27, 1846

Battle of Dominguez Rancho – October 7, 1846

First Battle of Tabasco – October 24-126, 1846

Battle of Natividad – November 16, 1846

Battle of San Pasquel – December 6, 1846

Capture of Tucson – December 16, 1846

Battle of El Brazito - December 25, 1846

Battle of Santa Clara – January 2, 1847

Battle of Rio San Gabriel – January 8, 1847

Battle of La Mesa – January 9, 1847

Battle of Canada – January 24, 1847

First Battle of Mora – January 24, 1847

Battle of Embudo Pass – January 29, 1847

Second Battle of Mora – February 1, 1847

Siege of Pueblo de Taos – February 3-4, 1847

Battle of Buena Vista – February 22-23, 1847

Battle of Sacramento – February 28, 1847

Siege of Veracruz- March 9-29, 1847

Scott's Campaign – Mar 9 – Sep 14, 1847

Battle of Cerro Gordo – April 18, 1847

First Battle of Tuxpan – April 18, 1847

Battle of Red River Canyon – May 26, 1847

Second Battle of Tuxpan – June 1847

Second Battle of Tabasco – June 16, 1847

Third Battle of Tuxpan – June 30, 1847

Battle of Las Vegas – July 6, 1847

Battle of Cienega Creek – July 9, 1847

Battle of Contreras (Padierna) – Aug 19, 1847

Battle of Churubusco – August 20, 1847

Battle of Molino del Rey – September 8, 1847

Battle of Chapultepec – September 13, 1847

Battle of Mexico City – September 13-14, 1847

Siege of Puebla – Sep 14 to Oct 12, 1847

Fall of Mexico City – September 15, 1847

Battle of Mulege – October 2, 1847

Battle of Huamantla – October 9, 1847

Bombardment of Guaymas – Oct 19-20, 1847

Bombardment of Punta Sombrero – Oct 31, 1847

Battle of La Paz – November 16-17, 1847

Battle of San Jose del Cabo – November 20-21, 1847

Battle of Santa Cruz de Rosales – Mar 16, 1848

The Battles Begin –

Upon the arrival of General Zachary Taylor's army along the Rio Grande River opposite Matamoros, Mexico, an earthwork fort was built March 26, 1846. Captain Joseph K. F. Mansfield, Chief Engineer, supervised construction of the fort under the authority of Major General Zachary Taylor. It was unofficially named Fort Taylor for the general and officially Fort Texas. A month later the fort would receive a permanent name change after events surrounding the siege of the fort by Mexican troops.

The first conflict of the war even before a declaration by the United States, even though Mexico had declared war, was that of Mexican forces led by Mexican General Anastasio Torrejon who attacked an eighty-man detail of the Second U. S. Dragoons led by Captain Seth Thornton on April 25, 1846, that became known as the *Thornton Affair*.

General Taylor received word that Mexican troops had crossed the Rio Grande River at two points into the disputed territory of Texas. Taylor sent Captain Croghan Ker of the Second Dragoon to investigate one of the incursions and Captain Thornton to the other. Captain Ker found no evidence of the Mexican Army while Captain Thornton and his dragoons were ambushed resulting in the death of eleven, wounding of six, and the remainder captured including Captain Thornton and his second Captain William J. Hardee. General Torrejon sent the six wounded dragoons back to General Taylor in a cart with a message that he could not care for them!

The attack on the U. S. troops prompted a response securing Santa Fe de Nuevo Mexico, the present State of New Mexico, along with Alta California that included California, Nevada, Utah, and portions of Arizona, Wyoming, Colorado and northern New Mexico. Both of these regions constituted the entire southwestern United States of today. All this action was prior to any declaration of war, but General Taylor immediately called for a U. S. Declaration of War that took place on May 13, 1846, as noted earlier.

From the large list of battles, skirmishes, sieges, and other actions during the Mexican War, it is easy to see that there was rapid succession of these events once the war commenced! General Taylor immediately moved out of Fort Texas on May 1 with a substantial force after the Thornton Affair in an attempt to meet the aggressor's head on. Remaining in command of the fort was the Seventh Infantry commanded by Major Jacob Brown supported by Company I of the Second U. S. Artillery with four 18-pounder guns and commanded by Captain Allen Lowd and Company E of the Third U. S. Artillery that was a field battery commanded by Lieutenant Braxton Bragg. Taylor had been gone two days when Fort Texas came under siege by a large Mexican Army around 1,600 men with several artillery guns led by Mexican General Mariano Arista commanding the Mexican "Army of the North." The *Siege of Fort Texas* began at sunrise on May 3, 1846, and continued periodically to May 9. It was essentially a bombardment that changed nothing except the eventual name of the fort. Major Brown was one of two defenders killed in the

bombardment and would be honored for his service by renaming Fort Texas as Fort Brown that remains the same to this day.

Meanwhile, General Taylor in search of the perpetrators who attacked, captured, and killed Captain Thornton's dragoons would be involved in the first named battle of the war. The *Battle of Palo Alto* would take place on May 8, 1846, involving nearly 2,300 American troops against Mexican General Mariano Arista's forces just under 4,000. Palo Alto was in the disputed territory of Texas several miles east of today's Brownsville, Texas. General Taylor had marched his force to Point (Port) Isabel near South Padre Island of today eighteen miles northeast of Fort Texas. Point Isabel was established as a supply depot March 24, 1846, at which time a fort was erected named Fort Polk. This fort was the work of Major John Monroe and the men of the Second U. S. Artillery charged with its defense. While at or near Point Isabel gathering supplies, General Taylor heard the sounds of artillery fire coming from the vicinity of Fort Texas. Assuming that Fort Texas was under attack, he immediately set his forces in motion to return to the fort.

Mexican General Marino Arista became aware of General Taylor's action and sent some of his force besieging Fort Texas to meet the U. S. force on its return. This action became the Battle of Palo Alto that commenced at 2 PM on Friday afternoon, May 8. The American forces involved in this action consisted of two brigades, First Brigade the "Left Wing" and the Second Brigade the "Right Wing." The First Brigade commanded by Lieutenant Colonel William Goldsworth Belknap was made up of a battalion of the First Artillery joined by Company D, E. G, I from the Fourth Artillery under Lieutenant Colonel Thomas Childs employed as infantry, Company A of the Second Artillery (Light) under the command of Captain James Duncan, the Eighth Infantry Regiment commanded by Captain William R.

Montgomery, and a 200 wagon supply train under Captain's George Hampton Crosman and Abraham C. Myers.

The Second Brigade commanded by Colonel David Emanuel Twiggs included the Fifth U. S. Infantry led by Lieutenant Colonel James Simmons McIntosh, Company C of the Third U. S. Artillery (Light) under Major Samuel B. Ringgold, the Third U. S. Infantry commanded by Captain Lewis M. Morris, the Third U. S. Artillery (Heavy) led by Lieutenant William H. Churchill, the Fourth U. S. Infantry commanded by Major George W. Allen, and finally a Squadron of the Second Dragoons with Captain's Croghan Ker and Charles A. May.

As pointed out the Mexican artillery commenced the battle on the afternoon of May 8 and General Taylor responded with more effective artillery fire of his own that was followed by ground assaults by Mexican lancers that were readily repulsed resulting in a large number of Mexican casualties. After dusk and during the night, General Arista began withdrawing his troops to the south in the direction of Fort Texas. General Taylor sent a force of around two hundred to determine the intentions of the Mexican Army that would soon result in the second battle of the undeclared war at least from the standpoint of the United States.

The Mexican Army easily took the brunt of this first battle losing one hundred two killed, one hundred twenty-nine wounded, and twenty-six missing. General Taylor's forces had four killed, forty-eight wounded, and two missing. The next battle would produce much of the same casualty results. On a positive note, many of the American soldiers performed admirably in the Battle of Palo Alto and were brevetted for their participation. Captains Charles A. May, James Duncan, and George H. Crosman were each breveted majors for their gallantry during the battle on that day.

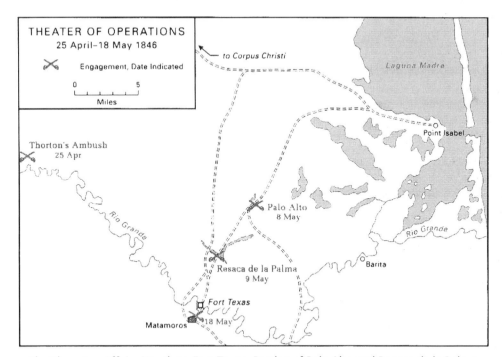

The Thornton Affair, Attack on Fort Texas, Battles of Palo Alto and Resaca de la Palma
Source: The U. S. Army Center of Military History (CMH -MH Pub 73-2 PIN: 081784-000)

Battle of Palo Alto Painting by Carl Nebel
Wikipedia (chg to B/W) {{PD-US}}

Depiction of the wounding of Major Samuel B. Ringgold during the Battle of Palo Alto May 8, 1846
Major Ringgold would die of his wounds three days later May 11, 1846
Library of Congress, Prints & Photographs Division, LC-USZ62-65

The *Battle of Resaca de la Palma* immediately followed the Battle of Palo Alto. The Mexican Army under the command of General Arista supported by Generals Romulo Diaz de la Vega and Pedro de Ampudia took up defense during the morning of May 9, 1846, with around 4,000 men in a dry riverbed called a resaca. Here they awaited the arrival of the American forces for which they would not be disappointed. Around 2 PM General Taylor arrived with a force of some 1,700 men most of the same from the Battle of Palo Alto Those artillery companies not directly supporting were assigned to the First Artillery Battalion as infantry. The Mexican troops thought they were hidden from observation by thick vegetation that proved anything but true.

A fierce artillery and ground assault ensued the moment General Taylor's troops arrived. Although out numbered in strength, the will of the American troops was apparently under estimated by the Mexican generals as they were met at every turn with overwhelming zeal that crushed the Mexican defenders forcing them to flee in haste leaving vast number of weapons including ten artillery guns and all types of equipment and supplies. The rout of the Mexicans can largely be credited to the Second Dragoons under Captain Charles A. May who were given the responsibility to silence the artillery. Not only did the dragoons accomplish their mission, they also captured Mexican General Romulo Diaz de la Vega in the process! As the Mexican soldiers hastily fled from the battlefield, some drowned as they attempted to cross the nearby Rio Grande River back to the safety of Matamoros. The number of men who drowned is uncertain, but it is known that one hundred fifty-four Mexicans were listed as killed, two hundred five wounded, and one hundred fifty-six missing that may include those that drowned. The Americans faired better with thirty-three reported killed in battle and eighty-nine wounded.

Captain Charles A. May and the Second Dragoons charging the Mexican artillery
in the Battle of Resaca de la Palma, May 9, 1846
Library of Congress, Prints & Photographs Division, LC-DIG-ds-05567

After this last battle, General Taylor moved his troops three or so miles to Fort Texas and would cross the Rio Grande River occupying Matamoros, Mexico, on May 18 five days after the United States made its Declaration of War. Bravery was noticeable again in the Battle of Resaca de la Palma and Captain Robert C. Buchanan of the Fourth U. S. Infantry and Captain Charles A. May of the Second Dragoons were brevetted to Major, Major James Duncan of Company A, Second U. S. Artillery, and Captain George W. Allen of the Fourth U. S. Infantry were brevetted to lieutenant colonel. Brigadier General Zachary Taylor was brevetted to major general after his success during both battles.

Before General Taylor marched his army into the northern portion of Mexico, on the west coast in California that was part of Mexican Alta California the U. S. Navy under Commodore John D. Sloat had assembled a vast armada of ships in anticipation of hostilities with Mexico just as the Army had assembled in Texas. On July 7, 1846, Commodore Sloat from his command ship, the frigate USS *Savannah*, ordered a landing party for the purpose of seizing Monterey. The seizure was the **Battle of Monterey** and occurred without firing a shot and California was declared for the Unites States!

USS Savannah launched May 5, 1842
Naval Historical Center, U.S. Navy

The U. S. Pacific Squadron was not done with just the seizure of Monterey. Attention would be focused next on Yerba Buena of that day that is San Francisco of today. The **Battle of Yerba Buena** occurred on July 9 two days after Monterey was seized. Neither the Battle of Monterey nor the Battle of Yerba Buena were battles, and, in fact, they resembled nothing like a battle since not a single shot was fired in either. Yerba Buena was seized under the command of U. S. Navy Commander John B. Montgomery who captained the USS *Portsmouth*.

USS *Portsmouth* launched October 23, 1843
Wikipedia {{PD-US}}

Back in Mexico, Brevet Major General Taylor continued his movement occupying Camargo in the north central region of Mexico on his approach to Monterrey and Tamaulipas in the east along the Gulf Coast both around July 14, 1846. The Mexican Army had retreated to what they believed were impenetrable sites and Monterrey was on that list. The Mexicans should have known better after their large force was defeated in both battles at Palo Alto and Resaca de la Palma.

The Mexican-American War began in Texas, but was not confined to that region. All Mexican lands were subject to conflict as seen in Alta California at Monterey and Yerba Buena. Santa Fe in present-day New Mexico was next to see conflict. Similar to the occurrence at Monterey and Yerba Buena where no shots were fired in their seizure, Santa Fe was approached August 15, 1846, by an American force identified as the *Army of the West* consisting of 1,700 regular and volunteer troops led by Brigadier General Stephen Watts Kearney and seized in the same fashion.

General Kearney's force included Company B, C, G, I, & K of the First U. S. Dragoons commanded by Major Benjamin Lloyd Beall; the First Missouri Mounted Regiment led by Colonel Alexander William Doniphan; and two companies of artillery. This seizure is named the *Battle of Canoncito* or *Battle of Santa Fe* even though there was no battle that occurred. New Mexico was declared a part of the United States. General Kearny was not through with his campaign to secure more of the Mexican territory for the United States. With a portion of his troops he marched on to California and would be involved in another battle in December.

Battle of Monterrey –

While action was taking place in California and New Mexico, General Zachary Taylor was marching an army exceeding six thousand troops toward Monterrey, Mexico, considered impregnable or at least that was what the Mexican generals thought! It is true that

Monterrey was well defended positioned on a flat open plain, mountains to the south and west, and a river to the south with a number of fortified structures surrounding the city. After the defeat of the Mexicans at the Battle of Resaca de la Palma, General Mariano Arista turned over command of his troops to General Francisco Mejia who marched to Monterrey. There he along with General Pedro de Ampudia now in command of the *Army of the North* prepared to defend the city against the U. S. forces. It is hard to keep a large army on the march a secret and the Mexican generals were obviously well aware of what was coming. They responded by reinforcing Monterrey with several thousand troops from as far south as Mexico City. Monterrey by the end of August 1846 had over 7,000 Mexican troops on hand.

General Taylor's army reached the outskirts of Monterrey around mid-morning on Saturday, September 19. The army was formed into four divisions, the first three with two brigades each, and the fourth only one. The First Division was directed by Brigadier General David E. Twiggs, the Second by Brigadier General William J. Worth, the Third under Major General William O. Butler, and the Fourth was commanded by Major General James Pickney Henderson[1] A head on assault of Monterrey was considered suicide. A better plan included enveloping the city thereby engaging the enemy from all sides simultaneously as well as cutting off any escape and the further chance of reinforcements coming from the south. Surrounding the city took most of Sunday the 20th, but the troops were in position early on the 21st.

Battle Plan for the Battle of Monterrey, September 21-23, 1846
The U. S. Army Center for Military History, CMH Pub 73-1 PIN: 081783-000

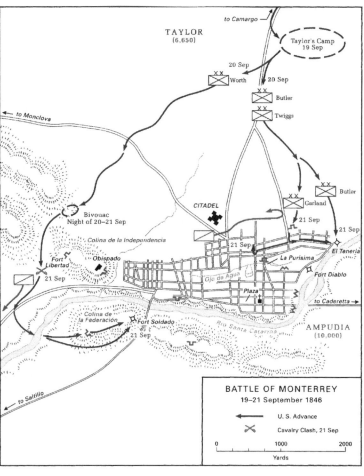

Two positions held by the Mexican Army would need to be neutralized by Brigadier General Worth if the attack on the city were to become successful. Both positions were high ground that gave a marked advantage to the occupier. One was called Federation Hill located southwest of the city and the other Independence Hill to the west of the city. A coordinated attack utilizing the Texas Rangers supported by the Fifth and Seventh U. S. Infantry Regiments were successful in expelling the Mexican forces from Federation Hill capturing several artillery guns in the process.

Brigadier General William J. Worth's Second Division attacking Independence Hill
at the Battle of Monterrey, September 21, 1846
Library of Congress, Prints & Photographs Division, LC-DIG-ds-05570

On the opposite side of the city, General Taylor hearing the sounds of battle jumped into action. His forces would have a harder time due to the flat terrain that offered little protection from both individual weapons fire and artillery. This assault would be a direct attack on the City of Monterrey that would evolve into street fighting that became a killing field. Strategically placed artillery weapons and snipers mowed down the U. S. troops as they tried to fight their way through the narrow streets. Finally, word came to pull back and regroup. This after two of the Engineer officers, Captain William G. Williams was killed and Captain Joseph K. F. Mansfield wounded although able to continue to direct the fight.

Other U. S, commands would receive crippling numbers of killed and wounded, but that would not dismay the overall command. By nightfall on September 21, General Worth was in firm control of the west and southwest portion overlooking the city and General Taylor with the First and Third Divisions were holding their own along the east side of Monterrey near the fortification de la Teneria. Hours before daylight on the 22nd, General Worth sent an assaulting party to take Independence Hill forcing the Mexican defenders to gradually retreat from their position. By mid-afternoon, the U. S. forces were in control of Independence Hill forcing the enemy to take refuge in the city proper.

Very late in the evening, September 22, Mexican General Ampudia abandoned his outer defenses pulling his troops into the city. This would mean another engagement in the streets of Monterrey. Lessons learned from the day before by the U. S. commanders on street fighting in the city called for new tactics. General Worth advanced his troops toward the city from the west and General Taylor did the same from the east hoping to drive the defenders into the center of the city. This time the troops would not adhere to the narrow streets, but knocked holes through the sides of the adobe buildings making their advance to the center. There was no escape for the Mexican soldiers who were driven to the central plaza. So too were the many civilians who had not evacuated probably thinking their army would prevail. With the American troops within two blocks of the central plaza, General Taylor called a halt to the operation fearing that many civilians would become casualties if continued.

"Lessons Learned"
Street fighting at The Battle of Monterrey on September 23 whereby troops
knocked holes through buildings to reach the central plaza.
Library of Congress, Prints & Photographs Division, LC-USZ62-62221

General Ampudia was surrounded and had nowhere to go at this point. A "white flag" was raised as the day ended on the 23rd and terms of surrender were proposed. Surrender terms were not easily achieved. At first, General Taylor flat out refused to accept General Ampudia's offer that called for the Mexican Army to retain all their weapons. It would take a commission to come to an agreement and that only after hours of negotiations. In the end, General Taylor agreed to allow the Mexican Army one week to abandon Monterrey, personal weapons could be kept, there would be an eight week cease-fire, and the American Army would not pursue further than fifty miles south during that time. Both commanders agreed to the terms and General Ampudia left Monterrey in the timeframe as accepted. Perhaps General Taylor could have sought more stringent terms of surrender, but his army had suffered greatly in those killed, wounded, and worn out. The Battle of Monterrey had taken its toll especially on Brigadier General Twiggs' First Division and Major General Butler's Third Division who had attacked over the open plain on the east and into the city streets. In addition, supplies of all sorts had diminished since leaving Fort Texas over four months earlier on May 18. It was time to pause and regroup.

Scene of the surrender of General Pedro de Ampudia to General Zachary Taylor, September 24, 1846, after the Battle of Monterrey, Mexico.
Library of Congress, Prints & Photographs Division, LC-USZ62-62222

The Battle of Monterrey was extremely costly in the lives of the men for both sides in the war. The Americans lost one hundred twenty killed, three hundred sixty-eight wounded, and forty-three missing. These numbers were the highest casualty count for the Americans in all conflicts combined to this point in the war. The Mexican Army on the other hand showed three hundred sixty-seven total killed and wounded if these numbers are accurate. There were undoubtedly civilian casualties the numbers of which are unknown. The Battle of Monterrey was definitely costly, but there would be a battle to come in February that would surpass these numbers.

California Again

The Battle of Monterrey may have been the focus in September 1846, but California would also see action. What would become one of several rare battle losses during the war, American forces near Los Angles were besieged by Mexican Captain (*Comandante General*) Jose Maria Flores in an attempt to drive them out of the region. This would become the *Siege of Los Angles* taking place September 22-30, 1846. The American forces had occupied the region since August 13, 1846, under U. S. Navy Commodore Robert F. Stockton. Stockton established a garrison under the command of Captain Archibald H. Gillespie, California Battalion, before departing for other duties. It was Captain Gillespie and his small contingent that were forced to surrender to Captain Flores. The Americans were allowed to leave on the merchant ship *Vandalia*. No casualties occurred during the conflict.

A battle that did result in casualties was the **Battle of Chino** fought September 26-27, 1846, that pitted approximately fifty Mexican militia otherwise called Californios against two dozen American militia led by Benjamin Davis Wilson. Wilson was an American who became a Mexican citizen in order to own land in California. He married into a Mexican family, but his loyalty was questioned. The Californios caught up with Wilson and his small group at the Rancho Santa Ana del Chino in present-day San Bernardino County, California. The engagement that followed resulted in the death of one Mexican and the wounding of two. Three of Wilson's men were wounded and all captured. They were held as prisoners for a time and eventually released.

On October 8, 1846, another engagement occurred between Mexican troops and Americans in the **Battle of Dominguez Rancho** that, too, would be a Mexican victory involving casualties. This brief battle was an attempt by Navy Captain William Mervine to recapture Los Angles that was lost only a week earlier. Captain Mervine in command of the USS *Savannah* landed ashore with just under three hundred Marines on October 7. The Mexican forces under Captain Jose Antonio Carrillo and General Jose Maria Flores were well prepared and aware of the landing. When Captain Mervine's Marines made their movement the next day, they were met with deadly fire causing the effort to retake Los Angles to be canceled. Captain Mervine and his Marines returned to the USS *Savannah* losing four killed and six wounded. There were no Mexican casualties reported.

U. S. Navy Home Squadron in Action –

The United States Navy undertook both a blockading measure of Mexico's coastline of the Gulf of Mexico and the capture of the coastal cities in an effort to deny commerce from reaching the country. This action began May 14, 1846, under Navy Commodore David Conner in command of the *Home Squadron*. That fall, Commodore Matthew C. Perry replaced Commodore Conner. Commodore Perry decided to further the blockade to the south in the Mexican State of Tabasco. Tabasco would have been a region to receive commerce by ships that could supply central Mexico, especially Mexico City. Perry left the Squadron command site at Anton Lizardo, Vera Cruz, for Tabasco on October 16 with seven ships including his flagship *Mississippi*.

The first stop for the fleet involved the capture of the coastal town of Frontera on October 23. Then Perry sailed up the Tabasco River known today as the Grijalva River. His objective was Tabasco also known as San Juan Bautista arriving the next day. This would become the **First Battle of Tabasco**. The defenders of the city had evacuated allowing occupation without a fight. For reasons unknown, Commodore Perry withdrew his forces that same evening permitting Mexican Lieutenant Colonel Juan B. Traconis to reoccupy the city and its defenses in buildings defying Perry to retake the city. Realizing that any further attempt to capture the city would achieve nothing, Perry sailed back to Frontera, but was attacked at several points along the way resulting in two killed, two wounded, and the drowning of two others. The Mexicans lost five men killed. Commodore Perry established a blockade of the region utilizing the USS *McLane* and USS *Forward* and would return to Tabasco June 16 resulting in a more successful outcome.

USS *Mississippi* (1841) Sidewheel Steamship in the foreground
Wikipedia {{PD-US}}

The U. S. Home Squadron was not done after the First Battle of Tabasco. More action would take place in the *Occupation of Tampico, Tamaulipas*, on November 14, 1846. Tampico is a port city along the Gulf of Mexico in the central portion of the country. A blockade or capture of the city would greatly impact commerce in Mexico. A fleet of ships under the command of Commodore David Conner prepared to attack Tampico November 14, 1846. The USS *Spitfire*, a sidewheel gunboat, was used as the flagship for Commodore Conner supported by at least the USS *Petrel* and USS *Vixen*. With little opposition, Tampico was seized as well as other settlements up the Panuco River. Several artillery pieces were captured and destroyed along with other military stores before returning to the Gulf waters. There would be more naval involvement along the Mexican shores of the Gulf of Mexico as the days of the war progressed.

Back to California et al

The future States of California, Arizona, and New Mexico saw conflicts the same as that in Mexico proper. The *Battle of Natividad* occurred on November 16 in today's Salinas Valley of California that was more a skirmish than a battle. Americans supporting the war effort were in the process of driving horses to the U. S. troops near Los Angles when they were attacked by Mexican partisans killing four of the Americans and wounding others, but did not stop the delivery of horses to the American command of Brevet Lieutenant Colonel John C. Fremont at San Juan Bautista, California.

A more significant episode occurred on December 6 called the *Battle of San Pasqual*. This was rightly called a battle involving around one hundred eighty troops led by Brigadier General Stephen Watts Kearny against slightly less than one hundred Mexican troops commanded by Major Andres Pico. This conflict took place near present-day San Diego. Involved in the battle was Company C, First U. S. Dragoons, of sixty men, Company K of the same command with twelve dragoons, Marine Captain Archibald Gillespie with thirty-nine troops from the California Battalion, and sixty-eight other troops consisting of Topographical Engineers, and staff.

A product of the Mexican War was the California Battalion organized by Commodore Robert F. Stockton July 23, 1846. Brevet Lieutenant Colonel John Charles Freemont was given command and Bvt Major Archibald Gillespie assigned as his second. The California Battalion would play an active role in supporting the U. S. forces in California leading to the *Treaty of Cahuenga* in January 1847 ending hostilities and securing California for the United States.

General Kearny with half his original force of the Army of the West, the other half sent back to Santa Fe, marched to the vicinity of San Diego where he planned to assist with the defense of the city threatened by a small band of Mexican soldiers. Plans to attack the Mexican force during the day of December 6 had to be moved up due to discovery of the plan. During a cold, rainy, early, and dark morning, the American forces began their movement on the Mexican troops, but surprise had been lost. The engagement that followed was anything but what had been planned. Poor communications led to misunderstandings that led to more casualties than should have occurred. The victor of the battle is in question. Some indications point to the withdrawal of Major Pico's forces as a reason to conclude this was an American victory. Comparing the number of casualties and especially those of officers, this could be considered a victory for Major Pico. The U. S. casualties included the death of Captain Abraham Robinson Johnston, commanding Company K, Second Dragoons; Captain Benjamin Daviess Moore in command of Company C, Second Dragoons; and Lieutenant William H. Emory, Corps of Topographical Engineers. In addition, fifteen others were killed and thirteen wounded to include Brigadier General Kearny who received a brevet promotion of major general for his involvement in the battle.

Captain Archibald Gillespie facing Mexican Lancers in the Battle of San Pasqual December 6, 1846
Wikipedia {{PD-US}}

In addition to the conflicts in California, the Mexican State of Sonora in present-day Arizona would see the presence of American troops on December 16, 1846, by none other than the Mormon Battalion led by Lieutenant Colonel Philip St. George Cooke. Tucson was the objective, but not so much for military purposes as it was for trade. The Mexican garrison of some two hundred soldiers under the command of Captain Antonio Comaduron willingly evacuated the post rather than take on the larger Mormon Battalion numbering just under four hundred. This action became known as the **Capture of Tucson** that was taken without opposition from the Mexican forces only to be withdrawn a day or two later and retaken by the previous defenders. No casualties occurred on either side.

Painting of the Mormon Battalion at the Gila River during their trek through Sonora
Wikipedia

As the year 1846 drew to a close, one last engagement would take place called the **Battle of El Brazito** that occurred December 25 at a point nine miles south of present-day Las Cruces, New Mexico. The First Regiment Missouri Mounted Volunteers commanded by Colonel Alexander W. Doniphan was ordered by Brigadier General Stephen Watts Kearney to Chihuahua, Mexico, where they would link up with Brigadier General John E. Wool heading the soon to take place Chihuahuan Expedition. Colonel Doniphan had paused his march in recognition of Christmas Day when a force of the Mexican Army led by General Antonio Ponce de Leon attacked.

The attack was no surprise to the Americans who saw a cloud of dust from the approaching army and prepared defenses. The Mexican Army may have had as many as five hundred soldiers, but they were up against a force just under nine hundred. The battle that ensued was devastating to the Mexicans who may have lost somewhere around fifty killed and three times that number wounded. Colonel Doniphan's forces suffered seven wounded. The number of troops involved and casualties for this battle is subject to question not unlike many that occurred during the war. Suffice it to say that the Mexican Army was decisively defeated in this battle!

The Mexican War in 1847

It did not take long for new battles to take place in 1847. For the year as a whole, there were twenty-six named battles, five sieges, and eleven other actions. January alone saw six battles and February was not far behind at four. Of the six battles in January, three each were in California and New Mexico.

The first battle of the Mexican War in 1847 was the **Battle of Santa Clara** that took place January 2 near present-day San Francisco. This encounter was more a skirmish than a battle resulting from a half dozen men from the *U. S. Sloop Warren* who had gone ashore for supplies and taken hostage by Californios. A rescue party sent to retrieve the men was engaged in brief action that lasted around two hours. In the end, four of the Californios were killed and like number injured. The Americans suffered two wounded.

On January 8, 1847, the back and forth military action for control of Los Angles was on again. On this date, American forces under Brigadier General Stephen Watts Kearny and Commodore Robert F. Stockton began action to retake Los Angles in the **Battle of Rio San Gabriel**. U. S. forces for this action included Company C, First U. S. Dragoons, commanded by a Captain Turner, sailors and marines, one unidentified artillery battery, and California volunteers. The name of the battle comes from the San Gabriel River over which the American forces launched their attack to reach Los Angles. This affair was complicated by the difficult task of crossing the river with artillery, but was successful ending once and for all Mexican control of the region. Before General Kearny and Commodore Stockton could celebrate their victory at Los Angles, there was one more obstacle that needed to be overcome. This was called the **Battle of La Mesa** on January 9 that was a mopping up operation following action of the previous day. The American victory was at a cost of three

American lives and eleven injured for both actions. Mexican losses are unknown but surely occurred. The loss of Los Angles sent Mexican General Jose Maria Flores packing back to Mexico.

The war with Mexico was not fought only in the country of Mexico as known today. Much of the current southwest United States was also Mexican territory. Mexico lost California after the Battle of Rio San Gabriel previously described, but the area of present-day New Mexico was still under control of the Mexican government. To hold this region, Mexican officials enlisted Native American Indians in an attempt to rid Americans from Santa Fe. This effort became known as the Taos Revolt that involved six conflicts spanning January 24 to February 4 and even into May 1847.

Mexican loyalists with the aid of Pueblo Indians planned an attack on Santa Fe that was discovered by Colonel Sterling Price commanding U. S. forces at Santa Fe. Colonel Price with his Second Regiment of Missouri Mounted Volunteers consisting of Companies D, K, L, M, and N; a battalion of Missouri infantry led by Captain Agney; Captain Ceran St. Vrain's Santa Fe Volunteers; and a battery of artillery commanded by Lieutenant Alexander B. Dyer of the Fourth U. S. Artillery intercepted the large enemy force at Santa Cruz de la Canada January 24, 1847, and quickly overwhelmed them. This became the **Battle of Canada**. The report of casualties varies by source, but there could have been as many as one hundred fifty of the Mexican and Indian force killed and perhaps four hundred captured. Those that escaped the carnage fled only to be encountered four days later. Colonel Prices' force may have had seven killed in this battle.

Also part of the Taos Revolt was the **First Battle of Mora** that occurred on the same day as the Battle of Canada, January 24. This episode was not a battle in the true sense of the word, but a military response to kidnapping and murder of eight civilian American businessmen by insurgent Mexicans led by Manuel Cortez of the town of Mora located equal distance to the east of Taos in the north and Santa Fe to the south. Captain Israel R. Hendley commanding a company of the Second Missouri Mounted Volunteers located at Las Vegas, New Mexico, responded to Mora with a force of approximately eighty soldiers. Once at Mora, Hendley was met with as many as two hundred armed rebels who were not going to respond kindly! Gunfire ensued between the two groups and Captain Hendley was struck and killed. The Missouri troops withdrew at this point, but would return a week later and avenge the death of Captain Hendley.

Just as there would be a follow-up episode to the First Battle of Mora, the Battle of Canada would see a second engagement on January 29 called the **Battle of Embudo Pass** that involved Colonel Price's forces against the Mexicans who fled his assault four days earlier. After the Battle of Canada, Colonel Price marched his force north along the Rio Grande River where he was joined by Company A, Second Missouri Mounted Volunteers, and Company G, First U. S. Dragoons. This was a mountainous region near the current town of Dixon. The result of this battle mirrored that of the previous driving the rebels even further into the countryside, but not before killing twenty and wounding around sixty. Colonel Price's losses amounted to one each killed and wounded. Price went on to lay siege to Taos lasting from February 3 and 4 ending with the surrender by Mexican loyalists ending the Taos Revolt at least for the time.

In the meantime, the **Second Battle of Mora** would occur February 1, 1847. This involvement was under the command of Captain Jesse I. Morin who quickly expelled the inhabitants from the village and destroyed all that was standing. The locals that survived fled to the north ending once and for all unrest in the region.

Battle of Buena Vista

The **Battle of Buena Vista** also called the **Battle of Angostura** was a major battle that occurred February 22-23, 1847, near the village of Buena Vista in the Mexican State of Coahuila located in the north central region of the country. This battle pitted an American force of nearly five thousand led by Major General Zachary Taylor against three times that number from the Mexican Army under the command of General Antonio Lopez de Santa Anna.

General Taylor had as his second in command Brigadier General John Ellis Wool who had previously commanded the Chihuahuan Expedition that was responsible for the capture of Saltillo. The entire American force included units of the First and Second U. S. Dragoons, Companies C and E from the Third U. S. Artillery, Company B of the Fourth U. S. Artillery, First and Second Regiments of Illinois Volunteers, Second and Third Regiments of Indiana Volunteers, Second Regiment Kentucky Volunteers, First Regiment Mississippi Riflemen, Regiment of Arkansas Mounted Volunteers, and Regiment of Kentucky Cavalry.

Mexican General Santa Anna's plan was to send waves of his army at the Americans overwhelming them by sheer numbers. This might have worked except for the fact that the site on which the battle was to take place was selected by General Wool providing a distinct advantage to the American defenders. Santa Anna might have also overlooked the ability of the U. S. command to shift military assets that became apparent once aggression commenced. The use of artillery and Dragoons also played a large part in suppressing the overwhelming number of Mexican soldiers.

The first day of the battle ended with no change in the disposition for either side. Day two saw little difference from the day before and ended with a heavy rain. No action took place on February 25 except the withdrawal of the Mexican Army ending the Battle of Buena Vista in essentially a draw. Although the battle had ended, the casualty count was staggering. Reports indicate that 591 Mexican soldiers were killed, 1,048 wounded, and nearly 2,000 missing. American losses show 267 killed, 387 wounded, and six missing. Senior American officers killed in the battle were Colonel John J. Hardin commanding the First Illinois Volunteers, Colonel William R. McKee and Lieutenant Colonel Henry Clay Jr. both of the Second Kentucky Volunteers, and Colonel Archibald Yell of the Arkansas Mounted Volunteers. All toll, there were twenty-eight officers killed in the two-day battle.

Major General Zachary Taylor surveying the battlefield during the Battle of Buena Vista.

Library of Congress, Prints & Photographs Division, LC-USZ62-6222

Gallant Charge of the Kentucky Cavalry under Colonel Humphrey Marshall during the Battle of Buena Vista.

Library of Congress, Prints & Photographs Division, LC-USZ62-62230

Prior to the Battle of Buena Vista, Colonel Alexander William Doniphan commanding the First Regiment Missouri Mounted Volunteers led a force of over 1,000 men south from El Paso to Chihuahua, Mexico, on February 8 in anticipation of linking up with Brigadier John Ellis Wool perhaps unaware that General Wool had orders that would involve him elsewhere. Instead, Colonel Doniphan would find himself facing a Mexican Army four times his number approximately fifteen miles north of Chihuahua in what would become the **Battle of the Sacramento River** named for the nearby river.

This battle took place February 28, 1847, and once again proved the superiority of the American forces. With the use of economy of force and precision artillery fire the Americans delivered deadly fire on the enemy resulting in at least 300 killed, a like number wounded, and forty or so captured. In contrast, Colonel Doniphan's command lost one man killed and eight wounded. The Mexican force withdrew from the area and Chihuahua was occupied by the American troops two days later. From here, Colonel Doniphan and his troops marched toward Saltillo south of Monterrey.

Scene of the Mexican lancers charge during the Battle of the Sacramento River, January 28, 1847
Library of Congress, Prints & Photographs Division, LC-USZ62-5222

The Siege of Vera Cruz

The land battles in the north of Mexico shifted in early March to a naval **Siege of Vera Cruz** far to the south along the waters of the Gulf of Mexico. The purpose of this action was to pave a route to Mexico City. The Siege of Vera Cruz would be followed by five major battles and a number of smaller engagements eventually leading to the conclusion of the war.

A new player in the war against Mexico was Major General Winfield Scott a seasoned officer who had seen active service in the War of 1812, Indians Wars, as well as other key assignments. General Scott assembled a force of nearly 14,000 and a naval armada of no less than seven gunboats under the command of Commodore David Conner and Matthew Calbraith Perry and at least seven smaller ships identified as the Mosquito Fleet commanded by

Commodore Josiah Tattnall. General Scott arranged his ground forces into three divisions with two brigades each in the first two and three brigades in the third. The First Division was made up of the Fifth, Sixth, and Eighth U. S. Infantry Regiments as well as the Second and Third U. S. Artillery. The Second Division saw the Second, Third, Fourth, and Seventh U. S. Infantry Regiments, U. S. Mounted Riflemen, and First U. S. Artillery. The Third Division consisted of volunteers commands of the Second New York Volunteers, South Carolina Palmetto Regiment, First and Second Tennessee Volunteers, First and Second Pennsylvania Volunteers, and Third and Fourth Illinois Volunteers. General Scott further established a separate command of Dragoons that included the First, Second, and Third U. S. Dragoons.

This large American force was assembled in late February 1847 and sailed for Vera Cruz March 2 arriving near the shores of the fortified city on March 9. Brigadier General Juan Esteban Morales defended Vera Cruz with slightly more than 3,000 soldiers. General Scott had no intention of an all out assault on the city, but planned a siege instead that would last to March 29 at which time a surrender was achieved not by General Morales but his second General Jose Juan Landero. The surrender was preceded by artillery fire causing severe damage to the fortified complex prompting the final outcome. Due to the campaign as a twenty-day siege, casualties were considered light on both sides although they did occur. On the American side thirteen were killed and fifty-five wounded. The Mexicans obviously suffered more due to the bombardment resulting in at least eight killed and perhaps many more along with some fifty wounded. In addition, there were civilian casualties whose numbers can only be speculated.

The "Mosquito Fleet" taking action off Vera Cruz
The ship in order left to right are the *Falcon, Reefer, Vixen, Petrel, Bonita, Spitfire*, and *Tampico*
Library of Congress, Prints & Photographs Division, LC-USZ62-132

Landing American troops at Vera Cruz March 9, 1847, in preparation for a siege of the city.
Library of Congress, Prints & Photographs division, LC-USZ62-14216

Battle of Cerro Gordo

The surrender of the Mexican forces at Vera Cruz offered Major General Scott the opportunity to begin his march toward Mexico City that he began April 2. In his way would be Mexican President and General Santa Anna who had assembled an army of some 12,000. The two armies would meet near the mountain pass of Cerro Gordo on the eastern slope of the Sierra Madre Oriental Mountain range where Santa Anna had established strong defenses around the foothills. This would become the first of six major battles known appropriately as the **Battle of Cerro Gordo**.

In spite of strong defensive positions and an army numbering 4,000 over that of the Americans, the battle would go to the Americans who used a flanking maneuver to destroy the enemy. The American forces reached the vicinity of Cerro Gordo on April 12. Through the expertise of the U. S. Army Corps of Engineers it was determined that the Mexican defenses could be flanked thereby lessening the chance of a catastrophic calamity. After assessing the plan, Major General David E. Twiggs in command of the Second Division led his force striking the Mexican defenders on April 18 who were quickly overrun resulting in many killed and captured. Again depending on the source, the number of American casualties may be about sixty-three killed and 367 wounded. Mexican losses were over 1,200 killed and wounded and over 3,000 captured. Most of the captured were paroled shortly after the battle with assurances they would not engage in further conflicts if there could be any belief that would happen!

Scene at the Battle of Cerro Gordo, April 18, 1847
Wikipedia (USPD – chg B&W)

"Colonel Harney's brilliant charge at the Battle of Cerro Gordo
Colonel William Shelby Harney commanded the Second U. S. Dragoons
Library of Congress, Prints & Photographs Division, LC-USZ62- 62226

With victory in hand, Major General Scott marched his troops on to Jalapa where he halted awaiting a resupply of materials and reinforcement before continuing his march to Mexico City. Along the Gulf coast the Navy Home Squadron under Commodore Matthew C. Perry continued blockading operations against the various Mexican ports along the Gulf of Mexico. On April 18 the village of Tuxpan, Mexico was the focus of the blockading action identified as the **First Battle of Tuxpan** that was anything but a battle. It was in fact more of an incursion or show of force although the Americans did suffer two killed and nineteen wounded in the effort. The town of Tuxpan was seized and at least two ships were left to block the Tuxpan River from future use, but this would not end the involvement of Tuxpan..

The first Battle of Tuxpan was followed by a **Second Battle** some time in early June and a **Third Battle** June 30. Both of these conflicts were caused by trouble with the local militia attempting to dislodge the American blockade force from their shores. The second battle resulted in the death of one sailor and the wounding of six others. The third battle was much the same with two Americans killed and five wounded. Mexican losses for all three battles are unknown.

Much of the war effort in the first half of 1847 involved the south central region of Mexico, but that did not mean that other areas were void of conflict. The Taos Revolt that was supposed to have ended in February once again reared its head on May 26, 1847, in the region of present-day New Mexico. The **Red River Canyon Affair** also called the **Battle of the Red River Canyon** involved American forces against Mexican militia supported by Apache, Kiowa, and Comanche Indians. The American Military force was commanded by Major Benjamin B. Edmundson (Edmonson) assigned to the Second Regiment Missouri Mounted Volunteers.

History has not been helpful in the description of the men who were involved in this battle. Several of the names have been misspelled and the commander is listed as a United States Army officer when he was assigned as noted to the Second Regiment Missouri Mounted Volunteers. Major Edmundson's name is also shown in other records as Edmunson. Another officer is identified as Captain Holaway who is actually Captain John Holloway in command of Company C of the same command as Major Edmundson. In fact, all the men involved in this episode were assigned to one of the Missouri Volunteer commands.

The battle description may be more accurate than the previous information. Major Edmundson with his force of combined cavalry and infantry entered a canyon identified as the Red River that was actually the Canadian River of that time and today. Due to the terrain, the cavalry force dismounted and all two hundred soldiers were on foot when they were attacked by approximately five hundred of the enemy. The engagement when back and forth for a time before the Americans managed an organized retreat on that first day. The next day the Americans moved forward to find the enemy had withdrawn from the canyon ending the conflict. Two more Taos Revolt connections would take place in July before this affair would finally end.

The war effort shifted again to the south along the Mexican coast along the Gulf of Mexico. Here on June 15, 1847, Commodore Matthew C. Perry and his Mosquito Fleet of the Home Squadron were involved in the **Second Battle of Tabasco** also called the **Battle of Villahermosa**. The First Battle of Tabasco occurred the year before October 24-26, 1846. Perry had received word that the Mexicans had beefed up defenses of the city of San Juan Baustista, current Villahermosa, and constructed obstructions on the Tabasco River that is known as the Grijalva River today.

Commodore Perry had at his disposal eight ships, slightly more than 1,000 Marines, and seven artillery pieces. His opposition was about six hundred soldiers under the command of Mexican Colonel Domingo Echagaray.

On June 14, the U. S. forces began their movement up the Tabasco River keeping a watchful eye for obstructions that might cause delays and subject the force to hostile gunfire.

Sporadic enemy attacks did occur on the Americans, but the ships moved up the river with only slight occurrences. The fleet reached their objective on June 16, captured the city, and sent the defenders fleeing inland. This action virtually ended Mexican's use of coastal ports along the Gulf of Mexico for resupply.

Commodore Perry landing his forces in the Second Battle of Tabasco, June 16, 1847
Library of Congress, Prints & Photographs Division, LC-USZ62-66

The Mexican militia forces to the north were not through with their interruption in the region against the American forces of the New Mexico Campaign. Two conflicts would take place in the first weeks of July 1847. The first was the **Battle of Las Vegas** (New Mexico) on July 6 and the second was the **Battle of Cienega Creek** three days later on July 9 near Taos. Both of these affairs are part of the Taos Revolt that would finally come to an end.

The Las Vegas Affair resulted from an earlier incident involving Mexicans who had stolen horses belonging to Captain Thomas M. Horine's cavalry command of the Second Regiment Missouri Mounted Volunteers. In an

effort to retrieve the horses, three men were sent out but never returned. It was thought they had been killed and was confirmed by a local woman. Major Edmundson organized a party of about sixty men to find and punish those who were responsible for the killing of his men. This military force marched to Las Vegas arriving on July 6 where they were met by armed hostiles who took up the fight. The Americans quickly charged and overwhelmed their enemy forcing them to flee into the countryside. Some ten Mexicans were killed and about fifty captured. After burning some of the buildings, the Americans returned to their former position with their prisoners who were tried for their crimes and some six hanged. In all this, the Americans suffered only three slightly wounded.

The Mexican Militia would have one last gasp against their American rivals. On July 9, a detachment of thirty-one men from Captain Jesse I. Morin's Battalion of Missouri Mounted Volunteers was attacked by approximately 200 Mexican Militia at a point some miles south of Taos, New Mexico. At first overwhelmed, the American detachment was able to regroup and seek cover along a bank of the Cienega Creek giving way to the name of the battle. From here they were able to inflict major casualties on their enemy and were eventually relieved by the appearance of Captain Samuel Shepherd's Company from the same command as that of Captain Morin's. The Americans suffered five killed and nine wounded almost all in the first attack. Mexican losses are unknown.

Battle of Contreas

With the Taos Revolt put down, the focus of the Mexican War shifted once again back to Major Winfield Scott's effort toward Mexico City. Over a period from August 7 to September 15, five battles would occur culminating in the capture of Mexico City. Mexico City lies in a bowl shaped valley surrounded by mountains making access by ground a special challenge. General Scott planned his approach carefully following a southern route starting near Contreras, a city south of Mexico City proper. The Americans had marched from Puebla, Mexico, in the east August 7 with a force in excess of ten thousand men. They approached Mexico City from the south then turned north by way of Contreras to Churubusco, Molino del Ray, and finally Chapultepec before reaching Mexico City. Each of these places resulted in a named battle. The **Battle of Contreras** also known as the **Battle of Padierna** would be the first to occur fought August 19-20, 1847.

It is safe to say that the Order of Battle was much the same for all four battles that preceded the capture of Mexico City. That Order of Battle consisted of four numbered divisions and the U. S. Dragoons. Major General William J. Worth commanded the First Division consisting of the First Brigade under Brevet Brigadier General John Garland. General Garland's force included the Fourth Infantry and the Second and Third Artillery. Brevet Brigadier General Newman S. Clarke was in charge of the Second Brigade. He had at his disposal the Fifth, Sixth, and Seventh U. S. Infantry Regiments.

Major General David E. Twiggs commanded the Second Division with Brevet Brigadier General Persifor F. Smith as the First Brigade commander and Brevet Brigadier General Bennet Riley the Second Brigade. The First Brigade included the U. S. Mounted Rifles, Third U. S. Infantry, and Captain Francis Taylor's Battery from the First U. S. Artillery. The Second Brigade was the Second and Seventh U. S. Infantry Regiments and Fourth U. S. Artillery. Major General Gideon Pillow was in charge of the Third Division supported by Brigadier General Franklin Peirce's First Brigade, and Brigadier General George Cadwallader in the Second. The Ninth, Twelfth, and Fifteenth U. S. Infantry Regiments along with Captain John B. Magruder's Battery from the First U. S. Artillery were assigned to the First Brigade. The Second Brigade saw the Eleventh and Fourteenth U. S. Infantry Regiments and a new organization just for the Mexican War, a Regiment of Voltigeurs and Foot Riflemen. The term voltigeurs comes from the French language that means leap. Soldiers assigned as Voltigeurs were supposed to be able to mount their horses with one leap.

The Fourth Division consisted primarily of Volunteers units whose mission was somewhat different from the previous three. Major General John A. Quitman commanded this division. Brigadier General James Shield was in charge of the First Brigade consisting of the Second Regiment New York Infantry, Second Regiment Pennsylvania Infantry, South Carolina Palmetto Infantry, and Captain Edward J. Steptoe's Battery from the Third U. S. Artillery. Lieutenant Colonel Samuel E. Watson commanded the Marine Brigade whose task was that of storming parties. The Dragoons were not assigned to a division and acted independently as needed. Brevet Brigadier General William S. Harney was charged with control over the First, Second, and Third U. S. Dragoons. Whether all these organizations were involved in each of the five battles is speculation, but they were available and could easily have been used!

General Scott's route crossed between Lake Chalco and Lake Xochimilco on a path toward San Agustin approximately twelve miles to the west. This route would take him just south of the Pedregal lava field that he would exploit to the surprise of the Mexican Army of the North commander, General Gabriel Valencia. Scott ordered Captain Robert E. Lee to build a road across the lava field in order to strike the enemy where least expected. This action enabled all the American forces to attack Contreras from all sides although it would take two days to complete the endeavor.

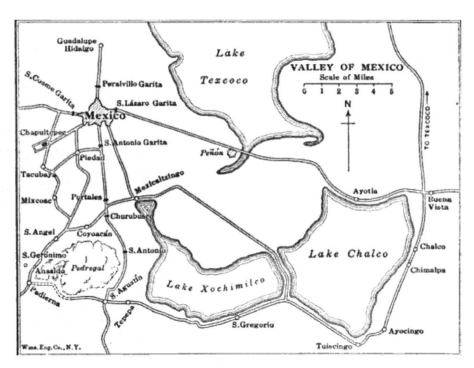

Map of the battle area south of Mexico City August 7 – September 15, 1847
Wikipedia

The Battle of Contreras was another victory for the Americans. There were, of course, casualties on both sides, but the original 7,000 or so Mexicans troops suffered major losses. By all counts, the Americans loss around sixty to three hundred killed or wounded, but the Mexicans estimates show 700 killed, 1,225 wounded, and 843 captured if these numbers are accurate. Mexican Gabriel Valencia withdrew his troops to San Angles and perhaps all the way to where the next battle would occur.

Battle of Churubusco

Only a day had passed when General Scott's army caught up with the Mexicans at Churubusco. Churubusco was on a direct line only five miles south of Mexico City. Defending Churubusco was none other than General Antonio Lopez de Santa Anna himself along with Major General Nicolas Bravo commanding the Army of the Center who was ordered to retreat from San Antonia about two miles south of Churubusco. This army numbered just short of 4,000 about half the size of the American force. Again, the Mexicans were no match for the determined and well disciplined Americans. Churubusco would fall that same day, but it was a pitched battle with the loss of many lives. The Americans suffered 133 killed and 865 wounded. The Mexicans on the other hand had 263 killed, 460 wounded, and 1.831 captured. Among the captured were three generals.

Scene depicting the Battle of Churubusco, August 20, 1847
Library of Congress, Prints & Photographs Division, LC-USZ62-41347

Major General Winfield Scott was close to the "gates" of Mexico City, but chose not to pursue further at the moment. Instead, he used this time to resupply and rest his troops, treat the wounded, and make preparations for what was to come next. After all, it had been a month since the army marched from Puebla and much had taken place in that timeframe! If surrender could be achieved from Mexican President and General Santa Anna, it would prevent further loss of life, but that was not about to happen!

Battle of Molino del Rey

It had been almost three weeks since the Battle of Churubusco and Major General Scott was ready for the next step in his conquest of Mexico City. Before that could happen two more hurdles lay in the pathway. The **Battle of Molino del Rey** was fought on September 8 on the outskirts of Mexico City between nearly all of General Scot's available forces and half that number of the Mexican Army. Some refer to this battle as the bloodiest of the war, but there were and would be other battles of equal proportion!

The purpose of this battle was to destroy what was believed to be a foundry for making cannons near an area called Molino del Rey (King's Hill) that was a collection of buildings used as mills for making flour and gunpowder. Also nearby was the earthen fort Casa de Mata and the hilltop fortified castle Chapultepec where a military academy was located. All three of these sites were within two miles or so of the capital of Mexico, Mexico City. The Mexican Army had their backs to the gates of their capital city and were ready for whatever was thrown at them. Not to be outdone, the Americans were ripe for a final assault on that city!

Major General Winfield Scott ordered a frontal assault on Molino del Rey using his infantry, artillery, and "Storming Parties." The Mexican troops were well entrenched and using their own artillery caused initial casualties to the Americans. As in previous battles, any Mexican advantage was soon overcome. After the initial impact of the battle, General Scott sent additional forces that tipped the balance in favor of the attackers. After nearly six hours of fighting, the Americans achieved their objective at a heavy cost. As many as 116 American soldiers were killed, nearly 700 wounded, and eighteen missing. By comparison, Mexican losses numbered 269 killed, approximately 500 wounded, and 685 captured. The next battle would see similar statistics.

Scene of the Battle of Molino del Rey, September 8, 1847
Library of Congress, Prints & Photographs Division, LC- USZ62-62215

Battle of Chapultepec

It would take one last battle to reach Mexico City and that would not be any easier than the last. This would be the **Battle of Chapultepec** on September 12-13, 1847. Chapultepec was a castle situated atop a high hill overlooking Mexico City. At the time of the Mexican War, the castle served as a military academy with around one hundred cadets ranging in age from thirteen to nineteen. The castle offered a commanding view of the city meaning that it could easily defend with its artillery of which there was sufficient. The elevation of Mexico City is listed as 7,380 feet and Chapultepec sits at 7,628 feet giving it a height of 248 feet higher than the city. If the Americans were going to capture Mexico City, Chapultepec would need to be taken first.

The terrain around the castle varied from a gentle slope on the west, moderate slope on the south, to steep slopes on both the east and north. The attack on Chapultepec would involve two "Storming Parties" using the west and south approaches to the objective. Captain Samuel Mackenzie, Second U. S. Artillery, formed the assault from the west and Major Levi Twiggs of the U. S. Marines from the south. The attack began at first light on Sunday morning August 12 with an artillery bombardment that continued throughout the daylight hours pausing overnight and resumed briefly the next morning for a few hours. At that time the ground assault commenced. Major General Gideon Pillow's Third Division led the attack from the west dividing his forces into three columns. When that stalled, Major General John A. Quitman's Fourth Division came into action. Within an hour from the start of the battle, the American flag was displayed over the castle. The gates of Mexico City were within reach of General Scott.

Scene of the "storming" of Chapultepec September 13, 1847
Library of Congress, Prints & Photographs Division, LC-USZ62- 129

None of the four battles leading to the capture of Mexico City were easy. The Battle of Chapultepec cost the lives of 130 Americans and wounding of slightly over 700. Two notable Americans killed in the battle were Colonel Truman B. Ransom commanding the Ninth U. S. Infantry and Marine Major Levi Twiggs who was mortally wounded leading one of the storming parties. Mexican losses were nearly 700 killed, around 200 wounded, and an equal number captured.

American troops on the assault during the Battle of Chapultepec, September 13, 1847
Library of Congress, Prints & Photographs Division, LC-USZ62-62209

Capture of Mexico City

Mexico City was protected with no less than seven gates into the city. Major General William J. Worth's First Division would attack the Belen Gate on the west side of the city and Major General John A. Quitman's Fourth Division took the San Cosme Gate south of the Belen Gate also on the west side. Mexican units defended various other gates such as the San Antonio, Nino Peridio, San Luzaro, Guadalupe, and Villejo were defended by various , but whether these gates were attacked is uncertain. As Generals Worth and Quitman breeched their respective gates late in the afternoon of September 14, General Santa Anna and what remained of his Mexican Army took refuge in the Ciudadela (citadel) that was a complex of factory buildings that could be defended much like a fort. Here they remained to the early morning hours of Wednesday, September 15 at which time all the Mexican troops that were able withdrew to the nearby Villa de Guadalupe Hidalgo that would be the site of the eventual treaty ending the war.

Although the Mexican Army had vacated the capital city, danger still loomed. When Santa Anna led his troops out of the city, he turned loose thousand of prisoners who brought sniper fire upon the American troops entering the city. Once this was under control, Major General Quitman marched into the city center to find all the Mexican forces had withdrawn. Soon after, city officials surrendered the city!

One person who played a vital role in the capture of Mexico City was Lieutenant Ulysses S. Grant who positioned a canon in a church belfry that brought effective fire on the Mexican defenders. Of course, Lieutenant Grant would become the General-in-Chief of the Union Army during the American Civil War not unlike many junior officers in the Mexican War who would become generals in the Civil War.

Lieutenant Ulysses S. Grant directing artillery fire during the Capture of Mexico city
Library of Congress, Prints & Photographs Division, LC-USZ62- 3911

Siege of Puebla City

Prior to the fall of Mexico City, Mexican General Joaquin Rea with 4,000 troops had been sent to Puebla City for the purpose of ending American occupation of the city and to cut supply lines supporting General Scott. At the time General Scott marched toward Mexico City on August 7, Brevet Colonel Thomas Childs, First U. S. Artillery, with 500 soldiers was left at Puebla City to protect the supply lines for the army coming from Vera Cruz. Puebla City also doubled as the site of a hospital for the sick and wounded of the American forces.

Late in the evening on September 13, Mexican General Rea entered Puebla City with his large force and was met with stiff resistance that began the **Siege of Puebla City** that would last one day short of a month. The Americans occupied three defensive positions within the city, the Convent, Fort Loreto, and the citadel of San Jose, and held off all attempts to retake the city. The citadel under the command of Lieutenant Colonel Samuel W. Black, First Pennsylvania Infantry, also served as the hospital for the soldiers. General Rea's attempt to get Colonel Childs to surrender and frequent assaults on the three defensive positions proved the Americans were not about to give up anytime soon!.

After the capture of Mexico City, Antonio Lopez de Santa Anna resigned his presidency retaining his general rank and marched his remaining army to Puebla City September 22 in an effort to force the surrender of the American forces. Again Colonel Childs defied a surrender request and the siege continued. Perhaps aware that an American relief force was preparing to march from Santa Cruz to Puebla City, General Santa Anna departed the city with most of the Mexican troops to meet the Americans head on. This would result in another battle to follow that would end the Siege of Puebla City on October 12, 1847.

Battle of Huamantla

Aware that Brevet Colonel Thomas Childs was under siege at Puebla City, Brigadier General Joseph Lane, Second Regiment Indiana Volunteers, organized a force of 2,700 men and marched to relieve Puebla. General Lane had at his disposal the Fourth Indiana Volunteer Infantry, First Pennsylvania Volunteer Infantry, four companies from the Ninth U. S. Infantry, six companies from the Second U. S. Infantry, a Mounted Detachment consisting of four cavalry companies one each from Texas and Georgia and two from Louisiana, and finally an artillery battalion. The supply train accompanying the force was under the guidance of the Fourth Ohio Volunteer Infantry, Seventh U. S. Infantry detachment, and Pratt's Battery from the Second U. S. Artillery.

Before reaching the site of the siege, the Americans received word that the Mexican troops were at Huamantle, a small village approximately thirty-five miles east of Puebla. General Lane attacked General Santa Anna's force of some 2,000 on October 9 leading with the four cavalry companies and sent the enemy fleeing to Queretaro over one hundred thirty miles northwest of Mexico City. Three days later, Brigadier General Lane marched his relief force into Puebla ending the siege.

Brigadier General Lane was not finished with action against his opposition. On October 19, 1847, General Lane routed Mexican General Joaquin Rea and his Light Corps in the **Atlixco Affair** some fifteen miles from Puebla. American casualties numbered one killed and two wounded. Mexican losses as usual were substantially higher with 219 killed and 300 wounded.

After this last battle, the war should have come to an end. Battle after battle resulted in victories for the American forces regardless of who was in command. Yet the beleaguered Mexican Army simply withdrew from the battlefield to fight another day. This in spite of major losses in killed, wounded, missing and captured. One thing that was clear, the conflicts that were yet to come involved smaller number of combatants resulting in smaller casualty counts.

The Pacific Coast Campaign

Along the Pacific coast there were several engagements involving the U. S. Navy and Marines stretching from the Baja California Sur to the coastline of the mainland. One of these was the **Battle of Mulege** fought October 2, 1847. This battle was a rare victory for Mexico if in fact it was even a battle at all! Another encounter occurred October 20 that involved the threat of **Bombardment of Guaymas** by U. S. Naval forces resulting in the evacuation of the Mexican garrison and U. S. control of the town thereafter. Another engagement took place October 31 near Mulege, Baja California Sur. This was a **Bombardment of Punta Sombrero** resulting from an attack on the USS *Libertad*. Other than flexing their muscles, neither side achieved much to boast about.

November 11 saw a large Pacific Squadron landing force **Occupy Mazatlan** without firing a shot.

A conflict of larger proportions involving the Pacific Squadron occurred November 16-17 in the **Battle of La Paz** near the tip of the Baja California Sur. The American garrison occupying La Paz came under attack by a force of some two hundred local militia. The engagement raged for several hours before ending for the day only to resume the next. In the end, the Americans held La Paz losing one man killed while inflicting six killed on the militia. Three days later on November 20 a small detachment of sailors, Marines, and twelve men from California who occupied San Jose del Cabo at the tip of Baja California Sur came under attack by approximately one hundred-fifty Mexican militia. This engagement that involved mostly cannon fire is appropriately called the **Battle of San Jose del Cabo** that began late in the day and through the night ending the morning of November 20 only to pickup again the follow evening without success. San Jose del Cabo remained in the hands of the Americans.

The End of the War

For much of October 1847 to February 1848, Mexican Captain Manuel Pineda Munoz engaged the American forces of the Pacific Squadron as they occupied sites along the Pacific coast. Each of Captain Munoz's efforts fell short of achieving much of anything, but try he did! Elsewhere in Mexico conflicts were nearly silent that would lead to peace negotiations and the signing of the **Treaty of Guadalupe Hidalgo** on February 2, 1848. This signing led to a **Truce on March 6, 1848**, that officially ended hostilities between Mexico and the United States, but did not stop all fighting especially when word failed to reach some troops in the field. A peace treaty had been signed, but ratification needed to take place to make things final. On May 30, 1848, the United States Senate ratified the treaty by a vote of 38-14.

Terms of the treaty gave the United States all of Texas and California, half of New Mexico, most of Arizona, Nevada, and Utah, and parts of Colorado and Wyoming. The United States agreed to pay Mexico $15 million perhaps for the land and offered citizenship to all Mexicans who resided in the territories now under control of the U. S. if they so desired. Most Mexicans accepted U. S. citizenship. A subsequent agreement known as the Gadsden Purchase of 1853 gave the last remaining lands of New Mexico and Arizona to the Unites States. The border of the United States with Mexico was complete!

Summary

The Mexican war began April 1846 and with battle after battle it seemed to drag on forever. Yet it was largely over after the capture of Mexico City in September 1847 though there were minor conflicts that raged on especially along the Pacific coast. Even after the signing of the Treaty of Guadalupe Hidalgo there were episodes by those who were dissatisfied by the outcome of the treaty. Antonio Lopez de Santa Anna went into self-imposed exile in Jamaica, then to Columbia, before returning to Mexico at the urging of the conservatives and church clergy to once again become President of Mexico. His tenure did not last and exile was again his way out.

The American military forces during this war proved beyond a doubt they were a force capable of achieving great success. Many junior officers would prove their worthiness and become senior commanders in wars to come especially the American Civil War. Of course, we can't forget those who paid the ultimate price with their lives in this war and those who suffered debilitating wounds that result from war.

[1] The Center for Military History, CMH Pub 73-1, PIN: 081783-000,- Gateway South, The Campaign for Monterrey

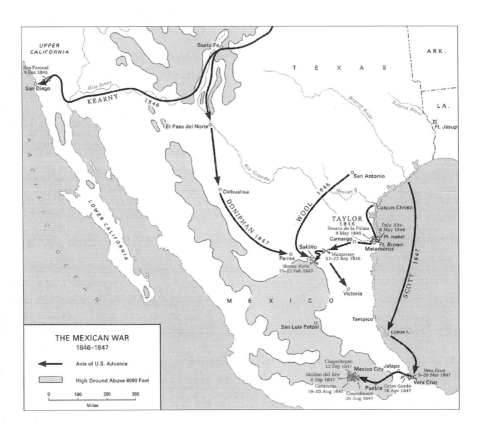

Map of the Mexican War 1846-1847
U. S. Army Center for Military History

American Civil War

A **War** that nearly tore this country apart was the American Civil War (ACW) fought over two underlying ideologies that separated the northern States from their southern counterparts! Many individuals will think and say that slavery was the main cause of the American Civil War that is only partially correct. What many disregard is the issue of States' Rights that was as much a concern for some in the 1860's as it is today! There is even a third cause for this war although it receives very little attention! This was the election of President Abraham Lincoln, a Republican, who was despised by the Democrat controlled southern States and vowed to defy his election. This may sound familiar to today's happenings except that most of the States that seceded from the Union in 1860-61 are now held by Republicans, and many of the northern States are the opposite!

The growth of the United States in the 1830's through the 1850's was in the northern and mostly industrial States while the southern States remained agrarian. The Northern States had more than the South in every category. The population and infrastructure was three times greater, industry was five times greater, and wealth was a staggering five to one in favor of the north. A larger population in one part of the country resulted in greater Congressional Representation in Washington, D. C. That representation would favor the ideology of the people it served resulting in the same issues of excessive control by Washington insiders as we face these days. The State of South Carolina was primarily an agrarian region that was impacted by the lack of States' Right more than any other Southern State causing them to withdraw from the Union as early as December 20, 1860. Georgia was in much the same state

of affairs as South Carolina, but did not have the political stalwarts to take up its case until after South Carolina raised the issue.

It is true that slavery was a factor in the cause of the American Civil War, and one by one slave states whether concerned with States' Rights or not would fall in line behind South Carolina in seceding from the Union. Mississippi was the first to follow South Carolina on January 9, 1861. The procession of States that followed was Florida January 10, Alabama January 11, Georgia January 19, Louisiana January 26, Texas February 1, Virginia April 17, Arkansas May 6, Tennessee May 6, and North Carolina May 20. Two States, Missouri and Kentucky, never withdrew from the Union, but had elements of their governments that proclaimed secession. Missouri's date is October 28 and Kentucky November 18. The Confederate Stars and Bars flag displays thirteen stars for the eleven seceded States and one each for Missouri and Kentucky.

The conflicts that raged during the American Civil War are numerous! It is almost impossible to document every event that involved combatants or at least it would take a monumental undertaking to cover each and every one. The focus of this endeavor will focus on the major campaigns and subsequent battles that mark our history. There is much written about the American Civil War and this author is no exception. However, the effort here is not to embellish each aspect, but to give the reader a worthwhile glimpse into the military history of the United States during the ACW showing how it has impacted our past as well as our future!

At the start of the ACW, the Regular United States Army consisted of approximately 16,000 troops of all ranks. There were ten infantry regiments, four artillery, two cavalry, two dragoons, and three mounted infantry. The majority of these organizations were on duty in the Western States and Territories manning the various forts and posts providing support for settlers, miners, and any other group or individual seeking a new life in the frontier regions at the risk of Indian attacks. This meant long, arduous, and dangerous duty for the soldiers often times without many of the comforts of life.

As the winds of war began to blow, a good number of Federal officers resigned their commissions and threw their support for the Confederate cause. This loss of officer corps would make a dent into the command structure, but those gaps would soon be filled by younger and eager replacements. Within days of the Confederate bombardment of Fort Sumter, South Carolina, April 12. 1861, President Abraham Lincoln called upon the States for 75,000 troops to bolster the Union Army and provide protection for the Capital of the nation, Washington, D. C. One by one, new organizations of volunteers of all types (infantry, artillery, cavalry) were established and there was a flurry of recruitment to fill up the ranks. Once organized, troops began to arrive in Washington by whatever means available. Some organizations were well equipped and dressed in full military uniforms. Others were not so lucky and might have joined an organization carrying their personal weapon for the lack thereof. A second call was issued by the President on May 4, 1861, for the establishment of nine new Regular Army regiments of three battalions with eight companies each that was two less than the previous ten in earlier organizations. These nine regiments would be organized over time with the Eleventh Regiment the first to come into existence on May 4, 1861.

While the Union organizations were being formed, the same situation of volunteer troops was duplicated by the fledging Confederacy that had no army of any sort at the beginning of the war. With much the same zeal as their counterparts in the North, Confederate organizations found no difficulty in filling their ranks with volunteers. By the time of the first battle in the war, ten of the original eleven seceded States had organizations ready to fight. Only Florida lacked participation in the First Battle of Bull Run on July 21, 1861, although individuals from Florida did serve. One stark difference from the Union Army to that of the Confederate Army was that the latter was made up almost exclusively of volunteer units. Regular Confederate Army units rarely existed although the term "Regular" was used even if they consisted of units from a State.

There were actually twenty-six named Confederate organizations established during the war. Of that number there were twelve Cavalry, nine of which were formed from State units. Nine Infantry organizations were formed all from consolidation of State units, and five Engineer units were organized consisting of individual recruits from the various seceded States serving primarily in regions where they were organized. Only two of the Confederate organizations were formed in 1861 while the majority was established in 1862 and 1863.

Major Campaigns of the American Civil War

1861

*Battle of Fort Sumter – Apr 12, 1861
*Manassas Campaign (First Bull Run) – Jul 21
*Battle of Wilson Creek – Aug 10,11861

1862

*Burnside's North Carolina Expedition - Feb-Jun 1862
*Sibley's New Mexico Campaign - Feb-Mar 1862
*Federal Incursion up the Cumberland and Tennessee Rivers- Feb-Jun 1862
  [Fort Henry Feb 6] [Fort Donelson Feb 11-16] [Shiloh Apr 6-7] [Corinth Apr 29 to Jun 10]
*Pea Ridge Campaign - Mar 1862
*Valley Campaign - Mar-Jun 1862
  [Kernstown Mar 23] [McDowell May 8] [Front Royal May 23] [Winchester May 25] [Cross Keys Jun 8] [Port Republic Jun 9]
*Peninsula Campaign - Mar-Sep 1862
  [Battle of Yorktown Apr 5 - May 4] [Williamsburg (Fort Magruder) May 5] [Eltham's Landing May 7] [Drewry's Bluff (Fort Darling) May 15] [Hanover Court House (Slash Church) May 27] [Seven Pines/Fair Oaks May 31-June 1] [Seven Days Jun 25 – Jul 1]
*Northern Virginia Campaign - Aug 1862
  [Cedar Mountain Aug 9] [Second Bull Run Aug 28-30] [Chantilly Sep 1]
*Maryland Campaign - Sep 1862 [Antietam Sep 4-20]
*Fredericksburg Campaign - Nov-Dec 1862

1863

*Vicksburg Campaign - Dec 26 1862 – Jul 4 1863
  [Chickasaw Bayou Dec 26-29] [Arkansas Post Jan 9-11] [Grant's Bayou Operations Jan-Mar, 1863] [Grand Gulf Apr 29] [Snyder's Bluff Apr 29-May 1] [Port Gibson May 1] [Raymond May 12] [Jackson May 14] [Champion Hill may 16] [Big Black River Bridge May 17] [Siege of Vicksburg May 18-Jul 4]
*Chancellorsville Campaign – Apr 30-May 6
  [Second Battle of Fredericksburg/Marye's Heights – May 3]
*Battle & Siege of Vicksburg – May 18-Jul 4
*Gettysburg Campaign - Jun-Jul 1863
*Chickamauga Campaign - Aug to Sep 1863
  [Second Chattanooga Aug 21] [Davis's Crossroads Sep 10-11] [Chickamauga Sep 19-20]
*Chattanooga Campaign – Oct to Nov
  [Wauhatchie Oct 28-29] [Orchard Knob Nov 23] [Lookout Mountain Nov 24] [Missionary Ridge Nov 25]

1864

*Red River Campaign - Mar-Apr 1864
  [Mansfield/Sabine Crossroads Apr 8] [Pleasant Hill Apr 9]
*Bermuda Hundred Campaign - May 1864
  [Port Walthall Junction May 6-7] [Swift Creek May 9] [Chester Station May 10] [Proctor's Creek May 12-16] [Ware Bottom Church May 20]
*Grant's Overland Campaign - May-Jun 1864
  [Wilderness May 5-7] [Spotsylvania May 8-21] [Yellow Tavern May 11] [Meadow Bridge May 12] [North Anna May 23-26] [Wilson's Wharf May 24] [Haw's Shop May 28] [Totopotomoy Creek/Bethesda Church May 28-30] [Old Church/Matadequin Creek May 30] [Cold Harbor May 31 to Jun 12]
*Lynchburg Campaign - May-Jun 1864
  [New Market May 15] [Piedmont Jun 5] [Lynchburg Jun 17-18]

*Richmond-Petersburg Campaign - Jun-Dec 1864

  [Jerusalem Plank Road Jun 21-23] [Staunton River Bridge Jun 25] [Sappony Church Jun 28] [First Ream's Station Jun 29] [First Deep Bottom Jul 27-29] [Crater Jul 30] [Second Deep Bottom Aug 14-20] [Globe Tavern Aug 18-20] [Second Ream's Station Aug 25] [Chaffin's Farm Sep 29-30] [Peebles's Farm Sep 30-Oct 2] [Darbytown and New Market Roads Oct 7] [Darbytown Road Oct 13] [Fair Oaks & Darbytown Road Oct 27-28] [Boynton Plank Road Oct 27-28]

*Sheridan's Valley Campaign - Aug-Oct 1864

  [Guard Hill Aug 16] [Summit Point Aug 21] [Smithfield Crossing Aug 25-29] [Berryville Sep 3-4] [Third Winchester (Opequon) Sep 19] [Fisher's Hill Sep 21-22] [Tom's Brook Oct 9] [Cedar Creek Oct 19]

*Atlanta Campaign - May-Sep 1864

  [Rocky Face Ridge May 7-13] [Resaca May 13-15] [Adairsville May 17] [New Hope Church May 25-26] [Dallas May 26-Jun 1][Pickett's Mill May 27] [Marietta Jun 9-Jul 3] [Kolb's Farm Jun 22] [Kennesaw Mountain Jun 27] [Pace's Ferry Jul 5] [Peachtree Creek Jul 20] [Atlanta Jul 22] [Ezra Church Jul 28] [Utoy Creek Aug 5-7] [Lovejoy's Station Aug 20][Jonesborough Aug 31-Sep 1]

*Franklin-Nashville Campaign - Sep-Dec 1864

  [Allatoona Oct 5] [Johnsonville Oct 16-Nov 16] [Decatur Oct 26-29] [Columbia Nov 24-29] [Spring Hill Nov 29] [Franklin Nov 30] [Third Murfreesboro Dec 5-6] [Nashville Dec 15-16]

*Savannah Campaign - Nov-Dec 1864

1865

*Richmond-Petersburg Campaign Continued - Jan-Mar 1865

  [Hatcher's Run Feb 5-7] [Fort Stedman/Hares' Hill Mar 25] [Third Petersburg Apr 2]

*Carolina Campaign - Feb-Mar 1865

  [Rivers' Bridge Feb 3] [Aiken Feb 11] [Wyse Fork Mar 7-10] [Monroe's Cross Roads Mar 10] [Averasborough Mar 16] [Bentonville Mar 19-21]

*Appomattox Campaign - Mar-Apr 1865

  [Lewis's Farm Mar 29] [White Oak Road Mar 31] [Dinwiddle Court House Mar 31] [Five Forks Apr 1] [Sutherland's Station Apr 2] [Namozine Church Apr 3] [Amelia Springs Apr 5] [Sailor's Creek Apr 6] [Rice's Station Apr 6] [Cumberland Church Apr 7] [High Bridge Apr 6-7] [Appomattox Station Apr 8]

1861

The first year of the ACW was a time of military preparation for each side in the conflict as they tried to get their bearings! Organization and recruitment for military units was a high priority. Federal arsenals and forts in the seceded States were seized by local militia groups, the occupation of Fort Sumter by Federal troops in South Carolina would receive the first Confederate aggression, and the first major battle would take place a short distance from Washington, D. C., followed by smaller engagements elsewhere. Much, much more would come in the three and a half years to follow!

Battle of Fort Sumter, South Carolina

Of all the notable events during the American Civil War, the bombardment of Fort Sumter on April 12, 1861, has the ominous distinction of the start of the war. Major Robert Anderson, First U. S. Artillery, and his sixty-eight enlisted soldiers from Companies E and H occupied the vacant fort lying in the midst of Charleston Harbor on December 26, 1860. They had evacuated nearby Fort Moultrie on Sullivan's Island that same day deeming it indefensible.

Fort Sumter was a five-sided brick structure built on a man-made island protecting Charleston Harbor. Although construction began in 1829, workers were still at the task of completing the structure at the time Major Anderson and his troops sought protection behind its walls. South Carolina had seceded from the Union on December 20, 1860. The flag of the United States of America flying over Fort Sumter was unacceptable to both South Carolina and the Confederate government. Diplomatic efforts between the United States government in Washington and the Confederacy in Montgomery, Alabama, in the early stages of the war failed to defuse the situation. President Abraham Lincoln's resolve to retain Fort Sumter for the Union and to resupply the garrison prompted Confederate President Jefferson Davis to authorize bombardment of the fort.

Confederate General Pierre Gustave Toutant Beauregard led the Charleston Command. On orders issued by Confederate President Jefferson Davis, General Beauregard directed his command of the First Artillery Regiment, South Carolina Militia totaling approximately five hundred men to commence firing on Fort Sumter at 4:30 in the morning April 12, 1861. Ringing the island fort were multiple sites positioned with artillery to include Fort Moultrie that had been abandoned late in December by Major Anderson. The bombardment occurred for thirty-four hours. The defenders supplies of food and water were nearly exhausted. Defense of the fort seemed fruitless. Major Anderson agreed to accept the terms of surrender offered shortly after the bombardment began.

Surprisingly, there were no casualties on either side during the attack on Fort Sumter. However, a fifty gun salute to the flag granted to Major Anderson in the terms of surrender resulted in injuries to five soldiers and death to one when a magazine exploded. A second soldier would die later of wounds sustained from the explosion. Major Anderson and his troops surrendered Fort Sumter at 2:30 P. M. on April 13, 1861, and evacuated the site to board nearby transports on April 14th. The Confederate flag was raised over Fort Sumter that would begin a continuous siege until the Confederate flag came down February 1865. [1]

Manassas Campaign (First Bull Run)

If there were a battle that defined the outcome of the ACW, it would be the **First Battle of Bull Run** or **First Manassas** that occurred Sunday, July 21, 1861, near Manassas,

Virginia only a short twenty-five miles from Washington, D. C.! This was a battle could have ended the war before it ever got started, but instead, it would be the beginning of a four-year blood bath that should never have happened if the military leaders of the Federal Army (Union) had not been so sure of victory that they forgot to lead their troops albeit inexperienced and ill-equipped even for a Federal Army. Of course, there is the side of the Confederate troops that were not going to let the Union forces have their day. Pride surely prevailed that July day over incompetence and a false sense of superiority that proved humiliating for the Union Army when all was said and done.

The first major battle of 1861 would define the course of the war over the next four years. Public sentiment was clamoring for a response to a build-up of Confederate troops so close to Washington, D. C., prompting President Abraham Lincoln to order his field commander, Brigadier General Irvin McDowell, to put an end to the potential threat. General McDowell had slightly more than 35,000 troops many of whom where inexperienced led by equally inexperienced commanders. McDowell was reluctant to send his army into battle for fear of the outcome, but his orders were clear and thus he devised a plan to achieve what the President had ordered in spite of his concerns!

Later Portrait of Major General Irvin McDowell, promoted November 25, 1872

Library of Congress, Prints & Photographs Division, LC-BH82-4161

Opposing General McDowell was a nearly equal sized Confederate Army identified as the Army of the Potomac led by Brigadier General Pierre Gustave Toutant Beauregard with nearly 22,000 troops and the Army of the Shenandoah led by General Joseph Eggleston Johnston with almost 12,000 men. Neither army had the advantage of seasoned soldiers nor the necessary equipment to fight a battle, but a battle would ensue regardless. The Confederate troops could be considered less experienced than their Union counterparts, but they were determined to defend their ways with a greater zeal.

Brigadier General Pierre Gustave Toutant Beauregard
National Archives 111-B-1233

General Irvin McDowell's **Army of Northeastern Virginia** consisted of five Divisions and all but the Fourth were engaged to some extent in the battle. Most of the 35,000 Union troops available to General McDowell were volunteers from the various States that had responded to President Lincoln's call for 75,000 to defend Washington, D. C. Thirteen States responded with military organizations to include Connecticut (3), Maine (4), Massachusetts (3), Michigan (4), Minnesota (1), New Hampshire (1), New Jersey (7), New York (20), Ohio (2), Pennsylvania (2), Rhode Island (2), Vermont (1), and Wisconsin (1).

In addition there were twenty-eight companies of Federal troops involved in the battle. Nine of that number were artillery that included Companies G and I of the First U. S.

Field Artillery; Companies A, D, E, G, and M of the Second U. S. Artillery; Company E of the Third U. S. Artillery; and Company D of the Fifth U. S. Artillery. There was one composite infantry battalion consisting of Companies C and K from the Second U. S. Infantry; B, D, G, H, and F from the Third U. S. Infantry; and Company G of the Eighth U. S. Infantry. Major George Sykes of the Fourteenth U. S. Infantry was in command of the battalion. New to the military organization was a Marine Battalion of four companies (A, B, C, D) that was established just for the ensuing battle. Marine Major George Reynolds was the commander supported by Captain and Brevet Major Jacob Zeilin (Co A), Captain James H. Jones (Co B), Lieutenant Alan Ramsay (Co C), and Second Lieutenant William H. Carter (Co D). The final complement of Federal troops was a battalion of dragoons under the command of Major Innis N. Palmer of the Second Dragoons. The battalion consisted of seven companies: Companies A and E of the First U. S. Cavalry Companies B, E, G, I, of the Second U. S. Cavalry; and Company K of the Second Dragoons. Company E, Second U. S. Dragoons, was assigned as escort to Colonel Samuel P. Heintzelman of the Third Division; Company I, Second U. S. Dragoons, was assigned escort duty for Brigadier General McDowell; and Company K, Second U. S. Dragoons, was assigned escort duty for Colonel David Hunter of the Second Division. All other dragoon companies were assigned to the First Brigade, Second Division.

The Confederate Army was represented by volunteer organizations from the various States. No Confederate units had been established by the time of the First Battle of Bull Run. The Union **Army of the Potomac** consisted of eight brigades totaling some 22,000 troops in organizations from Alabama (2), Arkansas (1), Louisiana (5), Mississippi (3), North Carolina (2), South Carolina (7), Tennessee (1), Texas (1), and Virginia (23). There were thirty-one

organizations of infantry, six artillery, seven cavalry, and one ranger unit. The Confederate **Army of the Shenandoah** was organized into four brigades with approximately 12,000 troops organized into State units from Alabama (1), Georgia (2), Maryland (1), Mississippi (2), North Carolina (1), Tennessee (1), and Virginia (12). These twenty organizations included fourteen infantry, five artillery, and one cavalry unit.

In the early hours of Sunday, July 21, 1861, Brigadier General McDowell began a march of approximately 18,000 Union troops in an attempt to drive the Confederate forces from an area near the town of Manassas, Virginia, some twenty-five miles southwest of Washington, D. C. If this action were successful, the Union forces would be able to continue to the Confederate Capital City of Richmond and end the rebellion. In the early going this outcome looked favorable, but miscalculations and unforeseen situations changed the scenario in the opposite direction.

Union forces were faced by a nearly equal number of Confederate troops and the element of surprise or pure luck sent the Confederates on their heels at the start. Union artillery fire was extremely effective with their rifled guns against the Confederate smoothbore pieces and would have continued if it weren't for two situations that changed that advantage. The first was a decision to re-position the Union batteries closer to the enemy negating that advantage. The second was Confederate soldiers wearing blue uniforms that were mistaken for Union soldiers. Instead of engaging the blue clad soldiers, they were allowed to virtually walk into the Union batteries overrunning the artillerists and captured the guns. These two situations may have turned the tide in the battle as the inexperienced Union troops panicked and began to retreat in droves leaving behind everything they carried including their weapons.

As the Union soldiers left the battlefield, the roadways became clogged causing even more panic both among the troops and the many local citizens who came to watch the battle as if it was some sort of game. Buggy loads of citizens were caught up in the fray that hampered the withdrawal of troops causing some to be captured by their Confederate pursuers. This outcome could have been even worse if the Confederate command had been organized enough to take advantage of the situation! As it was, they too had dissention in the ranks and the First Battle of Bull Run would go down as a Confederate victory but no more! Casualties for both sides were great, but they could have been even higher under the circumstances. The numbers for Union losses show 481 killed, over 1,000 wounded, and some 1,200 plus missing or captured. Confederate numbers are similar at 387 killed, 1,582 wounded, but only thirteen missing. Of course these number may vary from source to source that is consistent with battlefield engagements. While both Armies in the First Battle of Bull Run were licking their wounds and assessing what had taken place in the battle, half way across the continent in Missouri another battle was brewing between Federal troops and the upstart Missouri State Guard that supported the Confederate cause.

Colonel Ambrose Burnside's Second Brigade, Second Division, at Bull run with the First and Second Rhode Island and Seventy-First New York Regiment with their artillery attacking the Rebel Batteries at Bull Run
Library of Congress, Prints & Photographs Division, LC-USZ62-10807

The First Battle of Bull Run, Retreat Sunday Afternoon, July 21, 1861
Library of Congress, Prints & Photographs Division, LC-USZ62-8376

Battle of Wilson's Creek, Missouri

Missouri was a State that found itself split in two on the issue of secession. One group supported the Union effort while the governor, Claiborne F. Jackson, and many of his followers were in support of the Confederacy. Governor Jackson deliberately forced the hand of the legislature by aggressive actions against Federal authorities for which he was officially removed as governor although he continued to act as though he was still in office. A number of military incidents occurred in Missouri in the early months of the war before Federal troops took decisive action against the secessionists that became the **Battle of Wilson's Creek**.

Recently promoted Union Brigadier General Nathaniel Lyon with the commands of the First, Second, Third, and Fifth Missouri Infantry, the First Iowa Infantry, First and Second Kansas Infantry, and several companies of Federal troops consisting of infantry, cavalry, and artillery set up camp near Springfield, Missouri, with the intent of stopping the secessionist movement. The Federal complement consisted of Companies B, C, and D of the First Infantry, Companies B and E of the Second Infantry, Companies D and I of the First Cavalry, Company C of the Second Cavalry, Company from the Third Cavalry (former Mounted Rifles), Company F of the Second Artillery, one Company of artillery recruits acting as infantry, and one company of Mounted Rifle Recruits acting as artillery. The total strength of all these forces was in excess of 5,000 men.

Prior to the Battle of Wilson Creek August 10, 1861, the Union forces were organized into four brigades. The numbering of the brigades, First through Fourth, was changed at the time of the battle adding to the confusion of which units were with which brigades. General Lyon divided his force into two columns, one in which he commanded and the other by Brigadier General Franz Sigel. Initially, General Siegel commanded the Second Brigade that lost its identity in this attack scenario. The organization of the First Brigade remained the same with Major Samuel Davis Sturgis, First US Cavalry, in command. The Third Brigade commanded by Lieutenant Colonel George L. Andrews, First Missouri Volunteer Infantry, became the Second Brigade in General Lyons column while the Fourth Brigade commanded by Colonel George Washington Dietzler became General Lyon's Third Brigade.[2]

Brigadier General Lyon's column in excess of 4,000 troops was to conduct a frontal attack on the Confederate position assigning Brigadier Franz Siegel a rear assault with just over 1,000 troop. This approach could have been suicidal considering the Confederate forces numbered around 12,000 troops. As it was, the initial assault was extremely effective driving the Confederates off their ground and causing much confusion at least for a time.

The Confederate forces that would eventually be involved in the Battle of Wilson Creek consisted of two separate commands. Brigadier General Benjamin McCulloch commanded the Confederate Western Army made up of units from Arkansas, Louisiana, and Texas numbering just over 2,700 troops. Many of the Arkansas units were State Troops and not officially under Confederate control. The second complement of troops that would face Brigadier General Lyon was the Missouri State Guard commanded by Major General Sterling Price with a combined strength of slightly more than 7,000. As was the case with the Arkansas troops, the Missouri State Guard supported the Confederate cause, but was not officially under Confederate control since the State had not seceded from the Union.

In the period leading up to the Battle of Wilson Creek, there had been several conflicts involving Union forces against the Missouri State Guard one of which was the capture of the Missouri Capital of Springfield by Brigadier General Lyon's forces. At the end of July 1861, the Missouri State Guard was camped some seventy-five miles southwest of Springfield with plans to recapture the city. It was at this site that Brigadier General McCulloch's Western Army joined the Missouri State Guard raising their total strength to 12,000.

General Lyon was aware of the presence and the intent of his nemesis Major General Sterling Price and took it upon himself to initiate an attack rather than give up Springfield even though he was outnumbered over two to one. That attack occurred early in the morning of Saturday, August 10, 1861, and was initially successful as already pointed our three paragraphs ago. Perhaps the battle would have continued to favor the Union troops if it weren't for several facts that mirror the First Battle of Bull Run.

Union artillery fire was initially effective in keeping Confederate counterattacks from achieving any ground as was the case in the First Battle of Bull Run. However, Confederate soldiers wearing grey uniforms the same as Brigadier General Franz Siegel's men were mistaken for the First Iowa Infantry allowing entry into the position without engagement resulting in the loss of ground and artillery guns. General Siegel and his forces were sent fleeing for their lives. This situation placed the Union effort squarely on the soldiers of Brigadier General Lyon and his column and tipped the balance of the battle in favor of the Confederates.

At 9:30 on the morning of the battle, Brigadier General Nathaniel Lyon after being wounded twice earlier was shot through the heart as he rallied the Second Kansas Infantry in a counterassault. The second in command, Brigadier General Thomas William Sweeney, was also wounded leaving command of the entire Union force to Major Samuel Davis

Sturgis, First US Cavalry, the highest ranking Regular Army officer of the command. Brigadier General Nathaniel Lyon has the daunting distinction of being the first Union general to die from battle wounds in the American Civil War. Even more disturbing is the fact that his body lay on the battlefield after the retreat of the Union forces only to be discovered by Confederate troops who temporarily buried him until his remains could be returned to Union authorities.

The Union effort looked bleak at this time and by 11:00 AM, the defensive positions that had been repeatedly attacked found the troops short of ammunition and worn out from the back and forth action from early that morning. The only recourse available was an organized retreat from the battle scene that began in earnest first to Springfield and then to Rolla. A Confederate pursuit never materialized at that time, but Major General Price and the former governor, Claiborne Fox Jackson, would continue their efforts against Union sites and eventually officially join the Confederate cause.

The casualty count for the Battle of Wilson Creek lists Union killed at 258, wounded 873, and 186 missing. Of those numbers, General Lyon's First Brigade suffered a total of 153 casualties, the Second Brigade had 359 casualties, and the Third Brigade suffered the most at 508 casualties. It was the Third Brigade that was made up of the two Kansas Infantry units in which General Lyon was rallying at the time of his death. Brigadier Franz Siegel's force of about 1,000 troops suffered 297 casualties many of which may have been the result of misidentifying the Louisiana unit with the similar color uniforms.

The Confederate Western Army and Missouri State Guard losses are 277 killed, 945 wounded, and 10 or so missing. Of those numbers, the Western Army had 498 casualties and the Missouri State Guard reported 724 total casualties.

Scene at the Battle of Wilson's Creek, August 10, 1861
Library of Congress, Prints & Photographs Division, LC-USZ62-14862

The fall of Brigadier General Lyon in the Battle of Wilson's Creek
Library of Congress, Prints & Photographs Division, LC-USZ62-7619

[1] Civil War Era Fortifications, South Carolina, p. 596.
[2] The War of the Rebellion: A Compilation of the Official Records of the Union and Confederate Armies, Vol. 3, p. 65

1862

The year 1862 was a far cry from the previous year in both preparation and military involvement. Both sides seem to have gotten their ducks in a row and the number of military engagements was proof of that effort. Ten major campaigns occurred during the year yet no major breakthroughs resulted during this time. There would be more units organized on both sides and some changes of existing organizations common with the analysis of campaign results. New commanders would be assigned for reasons of injuries or death and some would be removed for failure to achieve the desired results. There would be combat casualties as expected just as there would in each year as the war progressed. It wouldn't take long to get things underway.

Burnside's North Carolina Expedition

The first action of 1862 would be Brigadier General Ambrose **Burnside's North Carolina Expedition**. In the early months of 1862, Union General-in-Chief, Winfield Scott, was intent on stopping the influx of supplies for the Confederate cause as well as those sold to foreign countries that would help finance their war effort. This effort took on the name Anaconda Plan that was designed to blockade southern ports that were capable of shipping and receiving goods along the Atlantic Coastline as well as the Gulf of Mexico and up the Mississippi River. After some discussion on the subject, Brigadier General Ambrose Everett Burnside was tasked with the job of recruiting a force that could undertake the blockade. He went about organizing a force of men familiar with operations on the sea that became known as the Coast Division. The Coast Division consisted of three brigades commanded by officers known to General Burnside from his earlier years as a cadet at West Point. Brigadier General John Gray Foster commanded the First Brigade. General Foster graduated from West Point in 1846, fourth in his class of fifty-nine, and was a career officer spending much of his time as an Engineer Officer.

Brigadier General Jesse Lee Reno commanded the Second Brigade. General Reno also graduated from West Point as a classmate of General Foster graduating eighth in his class. General Reno would not survive the war. In the Battle of South Mountain September 14, 1862, near Boonsboro, Maryland, General Reno was mistakenly shot in the chest by a Union soldier and died that same day. The Third Brigade was under the command of Brigadier General John Grubb Parke also a graduate of West Point three years later in 1849. General Parke was commissioned as an Engineer Officer and served in the military until his retirement in 1889 serving his last two years as Superintendent of West Point

A Coast Division is of little use without the support of the United States Navy. This was accomplished by the naval assets of Rear Admiral Louis Malesherbee Goldsborough, a forty-five year veteran of the Navy with much military experience behind him. Admiral Goldsborough was placed in charge of the Atlantic Blockading Squadron in September 1861. A month later the Atlantic Blockading Squadron was divided into the North and South Atlantic Blockading Squadrons. Admiral Goldsborough commanded the North and Rear Admiral Samuel Francis Du Pont commanded the South Blockading Squadron. The North Atlantic Blocking Squadron would assist Brigadier General Burnside in his North Carolina Expedition.

The first objective of Burnside's Expedition was Roanoke Island protecting the entrance to Albemarle Sound. Roanoke Island was part of the Confederate District of Roanoke commanded by Brigadier General Henry Alexander Wise with slightly less than 1,500 troops. That number would increase to near 3,000 before Union General Burnside departed Fortress Monroe January 11 with 13,000 troops, eight Army gunboats, twenty U. S. Naval vessels, and a number of troop transport ships headed for Roanoke Island. Weather conditions hampered the expedition in the early going and the flotilla did not arrive at its intended objective until the early days of February. Even the arrival was met with difficulty due to the shallow water into Pamlico Sound. Many ships were required to lighten their loads to make the passage and some were unable to achieve this end.

Once in position, the Naval ships exchanged fire with the shore batteries in Forts Huger, Blanchard, Bartow, and Forrest on the first day of the battle, February 7. Later that same day, General Burnside's troops were landed to begin a land assault that would have to wait until morning due the lateness of the day. The complement of Union forces for the First Brigade included the Tenth Connecticut Infantry along with the Twenty-third, Twenty-fourth, Twenty-fifth, and Twenty-seventh Massachusetts. The Second Brigade was made up of the Twenty-first Massachusetts, Ninth New Jersey, Fifty-first New York, and Fifty-first Pennsylvania. The Third Brigade included the Eighth and Eleventh Connecticut, Ninth New York, and the Fourth and Fifth Rhode Island.

Once the Coast Division troops were ashore and had rested for the night, they began an all out assault on the four forts, the furthest first, cutting off all chances of retreat from those closer to the initial action of the day before. Some resistance was encountered, but determination and good tactical maneuvers resulted in the surrender of the Confederate forces that included the Second, Eighth Seventeenth (3 companies), and Thirty-first North Carolina, as well as the Forty-sixth and

Fifty-ninth Virginia. The Confederate naval assets of small ships appropriately identified as the "Mosquito Fleet" of seven ships were tracked down and destroyed two days later February 10, 1862, at what was called the Battle of Elizabeth City

The ease and swiftness of this military action was not without casualties on both sides. The Union First Brigade reported nineteen killed and 113 wounded. The Second Brigade had similar numbers with fifteen killed, seventy-nine wounded, and thirteen missing. The Third Brigade fared much better with seventeen wounded. while the Eleventh Connecticut of the Third Brigade was not engaged in the action. Confederate casualties mirrored that of the Union troops showing a combined twenty-three killed, fifty-eight wounded, sixty-two missing, but at least 2,500 were captured along with thirty of the thirty-two artillery pieces.

The outcome of this military action gave control of the North Carolina coast to Union forces for the remainder of the war. Fort Forrest was destroyed by its defenders to prevent its capture, but the other three Confederate forts were captured mostly intact and renamed as Union forts by General Burnside. Fort Bartow became Fort Foster, Fort Blanchard became Fort Parke, and Fort Huger acquired the name Fort Reno. Of course, each of these newly named forts was for the three brigade commanders of Brigadier General Ambrose Burnside's North Carolina Expedition.

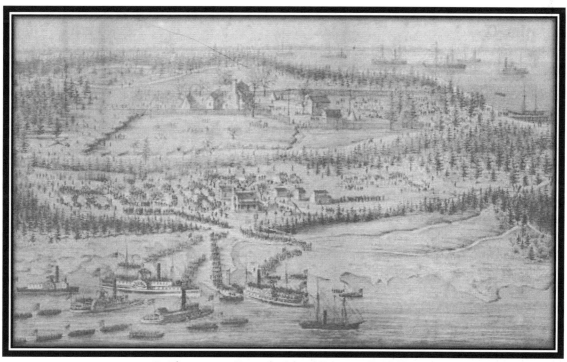

Battle scene at Roanoke Island February 7, 1862,
showing the many Union ships at the top and bottom involved in the attack.
Library of Congress, Prints & Photographs Division, LC-USZ62-3450

The attack on Roanoke Island was the first action taken by General Burnside during his North Carolina Expedition. Next would be New Bern along the Neuse River a considerable distance south off Pamlico Sound. New Bern was a railroad link of the Atlantic and North Carolina Railroad to the interior of the region and one that would be an important supply point for Confederate goods. The **Battle of New Bern** began March 13, 1862.

Gathering more ships than in the first engagement, General Burnside sailed south to the area of New Bern where his three brigades were essentially the same as in the Battle of Roanoke Island except for the Third Brigade that dropped the Ninth New York from its ranks. Confederates defending New Bern were all North Carolina units assigned to the Pamlico District of the Department of North Carolina under the command of Brigadier General Lawrence O'Bryan Branch. These units included the Seventh, Twenty-sixth, Twenty-seventh, Twenty-eighth, Thirty-third, Thirty-fifth, Thirty-seventh Regiments of Infantry along with the Nineteenth North Carolina Cavalry complimented and a Heavy Artillery Company plus a Special Battalion of Militia. The sum of these units numbered around 4,500 troops.

General Branch was aware of the loss at Roanoke Island and prepared his defense of New Bern expecting a water attack along the Neuse River that would be his undoing! Confederate Fort Thompson was an earthen fort protecting the approach to New Bern some seven miles down river and armed with thirteen artillery pieces all but three defending the river approach. Perhaps sensing that a river assault would meet with stiff resistance, General Burnside disembarked his force and approached the fort on foot from the land side overwhelming the occupants sending all the rebel troops in the area scrambling to New Bern where many boarded trains evacuating the area as quickly as possible. New Bern was

captured the next day. As quick as the battle occurred, it was not without casualties. Union losses were ninety killed, 380 wounded and one man missing. Confederate losses reported sixty-four killed, 101 wounded, and 413 captured or missing. New Bern would remain under Union control to the end of the war and a fort was quickly constructed named Fort Totten.

Next, General Burnside shifted his attention further south to the area of Morehead City and Beaufort, North Carolina, which was the terminus of the Atlantic and North Carolina Railroad. Protecting both towns was the former Federal Fort Macon that was a coastal Third System fort improved from the much earlier Fort Dobbs dating to 1756. Fort Macon was seized by local militia on April 15, 1861, along with five artillery guns and may have increased to as many as fifty guns under Confederate occupation. The effort against Fort Macon was primarily the responsibility of Brigadier General Parke and his troops of the Third Brigade.

Fort Macon was under the command of Confederate Colonel Moses James White and around 450 troops of the Tenth North Carolina State Volunteers of which slightly more than half were combat ready due to ill health. Colonel White graduated from West Point in 1858 and served in the Federal Army until his home State of Mississippi seceded from the Union. He then resigned his Federal commission and placed his services with the Confederacy as an artillery officer. Colonel White assumed command of Fort Macon on October 5, 1861.

The able bodied Confederate soldiers defending Fort Macon were few compared to General Parke's nearly three thousand troops, but capture of the fort would not be an easy task compared to the previous two engagements resulting in a **Siege of Fort Macon** that began March 23 and would take just over a month to complete on April 26.

On the morning of April 25, a Union bombardment began on the fort that would ultimately lead to its surrender and Union occupation the next day. The slightly over month long siege resulted in surprising small number of casualties for both sides. Union losses were two killed, five wounded, and eight captured. The captured may have been pickets (sentries) from the Ninth New Jersey Infantry who were attacked by rebel cavalry at sometime around April 7, but assigned to the Second Brigade not to the Third Brigade. The Second Brigade was not part of General Parke's troops involved in the siege of Fort Macon. Confederate casualties were equally light listing eight killed, sixteen wounded, and nearly 400 captured. Those captured were paroled with the understanding that they would not bear arms against the Union Army until properly exchanged that was a common practice in the early stages of the war that sometimes was violated.

Fort Macon showing the sallyport (entrance) c. 1940
Library of Congress, Prints & Photographs Division, HABS NC, 16-BEAUF.V,1--1

While the Third Brigade of Burnside's Expeditionary force was engaged in the siege of Fort Macon, Brigadier General Jesse L. Reno's Second Brigade was tasked with destroying the Dismal Swamp Canal Culpepper Locks near South Mills, North Carolina. The Dismal Swamp Canal provided access to open water for Confederate ironclads that could cause trouble for U. S. Navy ships. General Reno's 3,000 strong force sailed from Roanoke Island April 18 arriving near Elizabeth City late that evening and disembarked for an overland march to the lock. Nearing South Mills, the Union troops were met by a smaller force of Confederate soldiers from the Third Georgia Infantry, Ferebee's North Carolina Militia, an artillery battery, and a cavalry company all under the command of Colonel Ambrose Wright. The total of these troops was near 1,000. What resulted was the **Battle of South Mills** or the **Battle of Camden** fought on April 19. After a brief engagement,

Colonel Wright withdrew his forces a few miles from the action and General Reno declined to pursue due to the exhaustion of his force. Word that Confederate reinforcements were on their way prompted General Reno to abandon the mission marching his troops back to the transports and returned to Roanoke Island ending the mission. The brief encounter resulted in Union casualties numbering 112 of which the breakdown in killed and wounded was not given. Confederate numbers reported twenty-five total casualties.

The capture of Fort Macon on April 26 virtually ended Burnside's North Carolina Expedition although there were brief encounters to June. Nearly half of the Coastal Division along with Brigadier General Burnside returned to Virginia called upon for other duties. Brigadier General John G. Foster remained in North Carolina with approximately 8,000 troops and continued to attack various sites. At the same time newly assigned advisor to President Jefferson Davis, General Robert E. Lee began pouring troops into North Carolina realizing the importance of retaining the State for the Confederacy. North Carolina would see no other major campaign until the end of the war at which time Fort Fisher was the focus.

Sibley's New Mexico Campaign

On February 1, 1861, before the dawn of the Civil War, sympathetic Southern supporters in Texas would secure the state for the Confederacy. The Texas legislature, teeming with secessionists, voted one hundred sixty-six in favor of leaving the Union to eight against before the inauguration of President Lincoln. Texan citizens voted for secession on February 23, 1861, by a vote of 46,153 to 14,747. Texas was welcomed into the Confederate States of America on March 2, 1861.

Stationed at posts in Texas at the time of secession from the Union were two full U. S. infantry regiments (Third and Eighth - less Co G), the Second U. S. Cavalry regiment later renumbered as the Fifth, the Headquarters plus five companies (A, G, H, I, K) of the First U. S. Infantry, and five U. S. Artillery companies (F, K, L, M-First Regiment & M-Second Regiment). On February 18, 1861, Union Brevet Major General David E. Twiggs, commander of the U. S. Army's Department of Texas, issued GENERAL ORDER No. 5 that called for the surrender of all federal posts in Texas and their inventories to the Texas Commission, though it would take more than a month for Union commanders to comply with that order.

Brevet Major General David E. Twiggs
Commander, U. S. Army,
Department of Texas
Library of Congress,
Prints & Photographs Division,
LC-USZ62-92325

General Twiggs was dismissed from the U. S. Army for "treachery to the flag of his country." He accepted a commission as a Major General in the Confederate Army, but never served due to poor health.

While most of the Federal troops were successful in departing Texas by way of the coast, seven companies were captured on their transports at Saluria, Texas, before they could set sail. All seven captured infantry companies were immediately paroled once agreement was given not to engage in hostile action until exchanged for Confederate prisoners. They were allowed to board their ships and sailed to New York where they arrived on May 31, 1861.

The remaining companies of the Eighth U. S. Infantry never made it to the coast. Instead, they were captured near San Antonio, Texas, and became prisoners of war. The officers were paroled after nine months of captivity, but the enlisted remained prisoners until February 25, 1863.

The events of Texas secession from the Union were strikingly different from other Southern states. Surrendering of ordnance, quartermaster supplies, and other Federal assets was not uncommon. The prominent difference was capturing of Federal troops that had been avoided until Texas. This was further complicated by imprisonment of the officers and enlisted men for up to two years for the latter!

The Federal military presence in Texas in late 1860 and early 1861 was perhaps the greatest of any Southern state. This becomes particularly important when reviewing the events associated with the transfer of power due to the secession of Texas. While there may have been an appearance of cordiality on the surface, it was anything but civil in the delivery.[1]

One outcome of Texas joining the Confederacy was a plan offered by former Federal officer Major Henry Hopkins Sibley now Brigadier General in the Confederate Army to invade the southwestern territories all the way to California. This ambitious plan was devised soon after General Sibley was commissioned in the Confederate Army, approved a short time later, and got underway

in November 1861 after the organization and recruitment of a force numbering in excess of 3,000 men. That force became known as the Army of New Mexico and consisted of ten companies each of the Fourth and Fifth Texas Mounted Rifles, five companies initially of the Seventh Texas Mounted Rifles with five more to follow later, three companies organized as a battalion of the Second Texas Mounted Rifles, a Provisional Artillery Battalion, and several Arizona units. General Sibley's force left San Antonio in small detachments around October 22 headed for Fort Bliss near El Paso, Texas. The last group of detachments arrived at El Paso in late December and prepared for the next phase that was New Mexico.

Brigadier General Henry Hopkins Sibley
Officer of the Confederate Army
Library of Congress,
Prints & Photographs Division,
LC-DIG-cwpb-05992

New Mexico was held by Union troops under the command of Colonel Edward R. S. Canby commanding the Military Department of New Mexico. Colonel Canby had at his disposal a force at least as large to that of General Sibley plus a number of forts in the region and adequate supplies much greater than the Confederate troops.

The Union troops largely garrisoned at Fort Craig, New Mexico, consisted of Company D and G, First U. S. Cavalry; Companies C, D, G, I, and K, Third U. S. Cavalry; Companies B, D, F, I, and one unidentified company, Fifth U. S. Infantry; Companies C, F, and H, Seventh U. S. Infantry; Companies A, F, and H, Tenth U. S. Infantry; one artillery battery; the First, Second, Third, Fourth, and Fifth New Mexico Infantry, Company B of the Second Colorado Infantry; and the First and Second New Mexico Militia.

Most of these Union units were involved in the first action against the Army of New Mexico on February 21 called the **Battle of Valverde**. This battle was fought on ground near the Valverde Ford located near the Rio Grande River six miles north of Fort Craig. The battle was declared a Confederate victory, but achieved little other than bragging rights since the Union forces retreated to the safety of Fort Craig and would survive to fight another day. Neither side was spared casualties in the battle, but Colonel Canby's forces suffered the worst reporting sixty-eight killed, 160 wounded, and over two hundred captured or missing. Brigadier General Sibley's losses were less, but no less troubling. Thirty-six were killed, 150 wounded, and one soldier missing. These losses along with a shortage of supplies prompted the Army of New Mexico to abandon any further action against the well-fortified Fort Craig choosing to move north toward Albuquerque and eventually Santa Fe.

General Sibley's search for much needed supplies was met with virtual failure. His troops were suffering from lack of food supplies, potable water, transportation, and the need to tend to his wounded. In spite of these shortcomings, one more military engagement would occur March 28 in the **Battle of Glorieta Pass**. This battle too might have favored the Confederate force except that the supply wagons carrying what few supplies the Army of New Mexico still retained was destroyed by Union troops that all but ended any attempt of victory.

What started as an ambitious endeavor to secure New Mexico, Arizona, and California for the Confederacy turned out to be anything but what had been planned. An army on the march needs to be supported with supplies especially one who travels over long distances where the land does not provide for the shortages necessary for subsistence! The Army of New Mexico either failed to plan for their supply situation or more than likely suffered from the military action causing them to run short. Whatever the case, early military gains soon turned into attempts to save what lives they could having little or no supplies. The Army of New Mexico limped back to El Paso with no more than 1,700 survivors for the ordeal. It wouldn't take long for Union reinforcements from California to end any future attempts to secure New Mexico, Arizona, and California for the Confederacy!

Federal Incursion up the Cumberland and Tennessee Rivers

Union Major General Henry Halleck commanding the Department of the Missouri and Brigadier General Don Carlos Buell in command of the Department of the Ohio were being pressured to take action in their respective regions against Confederate forces under the command of General Albert Sidney Johnston. Two key sites were Confederate held Fort Henry situated on the Tennessee River and Fort Donelson on the Cumberland River some ten miles apart. Capture of these two forts would open river traffic to the Union

Army and allow further movement south to other Confederate held positions. The first to take action was General Halleck who dispatched Brigadier General Ulysses S. Grant from Cairo, Illinois, February 2 on a flotilla of ships under the command of Flag Officer Andrew Hull Foote landing his infantry forces north of the fort on both sides of the river in two waves February 4 And 5.

General Grant commanded a large force of some 15,000 troops nearly all volunteer units mostly from Illinois with a scattering from Iowa, Indiana, Missouri, Ohio, Kentucky, and Nebraska and only two Federal units, Company C of the Second U. S. Cavalry and Company I from the Fourth U. S. Cavalry. Seven ships made up Flag Officer Foote's complement including the USS *St. Louis*, USS *Carondelet*, USS *Essex*, USS *Cincinnati*, USS *Tyler*, USS *Conestoga*, and the USS *Lexington*.

Both Forts Henry and Donelson were under the command of Confederate Brigadier General Lloyd Tilghman assigned to General Johnston's Army of Central Kentucky. His combined force numbered just under 5,000 of which approximately 3,000 or so were garrisoned at Fort Henry, the remainder at Fort Donelson. It is known that the Tenth Tennessee Infantry was part of the garrison at Fort Henry as was the Fourth Mississippi Infantry. Fort Henry was defended with no less than seventeen guns of various caliber eleven of which covered the river approach and the other six the land side. All this defense was irrelevant as heavy rains in the early days of February caused the Tennessee River to rise so much that much of the fort was under water. After a naval bombardment of slightly over an hour, General Tilghman surrendered the fort on the afternoon of February 6, but much of the Confederate force had been sent to Fort Donelson long before that would be the next engagement February 13. General Grant arrived at Fort Henry with his infantry around 3:00 PM to find the fort had already surrendered to Flag Officer Foote.

Union Naval attack on Confederate Fort Henry, February 6, 1862, showing four iron-clad gunboats firing on the fort.
Library of Congress, Prints & Photographs Division, LC-DIG-pga-0395

With Fort Henry secured, the next move would be against Fort Donelson, the second of four eventual outcomes of this campaign. Fort Donelson was approximately ten to twelve mile march east of Fort Henry something that would be accomplished by General Grant and his troops. The Cumberland River would be the route for Flag Officer Foote and seven ships, five of which were involved in the attack on Fort Henry. The USS Essex was badly damaged in the battle and returned to Cairo as did the USS Cincinnati also damage and the USS St. Louis. The USS St. Louis returned to take part in the Battle of Fort Donelson along with two replacements ships, the USS Louisville and the USS Pittsburgh.

Fort Donelson was an earthwork fort similar to Fort Henry under the eventual command of Confederate Brigadier General John B. Floyd supported by Brigadier Generals Gideon J. Pillow and Simon Bolivar Buckner, Sr. The Battle for Fort Donelson would be dramatically different from the swift capture of Fort Henry! Fort Donelson was initially garrisoned by 5,000 troops with the arrival of the garrison from Fort Henry. That number would swell to around 17,000 with the arrival of reinforcements. The fort was supported by two river batteries, upper and lower, guarding against any river approach that played a significant role in the battle.

The Union ground troops departed from Fort Henry on February 12 awaiting the return of the Navy gunboats. Their march was not without some encounters by Confederate cavalry troops under the command of Brigadier Nathan Bedford Forrest, but these were only temporary delays. In the meantime, the U. S. Naval ships were making their way toward the Cumberland River in preparation for the attack on the fort. The first to arrive was the USS *Carondelet* who opened fire on the defenses testing the capability of the batteries and soon withdrew.

Sketch of the Ironclad USS *Cardondelet* approaching Fort Donelson defenses around February 12, 1862
Wikipedia

February 13 would see more probing action against the Confederate held Fort Donelson, but the real fight began around mid-noon on Friday, February 14 with the arrival of Union reinforcements from Fort Henry along with the Navy gunboats and transports pushing the number of troops in excess of 24,000 General Grant immediately ordered Flag Officer Foote to begin bombardment of the fort and its river batteries while the ground troops readied for the assault that would be delayed due to the damage inflicted on the Union ships by the two river batteries. February 15 saw the Confederate forces attempting a breakout that was partially successful only to fall back that would prove the end of Fort Donelson. The ground war was extremely costly to both sides

and February 16 would bring an end to the battle with the unconditional surrender of the fort by Confederate Brigadier General Simon Bolivar Buckner who was left to defend the fort alone as Brigadier Generals John B. Floyd and Gideon J. Pillow had made their escape before the surrender.

Casualty counts were high with Union totals of over five hundred killed, and nearly 2,000 wounded. Confederate numbers reflected some 327 killed, 1,127 wounded, and over 12,000 captured or missing. The Confederate prisoners were sent north to be held in prisons at various locations and General Buckner was held at Fort Warren in Boston until his exchange in August 1862.

Battle of Fort Donelson, February 16, 1862, showing Brigadier General Grant on the far left leading his troops mounted on his horse Cincinnati

Library of Congress, Prints & Photographs Division, LC-USZ62-14868

Following the fall of Forts Henry and Donelson, Union forces moved from two directions toward Confederate held Nashville, the capital of Tennessee. Major General Henry Halleck denied Brigadier General Grant the opportunity to join in this effort. Instead, Brigadier General William Bull Nelson who had arrived at Fort Donelson after the fort was in Union hands was instructed by General Grant to take Nashville. General Nelson commanded a division in Brigadier General Don Carlos Buell's Army of the Ohio. While General Nelson approached Nashville from Fort Donelson, General Buell did the same from Kentucky. By the time each Union force reached the city, the Confederate forces had evacuated Nashville and the city fell without a fight on February 25, 1862. Nashville was the first Confederate capital to fall into Union hands in the war.

Rivers at the time of the American Civil War were vital commerce routes as were rail lines crisscrossing the South connecting population centers. Control of these two transportation systems would provide a military advantage to the holder. Nashville was one of these important transportation centers and there were others that would see military involvement. Both Union Generals Grant and Buell were dispatched to the vicinity of Shiloh, Tennessee, for the purpose of securing the important rail system some twenty miles south at Corinth, Mississippi. Confederate General Albert S. Johnston was also aware of this plan and dispatched his forces that would lead to the **Battle of Shiloh** also known as the **Battle of Pittsburg Landing** April 6-7, 1862.

The battle that ensued began on the morning of Sunday, April 6, when some 40,335 Confederate soldiers surprised Union Brigadier General Ulysses S. Grant's 44,894 soldiers encamped along the west bank of the Tennessee River awaiting the arrival of Union Major General Buell's Army of the Ohio from Nashville. At first the Confederates drove the Union troops back from their positions only to see this change when the Union troops acquired more secure ground stopping the Confederate gains. At one point in this action, General Johnston was shot in the leg resulting in his death. His second in command Brigadier General Pierre Gustave Toutant Beauregard assumed command of the Confederate forces and the day ended in a stalemate. General Beauregard intended to conduct a final assault the next day, April 7, but was unaware that Union General Buell had arrived overnight increasing the Union forces to around 63,000. This outcome tipped the balance in favor of the Union troops and General Beauregard withdrew his forces ending the attempt to drive the Union troops from the area.

Scene at the Battle of Shiloh
April 6, 1862

Library of Congress,
Prints & Photographs Division,
LC-USZ62-3883

US Military History– American Civil War

The gunboats USS *Tyler* and USS *Lexington* on the Tennessee River in support of the Union troops in the Battle of Shiloh with other unidentified US Navy ships in the background.
Library of Congress, Prints & Photographs Division, LC-USZ62-15

The Battle of Shiloh was costly for both sides. Union numbers reported 1,754 killed, 8,408 wounded, and 2,885 missing or captured. Confederate casualties mirrored that of their adversaries showing 1,728 killed, 8,012 wounded, and 959 missing or captured. This battle would not end the effort to secure Corinth, Mississippi, by Union forces and would lead to the final campaign of the **Union Incursion of the Cumberland and Tennessee Rivers** in the **Siege of Corinth** also called the **First Battle of Corinth** from April 29 to May 30, 1862, leading to the capture of Corinth.

Corinth, Mississippi, was an important rail center for the Mobile and Ohio Railroad and the Memphis and Charleston Railroad linking other population centers in the South. The army that controlled Corinth would prove a distinct advantage in the war effort.

After the failed attempt to defeat Union Generals Grant and Buell at Shiloh, Confederate Brigadier General Beauregard's troops moved south to Corinth with around 65,000 troops and prepared for the onslaught of the Union

forces. That onslaught would come at the end of April 1862 not with just Generals Grant and Buell but also Union forces of the Army of the Mississippi under Major General John Pope swelling the total number of Union forces to over 120,000.

The previous battles at Fort Donelson and Shiloh were costly in the number of casualties prompting Union Major General Henry Halleck to take precautions not to engage in all out warfare against Corinth. Instead, the Union troops moved cautiously toward Corinth seizing one area at a time. This action would result in some casualties for both sides, but not to the degree seen previously.

Once the Union forces were within reach of Corinth, a siege was conducted against Confederate General Beauregard and his force already suffering from battle casualties and sickness plus a lack of day-to-day essentials. Realizing that continued resistance against a much larger force would endanger the safety and perhaps the capture of General Beauregard's Confederate troops, a withdrawal plan was initiated with the intent to deceive the Union generals into thinking that an attack was about to happen. Instead, the sick and wounded were placed on available trains and moved to safety followed by the able bodied troops along with artillery pieces and all the supplies that could be removed. In the end the siege proved successful although Corinth was absent of any Confederate soldiers at the time Union forces entered the town.

Union Major General Pope's Encampment before Corinth in May 1862
Wikipedia

Pea Ridge Campaign

No part of the United States in 1862 was free from military involvement during the American Civil War. Every State including those of the Confederacy was involved to some extent such as that seen in Tennessee in the last entry. The Pea Ridge Campaign was an effort to secure Arkansas and Missouri under Union control driving the Confederates out of the region. This was a short campaign in comparison to the previous and those to come, but this by no means makes it any less important.

Pea Ridge is an area in the far northwest corner of Arkansas a short distance from the Missouri State line. It was here that slightly over 10,000 Union troops under Brigadier General Samuel R. Curtis' Army of the Southwest later identified as the Army of Southwest Missouri, met 16,500 Confederates under Major General Earl Van Dorn's Trans-Mississippi District. The **Battle of Pea Ridge** took place over a two-day period, March 7-8, 1862, resulting in a Union victory.

Union forces under General Curtis were organized into four divisions. Units of all types included in the four divisions were thirteen from Missouri, eight from Illinois, five from Iowa, four from Indiana, and two from Ohio. No Federal units were included as part of the Army of the Southwest nor in the battle. Major General Earl Van Dorn organized his forces into a Right and Left Wing. The brunt of these units came from Missouri with a total of fourteen followed by Arkansas with thirteen, Texas with eight, Louisiana with one, and Confederate Indians units with four.

US Military History– American Civil War

The battle on the first day was a back and forth conflict that favored neither side. Some gains were made and soon after lost. There was much posturing and reposition of troops that occurred throughout the day ending late Friday, March 7, when assessment was taken of the day's events. Action resumed early the next morning, but was essentially over by 11:00 AM with General Van Dorn's troops in full retreat having lost all advantage on the battlefield. The smaller Union force had won the day and secured both Arkansas and Missouri for much of the remainder of the war.

Union losses in the Battle of Pea Ridge are reported at 203 killed, 980 wounded, and 201 missing.[2] Although two Union Division commanders, Brigadier General Alexander Asboth and Colonel Eugene A. Carr, were wounded in action they continued to command their troops and were instrumental in achieving the victory. Confederates on the other hand were less fortunate. Brigadier Generals Benjamin McCulloch and James M. McIntosh were killed and Colonel William Y. Slack was mortally wounded. In addition an estimated 2,000 Confederate soldiers were of the killed, wounded, captured, and missing.

Union assault on the final day of the Battle of Pea Ridge, March 8, 1862
Wikipedia

Valley Campaign

The Valley Campaign was primarily a Confederate operation attributed to Major General Thomas Jonathan "Stonewall" Jackson that took place in the Shenandoah Valley of central Virginia February 27 to June 9, 1862. This campaign involved six minor named battles against six Union general officers with General Jackson getting the best in all but the first conflict and that one proved of little consequence.

General Jackson was in command of the Valley District, one of three Confederate Districts established October 22, 1861, as part of the Department of Northern Virginia. The Valley District was formerly called the Army of the Northwest. While the Potomac and Aquia Districts, the other two, ceased operations early in 1862, the Valley District remained in service to the end of the war indicating its importance in the war effort. There were nine command changes for the Valley District during its tenure with two commanders, Major General promoted to Lieutenant General Jubal Anderson Early and Brigadier General John Daniel Imboden, serving two different times.

Portrait of Major General Thomas Jonathan "Stonewall" Jackson
Officer of the Confederate Army
Library of Congress, Prints & Photographs Division, LC-DIG-cwpb-07475

The Valley Campaign began February 27, 1862, with the arrival of some 35,000 Union troops under Major General Nathaniel Prentice Banks' Department of the Shenandoah into the region of Virginia west of the Potomac River where suspected Confederate troops were positioned. The Department of the Shenandoah was organized July 25, 1861, as part of the Department of the Potomac that itself became the Army of the Potomac July 26, 1861. General Bank's command was reorganized March 8, 1862, as the V Corps of the Army of the Potomac only to be reestablished as the Department of the Shenandoah on April 4. Before the last organizational change occurred, President Lincoln ordered all but about 9,000 of General Banks' soldiers back to Washington for protection of the city leaving but a scant number of troops to continue the mission. General Banks' original two divisions were thus reduced to only one commanded by Brigadier

General James Shields. That division fielded three infantry brigades, and one each cavalry and artillery brigade. All but one unit was from State organizations of Indiana, Ohio, Illinois, Pennsylvania, West Virginia, Michigan, and Maryland. Battery E of the Fourth U. S. Artillery was the only Federal unit within the First Division at the time of the first battle.

Portrait of Major General Nathaniel Prentiss Banks
Officer of the Federal Army
Library of Congress, Prints & Photographs Division, LC-DIG-ppmsca-08366

Confederate General Jackson in the early months of 1862 was headquartered at Winchester, Virginia, approximately seventy miles northwest of Washington, D. C. His total force numbered around 9,000, including units entirely from Virginia organized into three infantry brigades with one smaller cavalry unit. Each of the brigades were supported with Virginia artillery units.

As the Union troops began their approach into the valley, only 6,000 troops remained near Winchester. Upon receiving word of the Union troops nearing Winchester, General Jackson evacuated the city. In the meantime, General Banks sent his Division commander

Brigadier General Shields to reconnoiter the presence of Confederate troops near Winchester who reported back that they were nowhere to be found. General Jackson had in fact left Winchester, but given faulty intelligence on the number of Union troops, returned to an area south of Winchester called Kernstown. It was here that the first battle of the Valley Campaign occurred on, Sunday, March 23, 1862, named the **First Battle of Kernstown**.

The day prior to the battle, Union Brigadier General Shields was wounded in a skirmish so much so that command of the First Division was turned over to his First Brigade commander, Colonel Nathan Kimball. Colonel Kimball had 6,500 troops at his disposal twice the number of Confederate attackers under Major General Jackson. General Jackson's plan was ill advised perhaps due to poor intelligence that he received from his cavalry commander, Colonel Turner Ashby. Needless to say, the Confederate attack fell short of its intended goal that would be the only setback for General Jackson in his Valley Campaign. The Union victory if it can be called such does not reflect that outcome when comparing the casualties for both sides. Union losses were 119 killed, 446 wounded, and 22 captured or missing.[3] Confederate losses were 80 killed, 375 wounded, and 265 captured or missing.[4] Comparing the differences in the number of combatants on each side, it does seem that the Confederates did lose a higher percentage of combatants than the Union forces.

For much of the next two months, only sporadic incidents occurred in the Valley Campaign much to do with inclement weather. That lull changed when units of the Union Mountain Department commanded by Major General John C. Fremont arrived in the western region of the Shenandoah Valley threatening the Confederate supply depot at Staunton. Union Brigadier General Robert Huston Milroy commanding a brigade of the Cheat Mountain District of the Mountain Department advanced on the village of McDowell, Virginia, about twenty-five miles west of Staunton. Units of the Cheat Mountain District fluctuated over time, but at the time of the **Battle of McDowell** on May 8, 1862, the Twelfth, Twenty-fifth, Thirty-second, Seventy-third, and Seventy-fifth Ohio Infantry Regiments along with the Second and Third (West) Virginia Infantry and the Ninth Ohio Battery comprised the command. The total force numbered around 5,500 troops. On the day of the battle, Brigadier General Robert C. Schenck commanding the District of Cumberland within the Mountain Department arrived in support of General

Milroy bringing with him the Eighty-second Ohio Infantry and the Fifth (West) Virginia Infantry totaling about 2,700 troops. General Schenck was senior in rank to General Milroy and took command of the total force.

To prevent disruption of the Confederate depot at Staunton, General Jackson marched his force southwest about thirty miles from Swift Run Gap to counteract the Union threat. The village of McDowell is approximately one hundred miles southwest of Winchester near where the Battle of Kernstown occurred to start the Valley Campaign. General Jackson's force consisted of his own division comprised of the Tenth, Twenty-first, Twenty-third, Thirty-seventh, Forty-second, and Forty-eighth Virginia Infantry along with the First Virginia Battalion. Brigadier General Edward "Allegheny" Johnson's Army of the Northwest joined General Jackson bringing the Twenty-fifth, Thirty-first, Forty-fourth, Fifty-second, and Fifty-eighth Virginia Infantry Regiments along with the Twelfth Georgia Infantry. The total of both Confederate forces was about 6,000.

The battle lasted one day and in the end the Union forces withdrew from the battlefield ending the conflict. Except for the fact that the Union forces withdrew, this battle could have easily been declared a Union victory as the casualties for the Confederate troops were much higher. Confederate losses were reported at 75 killed, 423 wounded [5] Union numbers show 26 killed, 227 wounded and three missing.[6] The casualty numbers reported above are from the Official Records and vary from other sources consistent with battle reporting. Regardless of these numbers, General Jackson had achieved his first battle in the Valley Campaign that would not be his last!

It wouldn't take long for the next battle of the Valley Campaign. General Jackson's success at McDowell likely bolstered the moral of the Confederate troops as well as General Jackson himself. The push was now on to defeat Union Major General Banks who had taken a position at Strasburg, Virginia, fifteen miles southwest of Winchester. The First Maryland Volunteer Infantry under the command of Colonel John Reese Kenly as part of General Banks Department of the Shenandoah was located at Front Royal some eight or so miles southeast of Strasburg with just over 1,000 troops. It was here on May 23, 1862, that the **Battle of Front Royal** also known as the **Battle of Guard Hill** or the **Battle of Cedarville** occurred when the Union forces were attacked by three times the number of troops belonging to Major General Jackson's Army of the Valley.

Confederate Major General Jackson had at his disposal nearly 9,000 troops consisting of his own division and the division of Major General Richard S. Ewell. Of that number only 3,000 took part in the battle and they were a mix from each division command. Most notable was the Ninth Louisiana Infantry belonging to the Eight Brigade of Brigadier General Richard Taylor. Included in this brigade was Wheat's Battalion commanded by Major C. Roberdeau Wheat also known as the "Louisiana Tigers" well established for their audacious actions on the battlefield. Another Confederate command was the First Maryland Infantry under the command of Colonel Bradley T. Johnson. This organization is particularly significant due to fact that it faced a Union command of the same designation, First Maryland Volunteer Infantry, of which many soldiers were brothers, relatives, friends, and more, prior to the war effort! The First Maryland Infantry (CSA) took captive the First Maryland Volunteer Infantry (Union) on the day of the battle!

When all was said and done, Union Colonel Kenly and his First Maryland Volunteer Infantry were overwhelmed resulting in as many as 32 killed, 122 wounded plus some 691 captured. Confederate casualties on the other hand resulted in somewhere around thirty-six killed and wounded. As is true for many battlefield casualty counts, the numbers for both armies may have been different than reported in some sources. Regardless of this situation, the battle was a decisive victory for Confederate Generals Jackson and Ewell and sent Union Major General Banks and his Department of the Shenandoah in a hurry to Winchester to the north where the next battle would take place just two days later.

The **First Battle of Winchester** occurred May 25, 1862, when the vastly outnumbered Union Department of the Shenandoah commanded by Major General Nathaniel P. Banks would be defeated by Major General Thomas J. "Stonewall" Jackson and the Confederate Department of the Valley. The Department of the Shenandoah at this time in the war consisted only of the First Division commanded by Brigadier General Alpheus Starkey Williams with two brigades, a cavalry attachment, an artillery attachment and a cavalry brigade, about 6,500 troops. All units except Battery B, Fourth U. S. Artillery, were State volunteer organizations from Connecticut, Indiana, Maine, Maryland, Massachusetts, New York, and Pennsylvania. The Confederate commands were much the same as in previous engagements including those from Virginia, Alabama, Georgia, Mississippi, North Carolina, Louisiana, and Maryland.

Learning about the loss of the Union First Maryland Volunteer Infantry at Front Royal, General Banks moved his command north toward Winchester harassed all along the way by Confederate troops losing many of his supply wagons to the enemy. Arriving near Winchester, the Union troops took a meager stand although they were outnumbered and out gunned! The full force of Major General Jackson's Division and that of Major General Ewell's numbering around 16,000 men brought the battle to a fairly quick end forcing General Banks to save what forces he could and withdraw to the east across the Potomac River.

The Confederate troops so exhausted by their recent actions were unable to pursue ending this portion of the Valley Campaign, but not the last engagement! The First Battle of Winchester was an obvious loss to the Union command in more than just casualties, but the numbers show thirty killed, 121 wounded, and 1.023 captured or missing. Confederate numbers reflect around 225 killed, wounded, and missing.

The final nail in the Valley Campaign would take place on June 8-9 with the **Battle of Cross Keys** on the first day followed by the **Battle of Port Republic** the next. The outcome of both battles would end for the most part Union participation in the Valley Campaign and change the military effort in the region. The Battle of Cross Keys although not much of a battle was fought by approximately 15,000 Union troops under the command of Major General John Charles Fremont commanding the Mountain Department that would merge into the Army of Virginia at the end of the month on June 26, 1862. General Fremont was one of two Union commands sent to put an end to the Confederate control of the Shenandoah Valley or that was at least the plan.

The second command was that of Brigadier General James Shields, Shield's Division, Department of the Rappahannock, although General Shields was absent and command of the Division was under Brigadier General Erastus Bernard Tyler. Shield's Division would not be involved until the Battle of Port Republic.

General Fremont would face Confederate Major General Richard Stoddert Ewell and his approximately 5,800 troops assigned to Major General Thomas J. "Stonewall" Jackson's Department of the Valley. The odds in the number of soldiers would seem to favor the Union forces, but that would prove otherwise in the end. General Fremont's forces were the aggressors, but were met with a volley of fire from the Confederate positions that set them back on their heels. The battle was brief but no less costly resulting in 114 Union soldiers killed, 443 wounded along with 127 captured or missing while Confederate casualties were reported at forty-one killed, 232 wounded, and fifteen missing.[7, 8.] By days end neither side made any further effort to continue the fight, and action turned to Shield's Division against Confederate Major General Stonewall Jackson at Port Republic.

Troops deploying for the Battle of Cross Keys, Sunday, June 8, 1862

Library of Congress, Prints & Photographs Division, LC-USZ62-7009

The Battle of Port Republic came on the heels of the Battle of Cross Keys with much the same result. Port Republic was a town at the time of the Civil War that is now an unincorporated community in Rockingham County, Virginia, approximately five miles south of Cross Keys also an unincorporated community. It was here that Union Brigadier General Shield's Division under the command of Brigadier General Erastus B. Tyler with about 3,500 troops organized into two brigades with cavalry and artillery support met the combined Confederate forces of Major General Stonewall Jackson's Division and Major General Ewell's Division totaling around 6,000 troops.

Confederate forces under General Jackson's leadership initiated action in the battle and quickly learned that they were outgunned suffering more casualties than expected. This might have continued except for the arrival of General Ewell's Division that tipped the balance in favor of the Confederates. By 10:30 AM on that Monday morning, Union General Tyler was compelled to withdraw his forces signaling an end to the battle providing a final victory for Major General Thomas J. "Stonewall" Jackson and the Confederate Department of the Valley in the Valley Campaign. All Union forces were withdrawn from the Shenandoah Valley at that time. Except for the captured and missing, the Union losses were less than those of the Confederates. Union reports show 67 killed, 393 wounded, but 558 listed as captured or missing while Confederate losses were reported as 78 killed, 533 wounded, and four missing.[9, 10]

Peninsula Campaign

The Valley Campaign was primarily a Confederate effort in the Shenandoah Valley of Virginia while the Peninsula Campaign was a Union effort in southeastern Virginia with the goal of capturing the Confederate Capital of Richmond, Virginia. This action occurred from March to July 1862 overlapping that of the Valley Campaign and featured the Union Army of the Potomac commanded by Major General George Brinton McClellan with over 100,000 troops against the Confederate Army of Northern Virginia of nearly equal strength commanded by General Joseph Eggleston Johnston.

As with nearly all campaigns, there were a number of named engagements that took place during this time to include the Siege of Yorktown from April 5 to May 4, Battle of Williamsburg or Fort Magruder May 5, Battle for Etham's Landing May 7, Battle of Drewry's Bluff or Fort Darling May 15, Battle of Hanover Court House or Slash Church May 27, the Battle of Seven Pines or Fair Oaks May 31 to June 1, and the Seven Days Battle Jun 25 to Jul 1 that included the Battle of Gaines Mill June 26 and the Battle of Malvern Hill July 1.

The effort of the Union led Peninsula Campaign was influenced by what was taking place in the Valley Campaign. Union troops deployed against Confederate forces in the Shenandoah Valley reduced the number of troops available to Major General McClellan in his quest to take Richmond. Even after the conclusion of the Valley Campaign, Union reinforcements were of little help to General McClellan due to precious time lost and far too many failures in the mission. The **Siege of Yorktown** was the first of those failures largely due to the time and resources spent all because of failed intelligence on Confederate troop strength and perhaps some clever tactics employed by the Confederate commander Major General John Bankhead Magruder. General McClellan employed heavy siege artillery batteries against a much smaller Confederate force that was as much as one forth the size of his own Union command.

The organization of the Army of the Potomac was primarily comprised of State commands although there were some U. S. Army units.

The General Headquarters included the Second U. S. Cavalry, one battalion each from the Eighth and Seventeenth U. S. Infantry, and Troop A and E of the Fourth U. S. Cavalry. A number of Federal artillery units were part of the Army of the Potomac. These included Battery E, G, H, and K of the First U. S. Artillery; Battery A, B, E, G, and M of the Second; Battery C, F, G, K, L, and M of the Third; Battery A, C, G., and K of the Fourth; and Battery A, D, F, I, and K of the Fifth U. S. Artillery. In addition to those cavalry units already identified, the First, Fifth and Sixth U. S. Cavalry Regiments served as the Cavalry Reserve. A unit of U. S. Engineers was also part of the command.

States represented in the Union Army of the Potomac included Connecticut, Maine, Massachusetts, Michigan, Minnesota, New Hampshire, New Jersey, New York, Rhode island, Pennsylvania, Vermont, and Wisconsin.

The Confederate Army of Northern Virginia included State commands from at least Alabama, Florida, Georgia, Kentucky, Louisiana, Mississippi, North Carolina, South Carolina, Tennessee, Texas, and Virginia.[11]

This nearly month long siege allowed Confederate General Johnston to increase the strength of his command reinforcing that of General Magruder. When the Confederate defenders finally decided it was time to evacuate Yorktown for a better defensive position, a month had been lost in General McClellan's plan costing 182 Union casualties and about 300 Confederate losses.

Major General George Brinton McClellan
Officer of the Federal Army
National Archives – 111-B-4624

General Joseph Eggleston Johnston
Officer of the Confederate Army
National Archives – 111-B-1782

The first full scale battle following the Siege of Yorktown was the **Battle of Williamsburg** also identified as the **Battle of Fort Magruder** fought May 5, 1862. Confederate Fort Magruder was the largest and main earthen work in a line of numbered redoubts and redans east of Williamsburg that extended across the peninsula from the James River in the south to the York River in the north. Fort Magruder was also identified as Redoubt No. 6 in this defensive line. There were, in fact, three defensive lines established across the peninsula in an attempt to prevent Federal forces from reaching Richmond to the west.[12]

Union Army of the Potomac forces committed for the battle included the III Corps commanded by Brigadier General Samuel Peter Heintzelman and the IV Corps commanded by Brigadier General Erasmus Darwin Keyes supported by Major Joseph Hotchkiss Whittlesey's Fifth U. S. Cavalry. The total number of Union troops was just over 40,000.

The Union forces would face elements of the Confederate Army of Northern Virginia numbering slightly less than 32,000 troops. These included the Second Division under the command of Major General James Longstreet supported by Brigadier General Richard Heron Anderson; Major General John B. Magruder's command; Major General Daniel Harvey Hill's Division; and Cavalry support from Virginia, Mississippi, and Louisiana. State commands represented included Alabama, Florida, Georgia, Louisiana, Mississippi, North Carolina, South Carolina, and Virginia.

Drawing showing the charge of Union Brigadier General Winfield Scott Hancock's First Brigade, Second Division, IV Corps, Army of the Potomac, at the Battle of Williamsburg May 5, 1862
Library of Congress, Prints & Photographs Division, LC-USZ62-44937

Confederate defense of Williamsburg was not meant to stop the Federal advance only to delay it from reaching Richmond. The Battle of Williamsburg was one of several such delaying efforts employed by General Johnston during the Peninsula Campaign. The battle began May 5 with Union General Hooker's III Corps leading the attack that was a fever pitched battle from the start. By the end action each side claimed victory, but little changed from the start other than a large number of casualties. Union initial reports indicated the loss of 456 killed, 1,410 wounded, and 373 either captured or missing. Incomplete reports of Confederate losses listed 167 killed, 606 wounded, and 133 missing.[13, 14]

Two days later, May 7, the **Battle of Etham's Landing** also called the **Battle of Barhamsville** or the **Battle of West Point** would take place along the Pamunkey River to the northwest of Williamsburg. This was a lesser battle than at Williamsburg as far as the number of troops involved and the circumstances surrounding its occurrence. Union Brigadier General William Buell Franklin in command of the First Division, I Corps, Army of the Potomac, was given instructions to send his troops on ships by way of the York River in an attempt to cut off the Confederate retreat after the inconclusive Battle of Williamsburg. The First Division was headed for Etham's Landing along the south bank of the Pamunkey River just west of its juncture with the York River very near the key river port of West Point.

Perhaps realizing that there could be Union efforts to cut off General Johnston from an organized retreat toward Richmond, three brigades of Confederate Brigadier General William Henry Chase Whiting's First Division as part of Major General Gustavus Woodson Smith's Reserve Corps were sent to the area where General Franklin would eventually come ashore at Etham's Landing. The First Brigade was a Texas Brigade under the command of

Brigadier General John Bell Hood consisting of the First, Fourth, and Fifth Texas Regiments along with the Eighteenth Georgia Infantry. The Second Brigade was that of Colonel Wade Hampton's South Carolina Legion and the Nineteenth Georgia Infantry Regiment. The Third Brigade unidentified was assigned as the Reserve.[15]

Soon after Confederate pickets observed Union troops landing from their boats, a decision was made to attack. That attack occurred around 7:00 AM and was fought in a heavily forested area causing difficulty for both sides. By 2:30 that afternoon, the Union troops had been driven back to their boats virtually ending all action. The outcome was more costly to the Union forces with a reported 194 casualties of which at least 46 were captured and sent to prisons in Richmond. Confederate losses were recorded as eight killed and forty wounded.

Having achieved little at Yorktown, Williamsburg, and Etham's Landing, Union Major General McClellan decided to send U. S. Navy ships up the James River in an attempt to attack Richmond from a different vantage point. This effort would take the U. S. Navy past a bend in the river known as Drewy's Bluff named for the owner of the land, Captain Augustus H. Drewry, on which a Confederate fort was constructed. Fort Drewry was the name given by Confederates and Fort Darling by the Union command. The action that followed would result in the **Battle of Drewry's Bluff** also called the **Battle of Fort Darling** that would prove no less successful than previous efforts.

Fort Drewry was an earthen fort seven or so miles down river from Richmond. It held two 8-inch and one 10-inch Columbiad artillery gun. Word was received May 13, 1862, that five Federal gunboats including two ironclads were making their way up the James River. In the lead was the USS *Galena* that was actually iron plate over wood followed by the second ironclad, the USS *Monitor*. Three wooden hull ships named the USS *Aroostook*, *Port Royal*, and *Naugatuck* followed behind. On May 15 the two ironclads approached the fort and opened fire. The artillery of Fort Darling responded. The first shot from the 10-inch Columbiad threw it off its mounting rendering it out of action until it could be remounted. The USS *Galena* had no trouble elevating its guns to reach the fort high on the bluff. The guns of the USS *Monitor*, however, were not designed to allow such elevation and thereby proved much less effective in its fire. As the battle ensued for several hours, ammunition supply from the defenders of Fort Drewry (Darling) became a concern. Captain Drewry ordered a thirty-minute pause to conserve his resources. This delay was interpreted by Lieutenant Jeffers of the USS *Monitor* as an opportunity to move the remainder of his ships into close range of the fort for what was believed to be a final blow. As the five Union gunboats simultaneously attacked the fort, Captain Drewry was urged by his men who were sustaining casualties to resume firing. He obliged ordering fire to concentrate on the wooden gunships. His men did as ordered and soon the 10-inch Columbiad was back in service making a direct hit on the USS Galena that was badly damaged by this time. Commander John Rodgers ordered the Union gunships to withdraw down the river out of range ending the engagement. [16]

There were casualties on both sides, but the men of Fort Drewry who reported seven killed and eight wounded fared much better than did the crew of the USS *Galena* that alone may have sustained thirty killed and wounded. One official report given by Union Navy Commander William Smith on May 19, 1862, reported twelve killed and thirteen wounded. Later reports may give rise to the thirty number for the USS *Galena*. Needless to say, General McClellan once again failed to achieve his plan that was the capture of Richmond.

Depiction of the Battle of Drewry's Bluff, May 15, 1862

Wikipedia

After the Battle of Drewy's Bluff, the military action shifted north. The anticipated arrival of reinforcements for General McClellan's Army of the Potomac prompted units of newly appointed Brigadier General Fritz John Porter's Provisional V Corps to be sent north to insure the safety along the route reinforcements would travel that might have been threatened by Confederate forces. This effort would result in the **Battle of Hanover Court House** or the **Battle of Slash Church** that occurred May 27 involving about 12,000 troops from Brigadier General George Webb Morell's First Division, Colonel Gouverneur Kemble Warren's Third Brigade of the Second Division, and a composite brigade of cavalry and artillery from Army of the Potomac Headquarters led by Brigadier General William Hemsley Emory.

The Confederate forces were initially thought to be 17,000 that actually numbered closer to 4,000 under Brigadier General Lawrence O'Bryan Branch's Fourth Brigade that was part of Brigadier General Ambrose Powell Hill Jr.'s Division in Major General James Longstreet's command. The brigade included the Seventh, Eighteenth, Twenty-eighth, and Thirty-seventh North Carolina infantry plus the Forty-fifth Georgia Infantry. Around noon on Tuesday, May 27, Union General Porter's forces clashed with that of Confederate Colonel Branch's brigade at a point called Peake's Crossing just south of the Hanover Court House. The fight was intense until General Porter ordered his reserves into action that drove the Confederates from the field.

The Battle of Hanover Court House was a clear victory for the Union forces as they outnumbered their opponents nearly four to one. If the casualty numbers can be trusted, Union losses reported 62 killed, 233 wounded, and 70 captured. Confederate losses show 50 killed, 150 wounded, and 730 captured many of whom were stragglers after the battle had ended.

Scene of the "Commencement of the Battle of Hanover Court House 1:45 PM" May 27, 1862.
Inscribed and perhaps difficult to read above the image from left to right are the words "Gen Porter Staff," "6th Regular Cavalry," "The Rebel Army," " Bensons Horse Artillery," and "Johnston's Infantry."
Library of Congress, Prints & Photographs Division, LC-USZ62-7007

NOTE: In the previous graphic, Benson's Horse Artillery was that of Captain Henry Benson in command of Battery M of the Second Regiment, U. S. Horse Artillery. Captain Benson would be mortally wounded July 1 during the Battle of Malvern Hill as part of the Seven Days Battle and die of his wounds August 11, 1862.

Only days had passed from the Battle of Hanover Court House when the next battle of the Peninsula Campaign took place May 31 called the **Battle of Seven Pines** or the **Battle of Fair Oaks**. This battle was a three-day affair ending on June 1 that had further implications on future events. It was also a costly battle in the number of casualties on both sides second only at that time to the battle of Shiloh fought April 6 7, 1862.

The Battle of Seven Pines brought Union Major General McClellan and the Army of the Potomac the closest to Richmond they had been in the Peninsula Campaign, but would not result in the ultimate goal of capturing the city. All 105,000 Union forces in five Corps were deployed in an area northeast of Richmond. The II, V, and VI Corps were between the Pamunkey River to the north and the Chickahominy River to the south. The Pamunkey River was used as a supply line for the command. The III and IV Corps were in a precarious position south of the Chickahominy River that would be difficult to reinforce by other Union Corps if overwhelmed by Confederate forces. Aware of this situation, Confederate General Johnston began his attack plan that might have succeeded if everything had gone as planned. It didn't!

From the very start, General Johnston's orders were either misunderstood or poorly implemented. Further, the march of Confederate troops was no secret to the Union command and preparations were underway to counteract the assault. Fierce fighting did take place and very late on the first day Confederate General Joseph E. Johnston was severely wounded when struck by a bullet followed by shrapnel. He had to be carried from the field. This incident clearly changed the action on the field. The Confederate Left Wing commander, Major General Gustavus Woodson Smith, assumed temporary command of the Army of Northern Virginia that lost most of its aggressiveness. The next day General Robert Edward Lee who was at that time a military advisor to Confederate President Jefferson Davis replaced General Smith as commander of the Army of Northern Virginia. This move not only changed the battle plan in this incident, but would change much of the Confederate war plans for the duration of the war.

At dawn on Sunday, June 1, a new Confederate military action took place under the leadership of General Robert E. Lee. Initial gains were made, but the Union command had brought up a large number of reinforcements that stalled the effort. By late mid-morning the battle had ended and the casualty count began. Return of Casualties in the Army of the Potomac at the Battle of Fair Oaks, or Seven Pines, Va., May 31-June 1, 1862" list 790 killed, 3,594 wounded, and 647 either missing or captured.[17] Confederate count for the Army of Northern Virginia show 960 killed, 4,749 wounded, and 405 missing or captured. Needless to say, the Battle of Seven Pines or Fair Oaks was no small battle in lieu of the number of casualties, but it would not end the Peninsula Campaign. Yet to come was the **Seven Days Battle** Jun 25 to Jul 1 that included six battles of various types to which the **Battle of Gaines Mill** June 26 and the **Battle of Malvern Hill** July 1 were two of the more major battles.

Pencil drawing of the wounded at the Battle of Seven Pines being loaded onto rail cars
It is unknown if these are Union or Confederate wounded, but most likely Union soldiers.
Library of Congress, Prints & Photographs Division, LC-USZ62-5243

The **Seven Days Battles** began Wednesday, June 25, with the first of six conflicts involving in excess of 100,000 Union troops and just over 90,000 Confederates. The first of these engagements was named the **Battle of Oak Grove** perhaps for the White Oak Swamp near where the battle took place. This battle also went by the name **Battle of French's Field** or **Kings' School House** although there are no record of these locations other than T. French's Grist Mill that may have been property owned by someone with the name French and there may have been a school house nearby by the name King's. At any rate, this first battle was a Union effort to move close enough to Richmond to establish artillery positions that could bring effective fire on Richmond.

The Union Army of the Potomac III Corps commanded by Brigadier General Samuel Peter

Heintzelman was given the mission of undertaking this mission. The advance of the III Corps with its two divisions that crossed an area known as the White Oak Swamp was met and halted by the Confederate Division of Brigadier General Benjamin Huger with three brigades involving troops from Alabama, Georgia, Louisiana, and Virginia. Later in the day a second attempt was made and this too failed to gain enough ground to implement an artillery position called for by Union Major General McClellan. By some accounts this battle is referred to as a minor battle, but the casualty count seems to speak otherwise. Union losses included 68 killed, 503 wounded, and 55 missing. Confederate losses totaled 66 killed, 362 wounded, and 13 missing.

The next day, Thursday, June 26, General Robert E. Lee now commanding the Confederate Army of Northern Virginia struck a blow against Union forces in the **Battle of Beaver Creek Dam** near the town of Mechanicsville, Virginia. As with many battles, there are other names than that of Beaver Creek Dam such as **Battle of Mechanicsville** or **Ellerson's Mill**. This battle did not go well for General Lee who met with stiff resistance from the newly established Union V Corps commanded by Brigadier General Fritz John Porter and his 15,000 (+) troops. By all standards this engagement was considered a major battle and the casualty count reflect this fact.

General Lee planned to push the Union forces as far as he could away from Richmond realizing that a prolonged siege would result in the fall of Richmond. If his plan had worked it would have saved the day, but as with many of the Civil War battles there always seemed to be something that went wrong and this case was no different! Confederate commands had been under heavy fighting and worn down. Orders were either not received or received too late to effectively implement the objective. All of the possible complications were present in this endeavor plus the Union forces were in a strong defensive position that crippled the Confederate attack. In the end, General Porter's men held strong against General Lee inflicting many more casualties upon the Rebel troops and stopping the Confederate objective. Union losses were forty-nine killed, 207 wounded, and 105 missing or captured. Confederate numbers were only totaled at 1,484..

Sketch of the Union troops involved in the Battle of Beaver Creek Dam, (aka Battle of Ellerson's Mill)
Thursday, June 26, 1862
Wikipedia {{ PD-1923 }}

There was no relief in military action during this time in the Peninsula Campaign. The Battle of Beaver Dam Creek was a major battle followed the next day by another major battle called the **Battle of Gaines Mill** that also went by the names **First Battle of Cold Harbor** or **Battle of the Chickahominy River**. Once again Confederate General Robert E. Lee initiated action against the Union V Corps of Brigadier General Porter just as he had done the day before resulting in nearly the same outcome. General Lee was determined to either defeat the Union forces or push them from the vicinity of Richmond. The Union V Corps was south of the Chickahominy River threatening the security of Richmond. With a force of nearly 60,000 troops, General Lee assaulted the defensive position of the Union line of some 34,000 troops early in the morning on June 27. Union resistance was fierce and again there were problems with the Confederate forces meeting the requirements of General Lee. Confederate casualties mounted throughout the day and coordination on the battlefield was hurting the chances of achieving anything of substance. Finally at the end of day's light, Confederate forces were able to disperse the Union defenders from their position forcing them to cross the Chickahominy River by any means available, but it was done in an organized manner. After constant fighting, General Lee's troops were in no condition to pursue against the Blue Coats.

Confederate General Lee may have achieved his objective, but it was a costly achievement as it was for Union General Porter and his V Corps. Confederate losses are put at 1,492 killed, 6,402 wounded, and 108 missing or captured. Union losses were somewhat lower but by no means insignificant. There were 894 reported as killed, 3,107 wounded, and a much higher 2,836 reported as missing or captured. These numbers seem staggering, but there were still five battles yet to happen in the Seven Days Battles.

Pencil drawing showing Union troops of the V Corps in the Battle of Gaines Mill on June 27, 1862
Library of Congress, Prints & Photographs Division, LC-USZ62-14330

At the time the Battle of Gaines Mill was raging, a lesser battle called the **Battle of Garnett's and Golding's Farms** occurred that was more a skirmish than a battle. This was a Confederate probing action near the Garnett Farm on the 27th and the Golding's Farm the next day. Both actions involved Union Brigadier General Winfield Scott Hancock's First Brigade of the Second Division, VI Corps, against Confederate Major General John Bankhead Magruder's Reserve forces of Brigadier General Robert Toombs' and Colonel George Thomas Anderson's Brigades of Brigadier General David Rumph Jones' Division. Each Confederate attempt was repulsed resulting in slightly less than 200 Union casualties and 438 Confederate losses.

The Battle of Garnett's and Golding's Farms was a minor involvement and the next engagement was also minor only in the number of casualties, not the number of troops involved! This was the **Battle of Savage's Station** fought June 29 as General McClellan's Army of the Potomac was finally abandoning their ambitious goal of capturing Richmond, Virginia. The Army was withdrawing toward the James River to the south for their eventual return to the area of Washington, D. C.

The Union Army of the Potomac's II Corps commanded by Brigadier General Edwin Voss Sumner was the rear guard of the Army's withdrawal.. As in the Battle of Garnett's and Golding's Farms, Major General John Bankhead Magruder's Reserve forces of the Army of Northern Virginia attacked General Sumner's troops at a point along the Richmond & York Railroad called Savage's Station. A portion of the Union forces fought as they withdrew resulting in a large number of casualties mostly to those units in contact. The intensity of the fighting caused the Union wounded to be left on the field as well as with many supplies as Confederate troops overran the ground. Much of the Union II Corps managed to accomplish their withdrawal except for their wounded and the loss of supplies.

Union forces on the day of the Battle of Savage's Station, June 29, 1862.
Library of Congress, prints & Photographs Division, LC-USZ62-82884

Confederate General Lee was not pleased with the outcome of the battle and made his displeasure known to General Magruder. However, General Magruder was not the only commander responsible for the outcome as others failed to arrive in time as planned. Regardless, over 1,000 Union casualties resulted from the fighting compared to just under 500 for the Confederates.

Union Field Hospital treating their wounded within Confederate lines after the Battle of Savage's Station
Library of Congress, Prints & Photographs Division, LC-B8171-491

Confederate General Lee was apparently intent on keeping the pressure on the Army of the Potomac as the Army worked their way to the James River. This is reflected in the **Battle of Glendale** also called the **Battle of Frayser's Farm** among a host of other names that took place on Monday, June 30, right on the heels of the Battle of Savage's Station.

Each Army in this battle involved 40,000 or so troops. The Army of the Potomac in its quest to reach the James River had only partially achieved their goal. About two-thirds, however, had made it past the White Oak Swamp Creek region and were near the small community of Glendale at the intersection of the Charles City road and the Quaker or Willis Church Road still some four miles from the James River. What followed was another of the misguided military engagements through faulty implementation this time on the part of Confederates for a multitude of reasons. Nearly seven days of constant fighting moving over sometimes difficult if not impossible terrain took a huge toll on troops from both sides leaving the Confederates short in their attempt to prevent the Federal forces from reaching the James River although there was a battle of two yet to come!

This battle resulted in casualties on both sides, but Confederate losses were greater reporting 638 killed, 2,814 wounded, and 211 missing. Federal numbers reflect 297 killed, 1,696 wounded, and 1,804 missing or captured.

Opening of the Battle of Glendale or Frayser's Farm showing artillery of Union Brigadier General Henry W. Slocum's First Division, VI Corps, in a fight against Confederate Major General Benjamin Huger's Division from the Army of Northern Virginia.

Wikipedia {{ PD-1923 }}

The last battle of both the Seven Days Battles and the larger Peninsula Campaign occurred July 1 at a point on the north side of the James River named Malvern Hill not so much for a hill, but for a home that stood on the site built in the seventeenth century by one Thomas Cocke and named for the Malvern Hills in England. The conflict that ensued was named the **Battle of Malvern Hill** as well as the **Battle of Poindexter's Farm** that involved the Union V Corps of Brigadier General Fritz John Porter and the remainder of the Army of the Potomac that had not yet boarded ships.

The battlefield gave a distinct advantage to the Union forces due to open ground over which Confederate General Lee would have to advance his troops. Union artillery units positioned on Malvern Hill were able to direct fire on the unprotected advancing troops resulting in one failed attempt after another. In addition to ground artillery batteries, Union gunboats positioned on the James River also added to the firepower against Confederate troops. Several waves of Confederate infantry assaults against the Union positions were beaten back giving rise to a decisive Union victory if for no other reason than Confederate forces failed to stop the Union Army of the Potomac.

There were reported failures on the part of some Confederate commanders under General Lee, but it is doubtful that if everything had gone as planned there would have been any change in the outcome due to the superior field position held by the Union forces. The actual number of casualties is speculation as both Armies lumped different battles together in providing casualty returns, but there were approximately 3,000 Union losses compared to over 5,500 Confederates.

Battle of Malvern Hill fought July 1, 1862, with view of the James River in the background.
Wikipedia {{ PD-1923 }}

With the Battle of Malvern Hill at an end, Major General George McClellan established a staging area down river at Harrison's Landing on the north side of the James River approximately eight miles by water. It was here that the Union troops would assemble marching overland burning bridges as they moved denying Confederate forces any attempt of further attack. Once in the staging area they could take stock of their needs, treat the wounded, and refit for the next engagement wherever and whenever it might occur.

Eventually the Army of the Potomac would return to Washington in support of other military actions to follow. It would take nearly two years before there would be renewed military involvement in the Virginia Peninsula.

Northern Virginia Campaign

Perhaps bolstered by denying Union Major General George B. McClellan's 105,000 man Army of the Potomac from capturing Richmond, Confederate General Robert E. Lee marched elements of his Army of Northern Virginia north toward Washington with the whole Army to follow. This action kicked off the **Northern Virginia Campaign** from late July to the first of September also referred to as the **Second Bull Run Campaign** or the **Second Manassas Campaign**. This length of this campaign was shorter than those already covered and with only three named battles. It did, however, show the resolve of the Confederate forces under their new commander, General Lee.

Portrait of General Robert Edward Lee
Officer of the Confederate Army and
Commander of the Army of Northern Virginia

Library of Congress, Prints & Photographs Division,
LC-B8172-0001

A new Union major command came on the scene June 26, 1862, named the **Army of Virginia** under the command of Major General John Pope. The Army of Virginia was a consolidation of the Mountain Department, Department of the Shenandoah, and the Department of the Rappahannock with the commanders of each of the three becoming the I, II, and III Corps commanders respectively.

The first battle of the Northern Virginia Campaign was the **Battle of Cedar Mountain** August 9, 1862, also called Slaughter's Mountain or Cedar Run involving the Union Army of Virginia's II Corps commanded by Major General Nathaniel Prentiss Banks and his 8,000 troops against the Confederate Army of Northern Virginia's Left Wing commanded by Major General Thomas Jonathon "Stonewall" Jackson with nearly 17,000 soldiers.

The Battle of Cedar Mountain was precipitated by Union General Pope's deployment of troops across Northern Virginia

partly to relieve pressure from Confederate forces against Major General McClellan's withdrawal after the Peninsula Campaign. Confederate General Lee responded to Union General Pope's action by deploying Major General Jackson's Left Wing. The battle that ensued saw gains and losses on both sides until a final Confederate attack broke the Union line forcing General Banks to order a retreat surrendering the field to the Confederates. Union losses totaled 314 killed, 1,445 wounded, and 594 missing. Confederate casualties included 231 killed and 1,107 wounded.

Confederate success at the Battle of Cedar Mountain gave rise to a major battle conducted August 29-30, 1862, that became known as he **Second Battle of Bull Run** also called the **Second Manassas**. Around 8:30 on the day prior to the beginning of the Second Battle of Bull run, the Army of Northern Virginia's Right Wing commanded by Major General James Longstreet skirmished with Union Brigadier

General James Brewerton Ricketts' Second Division of the III Corps, Army of Virginia. This action became known as the **Battle of Thoroughfare Gap** that was an attempt by the Union command to prevent General Longstreet from linking up with General Jackson's Left Wing. This was a Union Division 5,000 strong trying to stop an army five times its size that would not happen! This engagement was anything but a battle that did nothing to stop General Longstreet from linking up with the Left Wing of the Army of Northern Virginia.

Major General Longstreet's troops of the Right Wing, Army of Northern Virginia, movement through Thoroughfare Gap around August 28, 1862
Wikipedia {{ PD-1923 }}

Action in the Second Battle of Bull Run began August 29 at which time Union Major General Pope's 50,000 plus Army of Virginia launched a series of attacks against Confederate forces of Major General Jackson's Left Wing of the Army of Northern Virginia. The attacks met with little success causing many casualties on both sides. By noon, the Confederate Right Wing of the Army of Northern Virginia under Major General Longstreet arrived on the battlefield having marched by way of the Thoroughfare Gap. The entire Army of Northern Virginia was on scene numbering around 50,000 troops.

Major action in the battle occurred on Saturday, August 30, with Union General Pope once again attacking what he believed was only the Left Wing of the Confederate Army of Northern Virginia. In fact, the Union Army was opposed by the entire Army of Northern Virginia. Little matter that the Union III, V, and IX Corps of General McClellan's Army of the

Potomac had joined adding 25,000 troops to the Union force. Every Union attempt to break the ranks of the Confederate troops was met with devastating losses. Adding to this situation was faulty information giving General Pope reason to believe that Confederate forces were retreating when just the opposite was taking place. The back and forth battle raged on until Confederate General Lee decided that it was time to initiate an all out assault and in doing so he forced the Union command to order a withdrawal around early evening on August 30 that was done in an orderly manner yet it gave the battlefield and the victory to the Confederates.

Various sources reporting on the casualties in the Second Battle of Bull Run are all over the map. It is safe to say that Union casualty numbers were greater than those of the Confederates. To further complicate the actual number of casualties in this one battle, official returns on casualties lump together numbers of the several engagements of the Northern Virginia Campaign rather than breaking them down by battle. A best guess scenario might show total Union losses at anywhere from 13,000 to 15,000 and Confederate numbers of 8,000 to around 9,000. For a battle of this significance, casualty counts should have been more accurate!

"Advance of the right wing of Genl. Lee's army commanded by Genl. Longstreet on Genl. McDowell's corps. South of Baldface Hill along the ridge S.E. of the Warrenton turnpike" during the Second Battle of Bull Run. Library of Congress, Prints & Photographs Division, LC-USZ62-13993

Retreat of Union forces crossing the Stone Bridge Saturday evening August 30, 1862,
at the end of the Second Battle of Bull Run
Wikipedia {{ PD-1923 }}

The Second Battle of Bull Run or Second Manassas did not end the Northern Virginia Campaign. There was one more battle to fight. In an effort to cut off the retreat of the Union Army of Virginia, Confederate Left Wing commander, Major General Jackson, of the Army of Northern Virginia engaged the attached III and IX Corps of the Army of the Potomac on September 1 in the **Battle of Chantilly** or the Confederate name **Battle of Ox Hill**. This battle was similar to the Battle of Thoroughfare Gap in the disparity of troop numbers showing about 6,000 Union against 20,000 Confederates. Regardless of the troop disparity, all efforts to stop the Union retreat failed to materialize and the brief battle ended without success, but it was a devastating blow to the Union command when both Brigadier General Isaac Ingalls Stevens in command of the First Division of the IX Corps, Army of the Potomac, and Major General Philip Kearny, Jr. commanding the First Division of the III Corps also of the Army of Potomac were killed in the Battle of Chantilly. General Kearny was killed when he mistakenly rode into the line of Confederate soldiers as depicted in the following sketch. There were other Union losses amounting to around 1,300 and Confederate numbers about 800.

US Military History– American Civil War

Major General Philip Kearny attempting to escape after mistakenly riding into Confederate lines.

Wikipedia {{ PD-1923 }}

Maryland Campaign

Following the Confederate's successful Northern Virginia Campaign, General Lee marched his 55,000 troops across the Potomac River into Maryland in hopes of finding adequate supplies for his army and proving that Federal territory was not free from occupation. This began the Maryland Campaign that lasted only seventeen days, but produced the most horrific battle of the American Civil War and perhaps all of modern military history.

At the same time that the Confederate Army of Northern Virginia moved into Maryland, Union Major General George B. McClellan moved his 102,000 strong Army of the Potomac through the South Mountain passes to the southeast of General Lee. It was here on September 14, 1862, that the **Battle of South Mountain** was fought that involved around 28,000 troops of the Army of the Potomac against some 18,000 troops from the Army of

Northern Virginia. There are three gaps in the South Mountain range that is a continuation of the Blue Mountains in Virginia. General Lee's Confederate forces occupied each gap. **Crampton's Gap** to the southwest held by Confederate Major General Lafayette McLaws' Division was attacked by the VI and IV (-) Corps of the Army of the Potomac and was taken at a cost of 113 killed, 418 wounded, and 2 listed as missing or captured.[18] Two of the Union wounded may have been mortally wounded reducing the number of wounded and adding to the number of killed. Nearly half of Confederate Brigadier General Howell Cobb's Brigade of 2,100 soldiers involved in the fight were either killed or wounded if not captured. **Turner's Gap** and **Fox's Gap** very near each other to the right of Crampton's Gap were attacked by the Right Wing of the I and IX Corps of the Army of the Potomac with lesser results, but soon gave way as General Lee ordered a withdrawal toward the town of Sharpsburg to the west. Union casualties were reported as 325 killed, 1,403 wounded, and 85 missing or captured. Confederate numbers although not officially provided may have been 195 killed, 801 wounded, and 763 missing or captured.

Battle scene at Fox's Gap during the Battle of South Mountain September 14, 1862
Library of Congress, Prints & Photographs Division, LC-USZ62-12926

Sketch of Confederate dead at Fox's Gap the day after the Battle of South Mountain
Wikipedia {{ US-1923 }}

While action was taking place near South Mountain, Confederate Major General Thomas J. "Stonewall" Jackson had a mission to capture the Union garrison and supply center at Harper's Ferry located at the confluence of the Shenandoah River with the Potomac River. The 14,000 strong Union garrison at Harper's Ferry was commanded by Colonel Dixon Stansbury Miles, an 1824 graduate of the United States Military Academy and veteran of several earlier wars. Colonel Miles' garrison was outnumbered and outgunned by Confederate General Jackson's 20,000 plus force from the Army of Northern Virginia. After three days of fighting, a bombardment of enormous measure forced the garrison to offer surrender. Before surrender could be accomplished, Colonel Miles was struck by a shell fragment and died of his wounds the next day. Harper's Ferry had fallen at a cost of over 12,000 captured along with 44 killed and 173 wounded. Confederate losses totaled 39 killed and 247 wounded.

The surrender of Harper's Ferry to Confederate General Jackson permitted his 20,000 plus command to march north joining General Lee near Sharpsburg, Maryland. It was at Sharpsburg that the **Battle of Antietam** also called the **Battle of Sharpsburg** took place on September 17 pitting the Confederate Army of Northern Virginia against the Union Army of the Potomac. This was a one-day battle that resulted in a combined 22,000 casualties. Only the three-day Battle of Gettysburg July 1863 can compete with this casualty count! More than one-fourth of the total Confederate force became casualties in one form or another while a greater number but lesser percentage resulted in Union losses!

Union thrust in the Battle of Antietam showing the Antietam Creek Bridge
Library of Congress, Prints & Photographs Division, LC-USZ62-15599

Confederate General Lee had organized his force in a defensive line slightly east of Sharpsburg along Antietam Creek that ran primarily from north to south eventually emptying into the Potomac River. Union Major General Joseph Hooker's I Corps of the Army of the Potomac began the attack followed by others in a back and forth battle that left no mercy to those in the conflict. By nightfall the battlefield was littered with the bodies of the killed and wounded. By all measures, this could have been a decisive victory for the Union troops if Major General McClellan had pressed the issue but he did not. Six Corps were available to General McClellan, but he only utilized four of them for reasons unknown.

Failing to take advantage of the situation allowed General Lee to withdraw his forces across the Potomac River back to the safe zone he had come from. When the casualty totals were finalized, the Confederate killed numbered 1,567 with 7,752 wounded, and 1,018 missing or captured. Union losses were 2,108 killed, 9,549 wounded, and 753 listed as missing or captured. These numbers are staggering, but there would be more of the same in the years to come!

Union troops burying their dead after the Battle of Antietam
Wikipedia {{ PD-1923 }}

As deadly as the Battle of Antietam had proven to be, there was still one more battle to fight in the Maryland Campaign. That was the **Battle of Shepherdstown** or the **Battle of Boteler's Ford** that occurred September 19-20 between divisions of both the Union and Confederate Armies. This action initiated by Union forces may have been a test of intentions following the Battle of Antietam. It resulted in roughly three hundred plus casualties on both Armies, but gave assurances that the Maryland Campaign had come to an end. What had not come to an end was the fighting in 1862. That would not end until after the Fredericksburg Campaign in December. The length of time from the Battle of Antietam in mid-September to action in Fredericksburg in December gives rise to the devastation of the former battle and the need to heal!

Fredericksburg Campaign

The Fredericksburg Campaign was a Union effort to once again capture Richmond, but the campaign never materialized due to a battle that ended the purpose! Union Major General Ambrose Everett Burnside replaced Major General George B. McClellan as commander of the Army of the Potomac on November 9, 1862. General Burnside's tenure as commander would last only two and a half short months most likely due to his devastating lost in the Battle of Fredericksburg in the period of December 11-15. Major command changes were frequent occurrences in the Union Army while Confederate General Lee remained for the duration of the American Civil War.

General Burnside was game on once again going after Richmond and thought that an overland approach by way of Fredericksburg, Virginia, might do the trick. The plan was to rapidly capture Fredericksburg and march on to Richmond approximately forty-five miles south that did not happen. Fredericksburg was situated on high bluffs along the south side of the Rappahannock River that would require pontoon boats to cross. Failure of the boats to arrive caused a delay in the Union plan allowing the nemesis of past battles for Union forces Confederate General Lee to assemble his forces in Fredericksburg.

The Union Army was organized into three divisions identified as the Right Grand, Center Grand, and Left Grand amassing slightly more than 122,000 troops. The Confederate Army consisted of the First and Second Corps along with a Cavalry Division totaling 78,000 plus. Once sufficient pontoon boats were available, the Fifteenth and Fiftieth New York Engineers along with a Battalion of U. S. Engineers began assembling the several pontoon bridges across the Rappahannock River beginning Thursday, December 11. The Engineers were faced with weapon fire from Confederate Sharpshooters that became a killing field.

Union Engineers building pontoon bridges across the Rappahannock River December 11, 1862
Library of Congress, Prints & Photographs Division, LC-USZ62-7023

Eventually, landing parties were sent across the river in boats at which time street fighting occurred that helped to silence the sharpshooter. In early afternoon on Thursday, a portion of the Union Right Grand Division was able to cross the river using the pontoon bridges while the remainder of the Division did the same the next day. The Left Grand Division south of the city was able to cross the river on two pontoon bridges without much difficulty beginning December 11 and finished the next day. The Right Grand Division made its crossing on Saturday.

Wood engraving of Union soldier engaged in street fighting in Fredericksburg
Library of Congress, Prints & Photographs Division, LC-USZ62-132748

Once the entire Army of the Potomac had managed to land its troops on the Fredericksburg side of the river, the Army was faced with Confederate fire from the high ground of Marye's Heights that towered above Fredericksburg. One Union attack after another on the Confederates entrenched on Marye's Heights met with the same failure. Finally, General Burnside was convinced that further attempts to dislodge Confederate General Lee's troops would be fruitless and the a pause in the action took place. On the afternoon of Sunday, December 14, a truce was reached between the major commanders to tend to the wounded on the battlefield. The next day, Major General Burnside marched his army back across the pontoon bridges and ended the battle.

This was a decisive victory for Confederate General Lee and his troops, but perhaps the outcome might have been different if General Burnside had received his pontoon boats in a timely manner and crossed the Rappahannock River before Confederate reinforcements had arrived to defend Fredericksburg. This "what if" type of scenario played out throughout the American Civil War.

The disparity of losses between Union and Confederate troops is staggering, but not surprising due to the defensive posture undertaken by the Confederate forces. Union killed were 1,284, wounded, 9,600, and 1,769 missing or captured. Confederate losses were one-third showing only 408 killed, 3,742 wounded, and 7 either missing or captured. The Fredericksburg Campaign had failed to make it past the first major objective and new efforts would be seen in 1863.

The first wave of Union soldiers crossing the Rappahannock River in the Battle of Fredericksburg
Library of Congress, Prints & Photographs Division, LC-USZ62-11345

----

[1] American Civil War: Support Services of the Union Army, p. 51-52.

[2] The War of the Rebellion: A Compilation of the Official Records of the Union and Confederate Armies, Vol. VIII, p. 204-206.

[3] Ibid, Vol. XII, Part 1, p. 346.

[4] Ibid, p. 384

[5] Ibid, p. 476

[6] Ibid, p. 462

[7] Ibid, p.665

[8] Ibid, p. 784

[9] Ibid, p. 690

[10] Ibid, p. 787

[11] Ibid, Vol. XI, Part III, p. 479-484.

[12] Civil War Era Fortifications, Virginia, p. 754.

(13) The War of the Rebellion: A Compilation of the Official Records of the Union and Confederate Armies, Vol. XI, Part I, p. 450.

(14) Ibid, p. 569.

(15) Ibid, p. 629-633

(16) Civil War Era Fortifications, Virginia, p. 739

(17) The War of the Rebellion: A Compilation of the Official Records of the Union and Confederate Armies, Vol. XI, Part I, p. 762.

(18) Ibid, Vol. XIX, Pt. I, p. 183

1863

The year 1863 saw fewer named military campaigns, but that did not lessen the importance nor decrease the number of battles or casualties. The Vicksburg Campaign including the Siege of Vicksburg involved fourteen named conflicts that occurred over four months if not longer. Of shorter duration was the Chancellorsville Campaign with two battles besides the Battle of Chancellorsville itself. The Gettysburg Campaign involved seventeen named battles including the battle named for the campaign and that battle rivals the Battle of Antietam in the Maryland Campaign during 1862. Tennessee and Georgia were the sites of two campaigns in the second half of 1863 named the Chickamauga and Chattanooga that shifted attention away from Virginia that had been ravaged in earlier action.

Vicksburg Campaign

The Vicksburg Campaign involved action around Vicksburg, Mississippi, in the Western Theater of the American Civil War described as an area primarily west of the Appalachian Mountains and east of the Mississippi River. The exact dividing line other than the Mississippi River was vague and there were areas that overlapped with the Eastern Theater States of Virginia, Maryland, Pennsylvania, coastal portions of North Carolina, and Washington, D. C. proper. A third theater of operations during the war was the Trans-Mississippi Theater that included those States immediately west of the Mississippi River as well as States and territories further west

The ability of Union forces to freely navigate the length of the Mississippi River was hampered by the Mississippi River town of Vicksburg held by Confederate Lieutenant General John Clifford Pemberton's Army of the Department of Mississippi and East Louisiana. The Department of Mississippi and East Louisiana established October 1, 1862, became the Army of the Department of Mississippi & East Louisiana on December 7, 1862, under the same commander, Lieutenant General John C. Pemberton. To complicate matters, the new department name was also identified as Army of Mississippi or Army of Vicksburg and commanded by the same Lieutenant General Pemberton. The original name Department of Mississippi and East Louisiana would be reinstated after the fall of Vicksburg, July 4, 1863.[1]

Vicksburg was on the east side at a sharp bend of the Mississippi River located on a high bluff giving the defenders a commanding view of the river approaches. Union Major General Ulysses Simpson Grant in command of the Army of the Tennessee was charged with capturing Vicksburg that would involve both ground and naval assets. The dates for the Vicksburg Campaign are given as March 29 - July 4,1863, but there were U. S. Naval efforts to silence Vicksburg as early as May 1862 that were followed by later attempts without success.

Major General Ulysses S. Grant
Officer of the Federal Army
National Archive - 164

Lieutenant General John C. Pemberton
Officer of the Confederate Army
Library of Congress, Prints & Photographs
Division, LC-USZ62-130838

The Vicksburg Campaign involved more than just the town of Vicksburg. In fact, there were nine battles leading up to the Siege of Vicksburg that began May 18, 1862, two named expeditions of multiple days action, two battles occurring during the time of the siege operations at Vicksburg, and one battle that occurred on the same day Vicksburg fell to Union forces, July 4, 1863. The first battle actually occurred at the end of 1862, but is included in the 1863 timeframe due to its connection to the Vicksburg Campaign. The **Battle of Chickasaw Bayou** also named the **Battle of Walnut Hills** took place December

26-29, 1862. This was a Union attempt under the command of Major General William Tecumseh Sherman to neutralize Vicksburg that ended in total failure

General Sherman commanded slightly more then 30,000 troops of an Expeditionary Force, Right Wing, XIII Corps, all part of Major General Ulysses S. Grant's Army of the Tennessee. His goal was to capture Vicksburg. He would face Confederate Lieutenant General John C. Pemberton's nearly 14,000 well positioned and determined soldiers from the Army of the Department of Mississippi and East Louisiana.

Major General William Tecumseh Sherman
Officer of the Federal Army

National Archives – 111-B- 1769

The first wave of Union troops departed Memphis, Tennessee, December 20, 1862, on transport ships escorted by Navy gunboats under the command of Rear Admiral David Dixon Porter. The troops were landed on an island north of Vicksburg opposite Steel's Bayou not far from Chickasaw Bayou where the battle would eventually occur. This area was a complex of the two bayous and the Yazoo River emptying into the Mississippi River. It was also low ground subject to wet and swampy conditions making military efforts more difficult. Both Steele's Bayou and the Yazoo River would see later action in this campaign.

Once ashore, the enemy lines were probed for weak points that failed to materialize. Even an artillery bombardment failed to achieve any easy approach. The only option left was an infantry assault. Each and every attempt by the Union forces to breach the Confederate lines was met with stout resistance by the defenders. Even U. S. Naval efforts were not enough to silence the Confederate forces. Realizing that

further action would produce nothing more than additional casualties, General Sherman called off the operation. The Return of Casualties for General Sherman's Union troops were 208 killed, 1,005 wounded, and 563 either missing or captured.[2] Confederate returns reported fifty-seven killed, 120 wounded, and ten missing.[3]

The **Battle of Arkansas Post** also known as the **Battle of Fort Hindman** followed the Chickasaw Bayou affair January 9, 1863, and came to an end January 11. The effort against Fort Hindman was a deviation from efforts against Vicksburg that did not please Major General Ulysses S. Grant nor was it the design of President Lincoln. Union Major General John Alexander McClernand was given the green light to attack Vicksburg, but changed the goal without approval.

Fort Hindman also identified as Arkansas Post was situated along the north bank of the Arkansas River about twenty-five miles from the Mississippi River. Initially, it was a series of earthen breastworks. The threat of a major

Union assault prompted the construction of a larger and more formidable earthwork fortification established by the Confederates in 1862. The new fort was square shaped with walls one hundred ninety feet long and a bastion on each corner.[4] A twenty foot wide, eight foot deep moat was dug around the fort. The armament included four ten pounder Parrot rifles, four 6-pounder smoothbore rifles, and three 9-inch Columbiads. At its completion in November 1862 there were five thousand Confederate defenders under the command of Brigadier General Thomas James Churchill. The fort was named Fort Hindman for Confederate Major General Thomas Carmichael Hindman.

The Arkansas River was a major waterway of the region. The force that controlled the river could influence the military activity in the area. Early in the American Civil War, Confederates were in control of the river traffic. It would not take long to test the resolve of the fort's defenders. In December of 1862, the same year the fort was built, a Union steamer named the *Blue Wing* would attempt to pass the fort. The guns of the fort fired upon the steamer and quickly forced it to shore and surrender.

The Union Army knew full well the importance of traversing the Arkansas River unencumbered. Arkansas Post had to be captured. A combined force of 32,000 Union soldiers and sailors under the overall command of Major General John Alexander McClernand would undertake this mission. To accomplish this goal, General McClernand combined elements of the U. S. XIII and XV Corps, Department of the Tennessee, into what he termed the Army of the Mississippi. This force was further divided into two numbered Corps consisting of the 1st and 2nd Divisions from each of the original corps. Brigadier General George Washington Morgan commanded the I Corps (formerly the XIII) while the II Corps (formerly the XV) was under the command of Brigadier General William Tecumseh Sherman. Rear Admiral David D. Porter commanded the U. S. Naval forces. The plan called for a combined naval bombardment and ground assault. The force would sail the nearby White River on January 8, 1863, until reaching the Arkansas River. A short distance from the fort, the ground forces would disembark from the vessels and proceed to encircle the fort.

On January 9, 1863, the ground forces went ashore, but failed to be in position for the assault on the 10th resulting in the initial attack conducted by the naval forces. The Union gunboats including the USS *Baron de Kalb*, *Louisville, Cincinnati, Lexington, Rattler*, and *Black Hawk* began their bombardment on January 10. Although there was return fire from the fort, the flotilla received no significant damage. The next day at 1:30 PM the naval bombardment began again and the ground assault commenced. By 3:30 that afternoon the eleven guns of the fort were virtually silenced and surrender was imminent.

Confederate Brigadier General Thomas J. Churchill surrendered Arkansas Post. The number of Confederate prisoners varies from 5,000 to 6,500 that is typical of many of the statistics of the war. Admiral David Porter wrote there were 6,500 prisoners, but the Confederate force was supposedly only 5,000. Other than the Confederate captured, there may have been twenty-eight killed and 81 wounded. Union casualties reported 134 killed, 898 wounded, and 29 missing.[5] Fort Hindman was destroyed in the assault and Union control of the Arkansas River was now theirs.

Union gunboats bombarding Fort Hindman (Arkansas Post) January 11, 1863.
Library of Congress, Prints & Photographs Division, LC-USZ62-14000

Further Union attempts to capture Vicksburg would require a new approach in light of the failures to this point in the war. One plan named the **Yazoo Expedition** was a joint Army and Navy operation using the Mississippi Delta waterways avoiding the Mississippi River itself. This involved a cut in a levee from the Mississippi River leading to Moon Lake allowing naval vessels to pass into the Yazoo Pass to the Coldwater River and then to the Tallahatchee River (spelled Tallahatchie today) that flowed into the Yazoo River. The Yazoo River would give access to the region north of Vicksburg thereby avoiding the well-defended approaches on the Mississippi River.

The Union Army assets were the Army of the Tennessee under the command of Major General Ulysses S. Grant while Rear Admiral David D. Porter commanded the U. S. Navy Mississippi River Squadron. General Grant placed Brigadier General Leonard Fulton Ross commanding the Thirteenth Division, XIII Corps, in command of the Army assets. "The force on the Yazoo consisted originally of 4,500 men, under Ross. To this had been added 3,500 under Quinby (BG Isaac Ferdinand, Seventh Division, XVII Corps), who now commands."[6]

Lieutenant Commander Watson Smith was placed in command of the U. S. Navy for the expedition. At the disposal of Commander Smith was the flagship USS *Rattler*, a steamship, along with the steamers *Mamora*, *Signal*, *Romeo*, and *Forest Rose* followed by two ironclad gunboats USS *Baron De Kalb* and *Chillicothe*. The gunboat USS *Petrel* and two rams, USS *Lioness* and *Fulton* were added later in the operation. The Naval operation kicked off February 3 preparing to cut the levee, but the going was slow allowing Confederate General Pemberton time to have a fort built at the confluence of the Tallahatchee and Yalobusha Rivers that would prevent the expedition from achieving its goal. The Army assets would not follow until February 23 transported on twelve transports supplied with fifteen day's ration, 160 rounds of ammunition per man, and axes and spades to clear obstructions.[7]

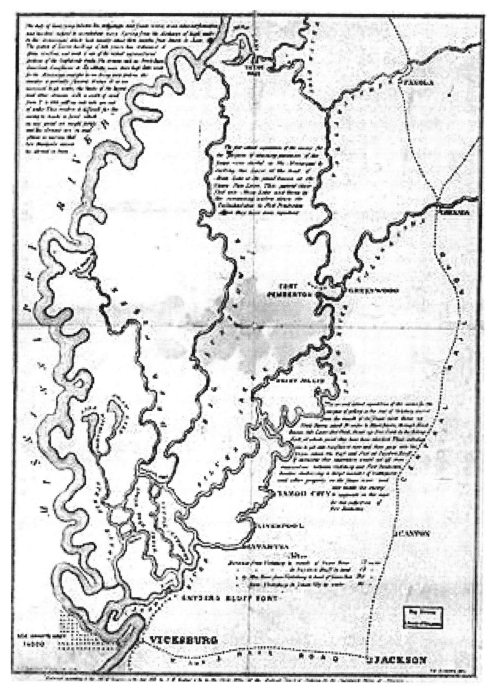

Period map of the Yazoo Expedition with Moon Lake at the top center to the right of the Mississippi River with the Yazoo Pass joining the Coldwater River to the right, then to the Tallahatchee River moving south before reaching Fort Pemberton at the confluence of the Tallahatchie and Yalobusha Rivers. The expedition could not pass Fort Pemberton falling far short of reaching the intended goal of the Yazoo River above Vicksburg.

Source: Wikipedia

The expedition did not reach the terminus of the Tallahatchie River near Confederate Fort Pemberton until March 11. In the meantime, Confederate Major General William Wing Loring with the aid of the Fifty-fifth Alabama Infantry Regiment constructed Fort Pemberton built of earth and cotton bales surrounded by water or flooded bottom-land that protected it from attack except by water. It was not particularly well defended, but its location posed a dilemma for any attacker.

On Friday, March 13, 1863, an assault was made on the fort. A Union flotilla consisting of the USS *Chillicothe* and *Baron de Kalb* took part in the action until their ammunition was exhausted at which time they withdrew. For the next two days, the fort was engaged with much the same results. On Monday, the USS *Chillicothe* was forced to permanently withdraw from the fight when all of its guns were damaged. Fort Pemberton had proven to be impenetrable. Thus, other ways would be necessary if the Yazoo River was to be used as a path to Vicksburg.

Before the Yazoo Expedition had even ended, a second was implemented called **Steele's Bayou Expedition** named for the bayou of that name. This expedition began March 14 one-day after the first attack was made on Fort Pemberton. This expedition mirrored the previous attempt in most everything except the starting point. Steel's Bayou was a waterway off the Mississippi River northwest of Vicksburg. It was miles closer than the Yazoo Expedition effort. It was still a joint Army/Navy operation, but as the previous, stopped short of attaining its goal.

U. S. Navy Rear Admiral David D. Porter was directly involved in this action commanding five gunboats and four mortar rafts. Following close behind were two transports carrying two brigades of Major General William T. Sherman's Fifteen Army Corps, Department of the Tennessee. The ships had little trouble moving through the wider Steele's Bayou, but reaching

Deep Creek posed a problem with a narrow waterway with overhanging trees that limited passage of the ships. This action was further complicated by Confederate troops who had cut trees across the creek both in front and behind the ships once they passed a certain point.

The situation looked bleak for any further movement toward Vicksburg and the narrow waterway made turning the ships around extremely difficult. The Union Eighth Missouri Infantry Regiment of Colonel Giles A. Smith's First Brigade, First Division, XV Army Corps, were called upon to clear the obstacles blocking the passage of the ships. This would prove to be no easy task especially with Confederate troops mounting an attack. General Sherman was still some distance away from the problem facing Rear Admiral Porter, but rushed to the scene in time to avert any further damage. The U. S. Navy ships and the Eighth Missouri were able to free themselves from their predicament and safely return to the Mississippi River ending the Steele's Bayou Expedition by March 27. With the failure of two expeditions attempting to reach Vicksburg from the north or right flank, Union General Grant changed his tactics to the south or left flank of Vicksburg.

The **Battle of Grand Gulf** took place April 29, 1863. Grand Gulf, Mississippi, was a community along the east side of the Mississippi River some twenty miles south of Vicksburg. Grand Gulf no longer exists. At the time of the American Civil War, Confederates had established two forts on the high bluffs overlooking the Mississippi River. Fort Cobun, manned by Company A, First Louisiana Heavy Artillery, under the command of Captain John B. Grayson, was situated northern most of the two forts closest to the river. Fort Cobun mounted one 8-inch Navy gun and two 32-pounder rifled guns. Fort Wade was approximately three-quarters of a mile to the south a slight distance inland under the command of Colonel William Wade of the First Missouri Artillery and Captain Henry Guibor's Missouri Battery. Fort Wade had one 8-inch Navy gun, one 32-pounder smoothbore, and four 6-pouner smoothbore guns. Both forts were earthen type established March 1863.

The Union attack on Grand Gulf was conducted by seven gunboats under the command of Rear Admiral David D. Porter. The U. S. Navy gunboats were the USS *Benton, Carondelet, Lafayette, Louisville, Mound City, Pittsburg, and Tuscumbia*. If the attack had been successful, Major General John A. McClernand's XIII Army Corps, Department of the Tennessee, would have landed from aboard

their transports and taken control of the area. The attack began at 8:30 in the morning and had silenced Fort Wade by 11:30. Fort Cobun was another matter and never taken having disabled the USS *Tuscumbia* in the action. Union Admiral Porter who determined that further action would not achieve the desired outcome call off the attack.

In action against Fort Wade as well as Fort Cobun, Confederate Colonel Wade was killed as were two others and Captain Guibor was among the wounded along with eighteen others. Union casualties reported eighteen killed and fifty-seven wounded most likely sailors on the gunboats involved in the action.

Union Ironclads in action during the Battle of Grand Gulf, April 29, 1863.
Wikipedia { US-1923 }}

Although Union Major General Ulysses S. Grant had changed his approach against Vicksburg shifting military action to the left flank, a Union feign was conducted against Snyder's Bluff north of Vicksburg to insure Confederate reinforcements would not be sent

to disrupt his Grand Gulf operations. The **Battle of Snyder's Bluff** was conducted April 29 to May 1, 1863. Union Major General William T. Sherman's Second Division commanded by Major General Francis Preston Blair, Jr., XV Army Corps, Department of the

Tennessee, combined with U. S. Navy Lieutenant Commander Kidder Randolph Breeze's eight gunboats to give Confederate Brigadier General Louis Hebert's brigade enough attention to keep them in place. After several feigns, the action was suspended having achieved its purpose.

Actions at this time in the Vicksburg Campaign were coming one after another. Evidence of this is the **Battle of Port Gibson** or **Thompson's Hill** May 1 the same day the Battle of Snyder's Bluff ended. Port Gibson, Mississippi, was not on or near the Mississippi River as in all the previous military actions. It was, however, an overland route to Jackson, Mississippi, that was a major railroad link that could provide troop reinforcements and necessary supplies for the Confederate troops in Vicksburg. The Vicksburg and Jackson Railroad running west from Jackson was part of the Southern Railroad to the east, and the New Orleans Jackson and Northern Railroad also identified as the Mississippi Central Railroad running north and south crisscrossed in the town of Jackson.

Union military action at this time would change from a naval involvement to ground action eventually allowing an approach to Vicksburg from the east. Union troops of the XIII and XVII Corps landed unopposed from transports at Bruinsburg, Mississippi, on April 30, 1863. From here they marched overland to the vicinity of Port Gibson where they "Met the enemy (11,000 strong) 4 miles south of Port Gibson at 2 a. m. on the 1st, and engaged him all day, entirely routing him, with the loss of many killed and about 500 prisoners, besides the wounded. Our loss about 100 killed and 500 wounded. The enemy retreated toward Vicksburg, destroying the bridges over the two forks of Bayou Pierre. These were rebuilt, and pursuit continued until the present time. Besides the heavy artillery at this place, four field pieces were captured, some stores, and the enemy driven to destroy many more. The country is the most broken and difficult to operate in I ever saw. Our victory has been most complete, and the enemy thoroughly demoralized.[8] On Saturday, May 2, Union forces moved into Port Gibson without finding any Confederates except their wounded. The four or so Confederate brigades in the engagement were commanded by Brigadier General John Stevens Bowen who would meet his fate July 13, 1863, not due to combat but dysentery.

Actual casualty returns for the Union forces reported 131 killed, 719 wounded, and twenty-five missing. Confederate losses were 68 killed, 380 wounded, and 384 missing that most likely includes those captured. These last numbers are those reported by Confederate sources that differ from the estimates given by Union Major General Ulysses S. Grant in the quote in the previous paragraph.

Before taking aim at Jackson, Mississippi, and the rail lines, Raymond, Mississippi, stood in the way where slightly more than 4,000 Confederate troops under the command of Brigadier General John Gregg would be engaged May 12 in the **Battle of Raymond** by the Union XVII Corps under Major General James Birdseye McPherson and his roughly 12,000 troops.

The Battle of Raymond began south of the town near Fourteen Mile Creek where Confederate General Gregg was under the impression that he held a distinct troop advantage over his Union opponents that soon proved to be untrue. What was thought at first to be a single Union brigade was actually the Third Division of the Union XVII Corps that had moved into position unbeknownst to General Gregg. What ensued was chaos and confusion by both sides, but more for the Confederate forces than those of the Union command. After back and forth fighting the realization that the Union force was much greater than had been envisioned, General Gregg was forced to retreat with his troops all the way to Jackson, Mississippi, where the next battle would occur. The Union Third Division suffered 66 killed, 339 wounded, and 37 missing or captured. Confederate Gregg's Brigade reported 73 killed, 251 wounded, and 190 troops among the missing or captured that may have been higher as the report was incomplete.

Sketch of the Battle of Raymond – Rebel charge on Union Major General John A. Logan's Third Division, XVII Corps, Army of the Tennessee.
Library of Congress, Prints & Photographs Division, LC-USZ62-137947

Military action over the next six days would include three named battles followed by the Siege of Vicksburg. The **Battle of Jackson** fought May 14 was not much of a battle. Few Confederate forces were available to defend Jackson and the command resolved to abandon the town rather than defend it that would most likely would have been a loss at any rate. Confederate Brigadier General John Gregg who had retreated to Jackson after the loss of Raymond was given orders to stall the Union assault until Jackson could be evacuated. The Union assault began a little before noon on May 14 and steadily pushed General Gregg's forces back. By mid-afternoon the evacuation of Jackson had been completed and General Gregg was given orders to disengage and retreat toward Vicksburg.

Although the battle was brief, that did not diminish the casualty count. The XV and XVII Army Corps of the Department of the Tennessee lost forty-two killed, 251 wounded, and reported seven missing. Only partial returns were reported for Confederate losses that may have been close to 900, but one Confederate brigade of Brigadier General States Right Gist who took part at Jackson reported 17 killed, 64 wounded, and 118 missing or captured.

Charge of the Seventeenth Iowa, Eightieth Ohio, and Tenth Missouri supported
by the First and Third Brigades of the Seventh Division, XVII Corps,
Department of the Tennessee, during the Battle of Jackson May 14, 1863.
Library of Congress, Prints & Photographs Division, LC-USZ62-13205

Only two days had passed when the two armies facing each other in the Vicksburg Campaign were at it again. The **Battle of Champion's Hill** or **Battle of Baker's Creek** occurred May 16 in an area that was a scant nine miles west of Jackson, Mississippi, about half way between Clinton, Mississippi, to the north and Raymond, Mississippi, to the south. This was no small battle involving 32,000 troops from the Union Army of the Tennessee's XIII Corps commanded by Major General John A. McClernand, XV Corps of Major General William T. Sherman, and Major General James B. McPherson's XVII Corps. The Confederate forces were three divisions from the Army of the Department of Mississippi and East Louisiana totaling 22,000 troops from Major General William W. Loring's Division, Major General Carter L. Stevenson's Division, Brigadier General John S. Bowen's Division.

The battle began in the early morning of May 16 and involved a concerted push by Union forces against their Confederate counterparts. It was a hard fought battle, but for whatever reason the Confederate troops were not able to stop the Union troops from gaining ground. A retreat order was given by the Confederate command to fall back to the Big Black River Bridge that would be the next battle. Union casualties for the battle show 426 killed, 1,842 wounded, and 189 missing. Confederate casualties were reported for only General Stevenson's and Bowen's Division. General Loring's Division was reported to have received only light involvement in the battle and may not have had any casualties. The Confederate numbers that were reported include 355 killed, 1,074 wounded, and 2,195 missing and or captured.

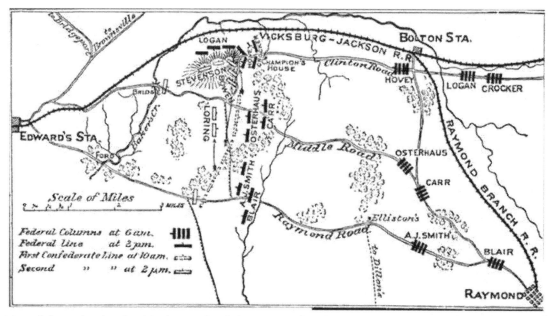

Map of the region involved in the Battle of Champion Hill with sites of other locations important at that time. The Champion House near Champion Hill can be found at the top beneath the words *Vicksburg-Jackson R. R.*

Wikipedia {{ PD-1923 }}

The Confederate Army of the Department of Mississippi and East Louisiana commanded by Lieutenant General John C. Pemberton was being pushed back toward Vicksburg with unrelenting attacks by Union Major General Ulysses S. Grant's Department of the Tennessee. The Confederate defeat at Champion Hill was followed the next day by the **Battle of Big Black River Bridge** or simply **Big Black**. The Big Black River was the last hope of stopping the Union advance if Vicksburg was to be saved. Here too, however, the outcome would be the same as previous when the Union XIII Corps overwhelmed Confederate Brigadier General John S. Bowen's troops desperately trying to hold their position but to no avail. Confederate troops were forced to cross the Big Black River in order to avoid capture that resulted in the drowning of untold number of soldiers. Some were lucky to cross by means of three ships anchored in such a way to offer a make shift bridge while others found their way over the Vicksburg and Jackson Railroad bridge

The number of Confederate soldiers was dwindling fast as each battle resulted in many captured as well as killed and wounded reported in the statistics for each battle. General Grant commented May 24, 1863, in a communication to General-in-Chief of the Union Army, Major General Henry Wagner Halleck, that, "In the various battles from Port Gibson to Big Black River Bridge, we have taken nearly 6,000 prisoners, besides killed and wounded, and scattered a much larger number."[9] Confederate losses in this latest battle amounted to only three killed and nine wounded, but 1,393 were listed as missing and or captured. Union losses were far more killed and wounded at twenty-nine and 242 respectively, but only two missing. There was only one place left as a refuge for Confederate General Pemberton and his troops and that was Vicksburg!

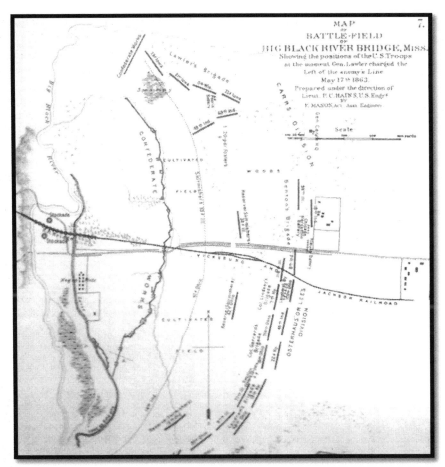

Map of the Battle of Big Black River Bridge May 17, 1863
The Official Military Atlas of the Civil War, Plate 37 -7, p. 115

Confederate General Pemberton was now confined at Vicksburg, Mississippi, with nowhere to escape. Not only was he surrounded, but his resupply was cut off painting a dim picture for any relief. A Union **Siege of Vicksburg** began May 25 after two unsuccessful Union assaults on the Confederate defenses and would continue until the total surrender of the Confederate forces on July 4, 1863. Ironically, July 4 was the same date that Confederate General Robert Edward Lee was forced to abandon his Army of Northern Virginia efforts after the stunning defeat at the Battle of Gettysburg.

The Union Department of the Tennessee consisted of five Army Corps with an estimated strength of nearly 80,000 troops at the time of the siege. They would face the Confederate Army of the Department of Mississippi and East Louisiana with some 33,000 men, about half the number that began the operation in late 1862.

Two assaults by Union forces were undertaken in mid-May that included the XV Corps of Major General William T. Sherman on the right, Major General James B. McPherson's XVII Corps in the center, and the XIII Corps of Major General John A. McClernand on the left. Neither of the two assaults was successful and, in fact, the majority of Union casualties for the Siege of Vicksburg occurred in these two early attacks that were repulsed, not during the siege operation that followed. At least 86 percent of those killed and 88 percent of the wounded from the time of the two assaults to the fall of Vicksburg occurred in the two failed attacks. Much of the reason for these casualty counts was due to the terrain around Vicksburg that was a series of hills, valleys, ravines, and the like dotted with fortifications of all types. Any assault would be extremely difficult just as it had proven to be. General Grant recognized that further efforts were unwise and reluctantly called instead for a siege.

Once a siege was undertaken, the Union forces formed a semi-circle around the six plus mile wide Confederate defensive line. This line extended from the Mississippi River on the south around to the bend in the river in the north. The same Corps alignment during the assault phase was involved in the siege operations. Two additional Union Corps, namely the IX Corps and XVI were added to the force structure swelling the total number of troops from 50,000 to the 70,000 mark. Further enhancing the Union siege was the U. S. Mississippi River Squadron that could now bombard Vicksburg from river approaches with limited return fire.

Due to the complex terrain surrounding Vicksburg, Union troops began digging trenches from which to fight. What ensued would be a war of attrition using largely artillery fire. The area around Vicksburg was filled with every kind of artillery weapon imaginable on both sides. Even today, the battlefield under the auspices of the National Park Services is dotted with the type of weapons used during the siege

Two examples of artillery weapons used at the Siege of Vicksburg that can be seen today at the Vicksburg National Battlefield

Over the forty days of the siege, the Union forces inched their way closer to the fortifications used by the Confederate defenders. While the Union troops benefited from adequate supplies of ammunition, rations, and any other comfort available, their Confederate counterparts had little of the same! Confederate Lieutenant General John C. Pemberton, Army of the Department of Mississippi and East Louisiana, confided the dire situation of his command to General Joseph Eggleston Johnston, Department of the West. "The enemy opened all his batteries on our lines about 3:30 this morning, and continued the heaviest fire we have yet sustained, until 8 o'clock, but he did not assault our works. My men have been thirty-four days and night in trenches without relief, and the enemy is within conversation distance. We are living on very reduced rations, and, as you know, are entirely isolated. What aid am I to expect from you?"[10] To General Pemberton's dismay with his dilemma, no aid was forthcoming. It was not so much that supplies were not available, but that they could not reach the Confederate forces due to the siege.

One Confederate effort to impede General Grant was an attack near Milliken's Bend along the Mississippi River fifteen miles north of Vicksburg. Milliken Bend was a supply depot for the Department of the Tennessee and the intent of the **Battle of Milliken's Bend** on June 7 was to disrupt the Union supply effort hoping to relieve the siege of Vicksburg. This effort failed with the help of the Twenty-third Iowa Infantry, the African Brigade, and the gunboats USS *Choctaw* and *Lexington*.

Another such Confederate effort to ease the siege at Vicksburg occurred in the **Battle of Goodrich Landing** June 29-30, 1863. Goodrich Landing was in Louisiana on the west bank of the Mississippi River a good distance north of Milliken's Bend. Similar to Milliken's Bend, Goodrich Landing was also a supply base for the Union Army. A fort was built to protect the supply base that received a demand to surrender. What followed was not so much a battle, but a series of skirmishes that at first gave the Confederate loyalists what they had demanded only to be thwarted by U. S. Naval power to reverse the outcome in the end. Confederate efforts to relieve the Siege of Vicksburg had no impact although supplies were captured, but would not reach Vicksburg.

On July 4, 1863, General Pemberton's Army and Department of the Mississippi and East Louisiana could no longer hold out against the Union forces and surrendered to Major General Ulysses S. Grant. The Confederates during the siege had lost 805 killed, 1,938 wounded, and 29,620 captured that included Lieutenant General John C. Pemberton. General Pemberton remained a prisoner until October 13, 1862, at which time he was exchanged and returned to Richmond, resigned his commission as a general officer, and remained there idle for a time before providing non-combat duty for the Confederacy. The large number of Confederate prisoners would have taken a toll on Union assets prompting General Grant to offer parole in hopes they would return to their homes and not take up arms again. They were paroled, but many were back in arms later that year.

Confederate Artillerymen on the ready!

View of trenches common during the Siege of Vicksburg. This depicts the area around Confederate Fort Hill that was the scene of major action at that time.
Library of Congress, Prints & Photographs Division, LC-USZ62-5558

Chancellorsville Campaign

The Vicksburg Campaign occupied attention in the Western Theater during the American Civil War, but action occurred elsewhere at the same time. The Chancellorsville Campaign was more a battle than a campaign that lasted all of seven days, but that made it no less important. There were three named battles and several skirmishes that occurred in the seven days with the primary event the **Battle of Chancellorsville** for which the campaign was named.

Major General Joseph Hooker assumed command of the Union Army of the Potomac January 26, 1863, replacing Major General Ambrose Everett Burnside after the disastrous Fredericksburg Campaign in late 1862. General Hooker had amassed an army of nearly 134,000

troops consisting of eight Corps including a Cavalry Corps. This large army would face the Army of Northern Virginia of just under 61,000 commanded by General Robert E. Lee. Not all of the troops would be involved at the same time in each of the three battles that ensued.

Chancellorsville was neither a village, nor a town, or even a community. Instead, it was a house operated as an inn early in the nineteenth century and later as a private residence of the George Chancellor family at the intersection of the Orange Turnpike and Orange Plank Road in 1863 approximately ten miles mostly west of Fredericksburg, Virginia. At the time of the battle the widow Frances Chancellor lived in the home with her children. The site today is on Ely's Ford Road just north of the intersection with Plank Road. The battle that occurred May 1–3 could have happened anywhere in this vicinity and would have taken on the name of that location just as it did Chancellorsville. The home was used as Union General Hooker's military headquarters at the time of the battle.

General Hooker's initial plan to unleash his Cavalry Corps on Confederate supply sources was scratched due to rainfall that made river crossings difficult. A second plan was to march three of his eight Corps south across the Rappahannock River at Kelley's Ford continue south to the Rapidan River crossing at the Gremanna and Ely's Fords and attack the Confederate Army of Northern Virginia at Chancellorsville. At the same time, two of Hooker's Corps would cross the Rappahannock River on the east at the U. S. Ford swelling the total force to 70,000 troops. Meanwhile one full Corps and a portion of another performed a diversion attack on Fredericksburg to the east.

Sketch of Major General Hooker's troops crossing the Rappahannock River at Kelly's Ford April 30, 1863
Wikipedia {{ PD-1923 }}

General Hooker had more than adequate manpower as well as firepower, but what began as a Union effort to end once and for all the Confederate Army of Northern Virginia became anything but after an enemy artillery shell fell on the Chancellor house where General Hooker himself was standing. The shell and subsequent fire destroyed the home and resulted in a concussion to General Hooker that may well have dampened his resolve to fight. After recovering from shell shock, General Hooker gave the order to retreat from the battle area ending the effort.

Photo showing destruction of the Chancellor House after the battle May 3, 1863.

Wikipedia {{ PD-1923 }}

A day prior to the retreat of the Union Army from Chancellorsville May 3, Confederate Lieutenant General Thomas Jonathan "Stonewall" Jackson commanding the Second Corps was on a reconnaissance mission to determine the strength of the enemy lines before conducting a flanking movement the next day. It was dark at the time when he was mistaken as the enemy, fired upon, and wounded by his own troops. The wound resulted in amputation of the general's left arm and died nine days later from complication of pneumonia. The loss of General Jackson was a blow to Confederates especially his close friend General Robert E. Lee. After General Jackson was wounded, command of the Second Corps fell upon his second in command Major General Ambrose Powell Hill, Jr. who shortly thereafter was wounded. The next in order of command of the Corps would have been Brigadier General Robert Emmett Rodes, but he

declined to command turning over command of the Corps to Major General Jeb Ewell Brown Stuart who also commanded the Cavalry assets of the Army of Northern Virginia.

Lieutenant General Jackson may have been the greatest loss in the Battle of Chancellorsville for the Confederates, but there were many other casualties. Initial Confederate reports were void of the missing and captured and even changed later when more accurate numbers came to light, but there were at least 1,581 who were killed and 8,700 wounded that may have been closer to 13,000 total when the final count was made. Union casualty numbers are more precise showing 1,082 killed, 6,848 wounded, and 4,214 missing or captured.

A Union soldiers killed at Chancellorsville was First Lieutenant Bryon Brewer of Company C, First U. S. Sharpshooters. Lieutenant Brewer was from Kent County, Michigan, near Grand Rapids. His father, Alonzo Brewer, graduated from the United States Military Academy in 1813 as a Third Lieutenant of Artillery and served until 1816.

The Brewer family lived on a farm that was later owned by this author and from whom two of the following records were received. Lieutenant Brewer may have been captured in the Seven Days Battle that explains his "Prisoner of War" record showing release at Centreville, Virginia, September 3-4, 1862. Corporal Job Brewer, brother of Byron, assigned to the Third Michigan Infantry, Third Brigade, First Division, III Army Corps, Department of the Potomac, was among the injured at the Battle of Chancellorsville. He survived his wounds and was discharged from service June 20, 1864, after the completion of his three year enlistment

Official Prisoner of War Record of Bryon Brewer showing release September 3-4, 1862

Excerpt listing officers killed in the "Return of Casualties during the Battle of Chancellorsville, May 1-3, 1863," from the *War of the Rebellion: A Compilation of the Official Records of the Union and Confederate Armies, Series 1, Volume 25 (Part I), p. 187*

Official War Record of Service for First Lieutenant Bryon Brewer assigned to Company C, First Regiment, U. S. Sharpshooters. His age is shown as 23 and the report was prepared at Petersburg, Virginia, August 20, 1864, long after his death May 3, 1863, at the Battle of Chancellorsville. His promotions are listed as Sergeant October 31, 1861 and Second Lieutenant August 31, 1862, on this record. Not on this record is the promotion to First Lieutenant October 4, 1862.

The First Regiment, U. S. Sharpshooters, was one of two numbered regiments of Sharpshooters in the United States Regular Army. The various Companies were organized in several States. Company C was organized in Michigan.

The reason for this report from Petersburg, Virginia, fourteen months after the death of Lieutenant Brewer may be the result of catching up on records that were unable to be done earlier. The First Regiment, U. S. Sharpshooters, was stationed at Petersburg as of June 16, 1864.

For the duration of the war, the First Regiment of U. S. Sharpshooters lost ten officers and 142 Enlisted men killed or mortally wounded and one officer and 128 Enlisted men by disease.

The **Second Battle of Fredericksburg** or the **Second battle of Marye's Heights** was fought May 3, 1863, just as the Battle of Chancellorsville unceremoniously ended. This battle may have been a diversion from what was taking place at Chancellorsville, but the timing resulted in little advantage. It may also have been retribution after the defeat of the Union Army of the Potomac at Fredericksburg in late December 1862. Regardless, Confederate troops continued to occupy the area especially the high ground of Marye's Heights. Confederate Major General Jubal Anderson Early commanding 8,500 troops of his own division of the Army of Northern Virginia was charged with its defense. On the date of the battle, Union Major General John Sedgwick with his 24,000 troops from the VI Corps along with Brigadier General John Gibbon's 3,000 or so men of the Second Division, II Corps, both of the Army of the Potomac attacked the Confederate defenses.

The Union forces attacked early on Sunday, May 3, and were successful in driving Confederate General Early's troops from the protection of the stonewall on Marye's Heights that afforded them protection, but the assault would take several attempts and there would be a price to pay in the number of casualties.

Confederate troops of Brigadier General Joseph B. Kershaw's Brigade of Major General Lafayette McLaws' Division, First Corps, Army of Northern Virginia, and Brigadier General Thomas Reade Rootes Cobb's Georgia Legion assigned to Brigadier General William T. Wofford's Brigade also of the First Corps, defending Marye's Heights from behind a stonewall May 3, 1863, in the Second Battle of Fredericksburg.
Library of Congress, Prints & Photographs Division, LC-USZ62-134479

Following the Union VI Corps capture of Marye's Heights driving off the Confederate defenders, Major General Sedgwick marched his forces west planning to link up with General Hooker at Chancellorsville. Before the link up could happen, General Sedgwick would again face units of Confederate General Early near Salem Church delaying his movement.

This engagement May 3 is called the **Battle of Salem Church** also called the **Battle of Bank's Ford**.

News of the loss of Marye's Heights reached Confederate General Lee who dispatched additional troops to prevent Union troops from reaching Chancellorsville. There was now a stalemate in the area of Salem Church located a short distance west of Fredericksburg and just south of Bank's Ford on the Rappahannock River. The next day, May 4, Confederate General Early recaptured Mayre's Heights and Union General Sedgwick sought advice from his commander, General Hooker. It was determined that the VI Corps should make a withdrawal that would take them to Bank's Ford. This crossing was achieved during the early morning hours of May 4, and the rest of the Union Army of the Potomac did the same over the next two days ending the Chancellorsville Campaign.

Due to the timing and the proximity of both the Second Battle of Fredericksburg and that of Salem Church, casualty counts are combined for both battles. Union losses were 493 killed, 2,710 wounded, and 1,497 missing or captured. Confederate reports do not give a breakdown of casualties for either of these two battles or even a combined total but they were likely equal to the losses of their Union counterparts. After all the Union troops had crossed to the safety of the north side of the Rappahannock River, they reassembled at their staging area before the campaign near Falmouth, Virginia. Union Major General Joseph Hooker would have one last go commanding the Army of the Potomac pursuing Confederate General Lee's Army of Northern Virginia on the march toward Pennsylvania. Due to General Hookers' differences with Headquarters of the Army, Major General George Meade replaced Major General Joseph Hooker as commander of the Army of the Potomac June 28, 1863, just as the Gettysburg Campaign was about to begin.

Gettysburg Campaign

Confederate General Robert E. Lee was apparently so emboldened by his small force defeating the much larger Union Army at Chancellorsville that he marched his force north to once again invade the Federal territory. This action would turn out to be a disaster costing many lives and nearly the destruction of the Army of Northern Virginia.

The Gettysburg Campaign began June 3 and continued to July 24 involving seventeen named battles to include one with the name of the campaign, namely the Battle of Gettysburg, occurring July 1-3, 1863. In addition, there were a host of smaller conflicts where Union and Confederate troops came in contact during the time of the campaign resulting as few as one casualty to as many as 176 just before the beginning of the Battle of Gettysburg on July 1. Eight named battles led up to the major Battle of Gettysburg and eight involved the retreat of the Confederate Army. All battles leading up to the Battle of Gettysburg and those that followed involved smaller units of both armies that would come together to fight the one major battle.

The first engagement of the Gettysburg Campaign was the **Battle of Brandy Station** or **Battle of Fleetwood Hill** June 9, 1863. This battle primarily involved cavalry units that occurred as a Union reaction to the presence of Confederate forces. The Union Cavalry Corps, Army of the Potomac, under the command of Brigadier Alfred Pleasonton, engaged the Cavalry Division of the Confederate Army of Northern Virginia commanded by Major General James E. B. Stuart. The strength of each was nearly the same with Union numbers around 11,000 and Confederates at 9,500.

Brandy Station was about four miles southwest of the North Fork of the Rappahannock River a good number of miles northwest of Fredericksburg, Virginia. Confederate General Stuart's troops were caught off guard by the Union cavalry that had crossed the Rappahannock River early Tuesday morning, June 9, and attacked the unsuspecting troops bivouacked near Brandy Station. By mid-afternoon the battle was over with no real gain except that the Confederate cavalry was still able to function. Union losses were greater than Confederates reporting 77 killed, 391 wounded, and 369 missing or captured. Confederate losses were 51 killed, 250 wounded, and 132 missing.[11-12]

Cavalry charge during the Battle of Brandy Station, June 9, 1863
Wikipedia {{ PD-1923 }}

The second battle of the Gettysburg Campaign was the **Second Battle of Winchester** fought June 13-15, 1863, resulting from the Confederate Army of Northern Virginia's movement north through the Shenandoah Valley toward Pennsylvania. The First Battle of Winchester was fought May 25, 1862, and there would be a third battle in 1864. Union troops from the Second Division, VIII Corps, Army of the Potomac, were garrisoned at Winchester in northern Virginia at that time in June. The Confederate Second Corps nearly double in size to that of the Union garrison was charged with clearing the way of Union troops as the Army of Northern Virginia marched north. That action was achieved in

this battle with the loss of 95 Union soldiers killed, 348 wounded, and 4,000 counted as missing or captured. Confederate losses show only 42 killed and 210 wounded. This was clearly a Confederate victory!

The rapid movement of troops at this time in northern Virginia required the use of cavalry units. The **Battle of Aldie** was just such a cavalry battle much the same as the Battle of Brandy Station, but with barely 3,500 troops combined. Aldie was a small village in 1863 roughly thirty miles east of Winchester, Virginia, that exists today. It was here June 17 that several Union cavalry units from Ohio, Massachusetts, Maine, and Rhode Island met five regiments of Virginia cavalry in an inconclusive battle that raged for several hours. The Union cavalry forces did not fare well losing 50 killed, 131 wounded, and 124 missing or captured. Confederate losses were not well reported, but may have been in excess of one hundred.

Each of the next four engagements leading up to the Battle of Gettysburg also involved cavalry units giving weight to the speed at which events were taking place. The **Battle of Middleburg** was next fought June 17-19. Here again, this involved units of division size and smaller without a conclusive outcome yet there were casualties as one might expect when warfare occurs. The **Battle of Upperville** occurred June 21. Aldie, Middleburg, and Upperville were communities aligned respectively east to west a few miles apart in northern Virginia as they are today. The Union command at this time was still unsure of the intent of Confederate General Lee resulting in probing actions by cavalry units instead of a major commitment. The answer to the question would soon come to light.

The Battle of Middleburg resulted in twenty Union soldiers killed, 75 wounded, 284 missing or captured. The majority in the last category were captured soldiers from the First Rhode Island Cavalry Regiment. The Union casualties at Upperville were twelve killed, 130 wounded, and 67 missing or captured. Confederate losses were listed by brigades but combined for both battles with 37 killed, 132 wounded, and 105 missing.

Wood engraving showing the Cavalry Battle of Upperville, June 21, 1863
Library of Congress, Prints & Photographs Division, LC-USZ62-93014

Following Upperville were two minor skirmishes that nevertheless were identified as battles. The first was a mix of Union infantry and Confederate cavalry identified as the **Battle of Fairfax Court House** June 27. This engagement was a chance encounter between Companies B and C, Eleventh New York Volunteer Regiment, and Confederate forces of the First North Carolina Cavalry. The Eleventh New York received the worst of the engagement, but casualties on both sides were in the teens. The second skirmish was a mirror image of the previous. This was called a **Skirmish of Sporting Hill** fought on June 30 near Camp Hill, Pennsylvania, close to Harrisburg and northeast of the eventual Battle of Gettysburg. The Confederate Eighteenth Virginia Cavalry Regiment clashed with the Twenty-second and Thirty-seventh New York Militia only to find they were outmatched and withdrew losing nearly forty in dead and wounded. Union losses were in the teens.

On the same date, June 30, as the Skirmish of Sporting Hill, a much larger cavalry engagement occurred near Hanover, Pennsylvania appropriately named the **Battle of Hanover**. Hanover, Pennsylvania, was about fifteen miles east of Gettysburg. Confederate Major General Jeb E. B. Stuart's Cavalry Division of the Army of Northern Virginia would engage elements of Union Brigadier General Hugh Judson Kilpatrick's Third Division, Cavalry Corps, Army of the Potomac. Mid Tuesday morning, June 30, the Eighteenth Pennsylvania Cavalry Regiment encountered mounted cavalry of the Thirteenth Virginia and an exchange of fire ensued. Other skirmishes took place all around Hanover and soon the area was filled with troops from both sides involved in fighting. Some of the action took place in the streets of Hanover. Union Brigadier General Elon John Farnsworth's First Brigade and Brigadier General George Armstrong Custer's Second Brigade were involved as were the brigades of Confederate Colonel John Randolph Chambliss, Jr. and Brigadier General Fitzhugh Lee, nephew of General Robert e. Lee.

In the beginning of the battle, Confederate troops were able to push back the Union cavalry and capture some of the supply wagons. Union reinforcements reversed this action and eventually forced the Confederate cavalry to withdraw from the battle. With both armies consisting of 5,000 or so troops, casualties would be expected although the number was much smaller than it could have been. Union records list nineteen soldiers killed, 73 wounded, and a much higher number of 123 missing or captured. Confederate losses may have been nine killed, 50 wounded, and 58 missing or captured although these numbers may reflect some casualties beyond those at Hanover. [13-14]

The intent of Confederate General Robert E. Lee and his Army of Northern Virginia was known at this point in the war and the **Battle of Gettysburg** would commence! The Army of the Potomac well in excess of 100,000 troops had gathered in the vicinity of Gettysburg, Pennsylvania, and would face off against a smaller but determined Army of Northern Virginia estimated around 75,000. The battle that ensued from July 1-3 would rival the one-day Battle of Antietam in the number of casualties and nearly resulted in the end of the Confederate Army of Northern Virginia.

Gettysburg in 1863 was a vibrant community of over 2,400 residents with thriving businesses of all types helped by no less than eight roads leading into town from all directions. A railroad link with Hanover completed in 1859 added to the towns' importance. The geography around Gettysburg included level plains dotted with hilly areas to the northeast and south that would become the focal points of the battle.

On July 1, the first day of the battle, only portions of each army were present around Gettysburg. One of those units was the Union First Division, Cavalry Corps, commanded by Brigadier General John Buford. The Union First Division soon after being engaged was reinforced by the I Corps on the left and the XI Corps on the right north of the town, but neither could hold the line against the Confederate Second and Third Corps. The Union troops were forced to flee through the streets of Gettysburg occupying the high ground south of town where they were able to hold their position. Cemetery Hill, Culp's Hill, Cemetery Ridge, Little Round Top, Round Top,

Devil's Den, Peach Orchard, and others are names that have become very familiar in topics associated with the Battle of Gettysburg!

On the second day of battle, both armies had swelled their ranks with the arrival of nearly all their available troops. One exception was that of Confederate General Jeb Stuart whose Cavalry Division was no where to be found to the dissatisfaction of General Lee. Union Major General George Gordon Meade's Army of the Potomac saw the arrival of its remaining Corps to include the II, III, V, VI, and XII. Both armies were poised for battle and would not be disappointed. The Union forces occupied the high ground in a somewhat upside down "U" shape north to south. Confederate troops were on three sides with only the south side open.

The battle on the second day would change little in the configuration as one Confederate assault after another was turned back even though there were partial gains but only temporary. Some of the reverses were due either to miscommunications or objectives too difficult to undertake. Also, the assaults did not take place until nearly noon that would be near the hottest part of the day in July taking a toll on the attackers. Remember too, the Union forces were in defensive positions and outnumbered the attackers nearly two to one. The number of troops should have been at least opposite to be an effective assault. Long after the Confederate attack had taken place on the second day, General Stuart arrived with his Cavalry Division too late to participate and was scolded by General Lee for his absence.

As the sun rose on the third day of the battle, July 3, casualties could be counted on both sides, but this day would prove to be even more devastating. The Union defensive positions changed slightly on July 3 extending further south to Round Top nearly forming a circle except for a small section on the southeast corner. The Confederate military plan for this day was fluid and eventually started with an artillery bombardment of the Union defenses that used large numbers of artillery shells with very little effect. The Union artillery command hunkered down during the bombardment and waited to unleash a lethal response on the Confederate attackers during the ground assault.

At 3 p.m on Friday July 3. the hottest part of the day, Confederate General George Edward Pickett commanding Pickett's Division, Lieutenant General James Longstreet's First Corps, began the infamous Pickett's Charge across the open ground facing the Union defenses among the hills south of Gettysburg. The Union artillery that had been mostly silent during the earlier Confederate bombardment opened fire on the infantry troops with deadly accuracy. The few Confederate soldiers that were able to reach the stone works defended by Union riflemen were lucky if they survived as the entire Confederate line gave way. General Pickett himself survived the charge, but fifty percent of his troops did not! This defeat ended the Battle of Gettysburg and all efforts from here were for General Lee to gather what was left of his Army of Northern Virginia and head back to the safety of Richmond. In the days following the Battle of Gettysburg, a slew of engagements would occur mostly involving small numbers of troops in pursuit of Confederate forces limping back to the area of Richmond, Virginia. This action would continue until August 1, 1863, at which time the Gettysburg Campaign ended. The Battle of Gettysburg alone resulted in a staggering 3,155 Union soldiers killed, 14,529 wounded, 5,365 missing or captured for a total of 23,049. The total Union casualties for all engagements during the Gettysburg Campaign were 3,642 killed, 16,576 wounded, 11,825 missing or captured totaling 32,043.[15] In comparison, Confederate casualty numbers only report the Battle of Gettysburg and may not be the full story. They show 2,592 killed, 12,700 wounded, 5,150 missing or captured for a total of 20,451.[16]

Union Major General Winfield Scott Hancock riding before his troops during the
shelling by Confederate troops prior to Confederate Major General George Pickett's Charge.
Library of Congress, Prints & Photographs Division, PC-USZ62-498

Confederate troops of Lieutenant General James Longstreet's command taken prisoner
by Union troops during the Battle of Gettysburg marching to the rear under guard.
Library of Congress, Prints & Photographs Division, LC-USZ62-79220

Chickamauga Campaign

Following the devastating Gettysburg Campaign experienced by Confederate General Lee's Army of Northern Virginia and the loss of Vicksburg to Major General Ulysses s. Grant, military action in north Georgia took center stage involving the Confederate Army of Tennessee and the Union Department of the Cumberland (aka Army of the Cumberland). The campaign lasted one month extending from August 21 to September 20, 1863. The culmination of the campaign was the Battle of Chickamauga, but the Second Battle of Chattanooga and the Battle of Davis' Cross Roads took place prior.

A predecessor to the Chickamauga Campaign was the brief Tullahoma Campaign conducted by Union forces under Major General William Starke Rosecrans' Army of the Cumberland. This campaign was conducted against the Army of Tennessee commanded by General Braxton Bragg that forced the Confederate troops to abandon middle Tennessee and take up occupation of Chattanooga, Tennessee.

Union Major General William Starke Rosecrans
Officer of the Federal Army
National Archives – 111-B-3646

Confederate General Braxton Bragg
Officer of the Confederate Army
Library of Congress, Prints & Photographs
Division, LC-USZ62-4888

General Bragg's stay in Chattanooga was not long arriving with his Army July 4 and abandoning the city September 8, 1863, not long after the **Second Battle of Chattanooga** conducted August 21. There was a prior battle for Chattanooga June 7-8, 1862, that involved a Union attempt to dislodge Confederate troops from the area that ended after a one day bombardment that changed nothing other than showing that Union troops could engage just about anywhere. The Second Battle of Chattanooga also began with a bombardment on August 21 only it lasted for several weeks. Union Major General Rosecrans sent Colonel John Thomas Wilder with his First Brigade of the Fourth Division, XIV Corps, Army of the Cumberland, along with the Eighteenth Indiana Light Artillery Battery commanded by Captain Eli Lilly, to the opposite side of the Tennessee River from Chattanooga as a diversion while the main Union Army would cross the Tennessee River west and south of Chattanooga.

Colonel Wilder with his brigade and the artillery battery arrived at a site named Walden's Ridge north of Chattanooga August 20 and "went with the balance of corps, three regiments and four pieces of artillery, to Chattanooga. We came within 50 yards of capturing a horse ferry-boat plying across the river. When we got into position on the river they had but three small pieces of artillery in position. Two steam-boats were lying at the landing, the largest of which we sank with shells before steam could be raised on it. The other, a small tow-boat, is, I think disabled. A pontoon-bridge of forty-seven boats was lying stretched up the river, ready to swing across the stream."[17]

Colonel Wilder kept up his attacks on the Confederate forces occupying Chattanooga and nearby Harrison landing for the remainder of August and into the early part of September confusing Confederate General Bragg into thinking that the bombardment was from the entire Union Army of the Cumberland who hunkered down in anticipation of the full attack at some point. Meanwhile, the Union Army of the Cumberland's five Corps less Colonel Wilder's small force were making their way across the Tennessee River west of Chattanooga. When General Bragg realized that he was about to be flanked, he abandoned Chattanooga marching his troops to meet the Union force now in Georgia.

Confederate artillery defending Chattanooga with one exception was of small caliber unable to reach Union Colonel Wilder's troops north of the Tennessee River. One 32-pounder did wound one Union soldier of Captain Lilly's artillery battery and there may have been other casualties, not reported. Confederate casualties are known to have been at least two killed and several wounded along with forty men taken as prisoner.[18] There may have been more! This ended the Second Battle of Chattanooga and action shifted to attempts by Confederates to stop the Union Army of the Cumberland that had advanced into northern Georgia.

An encounter of minor significance was named the **Battle of Davis' Crossroads** fought September 10-11 involving the Union Major General James Scott Negley's Second Division, XIV Corps, Army of the Cumberland supported by units of the First Division against the Division of Confederate Major General Thomas Carmichael Hindman, Jr. of Lieutenant General Leonidas Polk's Corps. While there was contact and gunfire was exchanged, nothing much came of the contact that would see a dramatic change one week later in the **Battle of Chickamauga** fought September 19-20.

The Battle of Chickamauga was fought between the Union Army of the Cumberland with its 60,000 troops against the Confederate Army of Tennessee and some 65,000 troops. This battle rivals the Battles of Antietam and Gettysburg in the number of casualties, perhaps slightly less but not by much! The battle was named for the Chickamauga Creek around which it was fought. Battlefield miscues on the part of Union Major General Rosecrans permitted Confederate forces to breach a weakness in the Union line on the second day that had been stopped on previous attempts. Union forces were able to reestablish their presence occupying high ground, but soon after relinquished the terrain retreating to Chattanooga ending the battle.

The Battle of Chickamauga has been declared a Confederate victory based mostly on the retreat of Union forces that might have been the reverse if the casualty numbers are any indication. Union casualty numbers are large, but Confederate casualties were even greater. Union casualties totaled 16,170 that included 1,657 killed, 9,756 wounded, and 4,748 listed as missing or captured. Confederates losses on the other hand are consistently given as 18,454 showing 2,312 killed, 14,674 wounded, and 1,468 captured or missing.

Depiction of the Battle of Chickamauga, September 19-20, 1863
Library of Congress, Prints & Photographs Division, LC-USZ62-5452

Chattanooga Campaign

The Chattanooga Campaign came on the heels of the Chickamauga Campaign occurring September 21 through November 25, 1863, and was essentially a continuation of the latter campaign. After Union Major General Rosecrans' Army of the Cumberland retreated from the battlefield at Chickamauga, the Army occupied Chattanooga, Tennessee, that had been given up just over a month earlier by Confederate General Bragg. General Bragg remained in command of the Army of Tennessee that would now conduct operations against the Union defenders in Chattanooga just as the Union forces had done to his troops in August.

General Rosecrans' troops were at the mercy of Confederate forces that held the high ground around Chattanooga and small parties attacked and destroyed supply trains meant for the Union troops at Chattanooga. The Confederate plan was to starve the Union command into submission and it was slowing working. The beleaguered Union troops were suffering from more than just fatigue running out of just about everything necessary for a military force, but a change was in store that would reverse this situation.

Union Major General Ulysses S. Grant became commander of the Military Division of the Mississippi October 18, 1863, that consolidated operations of several Western Departments under one command that included the Departments of the Ohio, the Tennessee, the Cumberland, and Arkansas. Under General Grant, reinforcements would be channeled to Chattanooga and a plan was initiated to break the supply embargo. Two days after assuming his new role, General Grant appointed Major General George Henry Thomas as commander of the Department of the Cumberland replacing General Rosecrans who would play no further part in the campaign.

General Grant's first priority for the Department of the Cumberland was to get the troops much needed supplies. This effort resulted in the **Battle of Wauhatchie** fought October 28-29 named for Wauhatchie Station along the Nashville and Chattanooga Railroad. The battle also went by the name **Battle of Brown's Ferry** that was a slight stretch.

Brown's Ferry was along the Tennessee River approximately a mile and a half to the north of Wauhatchie Station where the battle occurred. The significance of Brown's Ferry is that it was a prelude to the battle in which the ferry site was seized October 27 by Union troops without much fanfare defeating the outmanned Fifteenth Alabama Regiment at the hands of Union Brigadier General John Basil Turchin's First Brigade, Third Division, XIV Corps, Department (Army) of the Cumberland and Brigadier General William Babcock Hazen's First Brigade, Third Division, IV Army Corps also of the Army of the Cumberland. Some casualties were reported. Union losses were four killed and fifteen wounded while the Confederates lost eight killed, several wounded, and six taken prisoner.

Sketch of Brigadier General Hazen's First Brigade troops, IV Corps, Army of the Cumberland, landing from pontoon boats at Brown's Ferry October 27, 1863.
Wikipedia [[PD-1923 }}

In the meantime, Union Major General Joseph Hooker in command of two divisions from the XI Corps and one from the XII Corps each recently transferred from the Army of the Potomac to the Department of the Cumberland arrived in the vicinity of Lookout Valley October 28 much to the surprise of

Confederate General Bragg. Before continuing General Hooker's march, he dispatched Brigadier General John White Geary's Second Division, XII Corps, with the task of securing the lines of communication around Wauhatchie Station.

Portrait of Major General Joseph "Fighting Joe" Hooker
Officer of the Federal Army
National Archives – NA 111-B-2775

What followed next was a two-hour long nighttime battle conducted by Confederate Lieutenant General James Longstreet's Corps assigned to the Army of Tennessee. Colonel John Bratton with his brigade were to attack the Union forces at Wauhatchie while the remainder of General Longstreet's Corps were to block Union General Hooker's remaining troops from coming to the aid of General Geary at Wauhatchie. In the beginning this plan had some success, but as with many Civil War battles, not everything went as planned.

In the end, Confederate troops were withdrawn due to a series of conflicting messages giving the victory to the Union forces. Union losses are accurately reported for both the XI and XII Corps as 78 killed, 327 wounded, and fifteen missing.[19] Confederate losses on the other hand are in question. In Colonel Bratton's Brigade alone there were reported 31 killed, 286 wounded, and 39 missing.[20] This of course does include casualties from the three remaining brigades of General Longstreet's Corps that participated in the conflict. It is conceivable that upwards of 1,000 Confederate casualties occurred in this battle! The immediate outcome of this first battle of the Chattanooga Campaign was the restoration of much needed supplies to the Union troops occupying Chattanooga and a precursor to the battles that would follow in the campaign.

There would be a nearly month long lull in action from the time of the Battle of

Wauhatchie while forces on both sides apparently assessed the strengths and weaknesses of each other. On November 24, 1863, the lull was over as Union Major General Joseph Hooker's XI and XII Corps now part of the Department of the Cumberland along with units from the IV and XV Corps attacked elements of the Confederate Army of Tennessee holding Lookout Mountain. This became appropriately named the **Battle of Lookout Mountain** resulting in a Union victory!

Union General Hooker had at his disposal about 10,000 troops and faced slightly less than 9,000 Confederate troops consisting of four brigades, two each from the divisions of Major General Benjamin Franklin Cheatham and Major General Carter Littlepage Stevenson, Jr. It would seem that Confederate forces holding the high ground in a defensive posture would have had a distinct advantage, but that advantage was not as great as it seemed.

What General Grant had planned as a diversion on Lookout Mountain when the real objective was nearby Missionary Ridge turned instead into a total Union victory dispelling the Confederate hold on Lookout Mountain. Those Confederate troops able to avoid capture by Union forces made their way to the lines of Confederate troops on Missionary Ridge.

Casualty counts for both the Union and Confederate Armies were not separated by battles for most of this campaign except those previously reported, but there were undoubtedly casualties in the Battle of Lookout Mountain that have a considerable range of accuracy from several hundred Union to slightly over one thousand Confederates. The Union Second Division of the XII Corps was the only command to provide casualty numbers for this battle listing twenty-two killed and 116 wounded and even those numbers may have changed later upon review from the units involved.

Sketch of the Battle of Lookout Mountain, November 24, 1863
Library of Congress, Prints & Photographs Division, LC-USZ62-15767

The capture of Lookout Mountain by Union forces that was meant only as a diversion to the pending attack on Missionary Ridge proved to be a significant victory nonetheless and may have placed doubt in the minds of the Confederate leaders to hold their current position resulting in a major Union victory in the **Battle of Missionary Ridge** the next day, November 25! Missionary Ridge was a complex of high ground to the south and east of Chattanooga running nearly parallel but much shorter in length than Lookout Mountain to the west that was opposite Moccasin Bend in the Tennessee River. Both high terrain features held a commanding view of the Union troops hunkered down in Chattanooga. Nearly 45,000 Confederate soldiers belonging to the Army of Tennessee commanded by General Braxton Bragg as already noted occupied Missionary Ridge including those that came from Lookout Mountain in the previous battle. The Confederate commands included two Corps under the leadership of Lieutenant General William Joseph Hardee and Major General John Cabell Breckinridge.

Nearly 60,000 Union troops of the combined Army of the Cumberland and the newly arrived XV Corps from the Army of the Tennessee led by Major General William T. Sherman each under the leadership of Major General Ulysses S. Grant's Military Division of the Mississippi would be involved in this battle. General Sherman's 20,000 troops had crossed the Tennessee River on pontoon boats early Tuesday, November 24, heading toward the north end of Missionary Ridge

View of Chattanooga, a pontoon bridge, and Lookout Mountain from the north side of the Tennessee River at some point in 1863, but not at the time of General Sherman's crossing November 24, 1863.
Library of Congress, Prints & Photographs Division, LC-USZ62-119562

General Sherman's troops were the first to test the strength of the Confederate line as they approached Missionary Ridge from the northern end. The Union troops were able to take what was thought to be the ridge area only to find that these were a few hills separated from the main ridge by a valley. In response to the Union effort, Major General Patrick Ronayne Cleburne's Division of General Breckinridge's Corps supported by Brigadier General Marcus J. Wright's Brigade of Major General Benjamin F. Cheatham's Division in Lieutenant General William Hardee's Corps were dispatched to oppose the Union forces. General Sherman's efforts to go further were stalled and both sides dug in for the duration of that Tuesday.

Wednesday, November 25, would be another story! Perhaps concerned that Union General Sherman would be overrun by Confederate General Bragg's forces, Union General Grant unleashed the Army of the Cumberland on the center portion of Missionary Ridge to include the valley area leading to the ridge itself. Sporadic successes were achieved in this action and total success was accomplished with the addition of General Hooker's assault on the southern end of the ridge sending Confederate troops in retreat to safety some twenty miles south.

Scene at the Battle of Missionary Ridge with Union troops assaulting the Confederate held ridge line, November 25, 1863

Library of Congress, Prints & Photographs Division, LC-USZ62-19441

Union commanders viewing action in the Battle of Missionary Ridge, November 25, 1863
Library of Congress, Prints & Photographs Division, LC-USZC4--2382

There would be one more battle to fight as Union troops pursued the retreating Confederate Army of Tennessee named the **Battle of Ringgold Gap** fought November 27, but the outcomes of the Chattanooga Campaign were etched in memory. Tennessee was in the hands of the Union Army to include Chattanooga that would serve General Sherman as a major supply hub for his Atlanta Campaign beginning May 1864, and Major General Ulysses S. Grant with this victory would become General-in-Chief of the Union Army March 12, 1864, promoted to the rank of Lieutenant General, and serve throughout the war in this capacity and beyond. A command change would also occur in the Confederate Army of Tennessee. General Braxton Bragg

would resign his command December 1, 1863, giving temporary control to Lieutenant General Hardee until December 27 at which time General Joseph E. Johnston assumed command.

For whatever reason that can't be explained, casualty numbers for the individual battles of the Chattanooga Campaign were not provided. Instead, the casualty records at least for the Union lump all the battles together that occurred over the two month long campaign. Union "Return of Casualties" report 753 killed, 4,722 wounded, 349 missing or captured for a total of 5,894.[21] Once again, Confederate casualties are speculation. There was no single battle casualty numbers nor combined totals, but may have been upwards of 8,000.

[1] American Civil War - Support Services of the Confederate Army, p. 127.

[2] The War of the Rebellion: a Compilation of the Official Records of the Union and Confederate Armies, Vol. 17, Part 1, p. 625.

[3] Ibid, p. 671.

[4] Civil War Era Fortifications, Arkansas, p. 66-67.

[5] The War of the Rebellion: A Compilation of the Official Records of the Union and Confederate Armies, Vol. 17, Part 1, p. 719.

[6] Ibid, Vol. 24, Pt 1, p. 64

[7] Ibid, Part 3, p. 62.

[8] Ibid, Part 1, p. 34.

[9] Ibid, p. 37-39.

[10] Ibid, Part 3, p. 967-968.

[11] Ibid, Vol. 27, Part I, p. 193.

[12] Ibid, Part 2, p. 719.

[13] Ibid, Part 1, p. 193.

[14] Ibid, Part 2, p. 713-714

[15] Ibid, Part 1, p. 193.

[16] Ibid, Part 2, p. 346

[17] Ibid, Vol. 30, Part 3, p. 122-123.

[18] Ibid, p. 123.

[19] Ibid, Vol. 31, Part 1, p. 76.

[20] Ibid, p. 233.

[21] Ibid Part 2, p. 80-88.

1864

The war effort in 1864 was not much unlike the past year at least until the later months in the year. There were a number of campaigns during 1864 mostly in the Eastern Theater between Confederate and Union Armies while the Western Theater and beyond was plagued by groups of bushwhackers whose aim was whatever disruption they could cause and hostile Native American Indians whose indiscriminate abductions and killings of men, women, and children alike occurred regardless of their stance on the war.

The latter half of 1864 was a time of reflection for Confederate General Robert E. Lee and his entire Confederate Army. Union blockades of southern ports from early in the war played heavily on the minds of the officers whose essential supplies for the men of ammunition, food, clothing, etc., was dwindling. Also on the minds of these officers was the morale of the soldiers on the front lines who had suffered much over the nearly three long years of the war. This is not to say that Union soldiers were any less stressed, but supply matters were much less a concern for the Union Army.

After repeated engagements in the first half of 1864, action at least in the Eastern Theater shifted to the stalemate of siege operations surrounding Petersburg and Richmond, Virginia. This event in the war would extend into the next year before there was an end to hostilities. Also of significance beginning late May was the Atlanta Campaign that dominated action in Georgia and South Carolina that made it even harder for the Confederate Army to continue in the war. The year 1864 would be a time of decisions for the leaders on both sides!

Red River Campaign

The Red River Campaign named for the Red River originating in the far western regions of Texas and Oklahoma then meandering through Louisiana from the northwest to the southeast was part of the Trans-Mississippi Theater during the war and the focus of this operation. The campaign was a Union initiative beginning in early March and continued until May 22, 1864. The mission of the campaign may have been ill advised and was certainly a failure. Union Major General Nathaniel Prentice Banks commanding the Army of the Gulf was charged with neutralizing the Confederate Army of Western Louisiana under the command of Major General Richard Scott "Dick" Taylor as well as maintaining control of the Red River in hopes of occupying much of east Texas.

It should be remembered that General Banks commanded the Department of the Shenandoah during the Valley Campaign in the first half of 1862 and did not perform well against Confederate Major General Thomas Jonathan "Stonewall" Jackson. The Union Department of the Shenandoah was merged into the Army of Virginia and General Banks was out of a job until he assumed command of the Army of the Gulf December 17, 1862. General Banks and General Taylor clashed with each other in similar actions prior to the Red River Campaign with mixed results!

The Red River Campaign kicked off March 10 when Division elements from the XIII and XIX Corps, Department of the Gulf, began their march north from New Orleans toward the Red River. At the same time, Rear Admiral David Dixon Porter commanding a naval fleet of twenty gunboats and transports carrying a 10,000 man detachment of the XVI and XVII Corps from the Army of the Tennessee departed Vicksburg on the Mississippi River heading toward the Red River and Alexandria then Shreveport, the capital of Louisiana and headquarters of the Confederate Trans-Mississippi Department.

U. S. Navy Ships of Rear Admiral David D. Porter with troops of Brigadier General Andrew J. Smith's Detachment from the Army of the Tennessee on board leaving Vicksburg, Mississippi, for operations in the Red River Campaign.   Wikipedia {{PD-1923 }}

The majority of military units comprising the Union Army (Department) of the Gulf were from the various northern States. There were, however, artillery batteries from the First, Second, and Fifth U. S. Artillery Regiments and several units identified as Corps d' Afrique, later United States Colored Troops (U. S. C. T) both infantry and engineer. These included the Third and Fifth Engineers whose designation changed April 4, 1864, to the Ninety-seventh and Ninety-ninth Infantry, U. S. C. T. respectively. Also part of the Department of the Gulf were the First, Third, Twelfth, and Twenty-second Infantry of which their designation also changed April 4 to the Seventy-third, Seventy-fifth, Eighty-fourth, and Ninety-second Infantry Regiments.

The Union Navy not surprisingly moved faster than General Banks troops marching from southern Louisiana and entered the Red River March 12 at which point the troops of the XVI Corps under the command of Union Brigadier General Andrew Jackson Smith were put ashore and pushed forward toward Confederate held Fort De Russy that controlled access up the lower Red River.

Fort De Russy was an earthen fort established in 1862 along the meandering Red River a few miles northeast of Marksville, Louisiana. The fort was built by and named for Confederate Colonel Lewis Gustavus De Russy, uncle of Union Colonel Gustavus Adolphus De Russy for whom another Fort De Russy was established in Washington, D. C.

After brief encounters after coming ashore that were overcome, the Union troops arrived near Fort De Russy on March 14 and later that afternoon captured the earthen fort and its Confederate garrison opening the way to Alexandria by way of the Red River. Union Major General Smith described the action. *"…At About 6:30 p. m. the order to charge was given, and the First and Second Brigades advanced under a scattering fire from the enemy, whose infantry were kept down by my skirmishers, and scaled the parapet within twenty minutes from the time the order to charge was given. The enemy then surrendered. Our loss was 3 killed and 35 wounded; total 38. Full lists of casualties and captures accompany this report. We captured 319 prisoners, 10 pieces of artillery, and a large quantity of ordnance and ordnance stores, marching during the day 26 miles, bridging a bayou, and capturing the fort before sunset. Among the pieces of artillery taken were two 9-inch Dahlgren guns, which were captured by the enemy, one from the steamer Indianola and one from the Harriet Lane…"*[1]

The capture of Fort de Russy opened the Red River all the way to Alexandria, Louisiana, that itself would be captured March 20. Although the Red River was now open to Rear Admiral Porter, the low water level of the river would cause problems for the ships in their movement toward Shreveport. Toward the end of the campaign, the water levels would require some engineer ingenuity to move the ships back to the Mississippi River.

The Red River Campaign to this point had gone very well, but the further the Union forces moved up the Red River, the more difficult the task became! Another concern for Union General Banks was word that the Detachment form the Army of the Tennessee would be required to return to its primary organization by the middle of April that placed pressure on completing the campaign as early as possible. By the end of March, Union forces were still some 60 plus miles from the ultimate goal of Shreveport. Weather had caused some delays and the boats on the Red River were also having difficulty, but the campaign marched on.

The Union Army of the Gulf crossing the Cane River March 31, 1864, during the Red River Campaign on their march to Shreveport and the Headquarters of the Confederate Trans-Mississippi Department.

Wikipedia {{ PD }}

As the Union troops pushed closer to Shreveport they would come in contact with Confederate Major General Richard Taylor's District of West Louisiana as part of the Trans-Mississippi Department. General Taylor had deliberately retreated from earlier positions before taking a stand near Mansfield, Louisiana, where the **Battle of Mansfield** or **Battle of Sabine Crossroads** would be fought April 8, 1864. As the battle began that Friday morning in April, the Confederate forces held a distinct strength advantage with around 9,000 men compared to approximately 6,000 for their Union counterparts. As the day progressed, both sides would increase their strength to the point they were near equal in the number of fighting men although the Confederate forces still held a slight advantage. That strength advantage may have had a part in the outcome of the battle in which Confederate General

Taylor was able to fend off any Union assault, and, in fact, able to capture a large number of Union soldiers in the process. Perhaps for this reason, this battle was declared a Confederate victory.

Other than the nearly 1,500 Union soldiers listed as missing or captured, the battle took its toll on both sides in killed and wounded, and, in fact, may have had more Confederate casualties than on the Union side. Though no official record exists for Confederate casualties, there is a general agreement in the number of 1,000 total for all categories. By the same general agreement, Union casualties are reported as 113 killed, 581 wounded, and 1,500 or so captured. There was a second battle the next day, August 9, named the Battle of Pleasant Hill for which there is a Union record of casualties for the two battles lumped together.

The **Battle of Pleasant Hill** was fought Saturday, August 9, as a continuation of the previous battle and ended on the morning of the 10th with the retreat of the Union Army and the end of the Red River Campaign. Pleasant Hill was over fifteen miles south and east of Mansfield where the Union force had retreated after the Battle of Mansfield. Confederate General Taylor in this battle was the attacker against his Union rival. The attack, however, did not go well for General Taylor who incurred many casualties. That is not to say that the Union casualties were insignificant, only less!

Union Major General Banks had apparently already determined that his campaign was not going to succeed and ordered his forces to withdraw. Confederate General Taylor was intent in pursuing his enemy prompting the battle that ensued on the afternoon on August 9 and continued to late that night. After midnight, Union General Banks was successful in breaking the engagement and his Union forces retreated to the vicinity of Grand Ecore along the Red River

Receiving word of General Banks' departure from plans to capture Shreveport, Rear Admiral David D. Porter turned his fleet of boats around and headed down river as well. This effort was a challenge due to the low water level in the Red River at that time. As the ships approached Alexandria, the water level prevented the ironclads from passing over the river rapids. Union engineers spent 10 days building artificial dams to raise the water level sufficient enough for the ships to pass.

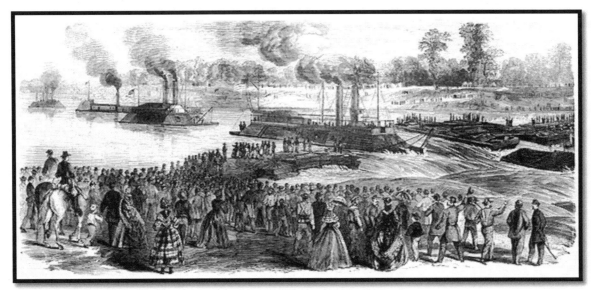

Union ironclads shown crossing over "Bailey's Dam" at Alexandria, Louisiana, near the conclusion of he Red River Campaign. The name Bailey's Dam came from Union Engineer Colonel Joseph Bailey who designed the project to raise the level of the river permitting the ironclads to pass the obstructions.
Wikipedia {{ PD-1923 }}

Once the ships were again on the way back to the Mississippi River, the ground troops of the Department of the Gulf also managed to make their way back to New Orleans.

However, harassment by Confederate troops continued along the way until the last engagement of the campaign occurred May 18 named the **Battle of Yellow Bayou** in which casualties were incurred on both sides. It did, however, bring to an end the Union Red River Campaign.

The Union forces of General Banks' Department of the Gulf finally arrived at the Atchafalaya River near Simmesport, Louisiana, Friday, May 20, signaling the official end of the Red River Campaign. It is unlikely that General Banks was aware that he had a new commander in Major General Edward Richard Sprigg Canby now commanding the newly organized Military Division of West Mississippi that included the Department of the Gulf and Department of Arkansas. General Banks would remain in command of the Department of the Gulf until June 3, 1865, and the department would disband just over three weeks later.

Scene at the Battle of Pleasant Hill, Louisiana, April 9, 1864
Library of Congress, prints & Photographs Division, LC- DIG-pga-05520

Bermuda Hundred Campaign

The Bermuda Hundred Campaign was one of three Union campaigns (Bermuda Hundred, Overland, Atlanta) each starting at nearly the same time. The Bermuda Hundred Campaign occurred May 6-20 around the small town of Bermuda Hundred along the west shore of the James River just above the confluence with the Appomattox River about fifteen miles southeast of Richmond, Virginia. Bermuda Hundred would become a Union supply depot around this time in the war. The Bermuda Hundred Campaign was conducted at the same time and in conjunction with Union Lieutenant General Grant's Overland Campaign against Confederate General Robert E. Lee's Army of Northern Virginia. The Bermuda Hundred Campaign was conducted to insure success of General Grant's campaign by preventing Confederate reinforcements from reaching the battle area of the Overland Campaign and disrupting enemy supply lines that could be used against the Union forces.

View looking south of Bermuda Hundred along the James River
Library of Congress, Prints & Photographs Division, LC-USZ62-13984

Five named battles were fought in the Bermuda Hundred Campaign involving the 33,000 man Union Army of the James commanded by Major General Benjamin Franklin Butler against Confederate General Pierre Gustave Toutant Beauregard commanding the Department of North Carolina and Southern Virginia also known as the Department of Virginia and North Carolina or simply the Department of North Carolina. General Beauregard's 18,000 or so troops consisted of a mix of young and elderly men and boys recruited from the Richmond area. This mix of "soldiers" may have been a window into outcomes to follow. The Union Army of the James was established April 28, 1864, from the XVIII Corps, Department of Virginia and North Carolina, and the X Corps from the Department of the South.

The XVIII Corps of the Union Army of the James boarded transports at Yorktown while the X Corps did the same from Gloucester Point and followed the former Corps by way of the James River to Bermuda Hundred arriving May 5. Shortly thereafter the first of the five battles occurred named the **Battle of Port Walthall Junction** May 6-7 that was a railroad station along the Appomattox River a short distance from the confluence with the James River. Port Walthall was an important commerce center served by a rail spur connected to the Richmond and Petersburg Railroad. Disruption of the rail system would prevent the Confederate government from receiving supplies or engaging in trade that might benefit both the government and the Army.

Word that Union troops were threatening the Port Walthall Junction and its railroad prompted Confederate leaders to dispatch the brigade of Brigadier General Johnson Hagood to the site. General Hagood's brigade consisted of the Eleventh, Twenty-first, Twenty-fifth, and Twenty-seventh South Carolina Infantry Regiments and the Seventh South Carolina Battalion. Action on May 6 involved only the Twenty-first and Twenty-fifth Regiments. The next day the Twenty-seventh joined the fight.

On May 6, Confederate General Hagood faced the Union First Brigade, Second Division, XVIII Army Corps, Army of the James, commanded by Brigadier General Charles Adam Heckman. The First Brigade consisted of the Twenty-third, Twenty-fifth, and Twenty-seventh Massachusetts Infantry Regiments, as well as the Ninth New Jersey Infantry Regiment. The engagement that Friday, May 6, was fairly swift with the Confederate forces pushing back General Heckman and his troops costing slightly more Union casualties than their counterparts. General Heckman's own words described the action in this first engagement. *"Upon being assured that at least two brigades of the enemy were opposing me in front, and as a general engagement was not desired, I engaged them for a time and retired in perfect order, the enemy keeping up a heavy fire, officers and men being perfectly cool and obeying every order with as much precision as if at dress parade. Never did the troops behave more nobly. I regret to state that owing to the limited number of stretchers allowed my command, in retiring I was compelled to leave a portion of my killed on the field to save the wounded. No ambulances were sent with my command, and not until after I had sent for them from the field did I have the transportation for the wounded—meeting the ambulances on the road."*[2] Union losses for the first day of action were eight killed and sixty wounded. Confederate reports list one killed and twenty-nine wounded Action would pick up the next day.

The second day of the Battle of Port Walthall Junction was a different story. Union Brigadier General William Thomas Harbaugh Brooks in command of the First Division, XVIII Army Corps, Army of the James, with a four brigade force consisting of the Second Brigade, First Division, XVIII Corps; Third Brigade, First Division, X Corps, Second Brigade, Second Division, X Corps; and Second Brigade Third Division, X Corps, overwhelmed the Confederate defenders at Port Walthall Junction forcing them to flee while tearing up the railroad tracks of the Petersburg and Richmond Railroad. Casualties were much higher in this action. Confederate killed were twenty-one, wounded 142, and thirteen missing. Union losses reported twenty killed, 229 wounded, and thirty missing

Confederate General Hagood and his troops retreated from Port Walthall Station after the battle of that name heading toward Swift Creek to the northwest south of Confederate held Drewry's Bluff and north of Petersburg. Swift Creek was a tributary of the Appomattox River that could be traversed at least part way by Union ships. On Monday, May 9, the two armies would be engaged in the **Battle of Swift Creek** also named the **Battle of Arrowfield Church**.

Simultaneous to the land battle, a Union Army "Naval Brigade" consisting of five gunboats under the command of Brigadier General Charles Kinnaird Graham made their way up the Appomattox River to protect the flank of the Third Division of the XVIII Corps heading for Swift Creek and the Richmond and Petersburg Railroad tracks. At least three of the five ships were the Army steamers *Samuel L. Brewster* and *Charles Chamberlain* along with the U. S. Navy *General Putnam*. Confederate held Fort Clifton, an earthen fort located on an elevated site on the west side of the Appomattox River, would prevent further movement on the river toward Petersburg. The armament included "heavy guns" of undisclosed caliber.

Around 9 a. m. on May 9, one of the five ships approached Fort Clifton and was fired upon driving it off. At 11 a. m. all five boats approached the fort and began a three hour battle after which four of the boats withdrew and one was disabled "by a hole put through her boiler" and later burned to prevent it from falling into enemy hands. The burned boat was not identified.

Meanwhile, ground action was taking place at both Swift Creek and Chester Station around the same time. The Union XVIII Army Corps set its sights on Swift Creek where a much larger Confederate force had assembled. Action here was intense, but lasted only for that Monday, May 9, after which the Union forces withdrew the following day. Confederate casualties for General Hagood's South Carolina Brigade were 31 killed, 82 wounded, and 24 missing. Union casualties for the Battle of Swift Creek are combined with all other conflicts during the Bermuda Hundred Campaign making it impossible to list any numbers other than to know there were casualties that occurred during the Swift Creek affair mostly with the First Division of the XVIII Army Corps of the Army of the James. All subsequent battles in the Bermuda Hundred Campaign will have the same issue with Union casualty counts unlike many other battles during the war.

Chester Station, served by the Richmond and Petersburg Railroad, was the objective of the Union X Army Corps May 10 and its total destruction was achieved in what was appropriately called the **Battle of Chester Station**. For such a lesser battle, casualties still occurred estimated at 280 Union soldiers in the killed, wounded, and missing where Confederate losses may have been twice that number. The destruction of the rail line at Chester Station that would hamper the ability of Confederate supply efforts was a major achievement for the Army of the James.

Next in the line of conflicts initiated by General Butler and his Army of the James was against Drewry's Bluff that had been unsuccessful in 1862 and would prove no better in this endeavor! Drewry's Bluff was the Confederate name for the fortification while the Union called it Fort Darling. Regardless of what it was called, it would not be captured in this **Second Battle of Drewry's Bluff** or **Battle of Proctor's Creek** May 12-16, 1864.

View of Drewry's Bluff (Fort Darling) with destroyed ship lying in the river.
Library of Congress, Prints & Photographs Division, LC-DIG-ds-05477

The near full force of the Army of the James could not dislodge Confederate General Beauregard from the site in spite of nearly two to one odds in military strength. Union General Butler was known to lack aggressiveness in a fight and did the same in this battle costing not just the battle, but also many Union casualties the numbers of which are not provided by the battle, but may have exceeded 6,000 combined for both armies. General Butler's Bermuda Hundred Campaign was virtually over at this point as the Army of the James returned to Bermuda Hundred allowing Confederate General Beauregard to release some of his force to the benefit of the Army of Northern Virginia.

The Union Bermuda Hundred Campaign was not quite over after the Battle of Proctor's Creek evidenced by the **Battle of Ware Bottom Church** on May 20 in which Confederate forces had pursued Union General Butler back to the region of Bermuda Hundred. This battle became a stalemate of entrenched troops on both sides with the occasional rush of troops followed by retreating to previous entrenchments. Consistent with almost all the Bermuda Hundred Campaign battles, casualty numbers are estimates and often given as a total on both sides. Casualty totals for the Battle of Ware Bottom Church may have been 1,500.

Union fortification line of Bermuda Hundred near Point of Rocks
showing encampment and soldiers below the trees.
Library of Congress, Prints & Photographs Division, LC-DIG-ppmsca-32743

Bermuda Hundred remained under Union control for the remainder of the war and was used as a supply depot as indicated earlier. Union Major General Butler relinquished temporary command of the Army of the James August 27 to September 7 and again December 14-25 before finally giving up command to Major General Edward Otho Cresap Ord January 8, 1865, eight days after the Army of the James was once again called the Department of Virginia and North Carolina. On January 31, 1865, the Department of Virginia and North Carolina was separated back into the separate Department of Virginia and Department of North Carolina.

Lynchburg Campaign

At the same time as the Bermuda Hundred Campaign was getting underway along the James River, the Lynchburg Campaign with the same purpose began in the Shenandoah Valley under Union Major General Franz Sigel's Department of West Virginia. General Sigel was instructed to disrupt the rail system at Lynchburg, Virginia, and engage Confederate forces sufficient to prevent reinforcements from impacting Grant's Overland Campaign against the Confederate Army of Northern Virginia.

General Sigel had at his disposal around 10,000 troops more than sufficient to accomplish his objectives when opposed by less than 5,000 Confederate troops of which a few were cadets from the Virginia Military Institute. General Sigel was soundly defeated in the first battle of the campaign failing to achieve the desired objectives put forth by Union Lieutenant General Grant that was reason his tenure in the Department of West Virginia only lasted from March 10 to May 21, 1864.

The **Battle of New Market** was fought May 15 pitting the Union First and Second Brigades of both the First Infantry and First Cavalry Divisions, Department of West Virginia, against the Confederate First and Second Brigades of an Infantry Division commanded by Major General John Cabell Breckinridge within the Trans-Allegheny Department aka Western Department of Virginia. The battle began before noon Sunday, May 15, when Confederate General Breckinridge advanced his force against the Union troops south of the village of New Market in the Shenandoah Valley of northwest Virginia. The larger Union force of slightly more than 6,000 was soundly defeated by just over 4,000 Confederate troops resulting in over 800 Union casualties to slightly more than 500 for Confederates.

Cadets from the Virginia Military Institute charging the Union line
in the Battle of New market, May 15, 1864
Wikipedia {{ PD-1923 }}

Before the next conflict in the campaign there would be a change in the players for both armies. Failure at the Battle of New Market resulted in the appointment of Major General David Hunter to the Union Department of West Virginia. This command change would prove successful at least in the next conflict, but failed in the end.

On the Confederate side, Brigadier General William Edmondson "Grumble" Jones was placed in temporary command of the Trans-Allegheny Department May 23 due to the absence of Major General Breckinridge. General Jones was not comfortable with his command assignment and agreed to remain until a more qualified officer could be assigned. On May 31, Colonel George Bibb Crittenden assumed command of the Department apparently at the request of General Jones who remained in the Department. It is uncertain if this change was authorized at the request of General Robert E. Lee.

AUTHOR'S NOTE: The Confederate command structure can be difficult to follow due to the many different names used for the same organization often times by the same individual. Case in point is the Trans-Allegheny Department that far too often is called by its earlier name the Department of Southwest Virginia, or later as the Department of Western Virginia, Western Department of Virginia, and finally Department of Southwest Virginia and East Tennessee. The last department name was actually officially adopted February 25, 1865, ending all other names associated with this group and even that name ended when the department was merged into the Department of Tennessee and Georgia April 19, 1865.

Major General David Hunter
Officer of the Federal Army
Library of Congress, Prints & Photographs Division,
LC-DIG-ppmsca-32331

Brigadier General William Edmonson "Grumble" Jones
Officer of the Confederate Army
Wikipedia {{ PD-1923 }}

After assuming command of the Union Department of West Virginia, Major General David Hunter pumped new life into his force as they continued their objective to Lynchburg. General Hunter and his 8,000 plus force made contact June 5 with Confederate Brigadier General John Daniel Imboden's Cavalry Brigade plus Harper's Valley Reserves totaling around 1,500 troops reinforced by additional 4,000 infantry under the command of Brigadier General William E. Jones. This fight would become the **Battle of Piedmont** fought June 5. Against heavy odds, the Confederate forces were overcome, but not without inflicting just under 900 Union casualties in all categories. Casualty numbers for the Confederates was approximately 500 in killed and wounded and 1,000 or more captured. A more significant loss to the Confederate forces was General Jones who was killed in the fight. The next day Monday, June 6, the Union *"forces under General Hunter entered Staunton without opposition, and were there joined by General Crook* (Brigadier George, District of Kanawha) *on the 7th or 8th. After destroying the railroads in the vicinity, supplies for the rebel army, and all the manufacturing establishments in the place, the united forces advanced on Lexington, at which place was destroyed the Military Institute, with considerable quantities of arms and ammunition; proceeded toward Lynchburg, arriving in the vicinity of that place on the 17th, and immediately engaged the enemy, capturing artillery from him."*[3]

The action described in the previous paragraph became the **Battle of Lynchburg** that took place June 17-18, 1864. It did not go well for General Hunter and his Union troops. The Union march from Staunton meant that the Department of West Virginia had to cross over the Blue Ridge Mountains to reach Lynchburg. Lynchburg was an important commerce center lying ninety miles west of Richmond, Virginia. The Orange and Alexandria Railroad and the Virginia and Tennessee Railroad connected Lynchburg with both the west and the east. Further, the James River flowed from west to east just north of the town. Capture of Confederate held Lynchburg would serve two purposes – disrupt the logistics and tie up Confederate troops from reinforcing the Army of Northern Virginia that was engaged against the Union Army of the Potomac.

Three factors influenced the outcome of the battle. Union forces had come some distance south in the Shenandoah Valley stretching their supply lines that were also targeted by bands of Confederate soldiers, failure of Union Major General Philip Henry Sheridan's Cavalry to reinforce General Hunter, and the arrival of the independent Confederate command officially the Army of the Valley District under Lieutenant General Jubal Anderson Early.

The Union Department of West Virginia at this point in the war consisted of two each infantry and cavalry divisions plus supporting artillery. Brigadier General Jeremiah Cutler Sullivan commanded the First Infantry Division and Brigadier General George R. Crook the Second. The First Cavalry Division was under the command of Brigadier General Alfred Napoleon Alexander Duffle while Brigadier General William Woods Averell had the Second. These Union forces faced an increasing Confederate Army utilizing earthen fortifications from which they defended Lynchburg. The Confederate forces consisted of much of the Army of Northern Virginia II Corps and both infantry and cavalry forces from Richmond that arrived June 18 complicating efforts of the Union command. Back and forth assaults by both armies came to a halt when the Union command came to the realization that they could not break the defenses and ammunition was running low. That evening Union General Hunter called off the attack and retreated into West Virginia bringing to an end the Lynchburg Campaign.

Consistent with Union casualty reporting of supporting campaigns such as Lynchburg, battle losses were lumped together covering a period of time not individual battles. For the period of June 10-23 that includes the Battle of Lynchburg and lesser engagements, there were 103 killed, 564 wounded, and 271 captured or missing.[4] Confederate losses are speculation at best, but we know partial numbers at least for the Battle of Piedmont and virtually nothing for the Battle of Lynchburg.

Grant's Overland Campaign

At this time in the war, May 1864, all but one military campaign was the effort of Union leadership causing the Confederate leaders to react accordingly. The Overland Campaign derived its name from the Union Army of the Potomac marching from its staging area south of Rappahannock Station toward Richmond, Virginia. As already noted, both the Bermuda Hundred and Lynchburg Campaigns were conducted to disrupt the Confederate logistics and prevent reinforcements from impacting the Overland Campaign. There was partial success in the disruption of the supply lines, but failed to prevent troop reinforcements from supporting the Confederate Army of Northern Virginia.

The Overland Campaign was the mastermind of Union General-in-Chief Ulysses Simpson Grant using the Army of the Potomac commanded by Major General George Gordon Meade. General Grant stated that he "*tried, as far as possible, to leave General Meade in independent command of the Army of the Potomac. My instructions for that army were all through him, and were general in their nature, leaving all the details and the execution to him.*"[5] General Grant's quote was actually the opposite of what he said as he was running the campaign whether or not he would admit such. Nevertheless, it was probably good that General Grant was in charge of the campaign or there might have been more carnage.

Major General George Gordon Meade
Officer of the Federal Army
Library of Congress, Prints & Photographs Division, LC-DIG-ppmsca-40718

The Army of the Potomac departed from its staging area early Wednesday morning, May 4, and crossed the Rapidan River by nightfall, a distance of twelve miles. There might have been as many as 127,471 troops present for duty with an additional 21,363 from the IX Corps to follow. The V and VI Corps crossed at the Germanna Ford, the II Corps at United States (Ely's) Ford, and the Cavalry Corps in advance of all three at an undisclosed river ford. In the meantime, the IX Corps of Union Major General Ambrose Everett Burnside was instructed to remain near Rappahannock Station until word was received that the main Army had crossed the Rapidan River. General Burnside received word of the crossing May 4 and immediately began his march to meet up with the Army of the Potomac.

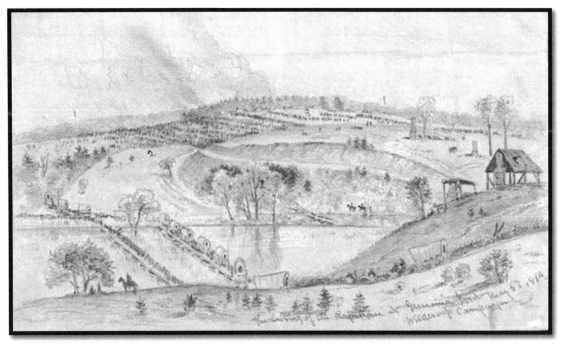

Drawing of he Union Army of the Potomac crossing the Rapidan River at the Germanna Ford
May 5, 1864, at the beginning of the Union Overland Campaign.
Library of Congress, Prints & Photographs Division, LC-USZ62-14327

Union General Grant's primary goal for the Overland Campaign was not to capture Richmond as some indicated, but rather to destroy the Confederate Army of Northern Virginia thereby breaking the back of the entire Confederate Army! This would be no easy task as General Grant quickly found out May 5 in the **Battle of the Wilderness**. Hardly had the Army of the Potomac crossed the Rapidan River when Confederate General Lee's forces of the Army of Northern Virginia engaged the V Corps of the Union Army of the Potomac. General Grant had hoped to surprise Confederate General Lee but that did not happen!

The Wilderness was just what it seemed, an area of dense woods and underbrush with narrow roads and pathways making any fight difficult. The battle raged on during the day as more Union Corps were flung into the fight. Darkness ended the first day of the battle with neither army gaining the upper hand. At 5 o'clock in the morning May 6, the battle resumed and continued throughout the day with the outcome the same as the previous day. That evening it was clear that this battle would achieve nothing positive for the Union command and orders were issued to move toward the area of Spotsylvania Court-House to the southeast. Union General Grant was not one to retreat from battle and go into encampment as many Union commanders had done in previous battles regardless of what had occurred. The Battle of the Wilderness was a costly battle for both sides in the war. Union losses show 2,246 killed, 12.037 wounded, and 3,383 missing or captured. A large proportion of the wounded were regarded as "slightly wounded." Confederate losses were somewhat less, but there were fewer troops engaged in the battle. Official reports recorded Confederate losses for the First and Second Corps of the Army of Northern Virginia as 1,128 killed, 4,974 wounded, and 156 missing or captured. What is missing in these numbers is the Third Corps that might make the total loss in excess of 11,000.

Battle of the Wilderness showing Union Brigadier General James Samuel Wadsworth and his Fourth Division, V Corps, Army of the Potomac, against the Confederate Army of Northern Virginia, May 5, 1864. General Wadsworth was mortally wounded in the battle and died three days later, May 8, 1864.
Library of Congress, Prints & Photographs Division, LC-DIG-ppmsca-20998

The loss for both armies in the two-day Battle of the Wilderness was staggering, but did not deter either commanding general from continuing the fight. Confederate General Lee and Union General Grant were determined and highly competent military commanders. General Lee may have been more amiable in his approach to battle or so it seemed while General Grant was hard charging at whatever the cost! The two generals had butted heads with neither achieving the desired outcome and would prepare to do the same again in the **Battle of Spotsylvania Court-House** that extended from May 8-21.

The fourteen-day engagement around the area of Spotsylvania Court-House did not mean that a continuous battle was taking place. Instead, engagements occurred periodically over the two weeks each of which resulted in more casualties for both sides in the campaign. Union General Grant had disengaged the Army of the Potomac after the Battle of the Wilderness and headed southeast toward the crossroads of Spotsylvania Court-House hoping to catch Confederate Lee's Army of Northern Virginia off guard. General Lee somehow learned of the Union plan and arrived first setting up defensive positions in anticipation of what would come. What is not acknowledged is how General Lee knew the Union forces were headed for Spotsylvania Court-House unless he was tipped off by either a captured Union soldier or a spy was within the ranks!

The first action of the Battle of Spotsylvania Court-House occurred May 8 in which the Union Army of the Potomac's V Corps commander, Major General Gouverneur Kemble Warren, and VI Corps commander, Major General John Sedgwick, attempted to take the position called Laurel Hill from the Confederate Army of Northern Virginia's First Corps commander Major General Richard Heron Anderson. This action failed! On May 10 an all out Union assault all across the Confederate line was attempted again without achieving the objective. Another assault occurred May 12 and again May 18 then May 19 with the same rejection. The size of each army in these latest engagements only changed by the loss of casualties from the previous battle and there would now be more losses. Official Records show the Union killed as 2,725, wounded at 13,416, and 2,258 missing or captured.[6] Confederate casualties vary from source to source with no official count. There may have been as many as 13,000 total losses.

Scene at one of the Battles of Spotsylvania Court-House, May 8-21, 1864.
Library of Congress, Prints & Photographs Division, LC-USZ62-5329

Other conflicts were occurring at the same time as the Battle of Spotsylvania Court-House quickly reducing the number of available combatants. The **Battle of Yellow Tavern** May 11 was a cavalry battle between Union Major General Philip Henry Sheridan's Cavalry Corps of the Army of the Potomac, against Confederate Major General Jeb E. B. Stuart's Cavalry Corps Army of Northern Virginia. During the engagement, General Stuart was mortally wounded and died the next day. This battle was a decisive victory for the Union Army! Two days later, May 12, the Union Cavalry was again in action in the **Battle of Meadow Bridge** or **Battle of Richmond Heights** against the same enemy although this time commanded by Major General Fitzhugh Lee and Brigadier General James Byron Gordon. This too was a Union victory resulting in the death of General Gordon commanding the Second Brigade of the Cavalry Corps who was mortally wounded and died six days later.

Except for individual engagements, the Union Army was having difficulty overcoming the Confederate forces and once again Union General Grant decided to change locations and headed further southeast toward the North Anna River and the important rail station of Hanover Junction. Confederate General Lee it seems had a crystal ball that was telling him every move of the Union Army allowing him to reach the North Anna River first to the obvious dismay of General Grant. The **Battle of North Anna** was actually a series of six smaller engagements fought for four days May 23-26 with inconclusive results although both armies would still suffer significant casualties. As the battles continued, both armies became smaller due to casualties of war and sometimes through enlistments that ran out at the time.

Military efforts in the region of the North Anna River would require river crossings by way of either existing bridges or pontoon bridges constructed where needed. One crossing point was the Chesterfield Bridge on the Telegraph Road over which Major General Winfield S. Hancock's II Corps would attempt to cross. The other was a pontoon bridge constructed upstream of the Telegraph Road over which the V Corps of Major General Gouverneur K. Warren would cross. The Chesterfield Bridge was taken by the Union II Corps, but was not crossed and a defensive position instead was set up on the north side. The V Corps using a pontoon bridge crossed the North Anna River without incident and established a bridgehead on the south side of the river. It would not take long before the Union V Corps was involved in conflict with the Confederate Third Corps commanded by Lieutenant General Ambrose P. Hill. The back and forth engagement eventually resulted in a stalemate as did the whole affair at the North Anna River.

By the third day of this engagement, May 25, it was clear that not much was going to change the outcome. A frontal attack like that at Spotsylvania Court-House would produce nothing but more casualties. Union casualty numbers for the Battle of North Anna are lumped with other engagements up to June 1 and totaled 3,986. Confederate casualty numbers are estimated somewhere around 1,500. Both these numbers have percentages relative to the number of troops engaged in battle.

It was again time for General Grant to disengage and find another area that might fulfill his plan to destroy the Confederate Army of Northern Virginia. Consistent with previous movements, the Army of the Potomac moved southeast about the same twenty-five miles as each change in the past taking them to an area around Cold Harbor. Cold Harbor was not what it seems! It was the intersection of two roads at which there was the Cold Harbor Tavern. Its primary significance was that the site was close to the Pamunkey River from which reinforcement and supplied could be attained.

The Telegraph Road with the Chesterfield Bridge over the North Anna River
showing Union soldiers on the south side of the river.
Library of Congress, Prints & Photographs Division, LC-USZ62-90718

View from the north side of the North Anna River of a canvass pontoon bridge constructed by the Fiftieth
New York Engineers near Jericho Mills in May 1864 at the time of the Battle of North Anna.
Library of Congress, Prints & Photographs Division, LC-USZ62-27820

US Military History – American Civil War

During the Battle of North Anna other smaller engagements were occurring. One of those conflicts was the **Battle of Wilson's Wharf** fought May 24 that saw Confederate Major General Fitzhugh Lee's Cavalry Division attack the Union supply station at Wilson's Wharf along the James River a good number of miles east of where previous battles in the Overland Campaign had been taking place, but close to Major General Benjamin Butler's Bermuda Hundred Campaign. The Confederate troops met stiff resistance from Brigadier General Edward Augustus Wild in command of the First Brigade, Third Division, XVIII Corps, Army of the James, consisting at one time of the First, Tenth, Twenty-second, and Thirty-seventh U. S. Colored Infantry. It may be that only the First and Tenth U. S. C. T. were involved in the fight. It is known that the Confederate forces included the First, Second, Third, Fourth, Fifth, Sixth, and Fifteenth Virginia Cavalry along with the First, Second, and Fifth North Carolina Cavalry and finally the Fifth South Carolina Cavalry. Union casualties for this action amounted to two killed, nineteen wounded, and one missing. Known Confederate losses included twenty-four killed, six wounded, and four captured. There were others killed and wounded that were removed from the battlefield before a count was made.

Three more minor conflicts toke place over three days from May 28-30 before the final battle of the Overland Campaign. The **Battle of Haw's Shop** or **Enon Church** was a cavalry affair May 28 approximately twenty miles southeast of the North Anna River. This conflict involved Confederate Major General Wade Hampton's Division of the Army of Northern Virginia Cavalry Corps against Union Brigadier General David McMurtrie Gregg's Second Division of the Army of the Potomac Cavalry Corps. Both armies with about 4,000 strong battled for nearly half a day that was deemed inconclusive in the end with slightly less than four hundred casualties for each army.

A more significant battle occurred May 30 called the **Battle of Totopotomoy Creek** that went by a slew of other names such as the Battles of Bethesda Church, Crumps Creek, Grove Road, and Hanovertown. Totopotomoy Creek was a tributary to the Pamunkey River approximately three miles east of Mechanicsville near where the Battle of Meadow Bridge occurred May 12. The Union V Corps of the Army of the Potomac was busy again this time against the Confederate Second Corps of the Army of Northern Virginia led by Lieutenant General Jubal Anderson Early. The battle that occurred on Friday was like so many in the past. One force would mount an attack and gain ground then receive a counterattack and lose the ground they had gained. This was complicated by errors in command that also changed whatever gains had been made. The battle ended with no advantage for either side, but did add to the casualty count that is lumped together with other conflicts from May 22 to June 1. The breakdown for this battle may have been just over 700 for the Union Army and slightly more than 1,500 for the Confederates.

While the Battle of Totopotomoy Creek was taking place, the First Division, Cavalry Corps, Army of the Potomac, commanded by Brigadier General Alfred Thomas Archimedes Torbet tangled with Brigadier General Matthew Calbraith Butler's Brigade in Hampton's Division, Cavalry Corps, Army of Northern Virginia. This conflict became known as the **Battle of Old Church** or **Battle of Matadequin Creek**. Old Church was just what it described, a church, and it was near the Matadequin Creek a short distance east of Totopotomoy Creek. This may be called a battle but it was more like a skirmish between two cavalry units resulting in less than 300 casualties total on both sides. It did, however, open the door to the final large battle of the Overland Campaign and a much more significant battle than the previous three.

Keeping with Union General Grant's pattern of southeastern flanking movements in an attempt to overrun the Confederate Army of Northern Virginia, Cold Harbor was next on the list. The **Battle of Cold Harbor** was a battle of all battles much the same as Antietam and Gettysburg! The major difference between Cold Harbor and the other two was the duration of almost two weeks from May 31 to June 12 compared to one day and three days respectively for each of the others. This nearly two week timeframe does not mean that constant fighting was taking place only that troops were deployed in some arrangement during this time. Make shift fortifications were constructed by both armies that would become the scene for the upcoming Siege of Petersburg and Richmond that would follow this campaign.

The Army of the Potomac crossing the Pamunkey River around May 31, 1864,
on the march to Cold Harbor prior to the battle May 31 – June 12.
Library of Congress, Prints & Photographs Division, LC-USZ62-79187

Cold Harbor was not a harbor at all! It was the site of a tavern named Cold Harbor situated at a crossroads one of which was the Mechanicsville Road where travelers could seek shelter (harbor) and be served a "cold" meal. It was approximately six miles east of Mechanicsville, Virginia, near where other conflicts had previously taken place. Both the Union and Confederate Armies had suffered massive casualties up to this point in the Overland Campaign, but both would receive reinforcements that bolstered their strength to near where they started the campaign May 4. The Union XVIII Corps from Major General Butler's Army of the James joined General Grant's Army of the Potomac. Confederate reinforcements included the Divisions of Major Generals John Cabell Breckinridge and Robert Frederick Hoke. The Union Army of the Potomac consisted of many State organized units with a few U. S. Regular units added to the mix. The Regular units included the First, Second, and Fifth U. S. Cavalry, the First and Second U. S. Sharpshooters, batteries from the Second, Third, Fourth, and Fifth U. S. Artillery, and a number of infantry companies from the Second, Fourth, Tenth, Eleventh, Fourteenth, and Seventeenth U. S. Infantry Regiments. In comparison, the Confederate forces of the Army of Northern Virginia consisted almost entirely of State organizations except for the First Confederate Battalion.

In the first few days of the Battle of Cold Harbor, the armies were engaged in testing each other's strength and objectives. The battle came to a head on June 3 well before dawn with a Union attack that was met with deadly resistance. This June day, Friday, resulted in a large number of casualties so devastating that General Grant ended all future assaults and reverted to trench warfare for the duration. What ensued was primarily face-to-face combat from the trenches with artillery bombardments added to the fight. As high as the casualty count was from the initial assault, the stalemate for the next nine days added far more to that number.

Union forces involved in the assault June 3 in the Battle of Cold Harbor.
Library of Congress, Prints & Photographs Division, LC-USZ62- 12912

Union soldiers throwing up breastworks during the Battle of Cold Harbor May 31 – June 12
Library of Congress, Prints & Photographs Division, LC-USZ62-7048

Union artillery unit firing
Coehorn mortars against
Confederate defensive lines
during the Battle of Cold Harbor

Wikipedia {{ PD-1923 }}

The outcome of the battle is declared a Confederate victory by some, but that may be an over statement. Union General Grant did withdraw his forces from the battlefield, but that is no different than had been done in every phase of this campaign and each of those occurrences was considered inconclusive. What is certain are the casualties for the battle that had Union killed as 1,845, 9,077 wounded, and 1,816 missing or captured.[7] Confederate losses may have been slightly over 5,000, but no official numbers are available.

The Battle of Cold Harbor virtually ended the Grant's Overland Campaign, but there were still two more conflicts that would take place before the campaign was declared over. The first was the **Battle of Trevilian Station** fought June 11, one day before the end of the Battle of Cold Harbor. This latest battle was another cavalry engagement between the two Cavalry Corps commanders from the two armies that is said to have ended as a Confederate victory that may well be true if the 1,512 Union casualties are any indication when Confederate losses were slightly more than 800. The final battle of the Overland Campaign called the **Battle of Saint Mary's Church** was also a cavalry affair that occurred as the Army of the Potomac headed for Petersburg. Confederate cavalry attacked Union cavalry units along the way without much impact either way. The Union Army of the Potomac and the Confederate Army of Northern Virginia would not be locked in an eleven-month siege involving Petersburg and Richmond, Virginia.

Atlanta Campaign

While Union General-in-Chief Lieutenant General Ulysses S. Grant was busy with his Overland Campaign in Virginia, his trusted loyal commander and friend, Major General William Tecumseh Sherman, was beginning his Atlanta Campaign May 7 that would involve a number of smaller unnamed engagements and several major named battles that would lead to virtual elimination of Confederate resistance in much of the South when combined with the Savannah Campaign that followed!

After the end of the Chattanooga Campaign in November 1863, General Sherman began preparation for an assault on Atlanta, Georgia, with the goal in mind to end all Confederate military control in the South in effect destroying the Confederate Army of Tennessee much the same as General Grant's plan to destroy the Confederate Army of Northern Virginia. Atlanta was important for many reasons one of which was its ability to supply Confederate forces by way of four railroads that crisscrossed the city (Western & Atlantic RR, Georgia RR, Macon & Western RR, and Atlantic & West Point RR). Control of this supply line would cripple if not destroy any chance of the Confederate Army to continue its existence in the South.

Chattanooga, Tennessee, under Union control and that of General Sherman after occupation in November 1863 became a major supply depot from which the Atlanta Campaign would be supported. General Sherman succeeded General Grant as commander of the Military Division of the Mississippi that was a military organization combining the assets of several major military departments under a single commander. General Sherman had at his disposal four Corps from the Army and Department of the Cumberland totaling 60,000 troops, three Corps from the Army of the Tennessee (his former command) with 24,000 troops, and the XXIII Corps from the Army and Department of the Ohio numbering 14,000 troops.

The objective of Union General Sherman was the Confederate Army of Tennessee under the command of General Joseph Eggleston Johnston. General Johnston had around 62,000 troops in four Corps one of which was cavalry. General Johnston would lose his command in July to General John Bell Hood after repeated defeats at the hands of the Union troops. Prior to that event, Confederate losses in late 1863 in the Chattanooga Campaign forced General Johnston to move his Army to the vicinity of Dalton, Georgia, and establish defensive positions in anticipation of further military involvement.

Union General Sherman's march to Atlanta would be a test of the tenacity of the Union resolve. Atlanta was in excess of one hundred miles south of Chattanooga over ground that ranged from mountains of sort to dense forests with many water crossings and swampy areas, but this was something that armies on both sides had faced at one time or another during the war and this effort would be no different!

The Atlanta Campaign may have officially started May 7, but there were skirmishes that occurred as early as May 1 as the Union troops geared up for action.

There was one aspect of the Atlanta Campaign that somewhat mirrored that of the Overland Campaign. Outright Union assaults on well defended Confederate positions was not the norm. The entire campaign could be characterized as a running battle in which Confederate positions would be engaged by one military organization while the remainder of the force would perform a flanking movement causing the Confederate leaders to fall back to secondary positions. This process was repeated over and over pushing the Confederate defenders closer and closer to Atlanta with each engagement. One such example was the **Battle of Rocky Face Ridge** also known as the **Battle of Mill Creek Gap** that occurred over several days in early May. When Union General Sherman determined that an all out assault on the ridge would produce nothing of significance, he ordered a flanking movement toward Resaca, Georgia, to the south. This action caused Confederate General Joseph E. Johnston to withdraw his forces toward Resaca where the two armies would meet in the **Battle of Resaca** May 13-15. While the battle was declared inconclusive for the combatants involved, it did cause Confederate General Johnston to find more defensible ground to the south and the process was repeated. The Battle of Resaca was no small affair where estimated casualties were around 2,800 for each side.

Depiction of the Battle of Resaca sometime between May 13-16, 1864
Library of Congress, Prints & Photographs Division, LC_USZ62-1265

The Union push toward Atlanta was working. The next engagement was the **Battle of Adairsville** May 17 approximately sixty miles north of Atlanta followed by the **Battle of New Hope Church** eight days later May 25-26 only twenty-five miles from

Atlanta. Adairsville was a minor involvement with few casualties, but at New Hope Church Union Major General Joseph Hooker's XX Corps, Army of the Cumberland, was caught off guard resulting in 147 killed, 1,214 wounded, and 304 missing or captured.[8] Confederate losses may have been as high as 276 killed and 1,729 wounded although that number may include other engagements at the time of the Battle of New Hope Church.[9] In an effort to offset the defeat at New Hope Church two nearly simultaneous actions were undertaken by Union General Sherman. The first action was the one-day **Battle of Pickett's Mill** May 27 that turned out no better than that at new Hope Church resulting in almost the exact same number of Union casualties as well as that for the Confederates. The second military action was the much larger **Battle of Dallas** that covered seven days beginning May 26 with the main battle occurring May 28. Dallas, Georgia, was a short distance southwest of New Hope Church

meaning the action was inching even closer to Atlanta. The Battle of Dallas was fought between Confederate Lieutenant General William Joseph Hardee's Corps of the Army of Tennessee and Union Major General John Alexander Logan's XV Corps of the Army of the Tennessee. This time the Union forces prevailed forcing the Confederates to move even closer to Atlanta. Casualty numbers were again high, but fewer Union losses around 2,400 compared to over 3,000 for the Confederates.

AUTHOR'S NOTE: Major commands for both Confederate and Union armies could have somewhat similar yet different names. Confederate armies often times lacked the word "the" such as the Army of Tennessee while Union armies included the word "the" as in the Army of <u>the</u> Tennessee. There are some exceptions to this situation, but mostly if there are no like named commands in both armies.

Union Major General John Alexander Logan encouraging his XV Corps, Army of the Tennessee, in the Battle of Dallas, May 28, 1864.

Wikipedia {{ PD-1923 }}

Union General Sherman and his three armies in their quest for Atlanta primarily followed the present day Interstate 75 route south from Chattanooga with slight variations due to terrain and conflicts with Confederate General Johnston's defensive positions. Along that route was Marietta, Georgia, a mere fifteen or so miles north of Atlanta where the **Battle of Marietta** took place that itself was a series of five named battles extending from June 9 to July 3, 1864. The Confederate Army had entrenched themselves around Marietta in anticipation of the arrival of the Union Army that had beleaguered them for a month from as far north as Dalton, Georgia. The first of the five conflicts was the **Battle of Pine Mountain** June 14 followed by **Gilgal Church** and **Pine Knob** June 15, **Kolb's Farm** June 22, and ending with **Kennesaw Mountain** June 27. It would take until July 3 for the Union forces to finally secure Marietta and drive the Confederate defenders to the defenses surrounding Atlanta.

Pine Mountain may not actually be a mountain, but it did have a commanding view of the countryside at just under 1,300 feet and was the sight of Confederate artillery in early June. The Battle of Pine Mountain was not a battle in the true sense, but rather an artillery engagement that took the life of Confederate Lieutenant General Leonidas Polk commanding the Third Corps of the Army of Tennessee. General Polk was observing action along with Generals Johnston and Hardee when struck by a Union artillery shell and fell at the spot. The Confederate position was abandoned the next day.

Lieutenant General Leonidas Polk
Officer of the Confederate Army
Killed in action, June 14, 1864, at the Battle of Pine Mountain.
Wikipedia {{PD-1923 }}

The **Battle of Gilgal Church** or **Lost Mountain** June 15 was part of a two-prong conflict that also involved the **Battle of Pine Knob** one mile to the east. The battle involved Confederate Major General Patrick Ronayne Cleburne's Division, Army of Tennessee, against that of Union Major General Hooker's XX Corps, Army of the Cumberland, and Major General John McAllister Schofield's XXIII Corps of the Army of the Ohio. The objective of the conflict was a Union effort to break the Confederate line that stretched between the two locations. The Union Second Division, XX Corps, under Brigadier General John White Geary attacked Pine Knob while Major General Daniel Butterfield's Third Division was responsible for Gilgal Church. The fighting began in late afternoon on Wednesday, June 15, and came to a halt by nightfall. Both attacks failed to achieve their desired objectives and General Geary's forces suffered as many as 500 losses while General Butterfield suffered around 150 casualties. Confederate losses were not provided.

The third engagement during the Battle of Marietta was the **Battle of Kolb's Farm** June 22. Kolb's Farm belonged to Peter Valentine Kolb who built his home in 1836 situated to the south of present-day Kennesaw Mountain National Battlefield Park. This was the site of the conflict between Confederate Lieutenant General John Bell Hood's Second Corps, Army of Tennessee, and Union Major General Hooker's XX Corps, Army of the Cumberland, along with the XXIII Corps of General Schofield's Army of the Ohio. The Battle of Kolb's Farm differed from most of the conflicts in the Atlanta Campaign in that Confederate forces took the battle to their Union foe rather than the other way around.

Lieutenant General John Bell Hood
Officer of the Confederate Army
Wikipedia

General Hood was mistaken in his analysis of the Union position. Union General Hooker was aware of General Hood's plan and established defensive positions that met the Confederate assault with more than they expected. Earlier probes by Confederate commanders provided no advantage and the main assault late in the afternoon was pummeled by Union artillery inflicting massive casualties numbering around 1,500. Union losses may have reached 350. General Hood's desire to be the aggressor would not end with this failure, but would be his demise in the end.

The last battle fought near Marietta on June 27 was the **Battle of Kennesaw Mountain**. Union General Sherman from the beginning of the Atlanta Campaign had avoided frontal assaults as much as possible in favor of flanking movements around the Confederate defenses. The Confederates defending Kennesaw Mountain west of Marietta was an impediment to reaching Atlanta and avoidance of a frontal assault was no longer an option. The Confederate Army had been pushed back to within fifteen miles of Atlanta and the concentration of those troops would make the going for the Union leadership much harder. The full complements of both the Union Military Division of the Mississippi and the Confederate Army of Tennessee would face off in this battle.

The battle opened shortly after 8 A. M. with an intense Union artillery bombardment followed by a like response from Confederate artillery units. Soon after a Union ground assault was launched against the well-defended Confederate positions that initially failed to dislodge them from Kennesaw Mountain. A flanking movement by Union Major General John M. Schofield's XXIII Corps, Army of the Ohio, was enough to threaten the security of the Confederate hold and they once again relinquished their defensive positions withdrawing toward Atlanta. The battle was by no means a Union victory in terms of casualties, but it did prove to win the day forcing a Confederate withdrawal. The general consensus shows 3,000 Union casualties compared to 1,000 Confederate

Confederate Troops dragging cannons up Kennesaw Mountain in preparation for the battle.

Wikipedia {{ PD-1923 }}

After the Confederate withdrawal from Kennesaw Mountain only one obstacle faced the Union Army from reaching Atlanta. That obstacle was the broad and deep Chattahoochee River that skirted around Atlanta on the north. Crossing the river would require bridging and ten pontoon bridges were built plus seven trestle bridges. In an effort to cross the river, the **Battle of Pace's Ferry** occurred July 5 that was more a skirmish than a full battle. Once the boats arrived, the river was crossed with limited resistance, but there was one more battle to fight before the Union Military Division of the Mississippi could set their sights on Atlanta. On July 18 before the next battle could be fought, Confederate Lieutenant General John Bell Hood replaced General Joseph E. Johnston as commander the Army of Tennessee. It would be up to General Hood to stem the tide of the Union assault on Atlanta that would be no easy task!

The test of General Hood's ability against Union General Sherman's Army would take but two days! It was the **Battle of Peachtree Creek** fought July 20 by the Union Army of the Cumberland under the command of Major General George Henry Thomas against two Corps of Confederate General Hood's Army of Tennessee. Both combatants had a strengh of around 20,000 with a slight advantage to General Thomas. Seven bridges were built over Peachtree Creek to accommodate the crossing of Union troops.

Major General George Henry Thomas
Officer of the Federal Army
Library of Congress, Prints & Photographs Division, LC-DIG-cwpbh-01069

Crossing the Chattahoochee River was a milestone achievement for the Union Army after more than two months of fighting in the campaign, but Confederate General Hood was not about to surrender Atlanta just yet even though the Federal Army was on the outskirts of the city. This would come to a head along Peachtree Creek that was a tributary to the Chattahoochee River apparently chosen for a Confederate stand against at least the Union Army of the Cumberland with the entire Union Military Division of the Mississippi on the march. *"On the 19th General McPherson [Army of the Tennessee] turned along the railroad into Decatur and General Schofield [Army of the Ohio] followed a road toward Atlanta, leading off by Colonel Howard's house and the distillery, and General Thomas [Army of the Cumberland] crossed Peach Tree Creek in force by numerous bridges in the face of the enemy's intrenched line; all found the enemy in more or less force and skirmished heavily."(10)*

On July 20 all of the Union Armies closed in converging toward Atlanta with the Army of the Cumberland facing the largest engagement around 4 p. m. with the XX Corps suffering the largest number of casualties, but no where that of the Confederate troops. Union General Sherman reported that "the enemy left on the field over 500 dead, about 1,000 wounded, and many prisoners" while his own losses were "1,500 killed, wounded, and missing." Many of that number were from the XX Corps. The Battle of Peachtree Creek was declared a Union victory, the second loss for Confederate General Hood but not the last!

Drawing of the Battle of Peachtree Creek from General Joseph Hooker's position.
Wikipedia {{ PD- 1923 }}

The Union victory at Peachtree Creek led to the **Battle of Atlanta** itself two days later that ultimately became a siege of the city that lasted until September 2. Atlanta was a fortified city with twenty-five lettered works A-Z less the letter "J" that ringed the city. Nearly all were open works resembling lunettes, redans, and batteries. Only Fort "D" for sure was a closed fortification. Though descriptions of each work are unclear, they were most likely earthworks by virtue of their sudden appearance late in 1863. Two of the lettered redoubts may have acquired names. One was called Fort Hood northwest of the city for which there is little information. Due to its location, it may have been lettered Redoubt X. It may have also gone by the name Fort Maxson. The other was Fort Walker that may have been Redoubt T or U. It was unnamed until the Battle of Atlanta in which Confederate Brigadier General William Henry Talbot Walker was killed. Fort Walker today is recognized with an historical marker in Atlanta's Grant Park.[11]

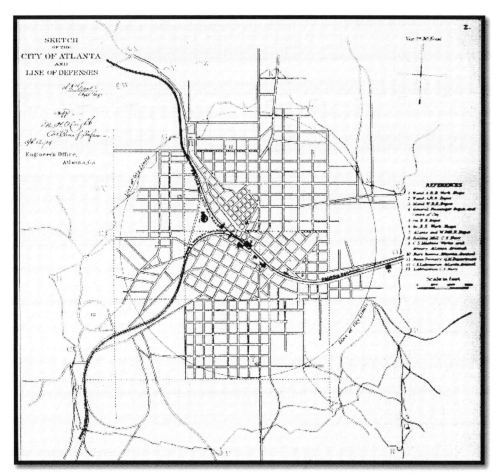

Sketch of the City of Atlanta (circle) and Line of Defenses (letters) April 12, 1864, highlighting the Confederate Redoubts A-Z beginning at the lower left clockwise around to "U" at the very bottom. Redoubts V-Z start outside the circle on the left below the signature to the top right of the sheet identification.
The Official Military Atlas of the Civil War. Series I, Vol. XXXII, p. 51 (2)

Confederate Redoubt on Peach Tree Street looking north. This may have been lettered Redoubt K shown at the top of the map on the previous page for the "Line of Defenses" of the City of Atlanta. Library of Congress, Prints & Photographs Division, LC-DIG-Stereo-2s01412

On the morning of July 22 as the Union forces continued their approach to Atlanta, General Sherman was somewhat surprised to find the whole Confederate defensive line abandoned. He "thought the enemy had resolved to give us Atlanta without further contest." That thought was quickly dispelled when the General "again found him occupying a line of finished redoubts which had been prepared for more than a year, covering all the roads leading into Atlanta, and we found him busy in connecting those redoubts with curtains, strengthened by rifle-trench abatis and chevaux-de-frise." [12]

From the site of the enemy occupying a series of redoubts, General Sherman concluded that the enemy was in force in Atlanta and meant to fight! By 10 a. m. Confederate artillery and musket fire rained down on the Union forces beginning the battle. Within two hours, Union Major General James Birdseye McPherson would be killed while responding to enemy movement on his flank. That movement was from the Confederate Corps of General William Joseph Hardee and the Battle of Atlanta was in full force! Throughout that Friday in July both armies were involved in intense action that would begin a siege of Atlanta lasting until September 2, 1864. Union losses on that day of battle were 3,722 killed, wounded, and prisoners. "The enemy left on the field his dead and wounded and about a thousand well prisoners. His dead alone are computed by General Logan at 3,240, of which number 2,200 were from actual count, and of these he delivered to the enemy under flag of truce sent in by him (the enemy) 800 bodies. I entertain no doubt that in the battle of July 22 the enemy sustained an aggregate loss of full 8,000 men." [13]

Major General James Birdseye McPherson
Officer of the Federal Army

Graduated first in his class at the
U. S. Military Academy in 1853.

Killed July 22, 1864, during the Battle of Atlanta while serving as commander of the Army of the Tennessee.

One of five Union Major Generals who fell in the war, but the only Department commander, the others commanding Army Corps.

Library of Congress, Prints & Photographs Division, LC-DIG-pga-13568

Union Major General William T. Sherman center facing left with right arm on the cannon surrounded by his staff of the Military Division of the Mississippi at some point during the Battle of Atlanta.
Library of Congress, Prints & Photographs Division, LC-USZ62-57016

After the Battle of Atlanta July 22, Atlanta was under siege, but that didn't stop other engagements from occurring around the city resulting from Confederate General Hood's attempts to dislodge Union forces and breakout. The first was the **Battle of Ezra Church** also called the **Battle of Ezra Chapel** or **Battle of the Poor House** July 28 in which the Union IV Corps, Army of the Cumberland, under Major General Oliver Otis Howard was given orders to cut off the supply route of the Macon and Western Railroad entering the city on the southwest side. The Union siege line extended on all but the southern end of the city permitting the Macon and Western Railroad to resupply the Confederate forces within the city. This would need to be stopped if the siege was to be effective!

Aware of the necessity of maintaining supply for his troops, Confederate General Hood sent Lieutenant General Stephen Dill Lee in command of General Hood's former II Corps to prevent any Union interference of this supply line. The Union and Confederate forces clashed with each other on Thursday afternoon in what General Hood had anticipated as a surprise encounter that was anything but a surprise that resulted in a Union victory causing as many as 3,000 Confederate casualties to slightly over 600 Union losses. This was the third defeat for General Hood in a short span of time.

Depiction of the Battle of Ezra Church showing Union soldiers firing on Confederate forces.
Wikipedia {{ PD-1923 }}

During the Union siege of Atlanta, Union forces established twenty-two consecutively numbered redoubts seven of which were previous Confederate positions. They were not, however, arranged in numerical order as for example Redoubt No. 7 was located on the west side of the city between and opposite the former Confederate works "C" and "D".

Redoubts No. 1 through No. 6 were inside an outer defensive line that started at No. 7 and continued to No. 22 on the opposite side east of the city.[14] Many of these redoubts were improved after occupation of the city as new defensive lines were established.

A second attempt to disrupt the supply lines of the Confederate forces took place in the **Battle of Utoy Creek** August 5-7 involving the Union XXIII Corps of the Army of the Ohio commanded by Major General John M. Schofield and the XIV Corps of the Army of the Cumberland led by Major General John McAuley Palmer against the Confederate Second Corps of the Army of Tennessee. The Confederate forces put up a determined defense forcing their enemy to give up the objective at a cost of over 800 casualties to around 170 losses. Four hundred of the Union casualties occurred on August 5 as the troops were "caught in the entanglements and abatis" attacking the Confederate defensive line. This battle would seem to be a decisive victory for the Confederate command although it is declared as inconclusive.

Scene of Union General William T. Sherman and officers of the Military Division of the Mississippi assessing action at some time during the Siege of Atlanta.
Library of Congress, Prints & Photographs Division, LC-USZ62-5335

Much of the action during the Siege of Atlanta revolved around the disruption of supply lines and each army was involved to some extent in this action. What didn't involve Corps size units was relegated to the cavalry.

One such action was the **Battle of Lovejoy Station** August 20 that was along the Macon-Western Railroad line that had been the focus of attention in the Battle of Utoy Creek. Lovejoy Station was some thirty miles south of

Atlanta necessitating a mounted cavalry force to quickly cover the distance and take action against the railroad. Union Brigadier General Hugh Judson Kilpatrick's Third Division, Department of the Cumberland, was tasked with this mission. The raid by the Union cavalry troops first struck the rail system of the Atlanta and West Point Railroad at 3:30 a. m. Tuesday, August 19, then a supply depot near Jonesborough on the Macon and Western Railroad, and finally reached Lovejoy Station August 20 also on the Macon and Western Railroad. While in the process of destroying the railroad Confederate forces attacked the Union Cavalry and a fight ensued that lasted into the early evening when the Union troops disengaged ending this action.

There would be one last gasp in the Atlanta Campaign known as the **Battle of Jonesbourgh** August 31 to September 1, 1864. This would be the crowning glory for Union General Sherman's effort to seize Atlanta and it would happen. Efforts to cut off the Confederate supply lines of the Macon and Western Railroad and that of the Atlanta and West Point Railroad had been only partially successful. Destruction of the rail systems were quickly repaired and General Sherman was determined to put an end to this occurrence once and for all!

The Union Army of the Cumberland with the IV, XIV, and Cavalry Corps plus the Army of the Tennessee and its XV, XVI, and XVII Corps with as many as 70,000 troops were to target the two rail systems and send the Confederate Army of Tennessee on the run if not destroyed. Confederate Lieutenant General John B. Hood countered with his First Corps (Hardee) and Second Corps (Lee) with no more than 25,000 troops. The strength difference would spell the outcome. The battle was intense, but General Hood in the end was forced to abandon Atlanta destroying all supplies and ammunition that could not be removed and take safety to the south with his troops that had not become casualties of combat to include capture. The Confederate Army of Tennessee had seen better days and General Hood would see a steady decline in his military role in the Confederate Army!

Photo showing the destruction caused by blowing up the Confederate Ordnance Train upon evacuation of Atlanta September 1, 1864. Many of the wheels of the train still lay on the track and only the smoke stacks of the "Rolling Mill" remain after the explosion.

Wikipedia {{ PD-1923 }}

The Union capture of Atlanta was complete and occupied by General Sherman's Military Division of the Mississippi on September 2. Atlanta would remain in the hands of the Federal Army for the remainder of the war.

Richmond-Petersburg Campaign

Following the largely unsuccessful Union initiated Overland Campaign by the Army of the Potomac, two assaults were made on the critical supply center of Petersburg, Virginia.. What some describe as the **First Battle of Petersburg** occurred on June 8 by the Union Army of the James under the command of Major General Benjamin Franklin Butler who also conducted the unsuccessful Bermuda Hundred Campaign a short time earlier. The Official Records of the Civil War do not identify this action as the first battle but rather an "engagement" giving first battle designation to the second effort beginning June 15.

Defending Petersburg was General Butler's nemesis Confederate General Pierre Gustave Toutant Beauregard's Department of North Carolina and Southern Virginia along the Dimmock line. The Dimmock defensive line was a series of earthen fortifications constructed in late 1862 for the defense of Petersburg named for Captain Charles Henry Dimmock who supervised the early construction. The Union attack on June 8 was a feeble attempt that fortunately resulted in less than one hundred fifty casualties combined with Confederate numbers slightly more than half the total.

Petersburg was a key supply center for Confederate forces with a complex of rail lines crossing the city. From the north was the Richmond and Petersburg Railroad followed by the Southside Railroad along the Appomattox River, the Norfolk and Petersburg Railroad from the east, and the Petersburg and Weldon Railroad from the south-southeast. A fifth rail line from the northeast was the City Point Railroad, but that was under the control of Union forces occupying the City Point Depot. For the reason of so many rail systems capable of supporting the Confederate cause, Union General Grant was determined to cut off that supply source as quickly as possible resulting in the surrender of the Army of Northern Virginia (AVN). That was the plan, but that would not come with ease as General Butler's Army of the James had already experienced. Next would come the real **First Battle of Petersburg** June 15-18 that was exactly the opposite from the previous attempt in the amount of military involvement but not the outcome!

The combined Union Army of the Potomac and Army of the James with upwards of 60,000 troops fought against the Confederate Army of Northern Virginia that mustered slightly less than 40,000 troops on the final day of the battle. The entrenched Confederate forces easily held their ground from their well-defended positions after repeated Union assaults resulting in enormous number of Union casualties compared to their own. When a final casualty tally was made, Union losses were nearly triple that of the Confederates showing nearly 12,000 in killed, wounded, and missing or captured.

Following the unsuccessful attempt to seize Petersburg, a siege was implemented against both Petersburg and Richmond that would last for nine and a half months until just before the surrender of the Confederate Army of Northern Virginia April 9, 1865. A siege of this length was out of the ordinary and may have been a window into the final outcome. Armies on both sides dug in for the long haul with as many as fourteen named battles designed to defeat the Confederate Army resulting in a rising number of casualties due to sporadic rifle and cannon fire, sickness, disease, and utter disillusionment!

Depiction of the Union XVIII Corps, Army of the James, storming the Confederate fortifications near Petersburg June 15 during the First Battle of Petersburg.
Library of Congress, Prints & Photographs Division, LC-USZ62-111178

The area around both Petersburg and Richmond was a maze of earthen fortifications on both sides in the war constructed for the protection of the combatants. Not all of the fortifications were in existence in the beginning, but the numbers grew as time passed. Some were so close to each other that the soldiers in the trenches could shout at each other. In the final tally, Petersburg had forty-one named forts with the vast majority, thirty-six, under Union control. There were an additional fifty-six Confederate numbered batteries plus forty-two numbered Union batteries. The thirty some mile siege line was inundated with defensive positions. Richmond had their share of forts but less than Petersburg. There were ten named forts all but two manned by Confederates plus seventeen numbered defensive Confederate positions along with twenty Confederate batteries and one Union battery.

The soldiers defending these positions were rotated in and out as the situation dictated. While one unit was in the trenches, another was on "rest and recuperation" waiting their turn to once again occupy the front lines. Troop concentrations varied as time passed and needs changed. Union forces at first were at low numbers around 15,000 and gradually increased as time passed to a high of 125,000 or so near the end of the campaign. Confederate forces never benefited from the high numbers compared to their enemy showing scant numbers early in the siege and around 50,000 total late in the campaign!

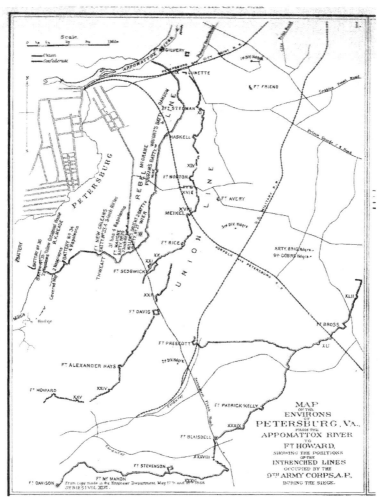

Map of the fortified positions involved in the Siege of Petersburg.
The Official Military Atlas of the Civil War, Plate 79-1, p. 198

The effort around Petersburg and Richmond was called a siege, but it was more accurately identified as trench warfare. A siege would constitute surrounding an enemy cutting off all essential resupply such as ammunition, food, water, and medical assistance as well as troop reinforcements and that was not the case in this situation. Confederate forces were able to both supply and reinforce their troops to and from Richmond to the northwest while Union forces did the same from their major supply depot at City Point, Virginia, to the northeast at the confluence of the Appomattox and James Rivers. Further, a siege does not typically involve battles and it has already been pointed out that as many as fourteen of these occurred in the five-months from June to November of 1864.

While siege lines were implemented, Union efforts continued to attack at any point that would break the hold on the Confederate defensive positions as well as disrupt if not totally destroy supply lines such as the railroads. The first of these attempts was the **Battle of Jerusalem Plank Road** also known as the **First Battle of the Weldon Railroad** occurring June 21-23. Keeping with Union General Grant's ambition to cut off supply avenues to the Confederate forces, the first attack of the siege was against the Weldon Railroad in which the Union II and VI Corps, Army of the Potomac, engaged the Confederate Third Corps of the Army of Northern Virginia. The numerical advantage in strength was clearly with the Army of the Potomac in excess of three to one, but little did that matter as the Confederate forces denied their enemy from achieving their goal at least for the present. Unfamiliar ground and difficulty in maintaining command integrity may have contributed in the failure to complete the mission. These two reasons may have also resulted in significant casualty numbers for the Union troops of just under 3,000 compared to around 500 for the Confederates.

While the previous battle did not turn out as General Grant had planned, it did result in the occupation of territory closer to Petersburg and this would be repeated with each assault against the Confederate defenses even though the siege was still in place. A Union Cavalry effort called the **Wilson-Kautz Raid** named for Brigadier General James Harrison Wilson assigned to the Cavalry Corps of the Army of the Potomac and Brigadier General August Valentine Kautz in command of the Cavalry Division, Army of the James, occurred from June 22 to July 1. The "Raid" was meant to operate deep in the rear of the Confederate lines and to do as much damage as possible to the rail systems as it could.

At least three named conflicts were offshoots of the Wilson-Kautz Raid effort. The first was the **Battle of Staunton River Bridge** taking place June 25. The bridge served the Richmond and Danville Railroad that was a vital supply route for the Confederate Army of Northern Virginia. The Union effort to seize and destroy the bridge failed resulting in slightly more than one hundred casualties against one-third that number of Confederates. The Union Cavalry forces then swung back east arriving near the Stoney Creek Station south of

Petersburg on June 28. It was here that the **Battle of Stony Creek Depot** occurred with the same outcome as had been experienced in the previous battle. A day later, Wednesday, June 29, the Union Cavalry force arrived at Ream's Station just south of the Weldon and Petersburg Railroad. It was here that the **First Battle of Ream's Station** occurred and again failed to achieve a significant outcome.

The two Union Cavalry commanders had started their mission with 5,000 or so troops and finished with no more than 4,000. In addition most of their wagon supplies had been lost, destroyed, or captured during the ten days and the force was lucky to find safety behind friendly lines after nearly being cut off. The Wilson-Kratz Raid was less than successful, but there was a more significant event to occur that had been in the works for some time!

Shortly after the Union siege line had been established at Petersburg, Lieutenant Colonel Henry Clay Pleasants commanding the Forty-eighth Pennsylvania Infantry Regiment proposed digging a tunnel under the Confederate defensive line, packing it with explosives, and blowing it up. Colonel Pleasants was a mining engineer in civilian life and many of the soldiers of the Forty-eighth were themselves miners. The plan was viewed with skepticism by the Union command, but was agreed to if for no other reason than to keep the troops busy on the front lines. The miners began digging at midnight June 25, 1864, and completed the tunnel by late July.

When the mine tunnel was finished the "main gallery" was 522 feet long with a "left and right lateral gallery" about forty feet each. Eight magazines were recommended in the two lateral galleries, four on each side with 12,000 pounds of powder. The 12,000 pounds of powder was reduced to 8,000 pounds at the time of ignition. The explosion was ready but a diversion was ordered before that would occur..

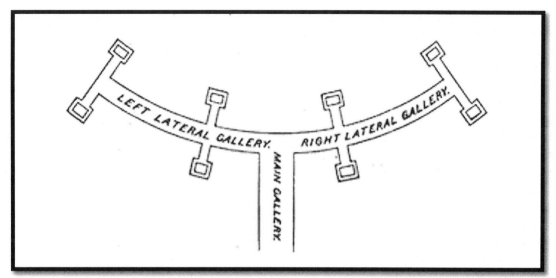

Sketch of the "Mine Shaft" provided by Major General Ambrose Everett Burnside, IX Corps, Army of the Potomac, showing the Main Gallery and Left and Right Lateral Galleries with the location of the eight magazines, four off each lateral.

The War of the Rebellion: A Compilation of the Official Records of the Union and Confederate Armies, Vol. 40, Part 1, p. 137

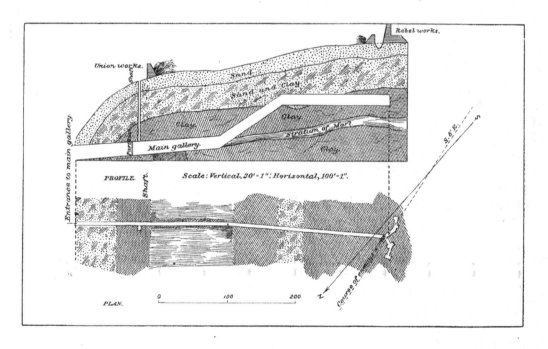

Drawing of the "mine" (tunnel) dug under Elliott's Salient. Elliott's Salient was named for Confederate Brigadier General Stephen Elliott, Jr. commanding a brigade of South Carolina Infantry Regiments.
The Official Military Atlas of the Civil War, Vol. 40, Part 1, p. 559.

Unsure of the outcome from the pending explosion of the mine shaft, Union General Grant ordered a diversion in order to draw Confederate troops from the Petersburg position known as Elliott's Salient. This effort resulted in the **First Battle of Deep Bottom** July 27-29 that went by a number of other names that included Darbytown the name of which would come up several times in the ensuing months in other Union attempts to drive the Confederate Army of Northern Virginia. from its defensive positions. Deep Bottom was a name given to an area at a bend in the James River approximately eleven miles southeast of Richmond. Union Major General Winfield Scott Hancock commanding the II Corps, Army of the Potomac, and Major General Philip Henry Sheridan, Cavalry Corps of the same army would be confronted by the Confederate First Corps, Army of Northern Virginia, commanded by Lieutenant General Richard Heron Anderson.

If greater gains could have been made by the Union commands it would have been a feather in General Grant's hat, but that was not the case. Confederate resistance was strong and the Union effort was terminated although it did help to draw Confederate reinforcements away from Elliot's Salient at Petersburg. Casualties for the Union forces were under 500 total in all categories. Confederate losses were slightly more at just under 700. The time was ripe to test the impact of the mine tunnel dug under the somewhat unsuspecting Confederate forces at Elliott's Salient. Somehow knowledge of the tunnel reached the Confederate command, but there was some doubt of its validity and only partial precautions were taken. Those suspicions would be borne out at 5:45 AM on the morning of Saturday, July 30, 1864, when the explosives were detonated! The action that ensued became the **Battle of the Crater** dubbed the **Second Battle of Petersburg** by Major General Burnside.

Scene of the explosion in what became known as the Battle of the Crater.
Library of Congress, Prints & Photographs Division, LC-USZ62-7056

The detonation of the explosives caused a crater 170 feet long, 60 to 80 feet wide, 30 feet deep and killed countless Confederate soldiers on duty at the time. The initial shock to the Confederate defenders was horrendous, but failure of the Union command to exploit this success resulted in a devastating loss of lives on both sides. Due to poor planning on the part of the Union commanders, many of the Union attackers poured into the crater where they became trapped by the depth of the walls becoming easy targets for Confederate riflemen who rushed to the scene. While the initial explosion resulted in immediate deaths to most of the soldiers of the Twenty-second South Carolina Infantry and many others of the Eighteenth South Carolina, their total number of killed may have reached 289 far less than Union losses reported at 504 killed, 1,881 wounded, and 1,413 missing or captured.[15]

Union General Grant's assessment of the Battle of the Crater was short sided. His remarks at 10:00 AM after the explosion gave the impression that it was a success and stated that, "Although just from the front, I have little idea of casualties. I think, however, our loss will be but a few hundred, unless it occurs in withdrawing, which it may not be practicable to do before night." [16] The Union casualty count far exceeded General Grant's comment!.

Two weeks after the largely failed Crater incident, it was back to another Union attack against Confederate positions. The **Second Battle of Deep Bottom** began August 14 and continued until August 20. Deep Bottom was just one of five names for this battle that pitted the Army of the Potomac II Corps under the command of Major General Winfield S. Hancock supported by the X Corps of the Army of the James commanded by Major General David Bell Birney against the Army of Northern Virginia First Corps commanded by Major General Charles William Field. Strength

advantage favored the Union command as in the past, but this proved no more successful than in previous engagements with close to 3,000 Union losses against 1,500 Confederates.

Battle after battle produced nearly the same outcomes and more casualties, but persistence was about to change this picture. The **Battle of Globe Tavern** August 18-21 that followed the Second Battle of Deep Bottom resulted in a Union victory, but casualty numbers still reached over 4,000 Union losses and slightly over 1,500 for the Confederates.. The **Second Battle of Ream's Station** August 25 reverted back to a Confederate victory with less casualties than the last at nearly 3,000 Union and 1,000 Confederate, but then it was back to favoring the Union effort in the **Battle of Chaffin's Farm** September 29-30 that involved efforts against Confederate held Forts Harrison, Johnson, and Gilmer near Richmond. Here too casualty numbers exceeded 3,000 Union to 2,000 Confederate. The capture of Confederate Fort Harrison by Union troops gave way to the **Battle of Peeble's Farm** September 30 to October 2 designed to relieve Confederate pressure against the new occupiers of Fort Harrison. This effort was a success, but did result in substantial casualties to the tune of 3,000 to 1,000.

For the remainder of 1864, there would be one more Union victory and two decisions for Confederates. The **Battle of Darbytown and New Market Roads** October 7 saw the Union X Corps, Army of the James, with support from the Cavalry Division of the same command engaged against two divisions from the Army of Northern Virginia. By previous engagements, this battle was tame accounting for less than 500 Union casualties compared to 700 for Confederates. Regardless, this was a Union victory, but the last during the 1884 Richmond and Petersburg Campaign.

Scene of the Battle of Chaffin's Farm showing the Union assault on Confederate Fort Harrison.
Wikipedia {{ PD-1923 }}

The final three battles of the Richmond and Petersburg Campaign for 1864 resulted in two Confederate victories and one draw. The first was the **Battle of Darbytown Road** October 13 that somewhat mirrored the previous battle in the number of casualties. The combined totals for both combatants were less than 1,000 about equal for each. The Battle of Fair Oaks & Darbytown Road also called the Second Battle of Fair Oaks was conducted October 27-28 pitting the Union Army of the James X and XVIII Corps against the Confederate First and Fourth Corps of the Army of Northern Virginia. This was a decisive victory for Confederate Lieutenant General James Longstreet's First Corps with only 100 casualties to over 1,500 Union losses. The final episode for the campaign was the Battle of Boydton Plank Road taking place the same dates as the previous battle. It ended much the same as many of the

campaign battles as far as casualty numbers in the low thousands for each.

The Richmond and Petersburg Campaign in 1865 would pick up where it left off the previous year and continue to near the end of hostilities for the American Civil War, but there were four other campaigns occurring in 1864 before reaching the final year of the conflict. Some of these campaigns involved a series of named battles while others were campaigns of themselves.

Sheridan's Valley Campaign

Sheridan's Valley Campaign was named for Major General Philip Henry Sheridan commanding the Middle Military Division made up of the Army of the Shenandoah. General Sheridan assumed command of each command August 6, 1864, after failures by previous commanders prompted Union Lieutenant General Grant to select General Sheridan to do what others had failed to accomplish. The Army of the Shenandoah was comprised of the VI Corps from the Army of the Potomac, two divisions from the XIX Corps from the Department of the Gulf, First and Third

.

Divisions from the Cavalry Corps of the Army of the Potomac, and five Provisional Divisions from the Department of West Virginia. It was the task of this command to pressure Confederate forces operating in the Shenandoah Valley in both Virginia and West Virginia from as early as May 1864.

Portrait of Major General Philip Henry Sheridan
Officer of the Federal Army
National Archives – 11-B-2520

Eight named battles occurred during Sheridan's Valley Campaign two of which can be considered major due to the number of casualties. Four were declared Union victories and four inconclusive. Both major battles were

Union victories. The combined strength of the Union Army of the Shenandoah was around 50,000 compared to the Confederate Army of the Valley at about 12,000 under the command of Major General Jubal Anderson Early

Portrait of Major General Jubal Anderson Early
Officer of the Confederate Army
Library of Congress, Prints & Photographs Division, LC-DIG-ds-01484

The first engagement of Sheridan's Valley Campaign was the **Battle of Guard Hill** or **Battle of Crooked Run** August 16. This was a Union cavalry fight against a Confederate infantry brigade and elements of a cavalry division. This battle was declared "inconclusive", but clearly seemed to favor the Union forces who captured perhaps three hundred Confederate infantry soldiers while sustaining less than one hundred casualties themselves. A similar fight occurred August 21 called the **Battle of Summit Point** initiated by Confederate Major General Early's forces against infantry divisions of the Union VI Corps that fought a delaying action as they moved to a safer position. Casualty numbers were light for this action.

A battle that was not much of a battle was the **Battle of Smithfield Crossing** that occurred over four days from Thursday August 25 to Monday August 29. Smithfield Crossing was about eight miles east of Charlestown, West Virginia, in the far northeast portion of the State. This too was an engagement of division size units on both sides amounting to very little change in the war and very few casualties.

Engraving of the events during the Battle of Summit Point August 21, 1864

Wikipedia {{ PD-1923 }}

The **Battle of Berryville** fought September 3-4 was another minor engagement between infantry divisions without much to-do! Berryville was in Virginia a short distance to the east of Winchester. There were casualties on both sides, but right around 300 for each army. The significance of the Battle of Berryville is what followed. The first major battle of the Sheridan Valley Campaign was about to happen. With both the Union Army of the Shenandoah and the Confederate Army of the Valley reinforced their respective commands as much as possible for the **Third Battle of Winchester** also known as the **Battle of Opequon** occurring September 19. Both the First Battle of Winchester fought May 25, 1862, and the Second June 13-15, 1863, were Confederate victories. The Third battle would turn the tide and become a Union victory, but not without paying a price!

The Confederate Army of the Valley order of battle for the Third Battle of Winchester included Major General John Cabell Breckinridge's Corps consisting of four infantry divisions (Breckinridge, Gordon, Rodes, and Ramseur), artillery assets, and Major General Fitzhugh Lee's Cavalry Corps of two divisions (Wickham, Lomax) with a combined total strength of 10,000-12,000 men. No regular Confederate units were involved in the battle.

Consistent with many battles, the Union forces were in greater number at 40,000 plus. The Union order of battle included the Army of the Shenandoah's VI Corps of three divisions (Russell, Getty, and Ricketts), artillery assets, Cavalry Corps with three divisions (Merritt, Wilson, and Averill attached from the Department of West Virginia for this battle), the Department of West Virginia's XIX Corps with two divisions (Dwight and Grover) attached earlier, and two divisions (Thoburn and Duval) from the Department of West Virginia attached for this battle. Several U. S. Regular artillery and cavalry units took part in the battle. These included Batteries K and L, First U. S. Horse Artillery; Batteries B, D, and L Second U. S. Horse Artillery; and Batteries B, L M, Fifth U. S. Artillery. United States Cavalry units that participated in the battle were the First, Second, and Fifth U. S. Cavalry Regiments.

Confederate Major General Early's Army of the Valley arrived first near Winchester in anticipation of the approach of the Union Army of the Shenandoah. He was able to establish defensive positions that would be engaged shortly before noon on Monday, September 19, 1864. Attacks and counterattacks were

conducted for a period of at least two hours with deadly outcomes before Union General Sheridan's forces forced the Confederate Army of the Valley into a hasty retreat. This was clearly a Union victory, but not much celebration was in order due to the loss of many soldiers including senior officers. The First Division commander of the VI Corps, Brigadier General David Allen Russell, was killed in the battle, and his replacement, Brigadier General Emory Upton was among the wounded as were Brigadier Generals John Baillie McIntosh and George Henry Chapman.

Action in the Third Battle of Winchester, September 19, 1864
Library of Congress, Prints & Photographs Division, LC-USZ62-300

The final tally of Union losses show 697 killed, 3,983 wounded, and 338 missing or captured for a total in losses as 5,018.[17] The Confederate Army of the Valley didn't fare any better in the number of losses in the Third Battle of Winchester. A major blow to General Early's command structure was the death of

Major General Robert Emmett Rodes commanding his own division. Another casualty was Brigadier General Archibald Campbell Godwin who was killed instantly by a shell fragment in his capacity of commanding a brigade. Cavalry Corps commander Major General Fitzhugh Lee was among the wounded as were brigade commanders Brigadier Generals William Terry and Zebulon York. One other notable Confederate casualty was Colonel George S. Patton, grandfather of General George Patton of World War II fame.

Confederate losses for this battle were 259 killed, 1,794 wounded with the number of missing and captured unreported.[18] The total losses may have reached over 3,000.

Union General Philip Henry Sheridan's final assault during the Third Battle of Winchester
Wikipedia {{ PD-1923 }}

The Union momentum from the Third Battle of Winchester was evidenced two days later, September 22, in the **Battle of Fisher's Hill** south of Strasburg, Virginia. Confederate Lieutenant General Jubal Anderson Early was doing all he could to stem the tide of his last defeat. His Army of the Valley took up positions on a complex of hills west of the North Fork of the Shenandoah River perhaps in hopes of redeeming his previous loss. Unfortunately, his force at one-fourth the size of the Union Army of the Shenandoah could not achieve that goal. The assault by the Union troops broke the Confederate line forcing them to retreat further south. Compared to the previous battle, casualty numbers were much diminished showing 528 Union losses to around 261 for the Confederates.

There was one more minor engagement October 9 called the **Battle of Tom's Brook** involving cavalry troops resulting in another Union victory albeit small compared even to the last battle. This engagement would lead to the final major battle of Sheridan's Valley Campaign rivaling the Third Battle of Winchester. The **Battle of Cedar Creek** occurred October 19 very near Middletown of that day and today. The battle was named for the nearby Cedar Creek but could have been called the Battle of Middletown.

Confederate General Early initiated the attack on the Union encampment of the Army of the Shenandoah. The attack was totally successful in the beginning driving the Union forces from their position causing the loss of both men and material. Often times seen in the Civil War, advantages were not exploited and the momentum lost. This was true in this case since General Early did not take up the pursuit and Union forces rallied to turn tails on the Confederates. A full out Union counterattack led by none other than Major General Sheridan was more than General Early's troops could handle losing all they had gained earlier and much of their own items as they retreated. By the time the final shot was fired in the battle, the Confederate Army of the Valley was doomed forever. A devastating blow had been delivered in Sheridan's Valley Campaign.

The rallying charge of Union Major General Philip Henry Sheridan at the Battle of Cedar Creek, October 19, 1864
Library of Congress, Prints & Photographs, LC-DivisionUSZ62-8354

Union losses in the last battle of the campaign amounted to 644 killed, 3,430 wounded, and 1,591 missing or captured totally 5,665.[19] On the other side of the coin, Confederate losses have not been officially reported, but a good number may be 2,910 total in all categories. The Union Army of the Shenandoah as part of the Middle Military Division would continue to exist to the end of the war with changes in command. Major General Philip H. Sheridan would relinquish command of both entities February 22, 1865, to Major General Alfred Thomas Archimedes Torbert. In turn, General Torbert would retain command of the Army of the Shenandoah to the end of the war, but relinquish command of the Middle Military Division March 7, 1865, to Major General Winfield Scott Hancock. Both organizations would come to an end June 27, 1865.

The Confederate Army of the Valley was not so lucky. General Early's army was established in May 1864 from the Second Corps of the Army of Northern Virginia. After the Army of the Valley's defeat at the Battle of Cedar Creek, the army was reduced to a quarter of its original strength losing three of the divisions that were released back to General Lee's Army of Northern Virginia. The army was without much of its war fighting materials and it was all but destroyed in February 1865 by the very Union Army of the Shenandoah that they had beaten badly in the waning months of 1864.

Franklin-Nashville Campaign

At much the same time that Major General Philip Henry Sheridan was conducting his Valley Campaign in Virginia and West Virginia, the Franklin-Nashville Campaign was taking place in and around those two cities in Tennessee and portions of Georgia. Military campaigns of 1864 were largely that of Union leadership, but that was not the case in this campaign. Confederate Lieutenant General John Bell Hood who had been pushed out of Atlanta during Union Major General William Tecumseh Sherman's Atlanta Campaign was looking to redeem himself and prove his worthiness to Confederate President Jefferson Davis. General Hood's mission was to threaten the Union supply lines from Chattanooga intended for General Sherman's Union forces. For this reason, this campaign is also called **Hood's Tennessee Campaign**.

After the disappointing loss of Atlanta to the Union forces under Major General William T. Sherman, Confederate Lieutenant General Hood marched his beleaguered Army of Tennessee to the vicinity of Lovejoy Station approximately twenty miles south of Atlanta. On September 13 he was busy reorganizing his command beset with the wounded and sick at the same time short of both food and funds to pay the troops. He implored Richmond to forward payment for his troops to "prevent dissatisfaction and desertion in consequence of the non-payment of the troops." He was also faced with a civilian population that could not feed themselves of which he was unable to subsist them. While these matters were foremost on General Hood's mind, he still needed to rally his troops and prepare for his next move. That move would materialize October 5 in the **Battle of Allatoona** or **Battle of Allatoona Pass** north of Atlanta as the Confederate Army of Tennessee moved north to disrupt the Union supply lines.

Eight named battles occurred during the Franklin-Nashville Campaign, but only the two named for the campaign were of major significance. The Battle of Allatoona was the first of the campaign that had minor consequences. Federal outposts were scattered along the route of the Western and Atlanta Railroad stretching from Chattanooga, Tennessee, to Atlanta, Georgia, to protect against any disruption. The Battle of Allatoona was just such an attack by Major General Samuel Gibbs French's Division from Lieutenant General Alexander Peter Stewart's Corps, Army of Tennessee.

The Confederate troops had partial success destroying some of the rail tracks and may have routed the Union garrison except for word that Union reinforcements were about to arrive prompting General French to call off the attack. As minor as the engagement might have been, Union losses were about thirty-five percent of the slightly more than 2,000 garrison troops. Confederate casualty number didn't fare much better at around twenty-seven percent of some 3,200 troops. Regardless of these numbers, this action proved that the Confederate Army of Tennessee was still in business and a force to be reckoned with at this late phase in the American Civil War.

Portrayal the Battle of Allatoona October 5, 1864.
Library of Congress, Prints & Photographs Division, LC-USZC2-497

After the somewhat failed attack at Allatoona, the entire Confederate Army of Tennessee moved through northwest Georgia toward Resaca, then Dalton, and finally into Alabama capturing several Union outposts along the way. Meanwhile, both the Union Army of the Cumberland under Major General George Henry Thomas and Army of the Ohio commanded by Major General John McAllister Schofield were moving closer to each other in Tennessee that gave concern to Confederate General Hood.

Confederate General Hood had sent his forces in different directions all with the mission of cutting the supply lines of the Union Army. He was intent on reaching Nashville, Tennessee, and action occurred October 26-29 near Decatur, Alabama, where the Confederate Army of Tennessee was looking for a place to cross the Tennessee River on their march to Nashville. This would become the **Battle of Decatur** involving the District of North

Alabama under the command of Brigadier General Robert Seaman Granger against the whole of the Confederate Army of Tennessee minus the Cavalry Corps. The Union District of North Alabama was a part of the District of Tennessee that was itself a part of the Department of the Cumberland.

General Granger defended Decatur with a series of well-protected trenches and one unnamed redoubt and one lunette. If Confederate General Hood was going to cross the Tennessee River near Decatur, he would have to silence the Union forces. On Friday morning, October 28, a small force of Confederate troops was deployed to break the Union hold on Decatur. This attack failed resulting in the capture of over one hundred soldiers and other casualties. Crossing the Tennessee River at Decatur looked bleak for General Hood. What saved the day for General Granger and his small force of around 5,000 against nearly all the Confederate Army of

Tennessee was Union gunboats plying the waters of the Tennessee River near Decatur along with a failed attempt to overrun the Union forces occupying the trenches. Fearing that crossing near Decatur would cause his troops more harm than good, Confederate General Hood chose to move his crossing further to the west at Tuscumbia, Alabama, where the Union gunboats were less of a threat. Units of the Confederate Army of Tennessee began crossing the Tennessee River at Tuscumbia, Alabama, October 30 and continued to move across the river through November 13 at which time the headquarters was established at Florence, Alabama.

As Confederate General Hood moved his army closer to Tennessee from Alabama, he gave orders to his Cavalry Corps commander, Major General Nathan Bedford Forrest, to conduct raids on Union supply depots around Nashville, Tennessee. One of those raids was called the **Battle of Johnsonville** that took place November 4-5. Johnsonville was on the east bank the Tennessee River some seventy miles due east of Nashville, Tennessee. An attack on this site proves the tenacity of cavalry units to conduct missions far from the main army they supported. Supplies shipped on the Tennessee River arrived at Johnsonville where they were transferred to the Nashville and Northwestern Railroad and sent to Nashville.

The raid on Johnsonville was extremely effective resulting in the loss of vast number of supplies and ships employed in transporting supplies and providing naval support on the Tennessee River. An Inspector-General report by Lieutenant Colonel William Sinclair dated January 7, 1865, gave credence to the destruction. This was not a very flattering report of the Union handling of the attack. Prior to the attack on Johnsonville, Tennessee, Confederate General Forrest's cavalry forces were in action near Fort Heiman October 28 situated on the Kentucky side of the Tennessee River "capturing the steam-boat Mazeppa and a barge bound from Cincinnati, Ohio, to Johnsonville, Tenn., with a valuable cargo of quartermaster's and subsistence stores. After having landed the cargo the boat and barge were burned. The greater part of the stores captured on the Mazeppa were taken away by the rebels in their wagons." [20] This action was followed in the ensuing days by naval engagements on the Tennessee River using captured Union navel vessels. Here, too, the Confederate cavalry troops were victorious destroying more of the Union gunboats and steamboats.

All this action culminated on November 4 when Confederate artillery batteries opened fire on Johnsonville and its complex of warehouses. Union gunboats defending the depot were struck and disabled when there was an order to burn the ships. The fires of the ships spread to the docks then to the warehouses destroying vast amounts of supplies. Attempts to extinguish the flames were in vain as the Union troops were subjected to weapons' fire from Confederates on the west side of the river. Confederate General Forrest had achieved more than was expected as a consequence of ill-advised orders from the Union leaders. There would be more Confederate artillery fire on November 5, but the damage had already been done. The Confederate troops came out of this engagement nearly unscathed reporting two men killed and nine wounded. Union losses, although uncertain, may have reached just below two hundred in all categories.

To complicate matters, Colonel Sinclair's report further stated, "That after the fire a general system of theft was inaugurated, stealing clothing, hospital stores, and anything they could lay their hands upon." Even a railroad agent "ran off with a train of cars loaded with clothing and some 400 men from gun-boats" who proceeded to steal these items. It was estimated that the total loss of supplies amounted to about $2,200,000. Blame for all the destruction and chaos was leveled on Union Colonel Charles Robinson Thompson, Twelfth U. S. Colored Infantry, and Captain Henry Howland, depot quartermaster at Johnsonville.

As the Confederate Army of Tennessee moved north from Florence, Alabama, into Tennessee they would be met by the Union Army of the Ohio first at Columbia, Tennessee, in a series of engagements occurring November 24-28 named the **Battle of Columbia**, next to Spring Hill, Tennessee, November 29. The Battle of Columbia primarily involved a series of small skirmishes biding time for the Union command to gradually fall back to safer positions. The **Battle of Spring Hill** fourteen miles north of Columbia was more intense with regard to casualties, but still not the magnitude to follow. Some indications are that there were three hundred fifty Union losses and about five hundred Confederates. What could have been a Confederate victory engaging more troops than the Union Army of the Ohio turned out to be the opposite perhaps due to missed opportunities.

Another missed opportunity for Confederate Lieutenant General John Bell Hood was at the **Battle of Franklin** November 30. Union Major General John M. Schofield's Army of the

Ohio had engaged in organized withdrawals from Columbia followed by Spring Hill all the while keeping the Confederates at bay until reaching Franklin, Tennessee. Here the size of both armies was about equal, but the Confederate Army of Tennessee was a long way from their source of supply. General Schofield had his troops dig in for a pending Confederate assault that came after 4:00 pm, Wednesday, November 30. One wave after another attacked the well-defended Union positions without breaking the line except for momentary gains only to be thrown back. By the end of the day, General Hood suspended his efforts planning to resume the next morning if that would even be possible.

Laying on the battlefield were six Confederate generals killed in action along with eight more wounded one of which had been captured. In addition, there were fourteen regimental commanders killed, another twenty-nine wounded, five more wounded and captured, and seven missing and these were only the officers. The total of Confederate killed was 1,750, 3,800 wounded, and 702 captured.[21] Union losses in the Battle of Franklin were reported as 189 killed, 1,033 wounded and 1,104 missing or captured. [22]

Scene depicting the Battle of Franklin, November 30, 1864.

Library of Congress, Prints & Photographs Division, LC-USZC4-1732

General Hood's plan may have been to take up the fight the next morning, but to his surprise the Union Army of the Ohio had slipped away in the night taking up positions near Nashville along with the Department of the Cumberland in what would be the undoing of the Confederate Army of Tennessee along with Lieutenant General John Bell Hood. Before that could happen, Confederate General Hood determined to make good on his plan to capture Nashville sent an infantry division and his Cavalry Corps on a mission to destroy blockhouses and railroads along the way to Nashville. This action assumed the name of the **Third Battle of Murfreesbourgh** (Murfreesboro) conducted December 5-7. The infantry division failed to achieve its objective, but the Cavalry Corps under Major General Nathan Bedford Forrest completed its mission although of little significance.

There was one last objective for Confederate General Hood and that was Nashville itself. The **Battle of Nashville** was fought December 15-16 and ended in failure for General Hood. The Army of Tennessee had suffered catastrophic losses especially at Franklin and this current battle would prove no different! Previously, General Hood had initiated action against the Union forces, but the tails were turned at Nashville. Union Major General George Henry Thomas with his Department of the Cumberland supported by assets from the Army of the Ohio, Department of the Tennessee, and naval ships of the Mississippi River Squadron numbering around 55,000 troops met the Confederate Army of Tennessee of 30,000 troops if even that!

The Cumberland River ran through Nashville giving access to U. S. Naval vessels that would see action in the days prior to the main battle. This action involved eliminating three Confederate artillery batteries that had harassed transport ships in the early days of December. A total of eight ships took part to some degree one of which was the U. S. S. Neosho that received some damage in its effort to silence the Confederate batteries.

The USS Neosho in action against three Confederate batteries along the Cumberland River below Nashville, December 6, 1864
Wikipedia {{ PD-1923 }} (NH 58894)

The Union defenses of Nashville were a complex of thirteen forts and redoubts on which construction began as early as September 1862 and continued to the time of 1864. Considering it ill advised to attack the Union defenses, Confederate General Hood established a line of defenses of his own playing a game of cat and mouse waiting for General Thomas to attack his positions. That would come but not just right away. Bad weather befell Nashville December 8 necessitating a delay in any military action, but that changed December 15 when Union forces started their attack. This went off with partial success, but not sufficient to call it a victory at least on the first day. Friday, December 16, was a different story in the outcome but primarily the same plan – attack the right in hopes of drawing Confederate troops from the left, then attack the left. This worked! By late Friday the Confederate Army of Tennessee was in full retreat to the south crossing the Tennessee River December 23 arriving at Tupelo, Mississippi, where General Hood turned over command January 23 of what was left of the Army of Tennessee to Lieutenant General Richard Taylor. General Taylor only retained control of the Army of Tennessee long enough to release the remnants of the army for the fight against Union General Sherman's March to the Sea Campaign. He then was assigned command of the Confederate Departments of Alabama, Mississippi, and East Louisiana.

Union forces assailing the ramparts of the Confederate defenses
in the Battle of Nashville, December 15-16, 1864.
Library of Congress, Prints & Photographs Division, LC-USZ62-1289

Savannah Campaign

The famous "March to the Sea" accredited to Major General William Tecumseh Sherman took place November and December 1864 culminating in the capture of Savannah, Georgia, and all points along the way. General Sherman's armies within the Union Military Division of the Mississippi occupied Atlanta, Georgia, September 2 and other than a brief affair with Confederate John Bell Hood used the time to rest and resupply his troops in preparation for what was to come!

The Savannah Campaign began November 15 as General Sherman hid his actual objective by sending troops in two directions one south and the other east. Ultimately they would converge on Milledgeville, the capitol of Georgia at that time. Milledgeville was taken without resistance as was the case with much of the march to Savannah where only brief engagements occurred with little or no harm to the Union forces.

Along the way very little of the infrastructure of Georgia was left intact. The Union troops lived off the land confiscating everything they needed to subsist. This may have been General Sherman's way of saying that the "South" deserved what they had caused, but whatever the reason the people of Georgia were left with little for themselves! After twenty-six days on the march, the Union command arrived near Savannah on Saturday, December 10.

The area around Savannah was heavily fortified with thirty-eight named fortifications and forty-three numbered batteries and lunettes. Perhaps the most notable was Fort Pulaski, but there was also Fort Jackson and Fort McAllister. Fort Pulaski played no part in the Savannah Campaign captured by Union forces April 11, 1862, crippling Savannah and the Confederacy from supply by way of the ocean. Forts Jackson and McAllister would be impacted by the current campaign.

Savannah was surrounded by water of all types to include rivers, lakes, marshes, and ocean bays that offered protection of sorts. That protection offered little to stop the Union Army and the first to feel the wrath was Confederate Fort McAlister on December 13. Fort McAllister had seen seven previous attacks that failed, all by Union naval ships on the Ogeechee River and all the fort's defensive armament guarded a river approach. On December 13 the fort was attacked from the land-side and captured after just a fifteen-minute battle. The rest of Savannah would fall much the same way. Savannah fell to General Sherman December 20 along with Fort Jackson. This outcome was a stunning loss for the Confederate cause and would give rise to other losses much the same way in the days and months to come.

---

[1] War of the Rebellion: A Compilation of the Official Records of the Union and Confederate Armies, Vol. 34, Part 1, p. 305-306.

[2] Ibid, Vol. 36, Part 2, p. 153-154.

[3] Ibid, Vol. 37, Part 1, p. 7.

[4] Ibid, p. 103-106.

[5] Ibid, Vol. 36, p. 18.

[6] Ibid, p. 188.

[7] Ibid, p. 180.

[8] Ibid, Vol. 38, Part 2, p. 14.

[9] Ibid, Part 3, p. 687.

[10] Ibid Part 1, p. 71.

[11] Civil War Era Fortifications, Georgia, p. 235, 243, 244.

[12] War of the Rebellion: A Compilation of the Official Records of the Union and Confederate Armies. Vol. 38, Part 1, p. 72.

[13] Ibid, Vol. 38, Part 1, p. 75.

[14] Civil War Era Fortifications, Georgia, p. 244.

[15] War of the Rebellion: A Compilation of the Official Records of the Union and Confederate Armies, Vol. 40, Part 1, p. 249, 788.

[16] Ibid, p. 17.

[17] Ibid, Vol. 43, Part 1, p. 118.

[18] Ibid, p. 557.

[19] Ibid, p. 137.

[20] Ibid, Vol. 39, Part 1, p. 860-863.

[21] Ibid, Vol.45, Part 1, 344.

[22] Ibid, p. 118, 381, 411.

1865

The year 1865 would bring to an end the American Civil War, but not before three new military campaigns would occur and the continuation of the Richmond and Petersburg Campaign that was now nearly six months old. This war had carried on too long for either side and resources were strained as was the enthusiasm for such a conflict! The war could have gone on longer, but perhaps wiser heads could see the futility of such an occurrence. This thought was echoed by the men in the trenches largely on the rebel side as one after another entered the Union lines seeking not only safety, but rations that were scarce plus payment for any weapons they brought with them. Confederate General Robert Edward Lee desperately called for supplies of all sorts on many occasions while at the same time addressed plans to evacuate both Petersburg and Richmond realizing that the Confederacy could not hold on much longer.

Carolina Campaign

The Richmond and Petersburg Campaign was still ongoing as the new-year began, but the Carolina Campaign to the south began late January under Union Major General William T. Sherman who had taken Savannah, Georgia, only weeks earlier, but was now ordered by Union General Grant to sail north in an effort to support the Army of the Potomac. General Sherman elected instead to march his army north setting his sights on Columbia, South Carolina, that he disguised in the same fashion when departing from Atlanta.

During the march to Columbia and then further north, there were a number of battles that occurred most of which were minor in their outcomes. General Sherman had a vast army consisting of the Army of the Tennessee, Army of the Ohio, and the XIV and XX Corps that would become the Army of Georgia on March 28, 1865. The combined strength of these armies was 60,000 plus and growing. The Confederate forces facing General Sherman were lucky to muster 15,000 troops under General Joseph Eggleston Johnston's Army of Tennessee that had been resoundingly beaten during the Nashville-Franklin Campaign in late 1864.

Union forces would need to cross many waterways marching through South Carolina just as they had in their march to Savannah. The **Battle of River's Bridge** occurred February 3 at one of these water areas named the Salkehatchir River where a vastly superior Union force around 5,000 met Confederate troops one-fifth in size. This battle was no contest and the Union troops marched on.

Union Colonel Clark Russell Wever's Second Brigade, Third Division, Right Wing, Army of the Tennessee, wading across the Little Salkahatchie River at the time of the Battle of River's Bridge, February 3, 1865
Library of Congress, Prints & Photographs Division, LC-USZ62-14311

The Battle of River's Bridge did nothing to stop the Union forces from their march to Columbia, but the **Battle of Aiken** February 11 did put a damper on the movement if only for the moment. Confederate Major General Joseph "Fighting Joe" Wheeler's cavalry contingent defeated Union Brevet Major General Hugh Judson Kilpatrick's Third Division Cavalry, XXIII Corps, Army of the Ohio serving as the Center of Major General Sherman's Military Division of the Mississippi. The defeat of the Union force was an embarrassment even though it did not stop the overall effort.

On Friday, February 17, 1865, the Union forces of General Sherman occupied Columbia, South Carolina. That same day the fate of Columbia changed due to fires that destroyed much of the city the origin of which is debated today. Some say that Union soldiers put a torch to the city others say it was accidental, and still others say withdrawing Confederates caused the fire to deny the assets of the city to fall into Union hands. It is doubtful that the real answer will ever be known!

On the same day that Union forces occupied Columbia, the coastal city of Charleston was evacuated and items were destroyed that could aid the Union Army. The next day in Columbia, what was left of vital military importance was also destroyed and Union forces were again on the move north.

Sketch of the "Burning of Columbia" February 17, 1865.
Library of Congress, Prints & Photographs Division, LC-USZ62-133068

In related action not officially associated with Union General Sherman's Carolina Campaign, Confederate held Fort Fisher situated at a key point along the North Carolina coast at the mouth of the Cape Fear River guarding the entrance to Wilmington was attacked unsuccessfully December 24, 1864, and then successfully January 13, 1865. The first attack was conducted by Union Major General Benjamin Franklin Butler's Department of Virginia and North Carolina (former Army of the James) supported by sixty ships led by Rear Admiral David Dixon Porter. The failure of General Butler to capture Fort Fisher led to his removal from command of the department and replaced by Major General Edward Otho Cresap Ord. General Ord named Major General Alfred Howe Terry to command a Provisional Corps of the Department of Virginia and North Carolina for the purpose of capturing Fort Fisher. General Terry with the support of Admiral Porter's North Atlantic Blockading Squadron attacked Fort Fisher January 13 and successfully achieved its capture January 15, 1865. Nearby Wilmington, North Carolina, with no less than twelve named forts and three batteries providing for its defense would fall to Union forces February 22, 1865, led by Major General John McAllister Schofield's Army of the Ohio and Major General Terry's Provisional Corps of the Department of Virginia and North Carolina.

FORT FISHER

Built by Confederacy. Its fall, Jan. 15, 1865, closed Wilmington, last important southern port for blockade running.

Photo of Fort Fisher showing earth mounds protecting gun emplacements. (2005)

The battles and capture of Fort Fisher and Wilmington were added to Union General Sherman's Carolina Campaign when the Center Army, the Army of the Ohio, took part in the capture of Wilmington.. The various commands that made up the Carolina Campaign were moving rapidly north into central North Carolina. Major General John M. Schofield with Major General Alfred Terry's Provisional Corps were instructed to move inland after the capture of Wilmington to link up with the Left and Right Wings of General Sherman's force at Goldsburgh (Goldsboro). The exception to this was Major General Jacob Dolson Cox Jr. who had participated in the capture of Wilmington as the commander of the XXIII Corps of the Army of the Ohio. General Cox was ordered "to proceed at once by sea to Beaufort and New Berne [New Bern], N. C., and assume command of the District of Beaufort" where upon he would organize the local troops together with the First Division of the XXIII Corps into a "Provisional Corps" not to be confused with General Terry's Provisional Corps of the Department of Virginia and North Carolina.

General Cox arrived at New Berne late on February 28 and began organizing his forces the following day. That force would consist of three divisions including the First Division, XXIII Corps, commanded by Brevet Major General Thomas Howard Ruger and two divisions listed under the District of Beaufort. These last two divisions were designated the First Division under the command of Brigadier General Innis Newton Palmer and the Second Division commanded by Brigadier General Samuel Powhatan Carter. The mission of General Cox's Provisional Corps was to insure the rail system of the Atlantic and North Carolina Railroad was intact in order to "open a base of supplies from Beaufort Harbor, and to press the reconstruction of the road and its protection till we should unite with the remainder of the grand army at Goldsborough (Goldsboro)."

General Cox's fighting force numbered 13,056 and would encounter action Mar 7-10 in the **Battle of Wyse Fork** also called the **Battle of Kinston** for the nearby North Carolina town approximately thirty miles inland northwest of New Berne. On the outskirts of Kinston to the east, Union forces were engaged against Confederate troops under General Braxton Bragg's Department of North Carolina and Southern Virginia that had retreated from Wilmington after its capture by Union forces. This battle held up the movement of Union General Cox for a few days, but Kinston was taken March 14 after General Bragg withdrew his troops in the face of ever increasing Union reinforcements. A March 30 report listed the Union casualty numbers at 65 killed, 324 wounded, and 953 missing or captured.[3] By General Cox's own account, May 16, Union casualty numbers were 57 killed, 265 wounded, and a much larger 935 listed as missing.[4] The high number of missing were mostly captured soldiers from the Fifteenth Connecticut Infantry, Second Brigade, Second Division, District of Beaufort, commanded by Colonel Charles Leslie Upham that occurred during action on March 8.

At the time of the Battle of Wyse Fork, a cavalry engagement took place March 10 called the **Battle of Monroe's Crossroads** also known as the **Battle of Fayetteville Road**. This action was minor in nature other than delaying the Third Cavalry Division, XXIII Corps, from entering Fayetteville. Casualties for this conflict for Union troops and Confederates are reportedly less than two hundred and one hundred respectively. Another battle March 16 during the Carolina Campaign was the **Battle of Averasborough** that pitted Major General Henry Warner Slocum's Left Wing of the Union Army of Georgia against Confederate Lieutenant General William Joseph Hardee's First Corps of the Army of Tennessee. Averasborough was a town along the Cape Fear River that no longer

exists. It was located near present-day Erwin, North Carolina.

The rapid movement of Union General Sherman's forces through North Carolina posed a threat to Confederate General Joseph Eggleston Johnston's Department of North Carolina and Southern Virginia of which he assumed command March 6. General Hardee was General Johnston's hope of stopping the Union advance if only delaying it for the time being. The scenario for this battle was much the same for other recent battles. Confederates would attack the Union lines to which there would be a Union counterattack only to be stopped followed by the arrival of Union reinforcements causing the Confederate troops to conduct a withdrawal from the battlefield. This action would lead to the final battle of the Carolina Campaign, but first there were the casualties to consider in this battle. Union losses were 95 killed, 533 wounded, and 54 missing for a total of 682.[5] Confederate losses were not reported but may have been around 500.

Most of the battles of the Carolina Campaign resulted in minor engagements, but that could not be said for the **Battle of Bentonville** March 19-21 that took place near Bentonville, North Carolina. This battle involved Union Major General Sherman's Military Division of the Mississippi Right and Left Wings with some 60,000 men consisting of two armies - the Army of the Tennessee, and the Army of Georgia. The Army of the Ohio, the Center Wing, was making its way to Goldsborough. The Confederate side under the command of General Joseph Eggleston Johnson had three armies with about 22,000 soldiers - Department of North Carolina and Southern Virginia; Army of Tennessee; and Department of South Carolina, Georgia, and Florida. At least one source refers to these three armies as the Confederate Army of the South, but there is no official recognition of that name. Confederate General Johnston's armies were the last gasp if the Union forces were to be stopped in North Carolina and beyond!

The Battle of Bentonville followed a similar course as previous battles with a Confederate attack on the Union line on the first day with some success. The next day there was sporadic fighting and Union reinforcements were added to the battlefield. The third and final day saw Union forces making headway against the Confederate line resulting in a number of casualties prompting Confederate General Johnston to conclude that the large Union force was more than his troops could handle and withdrew that evening. The losses for both the Confederate and Union commands in the Battle of Bentonville are reported in the Official Records. Confederate losses show 239 killed, 1,694 wounded, and 673 listed as missing or captured. Union casualties show 184 killed, 1,112 wounded, and 221 missing or captured.[6]

This event marked the last battle of Confederate General Johnston's three armies. Although not pursued by Union General Sherman, General Johnston surrendered to General Sherman April 26 at Bennett's House near Durham, North Carolina, after the surrender of Confederate General Lee's Army of Northern Virginia on April 9, 1865.

Drawing showing surrender of Confederate General Joseph Eggleston Johnston to Union Major General William Tecumseh Sherman, April 26, 1865, near the Bennett House at Durham, North Carolina.
Library of Congress, Prints & Photographs Division, LC-USZ62-15593

View of the Bennett House in which Confederate General Joseph E. Johnston surrendered to Union Major General William T. Sherman, April 26, 1865.
Library of Congress, Prints & Photographs division, LC-USZ62-99600

Richmond-Petersburg Campaign Continued

The surrender of Confederate General Joseph E. Johnston on April 26, 1865, may have brought to an end the Carolina Campaign, but the standoff along both the Petersburg and Richmond lines continued from 1864 into 1865 without an end in sight at least so it seemed in January 1865. Much of the time, when not engaged in battles across the lines, was spent improving the defenses plus wiling away the boredom sometimes conversing with the enemy in the opposite trenches. However, there were times when the boredom turned more deadly as was the case with the **Battle of Hatcher's Run** occurring February 5-7, 1865, that was one of three such engagements that marked the time to the end of the siege operation.

The Battle of Hatcher's Run had a slew of other names, but they all came down to the same goal of cutting off supply lines of the Confederate Army on the Boydton Plank road and the Petersburg and Weldon Railroad to the south-southeast of Petersburg. The effort was spearheaded by the Army of the Potomac II Corps under the command of Major General Andrew Atkinson Humphreys, the V Corps led by Major General Gouverneur Kemble Warren, and the Cavalry Corps Second Division of Brigadier General David McMurtrie Gregg. The combined strength of this Union effort was nearly 35,000 troops.

The Union initiative kicked off Sunday, February 5, by the Second Cavalry Division supported by both the II and V Corps. Some headway was achieved that day, but Confederate Major General John Brown Gordon and his Second Corps of the Army of Northern Virginia would disrupt the plans if only momentarily. The next day, February 6, Brigadier General John Pegram's Division from the Confederate Second Corps attacked the

Union V Corps. This attack produced limited results that were later reversed. General Pegram was killed later on this day. February 7 was not much different other than the establishment of more ground along the siege line by the Union forces. Little by little the Confederate defensive lines were being pushed closer to Petersburg but there was a cost to pay. Union losses in Hatcher's Run totaled 1,539 including 171 killed, 1,181 wounded, and 187 considered missing or captured.[1] Confederate losses are speculation but may have been nearly equal.

Pencil drawing of the Union V Corps in action February 7 at the Battle of Hatcher's Run.
Library of Congress, Prints & Photographs Division, LC-ppmsca-20888

The long and tiresome standoff along the Petersburg defensive line had apparently taken its toll with the Confederate high command! In what seems like a desperate move to end the stalemate, the Second Corps, Army of Northern Virginia, attempted to take the fight to their enemy by attacking Union Fort Stedman hoping to go all the way to the Union depot at City Point, Virginia, if possible. At 4:15 Saturday morning, March 25, 1865, Major General John Brown Gordon and his Corps attacked Fort Stedman and surprisingly captured the fort within fifteen minutes.

However, the capture was short lived as Union Major General John Grubb Parke's Third Division, IX Corps, Army of the Potomac rallied to the cause and retook the fort resulting in large losses for the Confederate Second Corps. There may have been nearly one-half of the original force of 10,000 Confederate soldiers counted among the casualties. It is known that Union losses were 1,044 consisting of 72 killed, 450 wounded, and 522 missing or captured more likely missing since the Confederate Second Corps was defeated in this action.[2]

Photo showing what remains of Union Fort Stedman (2005)

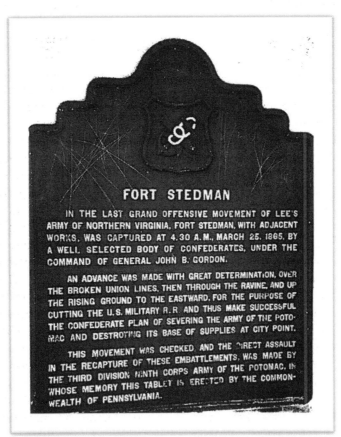

FORT STEDMAN

IN THE LAST GRAND OFFENSIVE MOVEMENT OF LEE'S ARMY OF NORTHERN VIRGINIA, FORT STEDMAN, WITH ADJACENT WORKS, WAS CAPTURED AT 4.30 A.M., MARCH 25, 1865, BY A WELL SELECTED BODY OF CONFEDERATES, UNDER THE COMMAND OF GENERAL JOHN B. GORDON.

AN ADVANCE WAS MADE WITH GREAT DETERMINATION, OVER THE BROKEN UNION LINES, THEN THROUGH THE RAVINE, AND UP THE RISING GROUND TO THE EASTWARD, FOR THE PURPOSE OF CUTTING THE U.S. MILITARY R.R. AND THUS MAKE SUCCESSFUL THE CONFEDERATE PLAN OF SEVERING THE ARMY OF THE POTOMAC AND DESTROYING ITS BASE OF SUPPLIES AT CITY POINT.

THIS MOVEMENT WAS CHECKED, AND THE DIRECT ASSAULT IN THE RECAPTURE OF THESE EMBATTLEMENTS, WAS MADE BY THE THIRD DIVISION NINTH CORPS ARMY OF THE POTOMAC, IN WHOSE MEMORY THIS TABLET IS ERECTED BY THE COMMONWEALTH OF PENNSYLVANIA.

Plaque displayed near Fort Stedman in the Petersburg National Battlefield
describing the action of the Confederate attack March 25, 1865. (2005)

US Military History – American Civil War

The failure of the attack on Union Fort Stedman signaled an end to the Confederate hold on Petersburg and Richmond that was not much of a surprise to Confederate General Robert E. Lee who had already made plans to evacuate the region. At this point in the war the Richmond and Petersburg Campaign becomes over-shadowed by the twelve-day Appomattox Campaign making it difficult to determine when one campaign ends and the other begins! Although the Siege of Petersburg was still occurring and would do so until April 2, the Appomattox Campaign shifted the focus away from Petersburg.

Appomattox Campaign

The Appomattox Campaign began March 29 as Union General Grant put in motion plans to end the siege of Petersburg. The Union Army of the Potomac, Army of the James, and Army of the Shenandoah with upwards of 114,000 troops began a movement west of Petersburg hoping to out flank and out maneuver the Confederate Army of Northern Virginia. Four engagements would occur before the siege could be broken. The first was the **Battle of Lewis's Farm** March 29 where a brief battle ensued resulting in few casualties, but the Confederates were forced to give ground leading to the next battle that would be the **Battle of White Oak Road** March 31 where the retreating Confederate force had gone from the previous battle. This last battle like so many had multiple names. It was also known as the **Battle of Hatcher's Run** that perhaps should have been the Second Battle of Hatcher's run since there already was a battle by that name fought February 5-7, 1865. Other names for this battle were **Battle of Gravelly Run**, **Boydton Plank Road**, and **White Oak Ridge**.

The Battle of White Oak Road had similar results to that of the Battle of Lewis's Farm except in the number of casualties. Union losses were much higher. The II corps of the Army of the Potomac suffered 51 killed, 323 wounded and 86 classified as missing. The Army of the Potomac V Corps had even higher casualty numbers. There were 126 killed, 811 wounded, and 470 missing combining the two Corps loss at 1,867.[7] The only numbers provided for the Confederates were the Fourth Corps, Army of Northern Virginia, listing ten killed, 80 wounded, and 97 missing that is far lower than other reports of as many as 800 casualties. Confederate Major General George Edward Pickett's Division from the First Corps, Army of Northern Virginia, also participated and may account for the other casualties but no report was provided.

At the same time the Union II and V Corps of the Army of the Potomac were engaged in the Battle of White Oak Road, Major General Philip Henry Sheridan's Army of the Shenandoah made up entirely of cavalry units attempted to swing north from Dinwiddie Court House along the Boydton Plank Road six and a half miles south of White Oak Road heading for the road junction of Five Forks five miles to the northwest. Five Forks was the intersection of five roads one of which was White Oak Road running east and west about six miles west of where the Battle of White Oak Road was taking place. Near Dinwiddie Court House, units from Confederate Major General George Edward Pickett's Division, First Corps, Army of Northern Virginia, and Major General Fitzhugh Lee's Cavalry Corps surprised General Sheridan in what became the **Battle of Dinwiddie Court House** March 31. The strength of both forces were about the same that should have made things about equal, but General Sheridan was caught off guard and needed help to survive. That help came late that evening and saved the day. Casualties for both the Union and Confederate forces were in the hundreds though Confederate losses were twice that of their enemy just shy of 800.

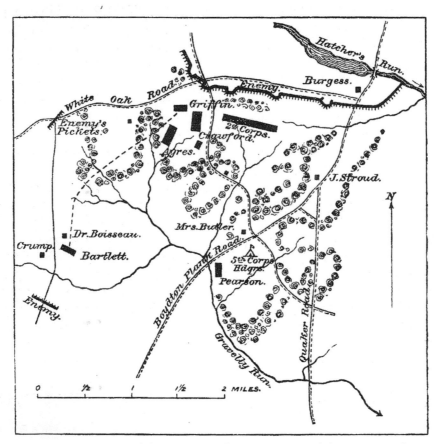

Sketch showing the position of the Union II and V Corps, Army of the Potomac, the evening of March 31 following the Battle of White Oak Road. Other key reference points are shown on the sketch such as White Oak Road, Hatcher's Run, Boydton Plank Road, and Gravelly Run. The War of the Rebellion: A Compilation of the Official Records of the Union and Confederate Armies, Volume 46, Part 1, p. 819

Following true to form, the **Battle of Five Forks** was next to occur April 1 fought between the same combatants as in the Battle of Dinwiddie Court House, but with the addition of the V Corps of the Army of the Potomac increasing the strength of the Union forces to around 22,000 doubling that of the Confederates that stayed the same from the last battle. The Battle of Five Forks resulted in a much different outcome than the day before. Union General Sheridan's Army of the Shenandoah coupled with the assets of the Army of the Potomac V Corps were all it would take to rout Confederate General Pickett's forces at Five Forks, exercise control over the South Side Railroad, and send a strong message to Confederate General Lee that the Union Army was close by! Casualties for this battle are all over the map, but one thing is clear, captured Confederate soldiers were in the thousands whether 3,000 or 6,000 and much if not all of its artillery was captured.[8] Unconfirmed and unofficial Union losses show 103 killed, 670wounded, and 57 missing for a total of 830.

Pencil drawing of Confederate Major General George Edward Pickett's last stand
during the Battle of Five Forks, April 1, 1865.
Library of Congress, Prints & Photographs Division, LC-USZ62-14304

The charge of Union Major General Philip Henry Sheridan's Cavalry during the
Battle of Five Forks, April 1, 1865
Library of Congress, Prints & Photographs Division, LC-USZ62-301

With all the military activity the last three days of March and the first day of April 1865, Petersburg had not yet fallen, but that would happen one day later, April 2, after the Battle of Five Forks in what is called the **Third Battle of Petersburg**, the **Breakthrough at Petersburg**, or the most devastating name, the **Fall of Petersburg**! The Confederate defense along the Petersburg line was a shadow of what it had been both at the end of 1864 and early 1865.

Numerous Union attacks at all points along the line and beyond had reduced both the territory defended and the defenders on the line. Adding to the combat losses for Confederates were injuries, sickness, and more devastating – desertions! Life for a Confederate soldier at this time in the war was not good! Many of the items of necessity such as rations, clothing, medicines, and shelter were lacking largely due to Union efforts cutting off supplies from reaching the soldiers. Adding to this dilemma was the capture of thousands of Confederate soldiers including many senior officers that included generals.

After a four-hour Union artillery barrage on the Confederate line at Petersburg, late in the evening of April 1 extending into the early hours of April 2, a ground attack began at 4:40 a. m. The Union forces were aligned with the IX Corps on the far right, VI Corps next to the left followed by the Department of Virginia (aka Army of the James) and then the II Corps on the far left. Union troop strength on the line was around 60,000 men facing about one-third that number of Confederate troops. It would take only thirty minutes and the VI Corps made a breakthrough of the Confederate line followed soon thereafter by the II Corps with the same result. A major blow to Confederate General Lee early in the battle was the death of Lieutenant General Ambrose Powell Hill killed while riding his horse by two unsuspecting Union soldiers who happened to be either in the right or the wrong place at that time.

Lieutenant General Ambrose Powell Hill
Officer of the Confederate Army

Killed in action April 2, 1865,
during the Third Battle of Petersburg

National Archive, 111-BA-1190

With the Union in full control of the battlefield, the II and VI Corps swung north toward Petersburg along the Boydton Plank Road pushing the Confederate forces ahead of them. One Confederate fortification after another fell to the vast number of Union attackers. Of the 214 or so Confederate defenders at Fort Gregg, 56 were reported killed and 129 wounded while inflicting as many as 714 Union casualties giving rise to the difficulty of attacking well fortified positions.[9]

Scene showing the Union XXIV Corps, Department of Virginia (aka Army of the James), in their attack on Confederate Fort Gregg to the left, April 2, 1865
Library of Congress, Prints & Photographs Division, LC-USZ62-12803

By mid-afternoon Sunday, April 2, Confederate General Lee issued an order to evacuate all of Petersburg and Richmond by 8:00 p. m. that evening and reassemble at the Amelia Court House over thirty miles to the west on the Richmond and Danville Railroad. By late that same evening, the government of the Confederacy had packed up and left Richmond for Danville, Virginia. These actions signaled the end of the Richmond-Petersburg Campaign!

Official casualty returns for this last battle are not available. The fluidity of action around Petersburg and the surrender of the Confederate Army of Northern Virginia soon after may have contributed to the lack of Union reports. Confederate casualty reports had been scarce for some time! Union General Grant provided a summary of casualties covering March 29 through April 9, but that is of little value due to the many engagements during that timeframe. If unofficial reports can be accepted, Union losses were shy of 4,000 while Confederate numbers are around 5,000 many of which were prisoners. Casualty reports for most if not all of the remaining battle of the American Civil War are not likely to materialize for the reasons already identified.

The Third Battle of Petersburg, April 2, 1865.

Library of Congress, Prints & Photographs Division, LC-USZC4-1620

The "Fall of Petersburg"

Library of Congress, Prints & Photographs Division, LC-USZC4-1520

On the same day as the Third Battle of Petersburg and for the next seven days, a total of nine named battles would occur as the Union forces pursued the Confederate Army of Northern Virginia as they desperately tried to regroup. Only one of the battles favored a Confederate outcome! The **Battle of Sutherland's Station** was the same day as the Third Battle of Petersburg, April 2. While the main Union thrust was on the Petersburg line, the Union First Division, II Corps, Army of the Potomac, commanded by Brevet Major General Nelson Appleton Miles swung to the west and attacked near the South Side Railroad in an attempt to cut off any hope of resupply for the Confederate Army. This mission was successful unofficially at a cost of just under 400 Union lives and 600 plus Confederate losses many of that number captured.

The Union cavalry was in a chase against the fleeing Confederate forces and caught up with the rear guard April 3 near **Namozine Church** approximately fifteen miles west of Petersburg resulting in a battle of that name. The action that followed was little more than harassing than anything else. This type of activity would continue over the next few days evidenced in the **Battle of Amelia Springs** April 5 proving only that the Union troops were on the heels of the Confederate Army and would not stop until they had achieved the end of the Confederate Army of Northern Virginia.

A large segment of the Union forces not just cavalry finally caught up to the main Confederate Army of Northern Virginia near Farmville and other points some fifty miles southwest of Petersburg April 6. It was not especially difficult to overtake the Confederate forces that were tired, hungry, injured, and extremely downtrodden! While recent encounters were considered skirmishes, this was a full scale battle or battles named the **Battle of Sailor's Creek** and a collection of other names like **Sayler's Creek, Lockett's Farm, Marshall's Crossroads, and Hillman's Farm** to name just a few. The reason for the different names was for different locations at which the battles occurred. Sayler's Creek was the same as Sailor's Creek, but the other names were from different sites sometimes miles apart at which different forces were engaged on that Thursday in April.

Union Major General Andrew Atkinson Humphreys' II Corps, Army of the Potomac, was engaged against Confederate Major General John Brown Gordon's Second Corps, Army of Northern Virginia, at Lockett's Farm a short distance east of Sailor's Creek. This involved a running battle that in the end resulted in the capture of many Confederate soldiers with those that escaped on the run.

Union cavalry forces under Major General George Crook, Second Division, Cavalry Corps, Army of the Potomac, encountered Confederate Lieutenant General Richard Heron Anderson in charge of the Fourth Corps, Army of Northern Virginia, at Marshall's Crossroads that took on a similar scenario as that at Lockett's Farm. And, finally, Union Major General Horatio Gouverneur Wright with his VI Corps, Army of the Potomac, fought Lieutenant General Richard Stoddard Ewell, Department of Richmond as part of the Department of North Carolina and Southern Virginia, at the Hillman Farm. The result of this action was the surrender of General Ewell's forces as well as himself. Less than three hundred of General Ewell's troops escaped capture that day.

Sketch of Confederate Lieutenant General Richard Stoddert Ewell's Department of Richmond within the Department of North Carolina and Southern Virginia at the time of their surrender, April 6, 1865, near Hillman's Farm approximately twenty-eight miles east of Appomattox Court House.

Wikipedia {{ PD-1923 }}

The Battle of Sailor's Station was not the only engagement April 6. A minor affair called the **Battle of Rice's Station** took place when Confederate Lieutenant General James Longstreet's First Corps, Army of Northern Virginia, made a stand against the Union XXIV Corps, Army of the James, commanded by Major General John Gibbon, near present-day Rice, Virginia, along the South Side Railroad a short distance east of Farmville. General Longstreet's troops were ordered to "dig in" awaiting the arrival of the Union force which they did. The Union troops came in contact with General Longstreet's entrenched troops during the morning hours and skirmished briefly before a stand down waiting for reinforcements. With knowledge of the devastating Confederate loss at Sailor's Creek, General Longstreet withdrew his force toward Farmville that evening ending the engagement.

Another engagement that began April 6 just to the north of Farmville was the **Battle of High Bridge** named for the South Side Railroad Bridge over the Appomattox River and a lower wagon bridge at the same location. The irony of this battle is that Union forces attempted to burn the bridge on Thursday, April 6, to prevent Confederate troops from crossing to the north side of the river, and Confederate troops attempted to burn the bridge the next day after crossing to prevent the Union troops from pursuing! Both efforts were unsuccessful, but the first effort resulted in heavy losses of Union soldiers to include the capture of some 800 or so.

In the final analysis, the Union pursuit continued so much so that Union General Ulysses S. Grant began the first of a series of messages to Confederate General Robert E. Lee encouraging the surrender of the Army of Northern Virginia. General Lee in return gave his analysis of the situation. The context of the first message and response follow.

April 7 – Headquarters, Army of the United States

General R. E. Lee, commander C. S. Army

"GENERAL: The result of the last week must convince you of the hopelessness of further resistance on the part of the Army of Northern Virginia in this struggle. I feel that it is so, and regard it as my duty to shift from myself the responsibility of any further effusion of blood by asking of you the surrender of that portion of the C. S. Army known as the Army of Northern Virginia." Very respectfully, your obedient servant, U. S. GRANT, Lieutenant-General, Commanding Armies of the Unites States.
(Official Records, Vol. XLVI, Part III, p. 619)

April 7 –

Lieut. Gen. U. S. GRANT, Commanding Armies of the United States:

"GENERAL: I have received your note of this date. Though not entertaining the opinion you express of the hopelessness of further resisting on the part of the Army of Northern Virginia, I reciprocate your desire to avoid useless effusion of blood, and therefore, before considering your proposition, ask the terms you will offer on condition of this surrender." R. E. LEE, General.
(Official Records, Vol. XLVI, Part III, p. 619)

The messages between the two commanders would continue for the next two days, but in the meantime the **Battle of Cumberland Church** April 7 would add to the bloodshed and suffering on both sides. The Confederate Army of Northern Virginia continued to withdraw to the northwest toward Appomattox under the constant pressure of the pursuing Union forces. Several miles north of the High Bridge the Battle of Cumberland Church would occur resulting in a Confederate victory if only for a moment and it was only a moment! The next day Saturday, April 8, Union Major General George Armstrong Custer's Third U. S. Cavalry Division, 4,000 strong, rode to Appomattox Station for the purpose of capturing several supply trains. Here General Custer engaged a mix of Confederate artillery and cavalry units that were no match against General Custer. The trains were captured and a number of prisoners were taken at few Union losses.

The dialogue between Generals Grant and Lee continued April 8. General Lee proposed a meeting to discuss the "restoration of peace" to which General Grant dismissed the idea reasserting his terms for General Lee's surrender. The day Sunday, April 9, 1865, has double significance. On one accord, the last battle fought by Confederate General Robert Edward Lee and his Army of Northern Virginia would occur in the early morning hours culminating in a decisive Union victory. That victory gave way to the second accord – the surrender of General Lee and his army! The terms of surrender are spelled out in the next message and accepted in the last passage.

April 9 – Headquarters, Armies of the United States, Appomattox Court-House, Virginia

General R. E. LEE, Commanding C. S. Army:

"GENERAL: *In accordance with the substance of my letter to you of the 8th instant, I propose to receive the surrender of the Army of Northern Virginia on the following terms, to wit: Rolls of all the officers and men to be made in duplicate—one copy to be given to an officer to be designated by me, the other to be retained by such officer or officers as you may designate; the officers to give their individual paroles not to take up arms against the Government of the United States until properly exchanged, and each company or regimental commander sign a like parole for the men of their command. The arms, artillery, and public property to be parked and stacked, and turned over to the officers appointed by me to receive them. This will not embrace the side-arms of the officers, nor their private horses or baggage. This done, each officer and man will be allowed to return to their homes, not to be disturbed by United States authority so long as they observe their paroles and the laws in force where they may reside." Very respectfully, U. S. GRANT, Lieutenant-General.*
(Official Records, Vol. XLVI, Part III, p. 665)

April 9 – Headquarters, Army of Northern Virginia

Lieut. Gen. U. S. GRANT, Commanding Armies of the United States:

"GENERAL: *I have received your letter of this date containing the terms of surrender of the Army of Northern Virginia as proposed by you. As they are substantially the same as those expressed in your letter of the 8th instant, they are accepted. I will proceed to designate the proper officers to carry the stipulations into effect." Very respectfully, your obedient servant, R. E. LEE, General.*
(Official Records, Vol. XLVI, Part III, p. 666)

General Robert E. Lee surrendered the Army of Northern Virginia to Lieutenant General Ulysses S. Grant at the McLean's house, Appomattox Court-House, Virginia, April 9, 1865. The formalities began shortly after 1:30 in the afternoon and were over by 4 P. M. This surrender was only that of the Army of Northern Virginia although General Lee commanded all of the Confederate forces. It would take approximately a month for all hostilities to cease as word reached commanders on both sides of the conflict in remote locations, but the American Civil War was over!

The room at the McLean House, Appomattox Court House, where Confederate General Robert E. Lee surrendered his Army of Northern Virginia to Union Lieutenant General Ulysses S. Grant, April 9, 1865
Library of Congress, Prints & Photographs Division, LC-USZ62-2480

---

[1] War of the Rebellion – A Compilation of the Official Records of the Union and Confederate Armies, Vol. 46, Part 1, p. 69.

[2] Ibid, p. 71.

[3] Ibid, Vol. 47, Part I, p. 62.

[4] Ibid, p. 979.

[5] Ibid, p. 66.

[6] Ibid, p. 1060, 76

[7] Ibid, Vol. 46, p. 677, 819.

[8] Ibid, p. 54.

[9] Pursuit to Appomattox – The Last Battles, Time-Life Books, p. 97.

Summary

The American Civil War was a black mark on the nation as a whole. Emotions over issues were allowed to overshadow the need for national unity and just plain common sense! As a consequence countless lives were affected in so many different ways. The loss of lives due to combat, disease, starvation, and accidents alone was approximately 620,000 for of all ages. The number of wounded was most likely three to four times or more than that number. The number of combatants who died from their wounds in the months and years after the war will never be known.

The casualties of war are not just those killed and wounded, but the non-combatants whose lives were affected by the loss of a bread winner or whose home and livelihood were torn apart due to the ravages of war! The South was particularly affected where much of the war took place. Homes were burned, crops destroyed, lives placed in an upheaval, and some civilians that became casualties of war through no fault of their own.

The years of the Civil War have long passed and a healing process should have taken place, but some today will not let go creating unrest for reasons only they can explain! Symbols of the American Civil War are historical in nature and nothing more! Many of the statues and monuments of and for Confederate leaders recognize not only their role in the American Civil War but their proud history of serving this country before the war and even after. It is long past time to put aside whatever differences there may be and work for the betterment of our proud country! It would be a shame if the current generation can't look upon the American Civil War as a tribute to the resolve of its people instead of the opposite! God Bless America!

PROUDLY DISPLAYED!

Bibliography

Government Publications -

United States War Department. The Official Military Atlas of the Civil War, Washington: Government, Inc. and Crown Publishing, Inc. 2003 edited by Barnes and Noble Publishing, Inc.

United States War Department. *The War of the Rebellion: A Compilation of the Official Records of the Union and Confederate Armies*; Washington D. C. Government Printing Office, 1880 - 1901.

Books –

Boatner, Mark mayo III. *The Civil War Dictionary*, Vintage Books, 1959

Chute, Joseph II. Jr. *Units of the Confederate States Army*, Gaithersburg, Maryland; Olde Soldier Books, Inc. 1987.

Dyer, Frederick H. *A Compendium of the War of the Rebellion*, Vol. 1 & 2. Des Moines, Ioaw: The Dyer Publishing Co., 1908.

Korn, Jerry and Editors of Time-Life Books. *Pursuit to Appomattox, The Last Battles*. Alexandria, Virginia: Time-Life Books, Inc., 1987.

Woltjer, Rodger. *American Civil War: Support Services of the Confederate Army*, Merriam Press, 2017.

Woltjer, Rodger. *American Civil War: Support Services of the Union Army*, Merriam Press, 2017.

Woodhead, Henry and Editors of Time Life Books. *Echos of Glory – Civil War – Battle Atlas*, Time Life Books, Alexandria, Virginia, 1996.

Internet Sources –

archive.org › stream › chronologicallis00webb › chronologicallis.

Army.mil/cmb-pg/books/R&H/R&H-1CV.htm

Army.mil/cmb-pg/books/R&H/R&H-2CV.htm

Army.mil/cmh-pg/books/R&H/R&H-1IN.htm

Army.mil/cmh-pg/books/R&H/R&H-2IN.htm

Army.mil/cmh-pg/books/R&H/R&H-3IN.htm

Army.mil/cmh-pg/books/R&H/R&H-4IN.htm

Army.mil/cmh-pg/books/R&H/R&H-5IN.htm

Army.mil/cmh-pg/books/R&H/R&H-6IN.htm

Army.mil/cmh-pg/books/R&H/R&H-7IN.htm

Army.mil/cmh-pg/books/R&H/R&H-8IN.htm

Army.mil/cmb-pg/books/R&H/R&H-1Art.htm

Army.mil/cmb-pg/books/R&H/R&H-2Art.htm

Army.mil/cmb-pg/books/R&H/R&H-3Art.htm

Army.mil/cmb-pg/books/R&H/R&H-4Art.htm

digitalcollections,fiu,edu/Tequesta/files/1969/60)_1_06.pdf

ebooks.library.cornell.edu

floridagenologytrails.com

history.amry.mil

legends of amrrica.com, Wyoming Indians Battles, p. 3

nativeamericannetroots.net

tamu.edu (Texas A& M Univeresity)

tshaonline.org (Texas State Historical Association)

usacac.army.mil/CAC2/CGSC/CARL/nafzinger/840XAA.pdf

Wikipedia, multiple sites

Index

F OR ease of identification, this Index will first include the names of individuals, Acts, Treaties, and items of historical importance followed by military entries of Battles, Forts, and Military organizations and the like. The army military ranks will be represented by the following: General – GEN, Lieutenant General – LTG, Major General – MG, Colonel – COL, Lieutenant Colonel – LTC, Major – MAJ, Captain – CPT, First Lieutenant – 1LT, Second Lieutenant – 2LT, Lieutenant – LT, Seargeant – SGT, and Private – PVT. Navy ranks will be Admiral – ADM, Rear Admiral – RADM, Commodore (Flag Officer) – COMDR, Commander - CMDR, Captain – CAPT, Lieutenant – LT, and Ensign – ENS. The letter (U) in front of a name is for Union and (C) for Confederate.

NAMES, ACTS, TREATIES, HISTORICAL IMPORTANCE:

(C) Ewell, MG Richard Stoddart – 263, 264, 265, 399, 400

-F-

Fannin, CPT James Walker Jr. – 186, 192, 194
Fanning, LTC Alexander C. W. – 139
(U) Farnsworth, BG Elon John - 314
Fauntleroy, MAJ Thomas T. - 150
Ferguson, MAJ Patrick (British) – 53
(C) Field, MG Charles William – 369
Filisola, GEN Vicente (Mexican) – 195, 196
First Continental Congress – 27
First Seminole War – 9
Flores, CPT Jose Maria (Mexican) – 209, 210, 214
(C) Floyd, BG John B. – 254, 255
(U) Foote, COMDR Andrew Hull – 253, 254, 255
Forbes, GEN John
(C) Forrest, BG, MG Nathan Bedford – 254, 379, 381
FORTS – see section after BATTLES
(U) Foster, BG John Gray – 246, 250
Foster, LTC William S. – 136, 137, 141
Franklin, Benjamin – 24, 29, 57, 58, 111
(U) Franklin, BG William Buell – 268
Frazer, Hugh McDonald – 193
Freeman, LT Edmund – 162
Fremont, Bvt LTC John Charles – 211, 212
(U) Fremont, MG John Charles – 262, 264
French and Indian War(s) – 9, 13, 15, 23, 36, 105, 111
(C) French, MG Samuel Gibbs - 377

-G-

Gadsden, LT James – 119, 122
Gadsden Purchase - 231
Gage, GEN Thomas – 29
Gaines, Bvt MG, MG Edmund Pendleton – 118, 121, 129, 130, 131, 132, 137
Garland, Bvt BG John - 223
Garner, CPT Hezekiah – 149

Garnett, MAJ Robert Selden - 170
Gates, MAJ William - 133
Gallatin, Albert - 101
Gates, MG Horatio – 29, 47, 48, 52
(U) Geary, BG John White – 321, 353
Gentry, COL Richard – 141
(U) Getty, BG George Washington - 373
(U) Gibbon, BG, MG John – 310, 400
Gibbs, MG Samuel (British) – 103
Gilleland, CPT Lewellen – 133
Gillespie, CPT, Bvt MAJ Archibald H. – 210, 212
Gist, Christopher – 11
(C) Gist, BG States Right – 299
George, King II – 10, 15
George, King III – 29
George, King IV – 102
(C) Godwin, BG Archibald Campbell - 374
(U) Goldsborough, RADM Louis Malesherbee – 246
(C) Gordon, BG James Byron – 343, 390
(C) Brown, MG John Brown – 373, 391, 399
(U) Grahm, BG Charles Kinnaird – 333
(U) Granger, BG Robert Seaman - 378
Grant, James – 189
Grant, LT Ulysses Simpson – 229
(U) Grant, BG, MG, LTG Ulysses Simpson – 253, 254, 255, 256, 257, 290, 291, 292, 294, 296, 297, 301, 303, 304, 317, 319, 322, 323, 324, 325, 331, 339, 341, 342, 343, 346, 347, 348, 349, 363, 368, 369, 384, 393, 397, 400, 401, 402, 403
Grattan, LT John Lawrence – 163
(C) Grayson, CPT John B. - 296
Green Mountain Boys – 36, 37, 46
Greene, BG, MG Nathanael – 28, 29, 33, 41
(U) Gregg, BG David McMurtrie – 345, 390
(C) Gregg, BG John – 298, 299
(U) Grover, BG Cuvier - 373
(C) Guibor, CPT Henry - 297
Gwinnett, GOV Button – 45
Gwynee, CPT Thomas P. - 153

Lowd, CPT Allen – 200
(U) Lyon, Nathaniel – 242, 243, 244, 245

-M-

Macdonough, CAPT Thomas – 96
Macomb, BG, MG Alexander – 96, 145, 146
Madison, President James – 70, 72, 73
Magruder, CPT John Bankhead – 223
(C) Magruder, MG John Bankhead – 265, 267, 275, 276
Magruder, Patrick – 72
Maloney, CPT Maurice – 167, 168
Mansfield, CPT Joseph K. F. – 199, 207
Marshall, COL Humphrey - 216
Martin, LT J. W. - 147
Mason, George – 29
Mason Bill No 2 - 70
Massachusetts Government Act – 27
Mawhood, COL Charles (British) – 43
May, CPT, Bvt MAJ Charles A. – 201, 203, 204
McArthur, BG Duncan – 101
McCall, LT George A. – 154
(U) McClellan, MG George Brinton – 265, 269, 270, 271, 272, 275, 278, 279, 280, 283, 286, 287
(U) McClernand, MG John Alexander – 292, 293, 297, 300, 302
(C) McCulloch, BG Benjamin – 243, 259
(U) McDowell, BG Irvin – 238, 240, 281
McIntosh, LTC James Simmons – 201
(C) McIntosh, BG James M. – 259
(U) McIntosh, BG John Baillie - 374
McKee, COL William R. – 216
McKenzie, CPT Samuel - 227
McKillop, CPT Alexander (British) – 66
(C) McLaws, MG Lafayette – 283, 310
McNeil, LT Winfield Scott – 140
(U) McPherson, MG James Birdseye – 298, 300, 302, 356, 358, 359
(U) Meade, MG George Gordon - 311, 315, 339
Medina, CPT Francisco (Mexican) – 185
Mejia, GEN Francisco (Mexican) - 206
Mellon, CPT Charles - 139
Mercer, BG Hugh – 43, 44

(U) Merritt, BG Wesley - 373
Mervine, CAPT William - 210
Mifflin, MAJ, MG Thomas – 35
Milam. COL Ben – 188
(U) Miles, COL Dixon Stansbury – 285
(U) Miles, Bvt MG Nelson Appleton - 399
MILITARY UNITS – see section after FORTS
(U) Milroy, BG Robert Huston - 262
Molasses Act 1733 - 23
Monro (Munro), LTC George – 15
Monroe, President James – 121
Monroe, MAJ John - 200
Montgomery, LT Alexander – 150
Montgomery, CMDR John B. – 204
Moore, CPT Benjamin Daviess - 212
Morales, COL Juan Esteban (Mexican) -190, 218
(U) Morell, BG George Webb - 270
Morgan, MAJ - 141
Morgan, BG Daniel – 53
(U) Morgan, BG George Washington - 293
Morin, CPT Jesse I. – 215, 223
Morris, CPT Lewis M. - 201
Morris, Robert – 29
Montcalm, GEN Louis-Joseph de (British) – 16, 20, 21
Montgomery, BG Richard – 33, 34, 37, 38
Montgomery, CPT William R. - 201
Moultrie, BG William – 51
Munoz, CPT Manuel Pineda (Mexican) - 231
Munroe, CPT - 141
Murry, John (Earl of Dunmore) – 112
Myers, CPT Abraham C. - 201

-N-

Napoleonic Wars – 87
Native American Indian Tribes, Chiefs, etc. –
  Abenaki - 111
  Algonquin – 17
  Apache - 172, 175, 190, 221
    Mangas, Chief – 171
    Cochise, Chief – 171
  Arapaho – 174, 175, 176, 178, 182
    Black Bear, Chief – 180, 181
  Arkiara - 122

_____

BATTLES - French & Indians Wars

BATTLES - Revolutionary War

BATTLES - Post Revolutionary War

BATTLES - War of 1812

Fort Detroit – 72
Fort Erie - 73
Fort George – 72, 77
Fort McHenry - 98
Fort Meigs (OH) – 72
Fort Niagara - 73
Fort Stephenson – 73, 80
Frenchtown – 72, 76, 91
Lake Borgne - 102
Lake Champlain – 73, 96, 97
Lake Erie (Put-In-Bay) – 73, 80, 87
Locolle Mills – 73, 87
Locolle River (First) – 72, 76
Lundy's Lane (Niagara Falls) - 73, 91, 92, 93
Maguaga – 72, 75
Malcolm's Mills – 73, 101
New Orleans – 73, 103, 117
North Point - 98
Oswego – 73, 89
Plattsburg – 73, 96, 98, 101
Queenston Heights – 72, 75
Raisin River (First) – 76, 115
Raisin River (Second) – 76, 115
Sackett's Harbor (First) – 72, 74, 76
Sackett's Harbor (Second) – 72, 78, 79, 90
Sandy Creek – 73 89
Stoney Creek – 72, 78, 80
Thames (Moraviantown) – 73, 83, 84
York – 72, 76, 77

BATTLES/WARS - Native American Indian

Antelope Hills Expedition – 106
Apache Pass – 106, 171
Apple River Fort - 124
Arikara War – 106, 122
Ash Hollow (Bluewater Creek) - 164
Bad Axe – 106, 125, 126
Bear River (Massacre) – 106, 172
Big Bend (Big Meadows) - 166
Black Hawk War – 106, 123, 126
Bloody Island Massacre – 106
Bridgewater - 147
Bushy Run – 111

Colorado War - 173
Canyon de Chelly – 107, 172
Cascades Massacre - 169
Cayuse War – 106, 158
Cherokee War (see Battle of Neches)
Cherry Valley Massacre - 113
Chickamauga Wars - 112
Colorado War - 107
Comanche Wars – 106
Coon Creek - 158
Council Hall Fight - 156
Council House Fight (see Btl of Plum Creek)
Coeur d'Alene War – 106, 170
Crazy Women's Fort - 180
Creek Wars (see Fort Mims Massacre)
Dade Massacre – 128, 129, 130, 137, 142
Dearborn - 115
Deerfield Massacre – 110
Devil's Hole Massacre – 111
Dunlawton - 130
Enoch Brown Massacre - 112
First Adobe Walls – 107, 175
First Kellogg's Grove – 124
First Loxahatchee River – 142, 143
First Seminole War – 106, 117, 118, 119, 121, 122
First Wahoo Swamp – 136, 137
Fort Dearborn – 106
Fort Dearborn Massacre – 115
Fort King - 147
Fort Mims Massacre – 106, 115, 117
Fort William Henry Massacre – 106, 111
Four Lakes – 106, 170
Frenchtown – 106, 115
Gnadenhutten Massacre – 106, 113
Grattan Fight (Massacre) – 106, 163
Great Raid of 1840 - 157
Great Swamp Fight – 110
Gunnison Massacre - 159
Hatchee-Lustee - 138
Haw Creek Affair - 154
Horseshoe Bend – 106, 116, 117, 118, 124
Hungry Hills - 165
Indian Massacre 1622 – 107, 108
Jamestown Massacre – 106

BATTLES - Texas War of Independence

BATTLES, etc. - U. S. – Mexican War

Petersburg (Siege) - 393

Richmond-Petersburg – 236, 369, 384, 390, 393

BATTLES – ACW

FORTS - Texas War of Independence

FORTS - US – Mexican War

FORTS - American Civil War- ACW

A-Z (lunettes, redans, batteries) GA - 357
Arkansas Post (Hindman) AR – 292, 293, 294
Bartow NC (Foster) – 246
Blanchard NC (Parke) – 246
Bliss TX – 251
Clifton VA - 333
Coburn MS – 296, 297
Craig NM – 252
"D" GA - 357
De Russy DC - 328
De Russy LA - 328
Donelson TN – 254, 255, 256, 257
Drewry VA (Darling) – 268, 269, 334
Fisher NC – 386, 387
Forrest NC – 246
Gregg VA - 397
Heiman KY - 379
Henry TN – 254, 255, 256
Hood GA - 357
Huger NC (Reno) – 246
Jackson GA - 383
Macon NC – 248, 249, 250
Magruder VA- 267
Maxon GA – 357
McAllister - 383
Monroe VA - 246
Moultrie SC – 237
Pemberton MS- 295, 296
Pulaski GA– 383
Stedman VA- 391, 392
Sumter SC – 233, 237
Thompson NC – 248
Wade MS – 296
Walker GA - 357
Warren MA - 255

CONTINENTAL Army

Continental Army – 36, 38, 39, 40, 43, 44, 47,
    48, 49, 50, 59
  First Continental Reg – 33
Continental Army Departments (Regions) -

-Canadian Dept - 34
-Eastern Dept – 34
-Highlands Dept- 35
-Middle Dept – 34, 35
-New York Dept – 34, 37
-Southern Dept- 34, 50, 51, 53
-Western Dept – 35
Continental Marine Corps – 36
Continental Navy – 36
Continental Militia –
  1st GA Reg – 45
  2nd GA Reg - 45

MILITARY MILITIA - Native American Indians

Alabama Militia – 138
Alabama (Caulfield's) Bn of Mtd Vol – 133, 138
Alabama (Lauderdale's) Bn of Mtd Vol – 142
Army of the Frontier – 124
California, 2nd Cav
  Co B – 171
  Co L – 180
  Co M - 180
California, 1st Inf
  Co E – 171
California, 3rd Inf
  Co K – 172
Colorado, 1st Cav - 174
Colorado, 3rd Cav – 174
Dakota, 1st Cavalry Bn
  Co A – 174
  Co B - 174
Florida Militia - 129, 146
Florida 1st Reg Mtd Vol - 162
Georgia – 1st Bn Foot Inf – 132
Illinois Militia – 123, 124, 125
Indiana Militia - 114
Indiana - Light Dragoons – 114
Iowa, 6th Cav – 174
Iowa, 7th Cav
  Co F - 180
Kansas, 11th Cav - 178
  Co A - 177

MILITARY MILITIA - Texas War of Independence

MILITARY MILITIA – US – MEXICAN WAR

MILITARY – Confederate State Cmds

Alabama, 15th Reg Inf - 320
Alabama, 55th Reg Inf – 296
Georgia, Cobb's Legion - 310
Georgia, 3rd Reg Inf - 249
Georgia, 12th Reg Inf - 262
Georgia, 18th Reg Inf - 268
Georgia, 19th Reg Inf - 268
Georgia, 45th Reg Inf - 270
Louisiana Tigers - 263
Louisiana, 9th Reg Inf – 263
Maryland, 1st Reg Inf - 263
Missouri St Gd – 244
Missouri, 1st Arty – 297
North Carolina, Freebee's Militia – 249
North Carolina, 1st Reg Cav – 313, 345
North Carolina, 2nd, 5th Cav 345
North Carolina, 10th, 19th, 26th, 27th, 31st, 35th Reg Cav - 248
North Carolina, 2nd Reg Inf – 246
North Carolina, 7th Reg Inf – 248, 270
North Carolina, 8th Reg Inf – 246
North Carolina, 17th Reg Inf- 246
North Carolina, 18th Reg Inf - 270
North Carolina, 28th Reg Inf- 248, 270
North Carolina, 31st Reg Inf- 246
North Carolina, 37th Reg Inf – 248, 270
South Carolina, Hampton's Legion - 268
South Carolina, 1st Arty Reg - 237
South Carolina, 11th Reg Inf - 332
South Caroline, 18th Reg Inf - 369
South Carolina, 21st Reg Inf - 332
South Carolina, 22nd Reg Inf - 369
South Carolina, 25th Reg Inf - 332
South Carolina, 27th Reg inf - 332
South Carolina, 7th Battalion - 332
Texas, 2nd Mtd Rifles - 251
Texas, 4th Mtd Rifles - 251
Texas, 5th Mtd Rifles - 251
Texas, 1st Reg Inf - 268
Texas, 4th Reg Inf - 268
Texas, 5th Reg Inf - 268
Virginia, 1st, 2nd, 3rd, 4th, 5th, 6th, 15th Cav - 345

Virginia, 18th Reg Cav - 314
Virginia, 10th Reg Inf - 262
Virginia, 13th Reg Inf - 314
Virginia, 21st Reg Inf – 262
Virginia, 23rd Reg Inf – 262
Virginia, 25th Reg Inf – 262
Virginia, 31st Reg Inf - 262
Virginia, 37th Reg Inf – 262
Virginia, 42nd Reg Inf - 262
Virginia, 44th Reg Inf - 262
Virginia, 46th Reg Inf - 246
Virginia, 48th Reg Inf – 262
Virginia, 52nd Reg Inf – 262
Virginia, 58th Reg Inf – 262
Virginia, 59th Reg Inf – 247

MILITARY – CSA Armies, Departments

Army of the Department of Mississippi and East Louisiana (formerly Dept of Mississippi & East Louisiana) – 290, 291, 300, 301, 302, 303, 304
Army of New Mexico – 252
Army of Northern Virginia (ANV) – 265, 267, 271, 272, 279, 280, 282, 283, 285, 305, 306, 307, 311, 312, 317, 331, 336, 340, 341, 346, 349, 363, 377, 389, 393, 397, 399, 400, 401, 402
   First Corps – 287, 310, 315, 342, 362, 368, 369, 370, 393, 400
   Second Corps – 287, 307, 314, 338, 362, 377, 390, 391, 399
   Third Corps – 314, 343, 366
   Fourth Corps – 370, 393, 399
   Cav – 314, 343, 345, 393
Army of the Shenandoah – 239, 240
Army of Tennessee – 317, 319, 323, 325, 349, 351, 354, 355, 377, 378, 379, 380, 384
   First Corps - 388
   Second Corps – 353, 360, 361
   Third Corps – 352
   Cav Corps - 381
Army of the Valley – 263, 338, 371, 373, 374, 375, 376, 377

MILITARY – Confederate Cmds –

MILITARY – Union State Cmds

MILITARY – Union Armies, Departments

Co H – 237, 266
Co I – 239
Co K – 250, 266, 374
Co L – 160, 250, 374
Co M - 250
2nd Arty Reg – 77, 79, 80, 129, 130, 133, 139, 142. 197, 200, 218, 223, 227, 328
  Co A – 127, 130, 132, 197, 204, 240, 266
  Co B – 127, 130, 132, 135, 266, 374
  Co C – 127, 128, 132, 160, 197
  Co D – 129, 130, 132, 134, 240, 374
  Co E – 132, 134, 160, 161, 197, 240, 266
  Co F – 128, 129, 130, 132, 160, 242
  Co G – 127, 130, 132, 160, 240, 266
  Co H – 127, 130, 132, 160
  Co I – 159, 160, 197, 200
  Co K – 159, 160
  Co L – 160, 374
  Co M – 240, 250, 266, 270, 271
3rd Arty Reg – 77, 130, 138, 144, 148, 151, 165, 201, 218, 223, 224, 347
  Co A – 134, 170, 197
  Co B – 128, 146, 150, 166, 170
  Co C- 129, 132, 134, 197, 215, 266
  Co D – 165
  Co E – 197, 200, 215, 240
  Co F - 266
  Co G – 149, 170, 266
  Co H - 129, 132, 134, 150, 165
  Co I – 132, 134, 150, 151, 197
  Co K – 145, 146, 147, 149, 150, 170, 266
  Co L – 169, 266
  Co M – 169, 170, 266
4th Arty Reg – 132, 142, 163, 214, 223, 347
  Co A – 135, 141, 266
  Co B – 138, 141, 142, 215, 263
  Co C – 134, 135, 138, 266
  Co D – 136, 138, 141, 142, 144, 200
  Co E – 137, 138, 200, 261
  Co F – 136, 138
  Co G – 138, 144, 166, 200, 266
  Co H – 136, 138, 141, 142
  Co I – 138, 144, 200
  Co K - 266

Co M – 161, 162
5th Arty Reg – 328, 347
  Co A – 266
  Co D – 240, 266
  Co F – 266
  Co I – 266
  Co K - 266
US Lt Arty – 77

Engineers US–

  Topographical – 212
  US Engineers – 266
  Battalion – 287

Signal US-

  Army Signal Corps – 180

Infantry US –

  1st Inf Reg – 123, 140, 141, 142
  Co A, G, K – 125, 250
  Co B – 125, 242
  Co C - 242
  Co D – 146, 242
  Co I – 147, 250
  2nd Inf Reg – 145, 218, 223, 230, 347
  Co B – 148, 154, 242
  Co C – 154, 240
  Co D – 151
  Co E - 242
  Co H – 145
  Co J - 154
  Co K – 147, 151, 154, 240
  3rd Inf Reg – 178, 197, 201, 218, 223, 250
  Co B, D, F, G, H – 240
  4th Inf Reg– 73, 114, 118, 119, 121, 128, 129, 130, 141, 166, 168, 169, 197, 201, 204, 218, 223, 347
  Co A – 167, 169
  Co B – 127, 128
  Co C – 154, 167
  Co D – 153, 154, 165

Printed in Great Britain
by Amazon